South Wind
Through the Kitchen

Part of Elizabeth David's kitchen.
On the dresser at the side of the cooker were knives and wooden spoons; she
always used the chair in front of the cooker, and sat here whilst writing.

SOUTH WIND THROUGH THE KITCHEN

The Best of Elizabeth David

COMPILED BY JILL NORMAN

MICHAEL JOSEPH

LONDON

MICHAEL JOSEPH LTD
Published by the Penguin Group
27 Wrights Lane, London w8 5tz
Viking Penguin Inc., 375 Hudson Street, New York, New York 10014, USA
Penguin Books Australia Ltd, Ringwood, Victoria, Australia
Penguin Books Canada Ltd, 10 Alcorn Avenue, Toronto, Ontario, Canada m4v 3b2
Penguin Books (NZ) Ltd, 182–190 Wairau Road, Auckland 10, New Zealand

Penguin Books Ltd, Registered Offices: Harmondsworth, Middlesex, England

This anthology first published in Great Britain 1997

Text copyright © The Estate of Elizabeth David
For extended copyright information *see* page xiii
Compilation of this anthology and Introduction copyright © Jill Norman 1997

Set in 10 and 11/14.25pt Postscript Monotype Ehrhardt
Typeset by Rowland Phototypesetting Ltd, Bury St Edmunds, Suffolk
Printed in England by Clays Ltd, St Ives plc

A CIP catalogue record for this book is available from the British Library

ISBN 0 7181 41687

The moral right of the author has been asserted

Contents

CONTENTS

Introduction

Elizabeth David was born in 1913, one of four daughters of Rupert Gwynne, Conservative MP for Eastbourne. Her mother was the daughter of the first Viscount Ridley. She had a conventional middle-class upbringing, with a nanny and governess, and later went to a girls' school where the food was decidedly inferior – 'nothing will surely ever taste so hateful as nursery tapioca, or the appalling boiled cod of schooldays'. At sixteen, she was sent to live with a French family in Passy, and if her studies at the Sorbonne did not leave any great impression, 'what stuck was the taste for a kind of food quite ideally unlike anything I had known before'. After eighteen months in Paris she spent some time in Munich, then returned to London to work briefly as a vendeuse at Worth before a spell at the Oxford rep and a short acting career at the Open Air Theatre in Regent's Park. In the late 1930s she went off to Italy where she met the writer Norman Douglas – the two became lasting friends in spite of the disparity in their ages, and Norman Douglas had a great influence on Elizabeth both as a writer and through his own approach to life.

She was living on the Greek Island of Syros at the beginning of the war, but when the Germans overran the country she was evacuated via Crete to Alexandria, where she worked for the Admiralty, and then moved to Cairo to run a reference library for the Ministry of Information. In Cairo she met and married Anthony David, an officer in the Indian army. At the end of 1945 she went to join him in New Delhi, but in India she became ill – the climate did not suit her – and after some months she returned to Britain.

Elizabeth David's first published work, *A Book of Mediterranean Food*, appeared in 1950, but her writing career had begun in the winter of 1946–7, in a hotel in Ross-on-Wye. She had returned to the deprivations of post-war Britain after several years of relative plenty in the Middle East and India, and although the hotel was at least warm and the staff pleasant, the food she described as 'produced with a kind of bleak triumph which amounted almost to a hatred of humanity and humanity's needs'. She revolted by writing down her memories of Middle Eastern and Mediterranean cooking, her private refuge from the cheerless reality of apathy induced by rationing. In 1949 a friend in the literary world offered to show her 'ragged' collection of notes and recipes to publishers. Most of them thought the idea of a cookery book when there was no food to cook at best absurd, but John Lehmann liked the material and agreed to publish it. He also commissioned John Minton to illustrate the book and design the striking jacket – a bright blue Mediterranean bay, and in the foreground tables holding fruits, a lobster, bowls of food, pitchers and bottles of wine.

The recipes were all authentic, collected in Provence, Italy, Corsica, Malta and in Greece. Even though scarcely any of the ingredients were available at the time (courgettes, fennel, aubergines were barely known, garlic and fresh herbs impossible to get), Elizabeth did not compromise or adapt her dishes – from the beginning she was meticulous in her description of foods and their regional differences. The book was acclaimed as a serious work on the food of the Mediterranean, with reviewers expressing their belief that once the shortages in Britain were lifted the work would become practical as well as inspirational.

The first Penguin edition, published in 1955 at 2/6d, brought the book to a very wide audience at the right time. Rationing had ended in 1954, and imports of olive oil, tahina, salame, pine nuts, chick peas and the like were beginning to trickle in. Many of Elizabeth's dishes were unknown in the Britain of the fifties, but over the years foods like paella, mousaka, ratatouille, hummus and gaspacho have become familiar in home kitchens, restaurants and supermarkets throughout the country.

The success of *A Book of Mediterranean Food* was followed in 1951 by *French Country Cooking*, another small book. In the introduction she dispelled the myth that all French families eat grand, rich meals ('the chances are that a food-conscious foreigner staying for any length of time with a French middle-class family would find the proportion of rather tough entrecôtes, rolled and stuffed roast veal and sautéd chicken exasperatingly high') and asserted that 'Those who care to look for it, however, will find the justification of France's culinary reputation in the provinces'. The rustic, peasant *French Country Cooking* was followed in 1960 by the more substantial, classic work on *French Provincial Cooking*, which dealt with 'sober, well-balanced, middle-class French cookery, carried out with care and skill, with due regard to the quality of the materials, but without extravagance or pretension' – a phrase which sums up precisely Elizabeth's own relentless pursuit of standards.

The two French books drew many English enthusiasts to France to explore the foods of the countryside (what is now called *cuisine du terroir*) 'at the riverside inns, the hospitable farmhouses of the Loire and the Dordogne, of Normandy and the Auvergne, in sea-port bistros, and occasionally also in *cafés routiers*'. As a result, pâtés and terrines, vegetable soups enriched with bacon and garlic, meat and poultry stews simmered in wine, and open tarts both savoury and sweet found their way into the repertoire of enterprising and creative British cooks. In the sixties many an amateur opened a small restaurant with little more than well-used copies of Elizabeth David, the necessary minimum of equipment and the will to succeed – as many of them did. In those days, more often than not, dinner parties, whether cheap and cheerful or stylish and sophisticated, were drawn straight from her books.

Meanwhile, Elizabeth had returned to live in Italy for a year, to research and collect material for her third book, *Italian Food*, which came out in 1954. This was still a difficult time for getting the right ingredients, but she urged her readers to try those recipes needing only everyday ingredients and not to attempt others until imports from Italy were more frequent. 'When an Italian has not the wherewithal to cook one of the traditional extravagant dishes she doesn't attempt to produce an imitation. She would not bother to make a ravioli stuffing with "fragments of cold joint" because the results would not at all resemble the dish as it should be, and would therefore be valueless.'

Elizabeth was one of the first writers to insist on the importance of regional differences in Italian food. The country was not unified until the later part of the nineteenth century, so to an Italian there was, and is, no such thing as Italian food: 'there is Florentine cooking, Venetian cooking, there are the dishes of Genoa, Piedmont, Romagna; of Rome, Naples and the Abruzzi; of Sardinia and Sicily; of Lombardy, Umbria and the Adriatic coast'. These provincial differences are clear to every discerning traveller, but at the time found no reflection in the Italian restaurants in Britain which merely served up the spaghetti, veal and chicken dishes the British had come to regard as Italian food. In the introduction to the Penguin edition in 1963 Elizabeth blamed other British cookery writers for their part in fostering these misconceptions. 'As I write this, I have just come across, in a respected monthly magazine, a recipe for a risotto made with twice-cooked Patna rice and a tin of tomato soup. What way is that of enlarging our knowledge and arousing our interest?'

Once *Italian Food* was delivered to her publishers Elizabeth started work on *Summer Cooking*, a smaller and less demanding collection of recipes for simple summer meals, cold buffets and picnics, drawn from old English dishes as well as those of the countries she had travelled in. She concentrated on herbs, fruits and vegetables in season, on light dishes of poultry or fish combined with vegetables and fruit (Filets de sole véronique: 'Wait until the muscat grapes come into season in August to make this dish. No other grapes will really do.')

By 1964 all five books were available in paperback, and finding an immense audience, especially among the young. During the years of writing the books Elizabeth also contributed to a variety of newspapers and magazines, having first been commissioned by Anne Scott-James to write a piece entitled Rice Again for *Harper's Bazaar* in 1949. At different times she was a regular contributor to *Vogue, House and Garden, The Sunday Times, Wine and Food, The Spectator* and *Nova*. Writing for *The Spectator* pleased her most, for there she was allowed to write a column about food, getting away from the standard formula of an introductory paragraph and a clutch of recipes. Her subjects were wide-ranging but topical, about the pleasures of good food, good wine, good cookery books, with occasionally 'harmless fun at the expense of restaurant guides or the baiting of public relations persons who made imbecile suggestions'.

With the launch of her kitchen shop in 1965 Elizabeth's writing came to an end, temporarily, but through the shop her influence on

Britain's cooks continued. She scoured Britain and the continent for the best in knives, earthenware, stoneware, cast-iron, soup pots, omelette pans, pepper mills, bread tins, plain white dishes. She had frequently written of the need for the right tools, and here they all were. Restaurateurs like Michel and Albert Roux (who had just opened their first restaurant nearby) shopped there for equipment that hitherto had had to come from France. Within a few months of the shop opening, kitchen shops sprang up everywhere, and thanks to her initiative we can now buy good cooking equipment and the right tools in department stores and specialist shops all over the country. Unhappily in 1973 she felt obliged to sever her connections with her business: she considered her standards were being compromised by her partners, who continued to run the business using her name.

During the years at the shop Elizabeth had written and privately published a few pamphlets on English cooking – potted meats and fish pastes, bread making, syllabubs and fools. Often thought of primarily as the writer who awoke British cooks to the pleasures of French, Italian and Mediterranean food, she had always had a passionate interest in English cooking, and owned a fine collection of old English cookery books which she read avidly. From this enthusiasm came the idea for a series of books which we rather grandiosely called *English Cooking, Ancient and Modern*. The first title was *Spices, Salt and Aromatics in the English Kitchen*, published in 1971. Drawing on her favourite authors – Eliza Acton, Marcel Boulestin, Mrs Leyel – on early writers about Anglo-Indian food such as Col. Kenney-Herbert, and on her own experiences in India and the Middle East she compiled a fine collection of English spiced and aromatic dishes, reviving for us old treats such as salt duck and spiced beef. Scholarliness was always present in Elizabeth's work, and in the English books it came to the fore. *Spices, Salt and Aromatics* contains much fascinating history, exploring the English relationship with the East, the trade cycles which led to the importing of oriental foods and the early attempts at recreating oriental dishes, particularly aromatic ones, as well as pickles and chutneys.

English Bread and Yeast Cookery, intended as the second title, took five years to write and outgrew the series. It is and will remain the definitive book on English baking, and at the time of publication

(1977) it had an immense influence. Eighty per cent of the bread sold in Britain came from factories – soft, white and sliced. The milling monopolies controlling the bread industry also supplied the characterless flour used to make most of the rest. The awfulness of English bread was nothing new. Eliza Acton noted in her own *Bread Book* (1857) that our bread 'was noted both at home and abroad for its want of genuineness, and the faulty mode of its preparation', and in *Practical Bread-making* (1897) Frederick Vine wrote: 'To describe some of the tackle sold as bread in London as anything else than batter would be to stretch a point in its favour'. In the 1970s a revolt against bland and soggy industrial bread was gathering momentum and people were starting to bake their own bread. They seized the bread book in their thousands, created a demand for flour from small millers, for supplies of yeast, for good bread tins. The industrial loaf is still with us, but look at the wide variety of other breads on sale in supermarkets, delicatessens and bakers, and thank Elizabeth.

In the last ten years of her life she became increasingly frail, suffering with broken limbs, having difficulty in getting about and eventually in standing and therefore in being able to cook – a source of great chagrin to her. She went on working on her book on the use of ice and the making of ices, doing painstaking research in a wide variety of books and journals. When she was well she worked at the kitchen table, always piled high with books. Later on she worked in bed, surrounded by precarious heaps of books and papers.

Writing was never easy for her. Her polished style came from writing and rewriting, always by hand, until she was satisfied with the result. She was constantly curious, marking pieces of useful information with slips of paper, a stickler for accuracy and the full acknowledgment of sources. She could have written on many other subjects: literature, travel and social history all feature extensively in her work: she had an unfailing knack of finding apposite passages to quote. The depth and breadth of her knowledge combined with her own elegant and literary style ensure that in future her own work will be similarly used by others.

Elizabeth was honoured with prizes, made Chevalier de l'Ordre du Mérite Agricole by the French in 1977, awarded the OBE in 1976 (she received the order from the Queen, who asked what she did.

'Write cookery books, ma'am,' said Elizabeth. 'That must be very useful,' replied Elizabeth II). In 1986 she received the CBE from the Prince of Wales, who confessed that his then wife liked Italian food. Honorary doctorates were conferred on her by the universities of Essex and Bristol. In 1982 she was elected Fellow of the Royal Society of Literature, perhaps the honour which pleased her the most.

When Elizabeth died on 22 May 1992, extensive obituaries appeared, from California to Greece. The memorial service on 10 September the crowded church of St Martin-in-the-Fields in London with family, friends, cooks, colleagues and readers – many of whom have chosen their favourite piece of Elizabeth's writings for this anthology, and contributed some personal tribute or anecdote.

Jill Norman
June 1997

Books by Elizabeth David

A Book of Mediterranean Food
First published by John Lehmann 1950. Revised editions 1955, 1958, 1965, 1988. New introduction 1991
Copyright © The Estate of Elizabeth David 1950, 1955, 1958, 1965, 1988, 1991

French Country Cooking
First published by John Lehmann 1951. Revised editions 1958, 1966
Copyright © The Estate of Elizabeth David 1951, 1958, 1966

Italian Food
First published by Macdonald and Co 1954. Revised editions 1963, 1969, 1977, 1987
Copyright © The Estate of Elizabeth David 1954, 1963, 1969, 1977, 1987

Summer Cooking
First published by Museum Press 1955. Revised edition 1965
Copyright © The Estate of Elizabeth David 1955, 1965

French Provincial Cooking
First published by Michael Joseph Ltd 1960. Revised editions 1965, 1967, 1970
Copyright © The Estate of Elizabeth David 1960, 1965, 1967, 1970

Spices, Salt and Aromatics in the English Kitchen
First published by Penguin Books 1970. Revised editions 1973, 1975
Copyright © The Estate of Elizabeth David 1970, 1973, 1975

English Bread and Yeast Cookery
First published by Allen Lane 1977
Copyright © The Estate of Elizabeth David 1977

An Omelette and a Glass of Wine
First published by Jill Norman at Robert Hale Ltd 1984
Copyright © The Estate of Elizabeth David 1984

Harvest of the Cold Months
First published by Michael Joseph Ltd 1994
Copyright © The Estate of Elizabeth David 1994

Editor's Note

In 1991 Elizabeth and I started talking about a volume of 'The Best of', and I wrote to a few friends asking for their ideas. Then Elizabeth's health deteriorated and the project was put to one side. After her death in 1992 my priority was to sort out the sheaves of manuscript and notes for the book on ice, and to see *Harvest of the Cold Months* through to publication.

At the beginning of 1996 the idea was revived. I wrote to many of Elizabeth's friends, and to chefs and writers known to have been influenced by her, asking them to select their favourite articles and recipes. Some sent notes explaining their choice or why Elizabeth was important to them, others provided an anecdote or a recollection about her; still more sent lists of recipes they have been using for years. Their names appear after the pieces they chose, as do their notes.

The texts used are those of the Penguin Cookery Library which incorporate Elizabeth's updatings and annotations. Metric measures and oven temperatures in celsius, fahrenheit and gas have been added to the recipes where necessary. The illustrations come from the original editions, and the illustrators are identified on page xv.

I would like to thank all the contributors: with their help; the book is incomparably better than if it had just been my own selection. Many wrote of the pleasure they had in re-reading the books. Their choices have introduced me to recipes and pieces I had not really noticed before, and I have cooked again dishes I had long forgotten. I hope that *South Wind Through the Kitchen* will give the pleasure of discovery and rediscovery to many readers.

My thanks also to Paul Breman, who has helped throughout with the selection and organization, and to Jenny Dereham who has edited the book with care and consistency.

The best of Elizabeth David was Elizabeth, herself. She was very old-fashioned, she loved conversation, five-hour-long lunches and, of course, wine – conversation and long lunches are unthinkable without a glass in hand. She was gifted with a wicked wit which was never cruel; she loved to laugh and it was infectious. Her writing, souvenirs of people and food, in particular, is a loyal and vibrant reflection of her conversation; the essays on Madame Barattero, Norman Douglas and the little Breton *bouchot* mussels are forever etched in my memory. When they met, Elizabeth was twenty-four, Norman Douglas seventy-two; a droll couple they must have been, moving from café to bistro, always arguing about food.

Elizabeth teased me mercilessly, claiming that my cuisine and my taste in wines were much too grand for the 'likes' of her. That was good for a laugh, too. She willingly drank the Montrachets, Chambertins, Lafites and Yquems that I sometimes imposed on her and I took care to serve her the simplest of food: she adored elvers, immersed in olive oil with a crushed garlic clove, a pod of cayenne and a pinch of grey sea salt, warmed only until they turned opaque and white, and creamy scrambled eggs packed with truffles. She admired a carefully composed cheese platter. And the conversation continued: we were often still at table at night fall.   Richard Olney

Introduction to
Mediterranean Food

The cooking of the Mediterranean shores, endowed with all the natural resources, the colour and flavour of the south, is a blend of tradition and brilliant improvisation. The Latin genius flashes from the kitchen pans.

It is honest cooking, too; none of the sham Grande Cuisine of the International Palace Hotel.

'It is not really an exaggeration', wrote Marcel Boulestin, 'to say that peace and happiness begin, geographically, where garlic is used in cooking.' From Gibraltar to the Bosphorus, down the Rhône Valley, through the great seaports of Marseille, Barcelona and Genoa, across to Tunis and Alexandria, embracing all the Mediterranean islands, Corsica, Sicily, Sardinia, Crete, the Cyclades, Cyprus (where the Byzantine influence begins to be felt), to the mainland of Greece and the much disputed territories of Syria, the Lebanon, Constantinople and Smyrna, stretches the influence of Mediterranean cooking, conditioned naturally by variations in climate and soil and the relative industry or indolence of the inhabitants.

The ever recurring elements in the food throughout these countries are the oil, the saffron, the garlic, the pungent local wines; the aromatic perfume of rosemary, wild marjoram and basil drying in the kitchens; the brilliance of the market stalls piled high with pimentos, aubergines, tomatoes, olives, melons, figs and limes; the great heaps of shiny fish, silver, vermilion, or tiger-striped, and those long needle fish whose bones so mysteriously turn out to be green. There are, too, all manner of unfamiliar cheeses made from sheep's or goat's milk; the butchers' stalls are festooned with every imaginable portion of the inside of every edible animal (anyone who has lived for long in Greece will be

2

familiar with the sound of air gruesomely whistling through sheep's lungs frying in oil).

There are endless varieties of currants and raisins, figs from Smyrna on long strings, dates, almonds, pistachios and pine kernel nuts, dried melon seeds and sheets of apricot paste which is dissolved in water to make a cooling drink.

All these ingredients make rich and colourful dishes. Over-picturesque, perhaps, for every day; but then who wants to eat the same food every day?

With this selection (it does not claim to be more) of Mediterranean dishes, I hope to give some idea of the lovely cookery of those regions to people who do not already know them, and to stir the memories of those who have eaten this food on its native shores, and who would like sometimes to bring a flavour of those blessed lands of sun and sea and olive trees into their English kitchens.

Mediterranean Food

Provence

Provence is a country to which I am always returning, next week, next year, any day now, as soon as I can get on to a train. Here in London it is an effort of will to believe in the existence of such a place at all. But now and again the vision of golden tiles on a round southern roof, or of some warm, stony, herb-scented hillside will rise out of my kitchen pots with the smell of a piece of orange peel scenting a beef stew. The picture flickers into focus again. Ford Madox Ford's words come back, 'somewhere between Vienne and Valence, below Lyon on the Rhône, the sun is shining and south of Valence Provincia Romana, the Roman province, lies beneath the sun. There there is no more any evil, for there the apple will not flourish and the brussels sprout will not grow at all.'

It is indeed certain, although the apple of discord can hardly be said to have been absent from the history of Provence, which is a turbulent and often ferocious one, that the sprout from Brussels, the drabness and dreariness and stuffy smells evoked by its very name, has nothing at all to do with southern cooking. But to regard the food of Provence as just a release from routine, a fierce wild riot of flavour and colour, is to over-simplify it and grossly to mistake its nature. For it is not primitive food; it is civilized without being over-civilized. That is to say, it has natural taste, smell, texture, and much character. Often it looks beautiful, too. What it amounts to is that it is the rational, right and proper food for human beings to eat.

Madame Léon Daudet, who, under the pen-name of Pampille, published many years ago a little collection of regional recipes called *Les Bons Plats de France*, goes so far as to say that 'the cooking of

4

Provence seems to me the best of all cooking; this is not said to hurt the feelings of other provinces, but it is the absolute truth.' Whether or not one agrees with Madame Daudet's wonderfully sweeping statement one should on no account be deceived by the often clumsy attempts of London restaurateurs to reproduce Provençal dishes. To them Provence is a name, a symbol to display to their customers; the string of garlic hanging on the wall is something like the equivalent of an inn sign. Nor must some ostentatious meal in a phoney Provençal 'oustalou' whose row of medals stands for price rather than true taste or quality be taken as representative. Provence does not consist only of the international playground of the coast. Northern and western Provence, the departments of the Vaucluse and the Basses Alpes, are still comparatively unsophisticated, and the cooking has retained much of its traditional character, the inhabitants relying on their own plentiful resources of vegetables, fruit, meat, game and cheese rather than on the imports from other provinces and from Algeria which supplement the more meagre resources of the coastal area.

Provençal food is perhaps best considered in terms of a meal such as that described, again, by Madame Daudet: 'I know of nothing more appetizing,' she says, 'on a very hot day, than to sit down in the cool shade of a dining-room with drawn Venetian blinds, at a little table laid with black olives, *saucisson d'Arles*, some fine tomatoes, a slice of water melon and a pyramid of little green figs baked by the sun. One will scarcely resist the pleasure of afterwards tasting the anchovy tart or the roast of lamb cooked on the spit, its skin perfectly browned, or the dish of tender little artichokes in oil . . . but should one wish, one could make one's meal almost exclusively of the hors-d'œuvre and the fruit. In this light air, in this fortunate countryside, there is no need to warm oneself with heavy meats or dishes of lentils. The midi is essentially a region of carefully prepared little dishes.'

This was written in 1919, but these little dishes of Provence are still to be found in country restaurants where they aren't falling over backwards to provide local colour; places where you may perhaps have the routine Sunday grilled or roast chicken but with it an interesting anchovy sauce, or a mayonnaise made unmistakably with real Provençal olive oil; or a *rôti de porc* with *pommes mousseline*, the interest lying in

6

the fact that that purée of potatoes will be good enough to serve as a separate course because the aromatic juices from the roast have been poured over it. It may be an hors-d'œuvre of anchovies and eggs, a salad of chick peas, a *pot-au-feu* or a beef stew which will be different from the *pot-au-feu* and the beef stew of other regions because of the herbs and the wine that have gone into it, even because of the pot it has cooked in. There will be vegetable dishes, too. The *haricots verts* are remarkable, although of course you won't get them on the crowded coast in August. Provence is now a great market garden centre, and from Cavaillon and Pertuis come melons, asparagus, artichokes, lettuces, courgettes, aubergines, peaches and cherries to enrich our own English markets. The little town of Le Thor supplies France with great quantities of table grapes; Carpentras is the centre of a lively trade in the local black truffles. The natural caves round about the astonishing red and ochre village of Roussillon are used for a large-scale cultivation of mushrooms; Apt provides peach jam and bitter cherry jam and most of the crystallized apricots we ourselves buy at Christmas time. It is also one of the few places hereabouts where you can still find the old traditional earthenware *gratin* dishes, saucepans and cooking pots of Provence.

Of course the inhabitants of Provence do not live upon *aïoli* and *grillades au fenouil* and *bouillabaisse*; in the hill villages of the Var and the Comtat and the Vaucluse you are lucky if you get fresh fish once a week; on the other hand nearly every village butcher makes his own sausages and pork pâtés, up in the Basses Alpes their own *pâté de grives*, too, and sometimes there will be locally cured ham, *jambon de montagne*. Once in the little town of Sault, on the lower slopes of the Mont Ventoux, I heard an old peasant lady getting very agitated because the shop assistant had inadvertently cut her a slice of ordinary commercial ham instead of the locally cured variety. The ham was for her dish of *petits pois* and that *jambon de Paris* would make it insipid, did Mademoiselle understand? Yes, Mademoiselle understood perfectly, and kept everybody in the crowded shop waiting while she cut the precise piece of ham required by the old lady.

In the season, in the villages of the Vaucluse, asparagus or wonderful broad beans will be a few francs a kilo, a basket of cherries or strawberries the same. Perhaps you may arrange for the bus driver to

bring you some *brandade* of salt cod out from Cavaillon or Apt for Friday lunch; at Les Saintes Maries and Aigues Mortes and other places isolated out in the marshes the travelling market stall called the Lion of Arles sets up in the Place and sells Arles sausage, charcuterie, and good butter. Perhaps a sheep farmer's wife will come down the hill with rabbits to sell, and the ewe's milk cheeses called *Banons*, wrapped in chestnut leaves or flavoured with the peppery herb called *poivre d'âne*, the Provençal version of savory.

Provence is not without its bleak and savage side. The inhabitants wage perpetual warfare against the ravages of the mistral; it takes a strong temperament to stand up to this ruthless wind which sweeps Provence for the greater part of the year. One winter and spring when the mistral never ceased its relentless screaming round our crumbling hill village opposite the Lubéron mountain we all seemed to come perilously near to losing our reason, although it is, of course, only fair to say that the truly awful wine of that particular district no doubt also contributed its share. It was the kind of wine which it was wisest to drink out of a tumbler so that there was room for a large proportion of water. I often wonder, when I hear people talking so enthusiastically of those fresh little wines of Provence, how they would feel about them if they had nothing else to drink. Most of them are made by the cooperative societies nowadays, and what they have lost in character they appear to have gained in fieriness. Of course, there are good wines in Provence but finding them is not easy, and the situation is further aggravated by the growing habit of Provençal restaurateurs of serving all white and rosé wines so frozen that any character they may have had has become unrecognizable.

Then there was the tragic spring of 1956 when it was not so much the mistral which had struck Provence as the terrible frosts of the preceding winter. Acre upon acre of blighted, blackened olive trees made the Provençal landscape almost unrecognizable. Hundreds of small farmers had lost their livelihood for years to come.

It does not do to regard Provence simply as Keats's tranquil land of song and mirth. The melancholy and the savagery are part of its spell.

French Provincial Cooking
chosen by Jacqueline Korn

When I started cooking 'seriously' at the beginning of the sixties, *French Provincial Cooking* was the book which inspired me more than any other. The piece about Provence seems to me to show Elizabeth writing at her best, conjuring up a different, exotic world where food was colourful and full of flavour, and eating was the most pleasurable of activities.

When I went to live in Rome in 1965 *Italian Food* was my bible. The Italian Store Cupboard from that book sums up the whole flavour of Italian food as well as Elizabeth's talent for sharing her excitement about ingredients and place. Looking through my notes from that time I see that a favourite dinner party menu which I would produce would be Melanzane Ripiene, followed by Costolette alla Bolognese, ending up with Monte Bianco.

Jacqueline Korn

HORS-D'ŒUVRE

From the luxurious pâté of truffled goose or duck liver of Alsace to the homely household *terrine de campagne*, from the *assiette de fruits de mer* of the expensive sea-food restaurant to the simple little selection of olives, radishes, butter, sliced sausage and egg mayonnaise of the *café routier*, an hors-d'œuvre is the almost invariable start to the French midday meal. The English visitor to France cannot fail to observe that the artistry with which the French present their food is nowhere more apparent than in the service of the hors-d'œuvre. So far from appearing contrived, or zealously worked on, each dish looks as if it had been freshly imagined, prepared for the first time, especially for you.

Now, since the main object of an hors-d'œuvre is to provide something beautifully fresh-looking which will at the same time arouse your appetite and put you in good spirits, this point is very important and nothing could be less calculated to have the right effect than the appearance of the little bits of straggling greenery, blobs of mayonnaise and wrinkled radishes which show all too clearly that the food has been over-handled and that it has been standing about for some hours before it was time to serve it. And the place for wilted lettuce leaves is the dustbin, not the hors-d'œuvre dish. What is the matter with a plain, straightforward half avocado pear, a mound of freshly boiled prawns, a few slices of good fresh *salame*, that they must be arranged on top of these eternal lettuce leaves? I swear I am not exaggerating when I say that in London restaurants I have even had *pâté de foie gras* served on that weary prop lettuce leaf. . . .

Now here are one or two ideas from France which have struck me as being particularly attractive for the service of an hors-d'œuvre.

To start with the north, where the ingredients obtainable are not so very different from our own, I remember the big airy first-floor dining-room of the Hôtel de la Poste at Duclair. At a table overlooking the Seine we sat with a bottle of Muscadet while waiting for luncheon. Presently a rugged earthenware terrine, worn with the patina of years, containing the typical duck pâté of the country, was put upon the table, and with it a mound of *rillettes de porc*; to be followed at a suitable interval with a number of little dishes containing plain boiled *langoustines* (we used to know them as Dublin Bay prawns before they turned into Venetian *scampi*), shrimps also freshly boiled with exactly the right amount of salt; winkles, a cork stuck with pins to extract them from their shells; sardines and anchovies both in their deep square tins to show that they were high-class brands. Then a variety of little salads each with a different seasoning, and forming, in white-lined brown dishes, a wonderfully imaginative-looking array, although in fact there was nothing very startling.

There were thinly sliced cucumbers, little mushrooms in a red-gold sauce, tomatoes, cauliflower vinaigrette, carrots grated almost to a purée (delicious, this one), herring fillets. The colours were skilfully blended but sober. The pale rose-pinks of the *langoustines*, the pebbly black of the winkles, the different browns of the anchovies and herrings and the dishes themselves, the muted greens of the cucumber and

cauliflower, the creams and greys of shrimps and mushrooms contrasted with the splash of red tomatoes, the glowing orange of the
carrots, and yellow mayonnaise shining in a separate bowl. Each of
these things was differently, and very sparingly, seasoned. Each had
its own taste and was firm and fresh. The shrimps and the *langoustines*
smelt of the sea. And with the exception of the duck pâté there was
nothing in the least complicated. It was all a question of taste, care,
and the watchful supervision of the proprietor. And although there
was such a large selection, larger probably than one would want to
serve at home, it had no resemblance at all to one of those trolleys
loaded with a tray of sixty dishes which may look very varied but in
fact all taste the same, and which almost certainly indicate that the
rest of your meal is going to be indifferent.

This is what food connoisseurs condemn when they say that a
mixed hors-d'œuvre is not only unnecessary but positively detrimental
to the enjoyment of a good meal; on the other hand, a nicely presented
and well-composed hors-d'œuvre does much to reassure the guests as
to the quality of the rest of the cooking, and to put them in the right
frame of mind to enjoy it.

I vividly remember, for instance, the occasion when, having stopped
for petrol at a filling station at Remoulins near the Pont du Gard, we
decided to go into the café attached to it, and have a glass of wine. It
was only eleven o'clock in the morning but for some reason we were
very hungry. The place was empty, but we asked if we could have
some bread, butter and sausage. Seeing that we were English, the old
lady in charge tried to give us a ham sandwich, and when we politely
but firmly declined this treat she went in search of the *patron* to ask
what she should give us.

He was an intelligent and alert young man who understood at once
what we wanted. In a few minutes he reappeared and set before us a
big rectangular platter in the centre of which were thick slices of
home-made pork and liver pâté, and on either side fine slices of the
local raw ham and sausage; these were flanked with black olives, green
olives, freshly-washed radishes still retaining some of their green
leaves, and butter.

By the time we had consumed these things, with wine and good fresh bread, we realized that this was no ordinary *café routier*. The *patron* was pleased when we complimented him on his pâté and told us that many of his customers came to him specially for it. It was now nearly midday and the place was fast filling up with these customers. They were lorry drivers, on their way from Sète, on the coast, up through France with their immense tanker lorries loaded with Algerian wine. The noise and bustle and friendly atmosphere soon made us realize that this must be the most popular place in the neighbourhood. We stayed, of course, for lunch. Chance having brought us there it would have been absurd to stick to our original plans of driving on to some star restaurant or other where we probably wouldn't have eaten so well (my travels in France are studded with memories of the places to which I have taken a fancy but where I could not stop – the café at Silléry where the still champagne was so good, the restaurant at Bray-sur-Seine where we had a late breakfast of raw country ham, beautiful butter and fresh thin *baguettes* of bread, and longed to stay for lunch – inflexible planning is the enemy of good eating). But here at Remoulins we stayed, and enjoyed a good sound lunch, unusually well-presented for a *café routier*.

We came back the next night for a specially ordered dinner of Provençal dishes, for the proprietor was a Marseillais and his wife the daughter of the owners of the house which had been converted from a farm to a restaurant-filling station. The young man was a cook of rare quality, and the dinner he prepared to order put to shame the world-famous Provençal three-star establishment where we had dined a day or two previously. But had it not been for the appearance of the delicious hors-d'œuvre, which was so exactly the right food at the right moment, we should have had our drink and paid our bill and gone on our way not knowing. . . .

Even simpler in composition was another hors-d'œuvre which was served us at a hotel at Les Saintes-Maries-de-la-Mer. It consisted simply of a very large round dish, quite flat, completely covered with overlapping circles of thinly sliced *saucisson d'Arles*; in the centre was a cluster of shining little black olives. Nothing much, indeed, but the visual appeal of that plate of fresh country produce was so potent that we felt we were seeing, and tasting, Arles sausage and black olives for the very first time.

So you see one does not need caviar and oysters or truffled *foie gras* and smoked salmon or even pâtés and terrines and lobster cocktails to make a beautiful first course. One needs imagination and taste and a sense of moderation; one must be able to resist the temptation to overdo it and unbalance the whole meal by offering such a spread that the dishes to follow don't stand a chance; one must remember that eggs and vegetables with oil and mayonnaise dressings, and pâtés with their strong flavours and fat content and their accompaniments of bread or toast, are very filling but not quite satisfactory to make a meal of; so the different components of an hors-d'œuvre must be chosen with great care if they are to fulfil their function of serving as appetizers rather than appetite killers.

To translate all this into practical terms I would say that a well composed mixed hors-d'œuvre consists, approximately, of something raw, something salt, something dry or meaty, something gentle and smooth and possibly something in the way of fresh fish. Simplified though it is, a choice based roughly on these lines won't be far wrong.

French Provincial Cooking

MUSHROOM SALAD

½ lb (225 g) mushrooms, olive oil, lemon juice, garlic, parsley, salt and pepper.

Buy if possible the large rather shaggy-looking variety of mushrooms. Wash them but do not peel them. Cut them in thinnish slices, leaving the stalks on. Put them in a bowl, squeeze lemon juice over them, stir in a little chopped garlic, season with ground black pepper, and pour a good deal of olive oil over them. Immediately before serving salt them and add more olive oil, as you will find they have absorbed the first lot. Sprinkle with parsley or, if you have it, basil, or a mixture of fresh marjoram and lemon thyme.

This is an expensive salad to make, as mushrooms absorb an enormous quantity of oil, but it is extremely popular, and particularly good with a grilled or roast chicken. Variations can be made by mixing the mushrooms with a few strips of raw fennel or with a cupful of cooked green peas.

For an hors-d'œuvre, mix the mushrooms with large cooked prawns.

Summer Cooking

CORIANDER MUSHROOMS

This is a quickly cooked little dish which makes a delicious cold hors-d'œuvre. The aromatics used are similar to those which go into *with Tomato* the well known *champignons à la grecque,* but the method is simpler, and the result even better.

Ingredients for three people are: 6 oz (170 g) firm, white, round and very fresh mushrooms, a teaspoon of coriander seeds, 2 tablespoons of olive oil, lemon juice, salt, freshly milled pepper, and one or two bay leaves.

Rinse the mushrooms, wipe them dry with a clean cloth, slice them (but do not peel them) into quarters, or if they are large into eighths. The stalks should be neatly trimmed. Squeeze over them a little lemon juice.

In a heavy frying pan or sauté pan, warm the olive oil. Into it put the coriander seeds which should be ready crushed in a mortar. Let them heat for a few seconds. Keep the heat low. Put in the mushrooms and the bay leaves. Add the seasoning. Let the mushrooms cook gently for a minute, cover the pan and leave them, still over very low heat, for another 3–5 minutes.

Uncover the pan. Decant the mushrooms – with all their juices – into a shallow serving dish and sprinkle them with fresh olive oil and lemon juice.

Whether the mushrooms are to be served hot or cold do not forget to put the bay leaf which has cooked with them into the serving dish. The combined scents of coriander and bay go to make up part of the true essence of the dish. And it is important to note that cultivated mushrooms should not be cooked for longer than the time specified.

In larger quantities, the same dish can be made as a hot vegetable to be eaten with veal or chicken.

Cooked mushrooms do not keep well, but a day or two in the refrigerator does not harm this coriander-spiced dish. It is also worth remembering that *uncooked* cultivated mushrooms can be stored in a plastic box in the refrigerator and will keep fresh for a couple of days.

No, a paper bag is much better as the mushrooms do not sweat.

Spices, Salt and Aromatics

TOMATES PROVENÇALES EN SALADE

Take the stalks off a large bunch of parsley; pound it with a little salt, in a mortar, with 2 cloves of garlic and a little olive oil.

Cut the tops off good raw tomatoes; with a teaspoon soften the pulp inside, sprinkle with salt, and turn them upside down so that the water drains out. Fill the tomatoes up with the parsley and garlic mixture. Serve them after an hour or two, when the flavour of the garlic and parsley has permeated the salad.

French Country Cooking
chosen by Sally Clarke

When I was twenty-one, freshly returned from a year of study in Paris, I wrote to Elizabeth David, whom I did not know, c/o 'the shop in Bourne Street', for advice. I had worked in three restaurants in Paris, spent three months at the Cordon Bleu school and decided that, as a result, I qualified as an informed and thoroughly capable 'writer'. The question was how to go about becoming one. As the weeks passed I forgot all about my desire to write. Then one afternoon, without warning, she telephoned me. I felt very stupid and a fraud – and, above all, I was shaking all over with nerves.

Although I went on, eventually, to become a restaurateur instead of a writer I shall never forget that day when she told me that to become a writer one needs to write and write and to keep sending the pieces to publishers and that one day, maybe one day, one may be accepted. Sound, sensible and obvious advice: very Mrs David, very to the point. Her guidance will continue to inspire generations as her thoughts and words speak of the pureness of the ingredient, the simplicity of their preparation, the importance of the seasons. How much I miss her.

Sally Clarke

PEPERONI ALLA PIEMONTESE

Cut some red, yellow or green pimentos, or some of each if they are obtainable, in half lengthways. Take out all the seeds and wash the pimentos. If they are large, cut each half in half again. Into each piece put 2 or 3 slices of garlic, 2 small sections of raw tomato, about half a fillet of anchovy cut into pieces, a small nut of butter, a dessertspoonful of oil, a very little salt. Arrange these pimentos on a flat baking dish and cook them in a moderate oven (180°C/350°F/Gas Mark 4) for about 30 minutes. They are not to be completely cooked; the pimentos should in fact be *al dente*, the stuffing inside deliciously oily and garlicky.

Serve them cold, each garnished with a little parsley.

Italian Food
chosen by Lindsey Bareham and Leslie Zyw

This is one of the simplest, most stunning and delicious dishes I know. It is something I make constantly, particularly when I am entertaining en masse. It's tucked away in the lengthy *antipasti insalate* section of *Italian Food* where it might have stayed had it not been for the eagle eyes and good taste of Franco Taruschio, who put it on the menu of The Walnut Tree when it opened near Abergavenny in 1963.

Some years later, Simon Hopkinson was introduced to Piedmontese Peppers by a chef who had worked for Franco (Peter Gorton, now at the Horn of Plenty at Gulworthy in Devon); he was so impressed by its stylish simplicity and powerful Mediterranean flavours that he 'saved' it for his first menu at Bibendum. That is where I first sampled it.   Lindsey Bareham

OLIVES

Italian olives present a fine variety of colours, shapes, sizes and textures. There are dark, luminous black olives from Gaeta; little coal-black olives of Rome, smoky and wrinkled; sloe-like black olives of Castella-mare, like bright black eyes; olives brown and purple and yellow from

Sardinia; Sicilian black olives in oil; olives of a dozen different greens; the bright, smooth, newly-gathered olives before they have been salted; the slightly yellower tinge they acquire after a week or two in the brine (how delicious they are before the salt has really penetrated); the giant green olives called *cerignola*, from Puglie; the bitter green olives with a very large stone known in Italy as *olive spagnuole* (Spanish olives); olives of all the greens of the evening sea.

As part of a simplified hors-d'œuvre, consisting of *salame*, tomatoes, and a country cheese, black olives are by far the best. If they seem too salt when bought, put them in a jar and cover them with olive oil. This is, in any case, the best way to store them at home. Generally speaking, for green olives, the small oval ones are the best. They can be kept in the same way as the black; and, if you like, add a little cut garlic to the oil and a piece of chilli or dried red pepper.

Italian Food
chosen by Annie Davies

When I went to work for Elizabeth at her shop in Bourne Street in 1970 I had read all her books without cooking a single meal. Via them I had journeyed through France and around the Mediterranean; *Italian Food* I especially loved. Like her books, the shop was a demonstration that food could be something more than just eating, and preparing meals more than just cooking: the aesthetic element was as strong as the gastronomic. Elizabeth was acutely sensitive to the look of things, particularly shapes and colours, the raw ingredients, the utensils used to cook them and the dishes to serve them in. It still seems to me that the books can be read for themselves, miles from any kitchen, such is the power of her writing and her ability to evoke not only the pleasure of cooking and eating, but the simple beauty of food and wine.

Annie Davies

ŒUFS DURS EN TAPÉNADE

An interesting Provençal hors-d'œuvre.

To make the *tapénade*, called after the capers (*tapéno* in Provençal) which go into it, the ingredients are 24 stoned black olives, 8 anchovy fillets, 2 heaped tablespoons of capers, 2 oz (60 g) tunny fish, olive oil, lemon juice.

Pound all the solid ingredients together into a thick purée. Add the olive oil (about a coffee-cupful, after-dinner size) gradually, as for a mayonnaise, then squeeze in a little lemon juice. It is an improvement also to add a few drops of cognac or other spirit, and sometimes a little mustard is included in the seasoning. No salt, of course.

Spread the prepared sauce in a little flat hors-d'œuvre dish, and put 6 to 7 hard-boiled eggs, sliced in half lengthways, on the top. The curious thing about this sauce is that it has a kind of ancient, powerful flavour about it, as if it were something which might perhaps have been eaten by the Romans. Well, it was invented less than a hundred years ago by the chef at the Maison Dorée in Marseille, although it must certainly have been based on some already existing sauce. The original method was to stuff the eggs with the *tapénade*, plus the pounded yolks. At la Mère Germaine's beautiful restaurant at Château-neuf du Pape, the *tapénade* is served pressed down into little deep yellow earthenware pots, like a pâté, and comes as part of the mixed hors-d'œuvre.

French Provincial Cooking

DOLMÁDES

Dolmádes, little rolls of savoury rice in vine leaves, are a favourite first course in Greece, Turkey and the Near East. Sometimes meat, pine nuts, and even currants are mixed with the rice. Here is the basic version:

For 3 dozen vine leaves you need about 2 teacups of cooked rice mixed with enough olive oil to make it moist, a little chopped fried onion, and a flavouring of allspice and dried mint. Blanch the vine leaves in boiling salted water. Drain them. Lay them flat on a board, outer side downwards. On the inside of each leaf lay a teaspoon of the rice, and then roll the leaf tucking in the ends as for a little parcel and squeeze this roll in the palm of your hand; in this manner the *dolmádes* will stay rolled up and need not be tied. When they are all ready put them carefully in a shallow pan, squeeze over plenty of lemon juice and add about a cup (enough to come halfway up the pile of *dolmádes*) of tomato juice or good stock. Cover with a small plate or saucer resting on top of the *dolmádes* and fitting *inside* the pan. The plate prevents the *dolmádes* moving during the cooking. Keep them just simmering for about 30 minutes. They are best eaten cold.

Mediterranean Food
chosen by Julia Drysdale

It was during the war, when Elizabeth was in Egypt, that her interest in Middle Eastern food began and developed into a lasting love. She knew strange little restaurants dotted around London where she would take you, tell you what you were going to eat and then conduct a voyage of discovery through each dish. Lebanese was probably her favourite, but Greek and Turkish followed closely. Julia Drysdale

LE SAUSSOUN, *or* SAUCE AUX AMANDES DU VAR

From Roquebrune in the Var comes this curious sauce which, served as an hors-d'œuvre to be spread on bread, or in sandwiches for tea, has a cool, fresh and original taste.

Pound 4 fresh mint leaves to a paste, then add 4 anchovy fillets. Have ready 2 oz (60 g) finely ground almonds, about 2 fl oz (60 ml) olive oil, and half a coffee-cup (after-dinner size) of water. Stir in these three ingredients alternately, a little of each at a time, until all are used up. The result should be a thick mass, in consistency something like a very solid mayonnaise. Season with a little salt if necessary, and a drop of lemon juice.

French Provincial Cooking

AUBERGINE PURÉE

Grill or bake 4 aubergines until their skins crack and will peel easily. Sieve the peeled aubergines, mix them with 2 or 3 tablespoons of yoghourt, the same of olive oil, salt, pepper, lemon juice. Garnish with a few very thin slices of raw onion and chopped mint leaves. This is a Near Eastern dish which is intended to be served as an hors-d'œuvre with bread, or with meat, in the same manner as a chutney.

Summer Cooking
chosen by Jonna Dwinger

MAURITIAN PRAWN CHUTNEY

4 oz (120 g) peeled prawns, a green or red pimento or half a small hot green or red chilli pepper, olive oil, salt, cayenne, green ginger or ground ginger, lemon or fresh lime juice, 4 spring onions.

Pound the peeled prawns in a mortar with the chopped spring onions. Add the pimento or chilli, chopped very finely. Stir in enough olive oil (about 3 or 4 tablespoons) little by little, to make the mixture into a thick paste. Add a pinch of ground ginger, or a teaspoonful of grated green ginger, and, if mild peppers have been used, a scrap of cayenne. Squeeze in the juice of a fresh lime if available, or of half a lemon, and salt if necessary.

Although this is a chutney to be served with curries, it makes a delicious hors-d'œuvre served with hard-boiled eggs, or just with toast.

Summer Cooking

or trout

FILETS DE MAQUEREAUX AU VIN BLANC

One of the classic hors-d'œuvre of France, but very rarely met with in England.

or wine vinegar

Prepare a *court-bouillon* with a wine glass of white wine and one of water, an onion, a clove of garlic, a bay leaf, salt and ground black pepper, and a piece of lemon peel. Bring this to the boil, let it cook 5 minutes, then leave it to cool.

Put the cleaned mackerel into the cold *court-bouillon* and let them cook very gently for about 15 minutes; leave them to get cold in the *court-bouillon*. Split them carefully, take out the bones, remove the skin and divide each fish into about 6 or 8 small fillets, and arrange in a narrow oval dish. Reheat the *court-bouillon*, letting it bubble until it is reduced by half. When it is cool, strain it over the mackerel, and garnish the dish with a few capers and some chopped chives or parsley.

cool makes skinning easier.

Compare this recipe with Scottish marinaded herring fillets

French Country Cooking
chosen by Norma Grant

Taramosalata

COD'S ROE PASTE IN THE GREEK MANNER

in any Greek food shop

Cheap, easy, made in advance, an admirable standby. What you can do with a 2-oz (60-g) jar of smoked cod's roe, a few spoonfuls of oil and a potato is quite a revelation to many people.

For a 2-oz (60-g) jar of smoked cod's roe the other ingredients are about 4 tablespoons of olive oil, a medium-sized potato, lemon juice, cayenne pepper and water; and, optionally, a clove of garlic.

An hour or two before you are going to make the paste, or the evening before if it's more convenient, turn the contents of the jar into a bowl, break it up, and put about 3 tablespoons of cold water with it. This

23

softens it and makes it much easier to work. Drain off the water before starting work on the making of the dish.

Pound the garlic and mash it with the cod's roe until the paste is quite smooth before gradually adding 3 tablespoons of the oil. Boil the potato without salt, mash it smooth with the rest of the oil, combine the two mixtures, stir again until quite free from lumps, add the juice of half a lemon and a scrap of cayenne pepper. Pack the mixture into little pots or jars. Serve chilled with hot dry toast. Enough for four.

Also freezes.

This little dish, or a similar one, is now listed on the menus of scores of Cypriot-Greek taverns and London bistros under the name of *taramasalata*. It is indeed very much akin to the famous Greek speciality, except that true *taramasalata* is made from a cod's roe much more salty, more pungent, and less smoked than our own. There is also a great deal more garlic in the Greek version, and very often bread instead of potato is used as a softening agent.

An Omelette and a Glass of Wine
chosen by George Elliot

POTTED CHICKEN LIVERS

This is a recipe which produces a rich, smooth and gamey-flavoured mixture, rather like a very expensive French pâté, at a fraction of the price and with very little fuss.

Ingredients are 4 oz (120 g) chicken livers (frozen livers are perfectly adequate), 3 oz (90 g) butter, a tablespoon of brandy, seasonings.

Frozen chicken livers are already cleaned, so if they are being used the only preliminary required is the thawing-out process. If you have bought fresh livers, put them in a bowl of tepid, slightly salted water and leave them for about a couple of hours. Then look at each one very carefully, removing any yellowish pieces, which may give the finished dish a bitter taste.

Heat 1 oz (30 g) butter in a small heavy frying pan. In this cook the livers for about 5 minutes, turning them over constantly. The outsides should be browned but not toughened, the insides should remain pink but not raw. Take them from the pan with a perforated spoon and transfer them to a mortar or the liquidizer goblet.

To the buttery juices in the pan add the brandy and let it sizzle for a few seconds. Pour it over the chicken livers. Add a teaspoon of salt, and a sprinkling of milled pepper. Put in the remaining 2 oz (60 g) butter, softened but not melted. Pound or whizz the whole mixture to a very smooth paste. Taste for seasoning. Press into a little china, glass or glazed earthenware pot or terrine and smooth down the top. Cover, and chill in the refrigerator. Serve with hot crisp dry toast.

If to be made in larger quantities and stored, seal the little pots with a layer of clarified butter, melted and poured over the chilled paste.

Rum (white, for preference) makes a sound alternative to the brandy in this recipe. Surprisingly, perhaps, gin is also very successful.

N.B. Since this dish is a very rich one, I sometimes add to the chicken livers an equal quantity of blanched, poached pickled pork (*not* bacon) or failing pickled pork, a piece of fresh belly of pork, salted overnight, then gently poached for about 30 minutes. Add the cooked pork, cut in small pieces, to the chicken livers in the blender.

An Omelette and a Glass of Wine
chosen by Jonna Dwinger and George Elliot

POTTED TONGUE

To my mind this is the best and most subtle of all English potted-meat inventions. My recipe is adapted from John Farley's *The London Art of Cookery* published in 1783. Farley was master of the London Tavern, and an unusually lucid writer. One deduces that the cold table at the London Tavern must have been exceptionally good, for all Farley's sideboard dishes, cold pies, hams, spiced beef joints and potted meats are thought out with much care, are set down in detail and show a delicate and educated taste.

Ingredients and proportions for potted tongue are ½ lb (225 g) each of cooked, brined and/or smoked ox tongue and clarified butter, a salt-spoonful of ground mace, a turn or two of black or white pepper from the mill.

Chop the tongue and, with 5 oz (150 g) (weighed after clarifying) of the butter, reduce it to a paste in the blender or liquidizer, season it, pack it tightly down into a pot or pots, smooth over the top, cover, and leave in the refrigerator until very firm. Melt the remaining 3 oz (75 g) of clarified butter and pour it, tepid, over the tongue paste, so that it sets in a sealing layer about one-eighth of an inch (3 mm) thick. When completely cold, cover the pots with foil or greaseproof paper. Store them in the refrigerator.

The amount given will fill one ¾- to 1-pint (400–550 ml) shallow soufflé dish, although I prefer to pack my potted tongue in two or three smaller and shallower containers.

Spices, Salt and Aromatics
chosen by Kit Chapman

PORK AND SPINACH TERRINE

Pâtés and terrines have become, during the past decade, so very much a part of the English restaurant menu as well as of home entertaining that a variation of formula would sometimes be welcome.

At Orange, that splendid town they call the gateway to Provence, I once tasted a pâté which was more fresh green herbs than meat. I was told that this was made according to a venerable country recipe of Upper Provence.

The pâté was interesting but rather heavy. I have tried to make it a little less filling. Here is the result of my experiments:

1 lb (450 g) uncooked spinach, spinach beet or chard, 1 lb (450 g) freshly-minced fat pork, seasonings of salt, freshly milled pepper, mixed spices.

Wash, cook and drain the spinach. When cool, squeeze it as dry as you can. There is only one way to do this – with your hands. Chop it roughly.

Season the meat with about 3 teaspoons of salt, a generous amount of freshly-milled black pepper, and about ¼ teaspoon of mixed ground spices (mace, allspice, cloves).

Mix meat and spinach together. Turn into a pint-sized (550 ml) earthenware terrine or loaf tin. On top put a piece of buttered paper. Stand the terrine or tin in a baking dish half filled with water.

Cook in a very moderate oven (170°C/330°F/Gas Mark 3) for 45 minutes to an hour. Do not let it get overcooked or it will be dry.

This pâté *can* be eaten hot as a main course, but I prefer it cold, as a first dish, and with bread or toast just as a pâté is always served in France.

The interesting points about this dish are its appearance, its fresh, uncloying flavour and its comparative lightness, which should appeal to those who find the better-known type of pork pâté rather heavy.

You could, for example, serve a quite rich or creamy dish after this without overloading anybody's stomach.

Spices, Salt and Aromatics
chosen by Sabrina Harcourt-Smith

When I was an Army wife in Germany, Belgium, the Netherlands and lastly in Stockholm, I often found myself having to cook huge and sometimes impromptu buffet lunches, dinners and picnics. Happily, at an early stage in these travels, I discovered this magical dish. Aunt Liza was pleased to hear that it never failed to inspire discussion about the unusual additions of spinach and mace and, more importantly, second and third helpings.

Sabrina Harcourt-Smith

RILLETTES

1½–2 lb (675–900 g) belly of pork, with a good proportion of lean to fat, a clove of garlic, a sprig of fresh thyme or marjoram, salt, pepper, a pinch of mace.

Remove bones and rind from the meat, and cut it into small cubes. Put these into a thick pan with the chopped garlic, the herbs and seasoning. Cook on a very low heat, or in the slowest possible oven for 1½ hours, until the pieces of pork are quite soft without being fried, and swimming in their own fat. Place a wide sieve over a bowl, and pour the meat into the sieve so that the fat drips through into the basin. When the meat has cooled, pull it into shreds, using two forks. If you cannot manage this, chop the meat. But unless you are making *rillettes* in a large quantity, try to avoid using the electric blender. It gives the meat too compact and smooth a texture. Pack the *rillettes* into small earthenware or china pots, and seal them with their own

fat. Cover with greaseproof paper or foil. *Rillettes* will keep for weeks, and make an excellent stand-by for an hors-d'œuvre. Serve them with bread and white wine.

Summer Cooking

TERRINE OF RABBIT

A rabbit weighing about 1 lb (450 g) when skinned and cleaned, 1 lb (450 g) belly of pork, ¼ lb (120 g) fat bacon, thyme, salt, pepper, juniper berries, a little lemon peel, 2 tablespoons of brandy, mace, garlic, a bay leaf.

Have the rabbit cut into pieces, and simmer it in a little water for 20–30 minutes. When cold, take all the flesh off the bones, and chop it on a board with the pork (uncooked), 2 or 3 cloves of garlic, a good sprinkling of fresh thyme, about 8 juniper berries and a small strip of lemon peel. (If you have not a double-handled chopper, which makes this operation very easy, the meat will have to be put through a coarse mincer, but chopping is infinitely preferable.) Season the mixture fairly highly with ground black pepper, salt and mace. Stir in the brandy. Line the bottom of a fairly large terrine, or 2 or 3 small ones, with little strips of bacon. Put in the meat mixture. Put a bay leaf on top, and cover with another layer of strips of bacon.

Steam, covered, in a slow oven (150°C/300°F/Gas Mark 2) for 1½–2½ hours, according to the size of the terrines. When they come out of the oven put a piece of greaseproof paper over the terrines, lay a fairly heavy weight on top of them and leave them overnight.

Next day, the terrines can either be filled up with home-made aspic jelly, or simply sealed with pork fat. They are good either way, and make an excellent and inexpensive hors-d'œuvre.

Summer Cooking

BŒUF EN SALADE

Here is a recipe for a very simple cold dish made on a large scale, sufficient for one of the dishes of a buffet for about twenty people. It is only an extension of the salad made regularly in French households with the boiled beef from the *pot-au-feu*, but it makes very good party food. It looks attractive, the meat is in manageable pieces, the sauce makes it sufficiently moist without being too runny, and it has plenty of character without being outlandish.

Ingredients are about 4 lb (2 kg) stewing beef, a piece of knuckle of veal weighing about 3 lb (1.5 kg) including bone, 4 carrots, 2 onions, a bouquet of herbs, seasoning. The correct piece of beef is really ox muzzle or cheek, but this is not always obtainable, and shin or top rump can be used instead. Flank is also good but rather fat, and an extra pound is needed to allow for the waste when the fat is trimmed off after cooking. If possible have the meat, whatever it is, cut in one large piece, and tied into a good shape so that it will be easy to cut when cooked. For the sauce: 8 to 10 shallots, 2 oz (60 g) capers, 3 or 4 medium-sized pickled cucumbers, a little mustard, a very large bunch of parsley, ½ pint (280 ml) of olive oil, tarragon vinegar, 2 tomatoes, salt and pepper.

Put the beef and veal into a deep pan with the carrots, onions, and bouquet of herbs. Add 1 tablespoon of salt, cover with 7 or 8 pints (4–4.5 l) water, cook with the lid on the pan either in a very low oven or on top of the stove over a very gentle heat for 3½–5 hours, depending upon the cut of meat (ox cheek takes the longest) until the meat is quite tender. Remove both veal and beef, sprinkle them with salt and olive oil and leave until next day. Keep the stock for soup. To make the salad, cut the meat when quite cold into thin slices, narrow and neat, a little smaller than a business card. Mix the veal and the beef together.

The sauce takes time to prepare. The shallots must be chopped exceedingly fine with the parsley, which must be first washed in cold water and squeezed dry; when both shallots and parsley are chopped almost to a pulp stir in a little French mustard, salt, pepper, the chopped pickled cucumber and the capers. Add the olive oil gradually, and a very little tarragon vinegar. Mix the sauce very thoroughly with the meat. Lastly add the roughly chopped tomatoes, which are there mainly for appearance's sake. Leave for several hours before serving. Arrange in shallow dishes with a little extra chopped parsley on the top. There should be enough parsley in the sauce to make it quite thick and quite green.

This recipe can be applied to almost any kind of boiled meat or to fish and chicken, the quantities for the sauce being reduced in proportion to the amount of meat.

French Provincial Cooking
chosen by Jack Andrews

Paris

Although I did not realize it at the time, it was by way of Norman cookery that I first learned to appreciate French food. Torn, most willingly, from an English boarding school at the age of sixteen, to live with a middle-class French family in Passy, it was only some time later that I tumbled to the fact that even for a Parisian family who owned a small farm in Normandy, the Robertots were both exceptionally greedy and exceptionally well fed. Their cook, a young woman called Léontine, was bullied from morning till night, and how she had the spirit left to produce such delicious dishes I cannot now imagine. Twice a week at dawn Madame, whose purple face was crowned with a magnificent mass of white hair, went off to do the marketing at Les Halles, the central markets, where she bought all the provisions, including flowers for the flat. I don't think any shopping at all was done locally except for things like milk and bread. She would return at about ten o'clock, two bursting black shopping bags in each hand, puffing, panting, mopping her brow, and looking as if she was about to have a stroke. Indeed, poor Madame, after I had been in Paris about a year, her doctor told her that high blood pressure made it imperative for her to diet. Her diet consisted of cutting out meat once a week. With Friday a fish day anyway, this actually meant two days without meat. On Wednesdays, the day chosen, Madame would sit at table, the tears welling up in her eyes as she watched us helping ourselves to our *rôti de veau* or *bœuf à la cuillère*. It was soon given up, that diet. Her grown-up children, two of whom were afflicted with a tragic eye disease and were probably going blind, simply could not bear to watch her sufferings – although, of course, they were not prepared to go so far as to share in her privations. Denise, the only able-bodied daughter,

31

was the greediest girl I had ever seen. She worked as secretary to a world-famous Parisian surgeon, and came home every day to the midday meal. Before she took off her hat and coat she would shout out to Léontine to know what was for lunch. Munching through two helpings of everything she would entertain us to gruesome details of the operations performed by her employer.

It never occurred to me at the time to wonder whether she had really witnessed these harrowing sights or if it was just her own way of expressing her family's morbid preoccupation with death and disaster, which reached its peak every Thursday. For Thursday was Madame's *jour*, and not even the really remarkable turn-out of cakes and *petits fours*, mostly made by Léontine, reconciled us to the fact that courtesy demanded we put in an appearance and listen to stories of the appalling catastrophes which had befallen during the week *la cousine* Anne-Marie, Tante Berthe, her daughter Marguerite, mortally stricken with diabetes, and about half a dozen other ladies always dressed from head to foot in deepest black.

To make up for the ordeal of Thursday afternoon, the boarders (there were only three of us) soon got round to finding some pretext for not being present at Friday lunch. Ever since those days it has remained a mystery to me how people who were so fond of good food and who knew so much about it could endure to eat the boiled salt cod which was the regular Friday lunch. Grey, slimy, in great hideous flakes, it lay plonked on the dish without benefit of sauce or garnish of any kind. At that time I had not even heard of Provençal cooking, or of any of the excellent ways they prepare salt cod in the south, and did not of course know how the people of Provence would scoff at the very idea of a Norman cook producing a decent dish of *morue*. In any case, to avoid this horror, we used to treat ourselves to lunch in a students' restaurant near the Sorbonne, where we thought ourselves lucky to eat egg mayonnaise and a dish of *petits pois* without being questioned by the family as to what the morning's lectures had been about.

Another place where we enjoyed ourselves hugely was at the automatic restaurant, in the Boulevard St Michel I think, all shining chromium and terribly noisy, where we got a plate of ham and an orange out of a slot machine for a few francs. Eating here was forbidden by Madame, who considered that neither the *ambiance* nor the food was suitable for young girls. We used to memorize the menu posted up outside some approved restaurant so that we should have an answer ready when she questioned us. We seldom got away with it, of course, because we were never able to describe the food in the detail required. What appalling *ordures* had been in the so-called *vol-au-vent*? Were the *boulettes de viande* made from beef or veal or lamb? Ah, tiens, *des épinards à la crème*, and did they really contain cream or some horrible *sauce blanche*? *Vous ne le savez pas*? *Mais comment, chère Élisabeth*, you did not notice? No, *chère Élisabeth* had not noticed and did not care, for the fact was that although we enjoyed the good food in the Rue Eugène Delacroix, we were bored with the family's perpetual preoccupation with it, and there was little else to talk to them about; for when they were not actually eating or going to market, Madame and her eldest daughter were either wearing themselves out with long vigils in church or knitting for the poor. We felt stifled by the atmosphere of doom which seemed always imminent in the household, and spent more and more time in our rooms mugging up for our exams and thinking of every possible excuse for not coming in to meals.

So it was only later, after I had come home to England, that I realized in what way the family had fulfilled their task of instilling French culture into at least one of their British charges. Forgotten were the Sorbonne professors and the yards of Racine learnt by heart, the ground plans of cathedrals I had never seen, and the saga of Napoleon's last days on St Helena. What had stuck was the taste for a kind of food quite ideally unlike anything I had known before. Ever since, I have been trying to catch up with those lost days when perhaps I should have been more profitably employed watching Léontine in her kitchen rather than trudging conscientiously round every museum and picture gallery in Paris.

I do not think that the Robertots spent, as the French are always said to do, a disproportionate amount of their income on food. What with the bargains from Les Halles, the wine arriving in casks from Bordeaux, and cream and butter from their Norman property, their food was lovely without being rich or grand. Above all, as I see it now, it was consistent, all of a piece, and this of course was due to Madame's careful buying. There was none of that jerky feeling you get when the marketing is erratic or careless. So what emerges from those days is not the memory of elaborate sauces or sensational puddings, but rather of beautifully prepared vegetables like *salsifis à la crème*, purées of sorrel, and *pommes mousseline*. Many egg dishes, and soups delicately coloured like summer dresses, coral, ivory, or pale green, a salad of rice and tomatoes, another of cold beef, and especially, of course, Léontine's chocolate and apricot soufflés. On soufflé days Denise would suddenly find she was in a fearful hurry to get back to work. This meant that the soufflé was handed to her first. She not only saw to it that she got it before it had had a chance to sink, but if there was enough for a second helping she had first go at that too.

Sometimes I spent part of the Easter or summer holidays with the family at their little Norman farmhouse near Caen. Here a local girl, Marie, took over the cooking, while Léontine returned to her family in the country for what must have been a well-earned rest. The only vivid memory I have of the food in this peaceful and pretty house with its old-fashioned kitchen garden is of tasting mussels for the first time. They were served in a thick creamy sauce which no doubt had cider or white wine in its composition; this seemed to me a most mysterious and extraordinary dish, something which must be quite special to the family or perhaps thought up by Marie, the little village girl, so that when a year or two later I found *moules à la crème* on the menu at Walterspiel's in Munich, at that time one of the most famous restaurants in Europe, I was quite astonished and wondered how it had found its way from that obscure little Norman village all the way to Bavaria. To this day a dish of mussels is one of the first things I ask for upon landing in Northern France, and the last thing I eat before crossing the Channel to return to England, for although since that first time I have eaten mussels served in dozens of different ways in many parts of Europe and have cooked them myself hundreds of times, they never seem to have quite the *cachet*, the particular savour, of those mussels of Normandy, so small and sweet in their shining little shells.

French Provincial Cooking

Pleasing Cheeses

In food-song and travel-story the scene, the characters, and the opening dialogue are familiar enough: the inn is humble and is situated close to the banks of the radiant Loire. (In legend the Loire is always radiant. Quite often it actually is radiant. On this particular day it is super-radiant. The inn, ever-humble, of French cookery fables is, on this occasion, archi-humble.) The cook-proprietress is where she should be, in the kitchen, cooking lunch. Her own lunch, not ours. Frying-pan in hand, she is saying she has nothing for us, she hadn't been expecting customers; at this time of year there are visitors only at weekends. The customers reply never mind about lunch, they will drink a carafe of wine and perhaps Madame has some bread and sausage? Oh, if that is all monsieur and madame wish, would they be seated? One will attend to them.

Enter the cross-eyed daughter, bearing wine, plates and cutlery. She sets the oilcloth-covered table. Couldn't we eat out of doors? On such a beautiful day it seems sad to sit in the dank, scruffy room. The girl looks scared. She does not answer. We repeat our request. She shakes her head. Deaf as well as cross-eyed.

Oh well. We were thirsty and hungry. Not to make a palaver. Bread, butter, sausage and sliced raw ham were put before us. The loaf was very large, flat, brown-crusted, open-textured, a *pain de ménage*, the real household French bread such as is rarely produced nowadays in restaurants and inns. That bread alone was well worth the journey. We ate so much of it, it was so marvellous, that we hardly wanted the sausage and the ham, noticed only in passing that the wine wasn't up to much, and that the eggs in the omelette which presently appeared were spanking fresh and buttercup yellow – in the French countryside

35

one takes that for granted. And anyway, by now the son of the house had come in for his midday meal, turned on the television, created havoc out of the quiet day. Like his sister, the young man was cross-eyed, deaf and simple. His mother came in from the kitchen to ask if we'd like cheese or fresh cheese with cream. The two, please. We need not have bothered with the cheese proper. The fresh cheese with cream was all we, or at any rate I, wanted.

The telly faded, the shoddy oilcloth vanished, the beautiful sunshine we were missing was forgotten. There it was, the big glass bowl half-filled with soft, very white, very fresh milk cheese with its covering of fresh thick cream. It was just as I had remembered it for over thirty years, it was just as it used to appear at least once a week at lunch in the Paris household where I spent two years of my youth with a greedy Norman family: two years of study interspersed with the most trying of family meals, endless and infinitely to be dreaded but for the blessed beauty of the food. It was first class, not at all, as I later understood, ambitious or opulent, but of consistent quality, very fresh and, in effect, just very good French bourgeois food, carefully bought, traditionally cooked, presented with much visual taste. Sorrel soups we used to eat, and lettuce soups, delicate vegetables such as salsify and celeriac, golden melting potatoes, a nutmeg-flavoured rice salad with tomatoes, apricot soufflés, and the famous *fromage frais à la crème* invariably presented in a glass bowl with sugar and more cream, Norman cream (well, I said they were greedy), on the table.

So what did she mean, the proprietress of the lugubrious little *estaminet* on the banks of the lovely Loire, what could she have meant when she said she had nothing in the house for lunch? She had that astonishingly good bread, did she not, and she had the freshly made fresh cream cheese – goat's milk cheese and cow's milk cream, not too thick, not rich, not yellow, appearing cream coloured only because the cheese it half-concealed and half-revealed (you see the point of the glass bowl) was so muslin-white and new.

An Omelette and a Glass of Wine
chosen by Celia Denney

So much is said (and how rightly) of Elizabeth's renown for meticulous research, her crusade for ingredients of quality, her scorn of pretension, that often her gift as a story-teller is neglected. For atmosphere evoked in a phrase or two, for her wry humour and sense of fun, for her characteristic understatement and economy as a raconteuse, I have selected The Christmas Pudding is Mediterranean Food, Ladies' Halves, and Pleasing Cheeses.

Celia Denney

SOUPS

PASTA IN BRODO CON FEGATINI E PISELLI

I first came across this *minestra* in Verona; it is one of the nicest *pasta in brodo* mixtures, mild, soothing and freshly flavoured.

The quantities for two people are 1 pint (550 ml) chicken broth, 4 or 5 chicken livers, 6–8 oz (170–225 g) shelled green peas, about 1½ oz (45 g) fine *pasta* (it should be home-made, in short strips about the thickness of a match, but ready-made *pasta* will do), Parmesan cheese, a little butter.

If using ready-made *pasta*, first cook it for 5 minutes, with the green peas, in plenty of boiling salted water. Drain it, and then heat the broth to boiling point and put in the *pasta* and the peas, which should be young and very fresh, so that they will be cooked at the same time as the *pasta*. Clean and chop the chicken livers, not too small. Heat them through in the butter, and add them to the *pasta* and broth, with their butter. Add some grated Parmesan when the broth is ready to serve.

Italian Food

BROAD BEAN SOUP

2 lb (900 g) broad beans, a few lettuce leaves, 2 or 3 spring onions, 1 pint (550 ml) of light veal or chicken stock, butter.

Boil the broad beans in salted water with the shredded lettuce leaves and onions. Be careful to take them from the heat the minute they are cooked or the skins will turn brown and spoil the colour of the soup. Strain them, reserving a small cupful of the water. Sieve them, put the purée into a clean pan and stir in the stock and the water which was reserved. Heat up and before serving stir in a small lump of butter or 2 or 3 tablespoons of cream. Serves 4.

Summer Cooking

FRESH GREEN PEA SOUP

A teacupful of shelled green peas, 1 oz (30 g) ham, half a small onion, 1½ pints (850 ml) veal or chicken stock, the juice of a lemon, mint, 2 eggs, 2 fl oz (60 ml) cream, butter, salt, pepper, sugar.

Melt the butter; put in the finely chopped onion. Do not let it brown, only soften. Add the ham cut into strips, then the peas. Let them get thoroughly impregnated with the butter. Season with salt, pepper, sugar, and add a little sprig of mint. Pour over hot water just to cover and simmer until the peas are tender. Stir in the boiling cream. Remove from the heat and stir in the eggs beaten up with the lemon juice. Pour the boiling stock over this mixture, stirring all the time, or the soup will curdle. Serve at once. A lovely soup. Serves 4.

Summer Cooking

SOUPE MÉNERBOISE

½ lb (225 g) courgettes, 1 lb (450 g) tomatoes, 2 onions, several cloves of garlic, 2 small potatoes, a handful of shelled and peeled broad beans, fresh basil, 1½ oz (45 g) small pasta or broken-up spaghetti, olive oil, 2 yolks of eggs, Parmesan cheese.

In an earthenware casserole warm a coffee-cupful of olive oil. Into this put the sliced onions and let them melt but not fry. Add the courgettes, unpeeled, and cut into squares (it is best to prepare them an hour before cooking, salt them lightly, and leave them in a colander so that some of the water drains from them). Let them melt in the oil slowly for 10 minutes before adding all but two of the tomatoes, roughly chopped. When these have softened put in the potatoes cut into small squares and pour about 2 pints (1.1 l) hot water over the whole mixture. Simmer gently for 10 minutes until the potatoes are nearly cooked; then add the broad beans, the pasta and seasoning of salt and pepper.

In the meantime grill the remaining tomatoes, remove their skins;

in a mortar pound 3 cloves of garlic, then the tomatoes, and a small bunch of basil. Add the yolks of the eggs, so that you have a sauce somewhat resembling a thin mayonnaise. The pasta in the soup being cooked, stir a ladleful of the soup into the sauce, then another. Return the mixture to the pan, and let it heat gently, stirring all the time to prevent the egg curdling. At the last minute stir in two large spoonfuls of grated Parmesan cheese.

A substantial soup for 4–6 people.

Summer Cooking

PURÉE LÉONTINE

2 lb (900 g) leeks, 1 cup each of spinach, green peas, and shredded lettuce, 1 tablespoon each of chopped parsley, mint, and celery, ½ tumbler olive oil, lemon juice, salt, and pepper.

Clean and cut the leeks into chunks. Into a thick marmite put the olive oil and when it is warm put in the leeks, seasoned with salt, pepper and the lemon juice. Simmer slowly for about 20 minutes. Now add the spinach, the peas and the lettuce, stir a minute or two, and add 2 pints (1.1 l) of water. Cook until all the vegetables are soft – about 10 minutes – then press the whole mixture through a sieve. If the purée is too thick add a little milk, and before serving stir in the chopped parsley, mint and celery.

This soup turns out an appetizing pale green. Enough for 6 people.

Mediterranean Food

POTAGE DE TOPINAMBOURS À LA PROVENÇALE

Cook 2 lb (900 g) Jerusalem artichokes in 3 pints (1.8 l) salted water. Sieve, and heat up, adding gradually 10 fl oz (300 ml) milk.

In a small frying pan heat 2 tablespoons of olive oil and in this fry two chopped tomatoes, a clove of garlic, a small piece of chopped celery, a little parsley and 2 tablespoons of chopped ham or bacon. Let this mixture cook only a minute or two, then pour it, with the oil, into the soup. Heat, and serve quickly. Enough for 6 people.

Mediterranean Food

TOURIN BORDELAIS

The onion soup generally regarded as 'French', with sodden bread, strings of cheese, and half-cooked onion floating about in it, seems to me a good deal overrated and rather indigestible. But certainly onions make warming and comforting soups for cold nights, and are admirable when one is suffering from fatigue or a bad cold. This country recipe makes a soup which is very acceptable under such circumstances. It requires no stock, but is enriched with egg yolks. It makes enough for 4–6 people.

Slice 3 large mild onions into the thinnest possible rounds. In a heavy saucepan heat 2 large tablespoons of pure pork dripping, and cook the onions in this, stirring until they begin to soften. Then season with salt, cover the pan, and leave to cook very gently for about 30 minutes. The onions should be reduced almost to pulp, but should still be of a creamy yellow colour. Pour over 2 pints (1.1 l) of cold water, bring slowly to the boil, simmer 10 minutes. Beat 2 egg yolks in a bowl with a few drops of vinegar and some of the hot soup, return this mixture to the pan, and stir until very hot, but on no account boiling. Slices of French bread baked in the oven should be put into each soup plate and the soup poured over.

French Provincial Cooking

LA SOUPE AU PISTOU

A famous Niçois soup of which there are many versions, the essential ingredient being the basil with which the soup is flavoured, and which, pounded to a paste with olive oil, cheese and pine nuts makes the sauce called *pesto* so beloved of the Genoese. The Niçois have borrowed this sauce from their neighbours, adapted it to suit their own tastes, and called it, in the local dialect, *pistou*. It is the addition of this sauce to the soup which gives it its name and its individuality. Without it, the soup would simply be a variation of *minestrone*.

Here is the recipe given in *Mets de Provence* by Eugène Blancard (1926), a most interesting little collection of old Provençal recipes.

In a little olive oil, let a sliced onion take colour; add 2 skinned and chopped tomatoes. When they have melted pour in 1¾ pints (1 l) of water. Season. When the water boils throw in ½ lb (225 g) green French beans cut into inch lengths, 4 oz (120 g) of white haricot beans (these should be fresh, but in England dried ones must do, previously soaked, and cooked apart, but left slightly underdone), a medium-sized courgette unpeeled and cut in dice, 2 or 3 potatoes, peeled and diced. When available, add also a few chopped celery leaves, and a chopped leek or two. After 10 minutes add 2 oz (60 g) large vermicelli in short lengths.

In the meantime prepare the following mixture: in a mortar pound 3 cloves of garlic with the leaves of about 10 sprigs of very fresh basil. When they are in a paste, start adding 2 or 3 tablespoons of olive oil, drop by drop. Add this mixture to the soup at the last minute, off the heat. Serve grated Parmesan or Gruyère with it. Enough for four.

French Provincial Cooking
chosen by Gerald Asher

Your note got me re-reading Elizabeth's books and mulling over all that I have enjoyed and valued in them. I need hardly tell you, of all people, what pleasure I get from the writing itself – from her 'voice'. Whether at her most scholarly or her most snippy (take that, Walls sausages) she is always lucid, entertaining and informative. Her insight, her sure judgement, her knowledge – always the right reference, the appropriate quotation – have greatly influenced (and educated) me. She has sent me to authors I might never have discovered, and from her example I learned very early on that there is more to food and wine than food and wine. In one of her pieces she quotes Norman Douglas who said that whoever has helped us to a larger understanding is entitled to our gratitude for all time. On top of my boundless affection for Elizabeth, that is how I feel about her.

Elizabeth's recipes always reveal the dish behind the 'improvements'. I remember reading her recipe for Soupe au Pistou and being amazed that it didn't actually have to have every vegetable in the garden thrown into the pot. Her books and recipes have given me a feel for food I would not otherwise have had. I cook out of my head rather than from recipes, but hers have inspired a number of favorite dishes. I frequently cook a dish based on her lamb and aubergine recipe in *Salt and Spices*, and another of chicken gizzards and hearts inspired by a recipe for goose giblet stew in *French Provincial Cooking*.   Gerald Asher

ZUPPA DI PATATE

For four people prepare 10 oz (280 g) potatoes, 1 medium-sized onion, and 8 small slices of bread. You also need about 2 pints (1.1 l) broth, 3 tablespoonfuls of olive oil, thyme, salt, pepper, grated cheese, nutmeg, 2 oz (60 g) butter.

Cut the potatoes in thin strips, as if you were going to make very small chips. Chop the onion. Heat the olive oil in the saucepan, brown the onion, then add the potatoes and season them with salt, pepper, nutmeg and thyme. Pour over the boiling broth. In 15 minutes the soup will be cooked.

To go with it, prepare the following *crostini*: saturate the slices of bread with melted butter; spread them thickly with grated Parmesan and cook them in a moderate oven (180°C/350°F/Gas Mark 4) for 10 minutes.

This soup, which is good and so easy to cook, can be made with water instead of stock provided a little bacon or ham (about 2 oz/60 g) is cooked with the onion to give flavour.

Italian Food
chosen by Julia Caffyn

POTAGE AUX CHAMPIGNONS À LA BRESSANE

This is an old-fashioned way of making mushroom soup in which bread rather than flour is used for the slight amount of thickening needed. It is a soup with a very fine flavour, but it does need some sort of mild chicken, veal or beef stock.

For ¾ lb (350 g) mushrooms the other ingredients are 2 oz (60 g) butter, garlic, parsley, nutmeg, a thick slice of bread, 1¾ pints (1 l) stock, 3–4 oz (90–120 g) cream, seasonings.

Rinse the mushrooms in cold water and wipe them dry and free of grit with a soft damp cloth. Do not peel them or remove the stalks. Cut them in small pieces. Melt the butter in a heavy soup saucepan, put in the mushrooms and let them soften; when the moisture starts to run add a very small piece of chopped garlic, a tablespoon of chopped parsley, a little salt, freshly milled pepper, grated nutmeg or mace, and let the mushrooms continue to stew in the butter for several minutes.

A thick slice of crustless white bread should have been soaked in a little of the stock while the mushrooms were being prepared. Now squeeze out the moisture and add the bread to the mushrooms. Stir until the bread amalgamates with the mushrooms. Now add the stock, and cook for about 15 minutes until the mushrooms are quite soft. Put the soup through the coarse mesh of the *mouli*, then through the next finest one. Or better still, side-step these two operations by blending the soup in the electric liquidizer. You will not get the thick or smooth purée usually associated with mushroom soup, but rather a mixture of the consistency of thin cream broken by all the minuscule particles of the mushrooms. Return it to the rinsed-out saucepan and when it is reheated add the hot cream and another tablespoon of parsley, this time chopped very fine indeed. These quantities should make enough for four.

French Provincial Cooking
chosen by Joe Hyam

POTAGE CRESSONNIÈRE À LA CRÈME

A richer version of the potato and watercress soups found in household cookery all over France.

Peel 1 lb (450 g) potatoes and cut them into even sizes but not too small, or they will become watery. Even so elementary a dish as potato soup is all the better for attention to the small details. Boil them in 2½ pints (1.4 l) salted water, adding the stalks of a bunch of watercress. Keep the leaves for later. As soon as the potatoes are quite soft, after about 25 minutes, sieve the whole contents of the pan through the food mill, using the medium mesh. Mix a tablespoon of ground rice (*crème de riz*) or potato flour (*fécule*) to a paste with a little of the soup; add this to the rest, heat gently, and simmer for 25 minutes; sieve again, this time through the fine mesh. The result should be quite a smooth cream, more cohered than the usual potato soup in which the potatoes always tend to separate from the liquid. Before serving add a pinch of nutmeg, about 2 tablespoons of the finely chopped watercress leaves and a good measure of cream, say about ¼ pint (150 ml). The result is a soup of the delicate colouring and creamy texture of so many of the dishes which charmed me when I first experienced French cooking with a Norman family. Plenty for four.

French Provincial Cooking
chosen by Thane Prince

I have always had a passion for soup and so, on receiving *French Provincial Cooking* as a Christmas gift from my husband in the mid-'eighties, I turned first to that chapter. I had come late to Elizabeth's work and had a preconceived idea that her books might be unapproachable. They carried the epithet 'scholarly' and, knowing little then of Elizabeth's love of food, I had expected to find text that necessitated a degree in English. Instead, I just found someone who wrote simply but with great knowledge and with as great a delight in food as I had myself.

The text of the recipe for the Potage Cressonnière à la Crème charms me now as it did then – the precise instructions on how to cut the cubes of potato 'not too small or they will become watery' contrasting with the more relaxed advice on how much cream to add: 'a good measure'. That such a simple recipe could be so carefully written is for me the essence of Elizabeth David's magic.   Thane Prince

GAZPACHO

There are many versions of this Spanish summer soup; the basis of it is chopped tomato, olive oil and garlic, and there may be additions of cucumber, black olives, raw onion, red pepper, herbs, eggs and bread. The following makes a very good and refreshing *gazpacho*, enough for 4.

Chop 1 lb (450 g) of raw peeled tomatoes until almost a purée. Stir in a few dice of cucumber, 2 chopped cloves of garlic, a finely sliced spring onion, a dozen stoned black olives, a few strips of green pepper, 3 tablespoons of olive oil, a tablespoon of wine vinegar, salt, pepper, and a pinch of cayenne pepper, a little chopped fresh marjoram, mint or parsley. Keep very cold until it is time to serve the soup, then thin with ½ pint (280 ml) iced water, add a few cubes of coarse brown bread, and serve with broken-up ice floating in the bowl. A couple of hard-boiled eggs, coarsely chopped, make a good addition.

Summer Cooking
chosen by George Elliot

MINESTRA DI POMIDORO

Melt 1½ lb (675 g) chopped and skinned tomatoes in olive oil; add a clove of garlic and some fresh parsley or basil or marjoram. Cook for 5 minutes, then add 1 pint (550 ml) meat or chicken stock, salt and pepper, and a pinch of sugar. Cook for 5 minutes more only.

By this method the flavour of the tomatoes is retained, and the soup tastes very fresh.

Enough for four.

In the summer this soup can be eaten iced, accompanied by hot *crostini* (as for potato soup, p. 44).

Italian Food

Buffet Food

A very understandable mistake often made at buffet luncheons and suppers is the over-complication of the food and the diversity of dishes offered. Several fine dishes of attractively prepared food look hospitable and tempting, but it is bewildering to be faced with too many choices, especially if some are hot and some cold. The taste of the food is lost when you find four or five different things all messed up on your plate at the same time; so have as the most important dish something rather simple which everyone will like, and provide variety with two or three salads, so long as they are easy ones to eat.

An excellent centrepiece for a party of this kind, particularly for those who haven't time for cooking but do not want to resort to a professional caterer, would be a smoked turkey. Smoked turkey is not of course cheap, but all you have to do is unwrap the bird and put it on a dish; with its dark golden skin it makes a handsome appearance, carves easily into thin slices, there is no waste, and the brown and white meat are equally delicious. The salads to go with it should be rather mild, as any strong flavour will conflict with that of the turkey; the classic potato salad with a mayonnaise made with lemon juice instead of vinegar, raw sliced mushrooms with an oil and lemon dressing, cucumbers with a cream dressing, or cubes of crisp cold melon go well with smoked turkey.

If something soft and creamy, such as a chicken or ham mousse, is to be the main dish, have as a contrast crisp raw salad vegetables, cucumber, radishes, or fennel cooled in bowls of salted iced water and perhaps some hard-boiled eggs stuffed with a green or red mayonnaise; these are easy to eat and always popular.

For a less conventional supper party a *roulade* of beef or veal with

48

a colourful stuffing of eggs and parsley and ham, or a loin of cold roast pork well spiked with garlic and herbs make fine dishes. The main thing is for the hostess not to wear herself out for days beforehand, fussing about with aspic, making patterns with mayonnaise and sticking little things on sticks. If time is limited, buy good-quality ham, plenty of it, and make it interesting by serving something unusual with it, such as a bowl of the beautiful Italian fruits in mustard syrup (to be bought in Soho shops) or pickled peaches, plums or cherries, or Cumberland sauce, or avocado sauce.

Start with a hot soup which can be served in cups (a walnut soup, or a white fish soup) accompanied by hot biscuits. (Romary's celery or cheese sticks heated in the oven.) As dessert, an iced, thick fruit fool which can be served in bowls is better than a fruit salad which has to be chased all over a plate balanced on your knees.

The presentation of party dishes, and of course of all food, is an important point. Cold food should certainly have a lavish and colourful appearance, but to varnish it with gummy gelatine or smother it with whirls of mayonnaise seems to me a misconception of what makes for an appetizing appearance. The effect needed is not of food tormented into irrelevant shapes but of fresh ingredients freshly cooked and not overhandled. The most elementary hors-d'œuvre such as a plate of red radishes with a few of their green leaves, a dish of green and black olives and another of halved hard-boiled eggs (not overcooked), with butter and bread on the table, is ten times more tempting than the same ingredients got up in a pattern all on one dish and garnished with strips of this and dabs of that. You are, after all, preparing a meal, not decorating the village hall.

As for hot food, if it has not acquired an appetizing look during the cooking, a few blobs of cream or a border of mashed potatoes will do little to improve matters. There are of course ways of making good food look especially beautiful. The colour, size and shape of the serving dish is obviously important; food should never be crammed into too small a dish; serve rice and pilaffs on large shallow platters, not pressed into a deep glass casserole; for the serving of fish and of grilled chicken, which should be spread out rather than piled up, a long narrow dish is best.

See that the dishes are appropriate to the food. Peasant and country stews of beans or lentils, deep brown *daubes* of meat and game, onion and oil-flavoured *ragoûts* of pimentos or purple-skinned aubergines lose some of their particular charm (and also get cold) if transferred from the earthen pots in which they have cooked to a smart silver entrée dish, and all the delicious brown bits on the bottom and sides of the dish are lost. Dark glowing blue china, the dark brown glaze of slip ware pottery and plain white always make good backgrounds for food; it would be an admirable thing if contemporary porcelain and pottery designers would pay a little more attention to these matters; does it ever occur to them that faded greens or greys, pale blues, washy yellows and garish reds do nothing to enhance the food which is to be served upon and eaten off their plates and dishes?

Summer Cooking
chosen by George Elliot

Oriental Picnics

I

'When I was going through the course of Garrison instruction, and accustomed to long days out surveying, I was partial to a galantine made of a small fowl, boned and rolled, with a block of tongue and some forcemeat introduced into the centre of it. A home-made brawn of tongue, a part of an ox-head, and sheep's trotters, well seasoned and slightly spiced, was another specialité.

'A nice piece of the brisket of beef salted and spiced, boiled, placed under a weight, and then trimmed into a neat shape is a very handy thing for the tiffin basket; and a much respected patron of mine recommends for travelling, a really good cold plum pudding in which a glass of brandy has been included.'

2

'The traveller's luncheon basket, and that of the sportsman are analogous. A friend of mine with whom I used to walk the paddy fields adopted the plan of taking out a digester pot, previously filled with stewed steak and oysters, or some equally toothsome stew. This he trusted to his syce, who lit a fire somewhere or other, in the marvellous way the natives of this country do, and, as sure as there are fish in the sea, had the contents of the pot steaming hot, at the exact spot, and at the very moment we required it.'
Extracts from *Culinary Jottings for Madras*, 'Wyvern' (Col. Kenney-Herbert) 1885

3

Charles Baskerville, the American painter, has described an Indian picnic given by the Maharajah of Jaipur, in 1937.

'Yesterday we spent the whole day picnicking . . . a lorry with lunch and bottles followed our car . . . one thing I particularly like about these outdoor luncheons is the cold fried fish. Besides the European food there are always some spicy Indian dishes . . . cold curry of boars' head (without the eyes) or peppery leaves of spinach fried in batter . . . of course a hamper of whisky, beer, gimlets, cider, and water is always taken along.'

4

My own experience of Indian picnics wasn't always quite so satisfactory. There was one in particular, a moonlight picnic near the Kutub Minar, the leaning tower near Delhi. There was nothing wrong with the transport, the food, or the moonlight; we had merely reckoned without the hordes of half-wild dogs which are a familiar feature of Indian outdoor life. Scarcely had we time to draw the cork of a bottle of the Rhinegold Australian hock which we were lucky to get in war-time India than we were surrounded by nearly every dog in the province; literally surrounded. They did not apparently want food, or at any rate not our food; they simply formed a circle round us at a respectful distance and stared and howled.

First we pretended not to notice, then we shoo-ed them away several times. They returned immediately, with reinforcements, re-formed their dreadful circle, and howled and stared and sniffed again, until they forced us to get into our cars and return to the city, leaving them in possession of their ruin.

5

In Egypt the picnic season starts sometime in March, with *Shem el Nessim*, the 'smelling of the Zephyrs', a day which is kept as a public holiday, when the whole population goes out to eat in the open air and greet the first day of spring.

An agreeable form of picnic in Cairo was the felucca party; on board a hired Nile sailing boat Arab servants would carry the food; there were copper trays of pimentos, small marrows and vine leaves stuffed with rice, large, round shallow metal dishes filled with meat and spiced pilaff, bowls of grapes and peaches and figs and melons cooled with lumps of ice, mounds of flat Arab loaves stuffed with a salad of tomatoes, onions and mint; there would be music and the wailing of Arab songs as the boat swung rather wildly about, the crew made Turkish coffee, and we drank the odd, slightly salty red Egyptian wine from the Mariut, one of the oldest wine-producing regions in the world.

Summer Cooking
chosen by Julia Caffyn and Veronica Nicholson

I have to declare a special interest in one of the 'oriental picnics' because I was one of the picnickers. I remember those enigmatic dogs well, circling us as we sat under the moonlit shadow of the 'Kut'b Minar', and have often tried to decide if this was the first time I had tasted E.D.'s food. I do remember asking her if her cook Bashir had taken a hand – all British memsahibs at this time employed an Indian cook. 'Oh no,' she replied, 'Bashir is only allowed to scramble eggs.'

Veronica Nicholson

All of Elizabeth's friends have stories to tell about her picnics which ranged between disaster and triumph. Any reason for an outing to a library, gallery, museum or house either in London or further afield was seized upon. When she was writing the bread book a lot of the resources were to be found at the handsome newly built Guildhall Library which opened in October 1974. When the first visit was proposed I asked if she intended to spend just the morning, or the whole day in the library. It was decided that a full day would be required, consulting the catalogue, making notes, ordering books, and so on. Then came the important matter of lunch. Elizabeth telephoned me to say that there was a dearth of anywhere in the City where lunch would be possible. So, a picnic was in order. The formula was of long standing. Elizabeth would bake the bread, bring butter and cheese, fruit and a bottle of wine. My contribution was to cook a Tian in the dish she had given me, according to her perfected recipe, quoted in *Mediterranean Food* from *La Cuisine à Nice* by H. Heyraud.

The next day we set out from Halsey Street in good time and struck lucky. There was a parking place in an extraordinary little square behind the library. The buildings were all high-rise, towering over the square – but to Elizabeth's delight, there in the middle, was a long rectangular pool with varied planting. This included a bushy shrub over-hanging the water which was immediately put to use. String was always a vital part of picnic equipment, and so the bottle of white wine was lowered into the pool, and attached to the shrub.

That done, we repaired to the library and made a start on the catalogues and the ordering of books. At the end of the morning we returned to the square and set out rugs and cushions, a tablecloth, and then the picnic. Fortunately the wine was still in place, nicely chilled. The sun shone, the food and wine were delicious – useful work accomplished. Altogether a most satisfactory start to a range of similar picnics during that summer of the Guildhall Library run. (And the bottle of wine was always to be found in place.)

April Boyes

English Picnic Meats

English military gentlemen are traditionally fond of their wine and food, and often uncommonly well informed about cookery and the management of the kitchen. Several regular army officers have written successful cookery books. Among the better known are Colonel Kenney-Herbert's *Culinary Jottings for Madras* (1885) – an indispensable book for curry addicts – and his *Commonsense Cookery*, written after his retirement when he opened a cookery school in Sloane Street, London. On pages 252–6 Colonel Kenney-Herbert's work is described in more detail.

The late Sir Francis Colchester-Wemyss, in common with Colonel Kenney-Herbert, had served in India (indeed it would have been difficult in those days for a professional soldier to avoid doing so) and in *The Pleasures of the Table* (1931, reprinted 1962) hints that his interest in cookery was a by-product of army life in British India. An early necessity to come to grips with the recipes which as mess secretary he attempted to transmit to his regiment's Hindustani cooks fostered an innate interest in food and wine.

Similar unexpected beginnings may well have been responsible for a whole school of cookery-writers whose books would make an entertaining and uniquely English collection (in France it is doctors and engineers who are the great amateurs of cookery writing), in which would certainly figure the works of a Major L—author of *The Pytchley Cookery Book* (1886), and *Breakfasts, Luncheons and Ball Suppers* (1887). Both these books contain diverting dissertations on racing, shooting and travelling luncheons.

Major L's luncheon basket, which he himself designed with the assistance of Messrs Farrow & Jackson, the firm still famous for the supply of wine bins and cellar fitments, played an important part in the major's life. Among other sensible innovations the basket was designed to hold a pint bottle of champagne or claret, and one of sherry or Salutaris water. As he observes 'in the summer the dust and heat make one thirsty, hot and uncomfortable. A good lunch and a glass of good champagne assist to while away the tediousness of the journey, oil the wheels of life, and improve the temper.'

Whether, in the dust and heat, the major contrived to get his champagne and his Salutaris water cooled to a suitable temperature he does not relate (our grandfathers, forever on the march with their champagne and travelling provisions, would have appreciated today's insulated picnic bags), but goes into some detail as to the solid content of the luncheon basket. It was to include, among other trifles, beefsteak or chicken pie, fillets of chicken, grouse or pheasant, cold stewed beef, lamb cutlets in aspic, slices of galantine, lemon biscuits, cakes of all sorts, mince pies and plum pudding. Inclusion of that last item betrays Major L's Indian service days.

They were right about the plum pudding, those Victorian officers. It does make a marvellous travelling and picnic dish, and, to me, is rather more welcome in the open air than ever it is on the Christmas table.

Spices, Salt and Aromatics
chosen by Anne Wilson

Elizabeth David had a tremendous knowledge of cookery books from earlier centuries, and when she wrote about English food she liked to draw on them not only for recipes, but also for ideas and attitudes to food. This passage shows her sharing with her readers her appreciation of the serious approach to picnics of some of our Victorian forebears.

Some time after the end of World War Two, the American army in Europe released surplus army rations which found their way onto the market in some European cities. Greece had undergone years of food shortages, first under German occupation and then through her own civil war. But the Greeks seemed to have little appetite for the individually-canned American plum puddings (one generous helping, and a tiny tin-opener supplied with each can) which lay about piled in tubs outside the food shops of Athens. Food in general was expensive in Greece, and the puddings were on sale for the *drachmae* equivalent of one or two English old pennies; but the local population did not respond.

We were students visiting Greece for the first time, and our budget did not stretch far beyond bread, olives, oranges and the hard-boiled eggs sold ready cooked in the bars. We found the plum puddings a useful dietary supplement, providing some extra energy for all the walking and sight-seeing.

Anne Wilson

EGGS AND CHEESE

POACHED EGGS

This is what Dr Kitchiner, author of the *Cook's Oracle* (1829) has to say about poached eggs: 'The cook who wishes to display her skill in Poaching, must endeavour to procure Eggs that have been laid a couple of days, those that are quite new-laid are so milky that, take all the care you can, your cooking of them will seldom procure you the praise of being a Prime Poacher: You must have fresh Eggs, or it is equally impossible.

'The beauty of a Poached Egg is for the yolk to be seen blushing through the white – which should only be just sufficiently hardened, to form a transparent Veil for the Egg.'

My own method for poaching eggs I learnt from a cookery book published by the Buckinghamshire Women's Institute, and it has proved infallible.

First boil a saucepan of water, and into this dip each egg whole, in its shell, while you count about thirty, then take it out. When it comes to actually poaching the eggs, have a pan of fresh water boiling, add a dessertspoon of vinegar, stir the water fast until a whirlpool has formed, and into this break the eggs, one at a time. 1–1½ minutes cooks them. Take them very carefully out with a draining spoon. They will be rounded and the yolks covered with a 'transparent Veil' instead of the ragged-looking affair which a poached egg too often turns out to be, and the alternative of the egg-poaching pan, which produces an over-cooked sort of egg-bun, is equally avoided.

It is interesting to note that Dr Kitchiner instructs his readers to place poached eggs on bread 'toasted on one side only'. How right he is; I have never been able to understand the point of that sodden toast. . . .

Try serving poached eggs on a piece of fresh, buttered bread; alternatively on a purée of some kind – split peas, sweet corn, or mushrooms, with pieces of fried bread around, but not under, the egg.

French Country Cooking
chosen by Prue Leith

I remember marvelling at the quality of the writing, sitting entranced on a radiator as a bed-sit cook – and quite forgetting to poach the eggs at all. A constant danger with E.D. is being distracted from the actual cooking.

Prue Leith

ŒUFS EN MATELOTE

Cook ½ pint (280 ml) red wine with herbs, onion, garlic, salt and pepper. Boil for 3 minutes and take out the herbs. In the wine poach 6 eggs, put them on slices of fried bread rubbed with garlic. Quickly reduce the sauce and thicken it with butter worked with flour and pour over the eggs. For 3 people.

Mediterranean Food
chosen by Jonna Dwinger

EGGS AND SPINACH

½ lb (225 g) spinach, 2 eggs, 2 tablespoons of cream and 2 of grated Gruyère or Parmesan for each person. Butter.

Clean and cook the spinach in the usual way. Drain it, and chop it, but not too finely. Arrange it in buttered fireproof egg dishes and heat it gently. Then put two eggs, either poached or *mollets* (eggs put into boiling water and cooked exactly 5 minutes, then shelled), into each dish. Cover with the cream and the cheese. Put in a hot oven (220°C/425°F/Gas Mark 7) for about 3 minutes.

This is a simplified version of the well-known *œufs Florentine*, in which the poached eggs are thickly covered with sauce Mornay (cheese-flavoured béchamel) which is then browned in the oven; a dish which always seems to me rather cloying, but there are those who prefer white sauce to fresh cream.

Summer Cooking

PETITS SOUFFLÉS AUX COURGETTES

1 lb (450 g) courgettes, 2 whole eggs and 2 extra whites, 5 tablespoons of grated Gruyère cheese (1½–2 oz/45–60 g), a *béchamel* sauce made from 1 oz (30 g) butter, 2 tablespoons of flour, and a scant ¼ pint (150 ml) warmed milk, the whole well seasoned with pepper but not too much salt until after the cheese has been added.

Prepare the courgettes as explained on page 208, and when they have been salted and drained, cook them in a heavy saucepan with a ladle of water until they are quite soft and the liquid evaporated. If they dry up before they are soft add more water, but only a very little, because the object of this operation is to extract the moisture from the vegetables, not to add more. Sieve them and stir the resulting purée into the prepared *béchamel*. Add the cheese; then, off the heat, the well-beaten yolks. Leave to cool before folding in the whites, beaten until they stand in peaks. Turn into miniature buttered soufflé dishes, filling them within half an inch (12 mm) of the top. Stand them in a baking tin containing water, cook in a pre-heated, moderate oven, 180°C/350°F/Gas Mark 4, for approximately 23 minutes. They should be well risen but still creamy in the centre. These quantities fill 6 little dishes of about 4 oz (120 g) capacity.

I first had these little soufflés at a lorry drivers' restaurant about three miles from the Pont du Gard. They came after cooked ham and cold vegetables served with a powerful *aïoli*, and were followed by a *bœuf à la gardiane* garnished with heart-shaped *croûtons* of fried bread. Then came a home-made ice with home-made almond *tuiles*. After which the local *marc* from Châteauneuf du Pape was a welcome digestive. It was not, I must add, the set meal of the café, but had been specially prepared for us by the proprietor, a Marseillais, at quite short notice. He had, I think, invented these delicious little soufflés himself.

French Provincial Cooking
chosen by George Elliot

OMELETTES

As everybody knows, there is only one infallible recipe for the perfect omelette: your own. Reasonably enough; a successful dish is often achieved by quite different methods from those advocated in the cookery books or by the professional chefs, but over this question of omelette-making professional and amateur cooks alike are particularly unyielding. Argument has never been known to convert anybody to a different method, so if you have your own, stick to it and let others go their cranky ways, mistaken, stubborn, and ignorant to the end.

It is therefore to anyone still in the experimental stage that I submit the few following points which I fancy are often responsible for failure when that ancient iron omelette pan, for twenty years untouched by water, is brought out of the cupboard.

First, the eggs are very often beaten too savagely. In fact, they should not really be beaten at all, but stirred, and a few firm turns

with two forks do the trick. Secondly, the simplicity and freshness evoked by the delicious word 'omelette' will be achieved only if it is remembered that it is the *eggs* which are the essential part of the dish; the filling, being of secondary importance, should be in very small proportion to the eggs. Lying lightly in the centre of the finished omelette, rather than bursting exuberantly out of the seams, it should supply the second of two different tastes and textures; the pure egg and cooked butter taste of the outside and ends of the omelette, then the soft, slightly runny interior, with its second flavouring of cheese or ham, mushrooms or fresh herbs.

A 10-inch (25-cm) omelette pan will make an omelette of 3 or 4 eggs. Beat them only immediately before you make the omelette, lightly as described above, with two forks, adding a light mild seasoning of salt and pepper. Allow about ½ oz (15 g) butter. Warm your pan, don't make it red hot. Then turn the heat as high as it will go. Put in the butter and when it has melted and is on the point of turning colour, pour in the eggs. Add the filling, and see that it is well embedded in the eggs. Tip the pan towards you and with a fork or spatula gather up a little of the mixture from the far side. Now tip the pan away from you so that the unset eggs run into the space you have made for them.

When a little of the unset part remains on the surface the omelette is done. Fold it in three with your fork or palette knife, hold the pan at an angle and slip the omelette out on to the waiting dish. This should be warmed, but only a little, or the omelette will go on cooking.

An omelette is nothing to make a fuss about. The chief mistakes are putting in too much of the filling and making this too elaborate. Such rich things as *foie gras* or lobster in cream sauce are inappropriate. In fact, moderation in every aspect is the best advice where omelettes are concerned. Sauces and other trimmings are superfluous, a little extra butter melted in the warm omelette dish or placed on top of the omelette as you serve it being the only addition which is not out of place.

French Provincial Cooking

OMELETTE FINES HERBES

Prepare 1 tablespoon of mixed finely chopped parsley, tarragon, chives and, if possible, chervil. Mix half of this, with salt and pepper, in the bowl with the eggs, and the other half when the eggs are in the pan. If you like, put a little knob of butter on top of the omelette as it is brought to the table.

French Provincial Cooking

OMELETTE À LA TOMATE

One tomato, skinned and chopped small, cooked hardly more than a minute in butter, with salt and pepper, is added to the eggs already in the pan.

French Provincial Cooking

OMELETTE AU LARD

Add a tablespoon of finely-chopped bacon softened a minute or so in its own fat, to the eggs already in the pan; take care not to salt the eggs too much.

French Provincial Cooking

OMELETTE À L'OSEILLE

One of the nicest of summer omelettes. Wash a handful of sorrel; chop it. Melt it in butter; add salt. In five minutes it is ready to add to the eggs.

Summer Cooking

OMELETTE AUX CROÛTONS ET FROMAGE

In butter fry a handful of little squares of bread; keep them hot on a plate.

Pour the beaten eggs for the omelette into hot butter in the omelette pan, put in the *croûtons*, then 2 tablespoons of grated cheese. Fold the omelette over quickly and slide it on to the hot dish.

The combination of the cheese and the *croûtons* of bread is particularly good.

French Provincial Cooking
chosen by Norma Grant

UOVA CON PURÉ DI PATATE
(*Poached eggs on potato purée*)

Have ready a very creamy and very hot potato purée. On top put poached eggs, and over the eggs strew a fair amount of grated Parmesan cheese. Delicious invalid food.

Italian Food
chosen by Lindsey Bareham

FONDUTA
(*Piedmontese cheese fondue*)

One of the most famous dishes of Piedmont, it is not to be confused with Swiss fondue.

For each person allow an egg and 3 oz (90 g) Fontina (a very buttery Piedmontese cheese; in England Gruyère will have to do instead). Cut the cheese into small dice and cover it with milk. Leave it to steep for at least 4 hours.

Put the cheese and any milk not already absorbed, the beaten eggs and a nut of butter in a double saucepan, adding salt and pepper. Cook gently, stirring all the time. The minute the cheese and eggs have amalgamated into a thick cream pour it into an earthenware or porcelain dish and cover it with very fine slices of white truffles. The combination of the cheese and the truffles is so remarkably right that there is really no substitute.

Italian Food
chosen by Lindsey Bareham

It wasn't long after I met and got to know Elizabeth David that I was embarrassed to have to admit that I didn't own a copy of *Italian Food*. We'd been talking about paintings, and Renato Guttuso (whom she loved) in particular, and what a pity, she said, that I hadn't seen his egg paintings. The conversation moved along and I forgot all about it until about ten days later a beautifully illustrated hardback edition of *Italian Food* arrived 'with the compliments of the author'. This was typical of Elizabeth. Needless to say, the first thing I did was check out those paintings (which *I* now love) in the egg section – and it was there that I discovered these two simple but utterly addictive dishes.   Lindsey Bareham

TARTE À L'OIGNON, *or* ZEWELWAÏ

This is the famous Alsatian speciality. It makes a truly lovely first course, and is enough for 4–6 people.

For the pastry: 4 oz (120 g) plain flour, 2 oz (60 g) butter or 1 oz (30 g) each of butter and meat dripping, 1 egg, salt, water.

For the filling: 1½ lb (675 g) onions, the yolks of 3 eggs, a good ¼ pint (150 ml) of thick cream, seasonings including nutmeg and plenty of freshly milled pepper, butter and oil for cooking the onions.

Make a well in the sieved flour, put the butter cut in small pieces, the egg and a good pinch of salt in the middle. Blend quickly and lightly but thoroughly, with the finger-tips. Add a very little water, just enough to make the dough moist, but it should come cleanly away from the bowl or board. Place the ball of dough on a floured board and with the heel of your palm gradually stretch the paste out, bit by bit, until it is a flat but rather ragged-looking sheet. Gather it up again, and repeat the process. It should all be done lightly and expeditiously, and is extremely simple although it sounds complicated written down. Roll it into a ball, wrap it in greaseproof paper and leave it to rest in a cold larder or refrigerator for a minimum of 2 hours, so that it loses all elasticity and will not shrink or lose its shape during the baking. This is one version of the *pâte brisée* or *pâte à foncer* used for most open tarts in French cookery. Without being as rich or as complicated as puff pastry, it is light and crisp. But those who already have a satisfactory method for tart and flan pastries may prefer to stick to their own. In spite of all the cookery rules, the making of pastry remains a very personal matter.

For the filling, peel and slice the onions as finely as possible, taking care to discard the fibrous parts at the root of the onions. Melt 2 oz (60 g) butter and a little oil in a heavy frying-pan. In this cook the onions, covered, until they are quite soft and pale golden. They must not fry, and they should be stirred from time to time to make sure they are not sticking. They will take about ½ hour. Season with salt, nutmeg and pepper. Stir in the very well-beaten yolks and the cream, and leave until the time comes to cook the tart.

Oil an 8-inch (20-cm) tart or flan tin. Roll out your pastry as thinly as possible (the great thing about this dish, as also the *quiches* of Lorraine, is that there should be a lot of creamy filling on very little pastry). Line the tin with the pastry, pressing it gently into position with your knuckle. Pour in the filling, cook in the centre of a fairly hot oven, with the tin standing on a baking sheet at 200°C/400°F/ Gas Mark 6 for 30 minutes. Serve very hot.

French Provincial Cooking
chosen by Alex Crawford

LA QUICHE LORRAINE

As in all regional dishes of ancient origin which have eventually become national as well as purely local property, there have been various evolutions in the composition of a *quiche*. Also called, in different parts of the province, *galette*, *fiouse*, *tourte*, *flon* and *flan*, a *quiche* is a flat open tart, and originally it was made of bread dough just like the Provençal *pissaladière* and the Neapolitan *pizza*. Gradually the bread dough came to be replaced with pastry while the fillings, of course, vary enormously, from sweet purple quetsch plums or golden mirabelles to savoury mixtures of onion, of chopped pork and veal, of cream flavoured with poppy seeds, of cream and eggs and bacon, of cream and cream cheese. According to its filling the tart will be called a *quiche aux pruneaux*, *quiche à l'oignon*, and so on. The one universally known as the *quiche Lorraine* contains smoked bacon, cream and eggs. Parisian, and English, cooks often add Gruyère cheese, but Lorrainers will tell you that this is not the true *quiche Lorraine*, whose history goes back at least as far as the sixteenth century.

There is, however, a time-honoured version containing a proportion of fresh white cream cheese as well as the cream, and it is perhaps this recipe which has caused the confusion. No doubt it is all largely a matter of taste, and for myself I find that whereas the combination of the mild flavour of white cream cheese with the smoked bacon of Alsace and Lorraine (which much resembles our own at its best) is quite attractive, that of Gruyère cheese with the same smoked bacon tends to be rather coarse and heavy. At any rate, here is a recipe for the plain cream and egg and bacon variety.

For the pastry the ingredients are 4 oz (120 g) plain flour, 2 oz (60 g) butter, 1 egg, salt, a little water. Cut the butter into little pieces and crumble it thoroughly with the sieved flour, adding a good pinch of salt. Break in the egg and mix the dough with your hands. Add enough water (2 to 4 tablespoons) to make the dough soft, but it should still be firm enough to come away clean from the bowl or board. Simply knead it into a ball, wrap it in greaseproof paper, and leave it for a minimum of 2 hours. When the time comes to use it, roll it out very thin, line an 8-inch (20-cm) flan tin with it, and with a fork prick the surface.

For the filling cut 6 thin rashers of streaky bacon into inch-wide strips. Cook them in a frying-pan for a minute so that some of the fat runs. Arrange them in circles on the pastry. Have ready ½ pint (280 ml) double cream mixed with the very well-beaten yolks of 3 eggs plus 1 whole egg, and well seasoned with freshly ground pepper and a little salt (taking into account the saltiness of the bacon). Pour this mixture over the bacon and transfer immediately to a pre-heated oven, 200°C/ 400°F/Gas Mark 6. Leave it for 20 minutes, then cook for another 10 minutes at a lowered temperature, 180°C/350°F/Gas Mark 4. By this time the filling should be puffed up almost like a soufflé, and golden brown. Let it rest a minute or two after you take it from the oven, to make it easier to cut, but don't wait until it has fallen before serving it.

French Provincial Cooking

QUICHE AU FROMAGE BLANC

For this version, well worth a trial, the filling consists of ¼ lb (120 g) fresh, unsalted, or slightly salted, cream cheese, beaten together with ¼ pint (150 ml) thick cream, the yolks of 3 eggs and 1 whole egg, plenty of freshly milled pepper, a little salt and 6 thin rashers of smoked streaky bacon. The pastry is made, the mixture is poured over the lightly fried bacon, and the *quiche* is cooked, all as in the preceding recipe.

To get a smooth mixture it is usually necessary to sieve the cream cheese.

French Provincial Cooking

The Markets of France: Martigues

One of the meals we all enjoyed most during our journeyings round the markets of France last summer was a lunch in the end-of-the-world little town of Salin-de-Giraud on the edge of the Camargue. After a pretentious dinner and a bad night – it is rare, I find, to get through even a fortnight's motoring trip in France without at least one such disaster – spent in a highly unlikely establishment disguised as a cluster of Camargue guardian huts, we left before breakfast and spent a healing morning lost in the remaining lonely stretches of this once completely wild, mysterious, melancholy, half-land, half-water, Rhône estuary country.

Much of the Camargue has now been reclaimed, roads and bridges have been built, and huge rice fields have been planted. They have been so successful that from an initial yearly production of about 250 tons during the middle forties these rice fields now yield 145,000 tons a year and supply France with the whole of her rice requirements. It has been a great triumph for France's construction and agricultural engineers, a dazzling testimony to the industry and enterprise of a people who so often appear, to those who do not know them, to be in a perpetual state of political and economic chaos. One cannot but rejoice for France, and wholeheartedly admire the determination and ingenuity which has turned an almost totally waste land into a productive and prosperous one.

Alas, though, for the animals and the wild birds, for the legendary beasts which frequented the Camargue, for the shimmering lonely stretches of water, for the still heart of this mournful mistral-torn and mosquito-ridden country. The harpies from Paris running the road houses which must inevitably multiply will be a worse scourge than

the mosquitoes. Owners of souvenir shops selling china Camargue bulls and plastic flamingoes and scarves printed with Provençal recipes will be more implacable than the mistral.

These rather gloomy thoughts were in our minds as we arrived, a bit soothed but still edgy, to find that the last ferry over the Rhône from Salin which would take us on to the road to Martigues had left at 11.30 and there would not be another until 2 o'clock. Forlornly we made our way to the local restaurant.

And there, instead of the omelette and the glass of wine which we had expected to swallow in a nervous hurry, we found the Restaurant La Camarguaise serving a well-chosen and properly cooked and comforting meal in a clean and high-ceilinged dining-room. The menu was 600 francs, and while the food was very simple it reminded me of what Provençal restaurants used to be like in the days before even the most ordinary of Provençal dishes became a 'speciality' listed on the menu as a *supplément* at 750 francs. There was an hors-d'œuvre of eggs and anchovies, there were hot grilled fresh sardines to follow, the vegetable course was *côtes de blettes*, the rib parts of those enormous leaves of the spinach family which we know as chard and which are much cultivated in the Rhône valley; the leaves themselves are cooked in the same way as spinach, the fleshy stalks and ribs were, on this occasion, sautéd in olive oil and flavoured with garlic and were delicious. The *bœuf Gardiane* which followed brought tears to our eyes; we had been overwrought and dropping with fatigue, and while the food we had already eaten had cheered and comforted us, it wasn't until the cover was taken off the dish of beef stew and we smelt the wine and the garlic and the rich juices and saw the little black olives and the branches of wild thyme which had scented the stew laid in a little network over the meat, that the tension vanished. We ordered more supplies of the cheap red wine and decided that the 2.30 ferry would have to go without us.

Well, God bless the French lunch hour. It must have been nearly 5 o'clock when, having finally got the cars across that ferry, we eventually drove into Martigues in dazzling late afternoon sunshine to see the fishing boats come in.

In this still picturesque village, beloved and painted by generations of English as well as French artists, so charmingly, proudly and absurdly known as the Venice of Provence – it is built on the Lagoon of Berre, west of Marseille – most of the inhabitants still live by fishing, and in spite of tremendous industrial development round about it is still comparatively unspoilt. It won't be for long. Martigues will soon be all but swallowed up in the new harbour constructions planned to stretch west from Marseille.

But for a little moment Martigues still stands, and we drink coffee on the quay as we wait for the boats to come in. Anthony is taking pictures of a faded blue warehouse door on which pink and coral and pale gold stars are hanging. They are starfish dried by the sun. Somewhere here in Martigues they are also drying something slightly more edible – the famous *poutargue*, compressed and salted grey mullet roes, a primitive speciality of Martigues whose origin goes back, they say, to the Phoenicians. It is made in Sardinia, too, and Crete, and for collectors of useless information, *poutargue*, or *botargo*, was among the dishes served at King James II's coronation feast. As a matter of fact we had some too, with a bottle of white wine for breakfast next day at M. Bérot's lovely restaurant the Escale, at Carry-le-Rouet, across the hills from Martigues and overlooking a real honest-to-goodness, · glorious postcard Mediterranean bay.

The children watching us are also watching for the boats, and they have spotted the first of the fleet coming in. So have the cats. The *Yves-Jacky* chugs into her berth, ties up; the skipper's wife, ready at her post, wheels her fish barrow aboard. Almost before you can see what has come up out of the hold the fish is loaded on the barrow and trundled off at breakneck speed, followed by the small boys and the cats. The auction in the market place on the quay has started.

A few minutes later, in quick succession, come the *Espadon* and the *St-Jean* and the *Bienvenue*. The boats are blue, the nets are black, and the whole scene does remind me a little of the Adriatic, even if not precisely of Venice.

None of the boats have sensational catches today. This part of the Mediterranean is terribly overfished. A large percentage of Marseille's fresh fish supplies is brought from the North Sea and Channel ports. But still there are some fine and strange-looking fish gleaming with salt water and sparkling in the sun. There's a brown and red and gold beast called a *roucaou*; it's a bit like the famous *rascasse* which goes into the *bouillabaisse*, but larger. Here is a boxful of tiny *poulpes*, a variety of squid which never grow big and which are exquisite fried crisp in oil. There's a *langouste* or two, and some kind of silver sea bream which they call *sarde* round here, and some *baudroie*, that fish with the wicked antennae-like hooks growing out of its huge head – the fish they call *rana pescatrice* in western Italy and *rospo* on the Adriatic, and angler or monk fish in England. The baby ones are as pretty and appealing as kittens with their little round heads. And there is a familiar friend, a gigantic turbot, and a long black fish with an arrow-shaped head. They call it *émissole* here, and to us it's a dogfish. There is a silver *loup de mer*, or sea-bass, and some big, rather touchingly ugly John Dories, called *St-Pierres* in France, because of the black St Peter's thumb marks on their sides.

Some of these big fish fetch big prices, two or three times as much as we would pay for them here, and they will go to the classy restaurants or the Marseille fish shops, but the boxes of little slithery bright pink fish called *demoiselles* and the miscellaneous collections of bony little rock fish, undersized whiting and other small fry, will go for very little. Most of the buyers are women – so is the auctioneer, a brawny, competent, good-humoured young woman with a Levantine cast of countenance and a thick Midi accent – who will re-sell them locally this very evening; any minute now the housewives of Martigues and Lavéra and round about will be turning them into *la soupe* or *la friture* for the evening meal.

An Omelette and a Glass of Wine
chosen by Paul Levy

Italian Fish Markets

Of all the spectacular food markets in Italy, the one near the Rialto in Venice must be the most remarkable. The light of a Venetian dawn in early summer – you must be about at four o'clock in the morning to see the market coming to life – is so limpid and so still that it makes every separate vegetable and fruit and fish luminous with a life of its own, with unnaturally heightened colours and clear stencilled outlines. Here the cabbages are cobalt blue, the beetroots deep rose, the lettuces clear pure green, sharp as glass. Bunches of gaudy gold marrow-flowers show off the elegance of pink and white marbled bean pods, primrose potatoes, green plums, green peas. The colours of the peaches, cherries and apricots, packed in boxes lined with sugar-bag blue paper matching the blue canvas trousers worn by the men unloading the gondolas, are reflected in the rose-red mullet and the orange *vongole* and *cannestrelle* which have been prised out of their shells and heaped into baskets. In other markets, on other shores, the unfamiliar fishes may be livid, mysterious, repellent, fascinating, and bright with splendid colour; only in Venice do they look good enough to eat. In Venice even ordinary sole and ugly great skate are striped with delicate lilac lights, the sardines shine like newly-minted silver coins, pink Venetian *scampi* are fat and fresh, infinitely enticing in the early dawn.

The gentle swaying of the laden gondolas, the movements of the market men as they unload, swinging the boxes and baskets ashore, the robust life and rattling noise contrasted with the fragile taffeta colours and the opal sky of Venice – the whole scene is out of some marvellous unheard-of ballet.

A very different kettle of fish, indeed, is the market of Genoa. Nothing will shake my conviction that Genova *la superba* is the noisiest city on earth. (This is nothing new; travellers have constantly remarked upon the fact.) The market-place will therefore be quite a rest; here one is oblivious of the uproar, spellbound by the spectacle of the odd fish which come up from these waters. Their names are descriptive enough: the angler or frogfish, the praying-fish, the sea-hen, the scorpion, the sea-cat, the sea-date, the sea-truffle, sea-snails, sea-strawberries, and a mussel with a hair-covered shell called *cozze pelose*. No wonder that anybody with a spark of imagination is prepared to put up with the ear-splitting din of Genoa, the crashing of trams and trains, the screeching of brakes, and even the agonized wailing of itinerant musicians in the taverns, in order to taste some of these sea beasts when they have been converted into *burrida*, the Genoese fish stew, or into the immense edifice of crustaceans, molluscs, fish, vegetables, and green sauce, which is known as *cappon magro*.

Along the coast at Santa Margherita the fish market is famous; here the fish are less forbidding and savage of aspect, but their brilliance of colour is phenomenal. Huge baskets are filled with what from a distance one takes to be strawberries but which turn out to be huge prawns (they are scarlet by nature, before they are cooked); dark green and grey *tonnetto*, gleaming silver with phosphorescence, are thrust head downwards, like so many French loaves, in a high basket; *moscard-ini*, brown and pale green, are arranged in rows, like newly washed pebbles; the tiny *calamaretti*, *fragoline di mare*, are black and grey (cooked in a wine sauce they turn a deep pink); the rose-coloured slippery little fish called *signorini* are for the *frittura*; the *scampi* are pallid compared to the brilliant prawns; an orange *langouste* is a tamed beast beside a black lobster, lashing furiously.

Another market with its own very characteristic flavour is that of Cagliari, in the island of Sardinia. Spread out in flat baskets large as cartwheels are all the varieties of fish which go into *ziminù*, the Sardinian version of fish soup: fat, scaly little silver fish streaked with lime green; enormous octopus, blue, sepia, mauve, and turquoise, curled and coiled and petalled like some heavily embroidered marine flower; the *pescatrice* again, that ugly hooked angler fish; cold stony little clams, here called *arselle*; *tartufi di mare*; silvery slippery sardines; rose-red mullets in every possible size, some small as sprats, like doll's-house fish; the fine lobsters for which Sardinia is famous. To eat the plainly grilled or fried fish in this island is an experience from which any town dweller, accustomed to fish which must have been in the ice at least a day or two, will derive great pleasure. The mullet, the thin slices of fresh tunny, the little clams, seem to have been washed straight from the sea into the frying pan, so fresh and tender is their flesh. In such conditions there is no necessity to create complicated sauces and garnishes; and, indeed, for the cooking of fish Italian cooks are mainly content to concentrate their skill on the arts of frying, grilling, and roasting.

Italian Food
chosen by Sybille Bedford, Veronica Nicholson
and Alice Waters

Elizabeth David's persona remains with us as that of a scholarly cook who read widely and deeply, and communicated in beautiful prose. Her biographical sketches give us convincing impressions of the periods and places to which they refer. She had a keen sense of the ridiculous, and her characters are often amusingly and charmingly described. She persuades us that Colonel Kenney-Herbert, a cavalry officer in India, is well worth reading and gives an excellent description of the memsahibs' kitchens in Delhi (disgraceful holes) which she saw when she was there at the end of the war.

For me Elizabeth's masterly writing is displayed at its best in her sensuous description of the fish and vegetable market at dawn in Venice where even the 'ugly great skate are striped with delicate lilac lights, the sardines shine like newly-minted silver coins' – the writing is very moving.

Veronica Nicholson

Oules of Sardines

What put the French fifty years ahead of any other nation when the sardine-canning industry developed in the nineteenth century was a combination of two circumstances; first, the fishermen of southern Brittany had evolved, for their own household consumption, a method of preserving their sardines which produced something more delicate than the primitive dried, salted and pressed fish of ancient Mediterranean tradition; they cooked their sardines in their own plentiful local butter or in olive oil imported from the south, packed them in clay jars called *oules*, and sealed them with more butter or oil. (The system sounds rather like the one used for preserving pork and goose in south-western France.) The delicacy came to be much appreciated by the prosperous shipbuilders and merchants of Nantes, the great trading port of the Loire estuary; and it was a Nantais confectioner, Joseph Colin, who in the early years of the nineteenth century first saw the possibilities of applying to the local method of preserving sardines the tinning process then being developed by a colleague, François Appert, by trade a confectioner-distiller, and by inclination an amateur chemist and scientist whose experiments with the preservation of food in bottles, jars and tins, hermetically sealed and then sterilized at high temperature, heralded the tinned-food era.

By 1824 Joseph Colin had established a sardine-tinning factory in the rue des Salorges at Nantes. The birth of the industry was attended by not unfamiliar wrangles, rivalries and complaints from the public. Colin's successful methods – he soon discovered that olive oil made the better preserving agent for sardines, and dropped the butter recipe – were almost immediately copied by competitors. In 1830 a Nantais restaurateur called Millet turned his establishment, situated in the heart of the residential quarter of the town, into a sardine-canning factory. The smell of the frying fish outraged the residents. Millet, brought to court in 1835, was forced to move his factory to the outskirts of the town. In 1838 another of Joseph Colin's rivals had the bright idea of taking into the firm a man who happened also to bear the name Joseph Colin; making him a partner, the firm proceeded to sell their products under precisely the same name as that of the originator. Another lawsuit followed – and put an end to the scandal.

For nearly fifty years sardine canning remained a French monopoly. It was not until the 1880s that competition from Spanish, Portuguese and American tinners, using cheaper processes and inferior grades of fish which were often not even true sardines, began to hit the French producers. By 1912 they felt driven into taking action to protect the industry from misrepresentation.

Sardines as understood in America and Canada were then and are still essentially a tinned product of which no equivalent in a fresh state exists in transatlantic waters; the only concession to exactitude obtained by the French from the American producers was that the place of origin of the tinned fish should be stated on their labels; and so the Americans have American-tinned herrings sold as Maine sardines, Canadian herrings labelled Canadian sardines, Norwegian sprats called Norwegian sardines and sometimes even Norwegian anchovies; so has arisen the confusion in the minds of the public as to whether or not there is actually and in fact any such animal as a sardine.

In England as well as in France matters are otherwise. The action brought in the English courts in 1912 by the French against an English importer selling Norwegian brisling (sprats) as sardines was finally settled in 1914 in favour of the French.

In England from that time on – which was presumably also the moment when the trade name of 'skippers' was invented for sprats – a sardine in a tin must be a sardine, and not a sprat or brisling, a herring or slid, a pilchard, an anchovy nor any other of the fish which belong to the same main family of *Clupeas*, but the *Sardinia pilchardus* or *Clupea pilchardus* Walbaum, the name by which the true sardine is now generally known. But just to add to the confusion there are several sub-divisions of the true sardine; the creature varies in numerous characteristics, as does the herring, according to the waters in which it is found, the food it eats, its degree of maturity. The Cornish pilchard is in fact a sardine, large and old and bearing only a small resemblance in appearance and flavour to the sardine of the Nantais canners, which is essentially a small and immature fish of which there are two main qualities, the finest not more than two years old – the age is indicated by rings on the scales – and measuring not more than seventeen centimetres from head to tail; the second, a year older and somewhat larger. The Portuguese sardine is again another variation, larger still and with one more vertebra than the Breton sardine.

A director of Philippe et Canaud, the oldest existing and largest-producing sardine-canning firm of Nantes, had stern words to say about the way the English treat sardines. 'Our fine sardines,' he said, 'should not be cooked. At an English meal I was given *hot* sardines, on cold toast. It was most strange. They were my sardines and I could not recognize them. The taste had become coarse. Perhaps for inferior sardines . . . but ours are best just as they are. A little cayenne or lemon if you like, and butter with sardines is traditional in France, although they are fat, and do not really need it. But, please, no shock treatment.'

One sympathizes. Shortages and much-advertised cheaper replacements have rather made us forget that best-quality French sardines are products of some delicacy, a treat rather than an everyday commodity. Production is small – about one-fifth of that of Portugal – the process is expensive, the hazards a perpetual worry. A member of the Amieux family and of the famous firm which bears their name told me something about the sardine-canning business. It is chancy, a gamble almost, even after 140 years of existence.

Sardines are migratory fish; their habits are notoriously unpredictable; the catch is seasonal; the factories operate approximately from May to October only; for several years there may be – and have been – shortages; then perhaps suddenly a glut. In a good year the Amieux firm will can up to 30,000 tons; in a poor one output may be as little as 6,000 tons. And since the sardine is one of the most perishable of all fish, depending for its delicacy upon its absolute freshness, the Nantais firms, who all deal in many other products besides sardines, have established special factories on the coast and close to the Breton and Vendéen fishing ports such as Douarnenez, the Ile d'Yeu, the Sables d'Olonne, St-Guénolé, Quiberon, Le Croisic, La Rochelle. Once into port, the sardine fishers rush their catches to auction; 15,000 kilos is the minimum quantity of any use at any one time to the Amieux factories. Raced from auction to factory, the sardines are decapitated and degutted, rinsed, plunged into a mild brine – made with salt from the Breton salt marshes – for anything from a few minutes to half an hour according to size; rinsed again, arranged on great grids, dried briefly in a current of warm air, rapidly fried (no more than a few seconds in the sizzling oil), drained, packed in their tins, covered with fresh olive oil selected by an expert taster for the purpose; the sardines are going to mature in that oil, and acquire some of its flavour; its quality is of prime importance. Finally, as required by French law, the sealed tins are stamped with code figures which indicate the date of tinning, and then sterilized at a temperature of 112°C.

In essentials, the present-day French process is the same as the one evolved by Joseph Colin, the sardine-tinning pioneer; other and cheaper methods have been tried; some, such as the Portuguese one of steaming instead of frying the sardines, have proved successful and popular, but the French canners consider that for finesse of flavour and texture, the olive-oil-frying system has never been equalled.

Ideally, the Nantais producers say, sardines in olive oil would be kept at least a year before they are passed on to the consumer; and after two years are at their best. Nowadays, though, unless one were to lay down stocks of sardines, one would not get them in this condition. The 1962 season has been a comparatively good one, but it follows five poor sardine years on the Brittany and Vendée coasts; the entire production has been going out to the wholesalers and retailers within months.

Dried and salted sardines were known it seems to the Romans. In the days of the Empire the Sardinians traded their product all over Italy and as far as Gaul. When the sardine fishing industry got under way on the Atlantic coasts of the Vendée and Brittany, round about the sixteenth century, much the same primitive methods of preservation must have been used. Henry IV, the Béarnais who so often crops up in the mythology of French gastronomy, was apparently inordinately fond of salt sardines. By the seventeenth century the French Treasury was already exacting taxes from the sardine industry which included among its activities the sale of by-products such as oil for lamps and for the tanners, obtained from pressed sardines, and manure from the debris of the fish to be salted.

An Omelette and a Glass of Wine
chosen by Derek Cooper

Having eaten tinned sardines since childhood I had no idea until I read E.D.'s piece in *The Spectator* in 1962 that these delicious little fish had much in common with port and claret – there were disappointing years and vintage years and the finest deserved laying down. This was E.D. at her best – informative, carefully researched, entertaining and calculated to enhance the enjoyment of food. That she should enthuse about a product most other writers would have dismissed – surely tinned sardines were something you had on toast in a seaside café? – added to the fun. Her ability to make you think more deeply about everyday foods – the good as well as the bad – had tonic properties. What a pity she never turned her abrasive eye on spaghetti in tomato sauce and canned baked beans.   Derek Cooper

FISH, SHELLFISH AND CRUSTACEA

COQUILLES ST JACQUES À LA BRETONNE

Allow 2, 3 or 4 scallops per person, according to size. Remove the little strip of skin and thick muscle on the outside of the white part. Rinse the white part and the red coral and drain well. Cut into small cubes. Allow 1 oz (30 g) butter and 1 heaped tablespoon of very fine, pale golden breadcrumbs per person. Butter the deep scallop shells with half the butter, then add half the breadcrumbs. Lay the scallops on top. Season them lightly with salt and pepper. Cover with the rest of the breadcrumbs, and the remaining butter cut in very small dice. Cook uncovered in a very low oven (140°C/280°F/Gas Mark 1) for 20 minutes. By the time the scallops are done the breadcrumbs have soaked up all the butter; they should be golden and just beginning to turn crisp, but still moist. Obviously, the breadcrumbs soak up a lot of butter, and if too little has been used, the dish will be dry. For those who like it, a scrap of finely chopped garlic or shallot and a little parsley can be mixed in with the breadcrumbs.

French Provincial Cooking
chosen by Sabrina Harcourt-Smith

One particular visit to my Aunt Liza's kitchen in the early 1960s remains firmly in my memory. She was preparing scallops with butter and breadcrumbs on her large kitchen table. These were the Coquilles St Jacques à la Bretonne which she had recently described in the shellfish chapter of *French Provincial Cooking*. As she arranged the scallops in their shells, her little black cat sat on the table and patted her arm impatiently until she said, 'Oh all right, Squeaker', and indulgently gave her one scallop, followed by another.

Sabrina Harcourt-Smith

COQUILLES ST JACQUES AU VIN BLANC

For 4 large scallops the other ingredients are 2 oz (60 g) streaky salt pork or unsmoked bacon, a shallot or two, butter, flour, a small glass of dry white wine, parsley.

Melt 1 oz (30 g) butter in a frying-pan, put in the finely chopped shallots and the pork or bacon cut into tiny cubes. Cut the cleaned scallops into larger cubes, season them with pepper but no salt, sprinkle them with flour, and put them in the pan when the shallots have turned pale yellow and the pork is beginning to frizzle. Let them cook very gently for 5–7 minutes. Take them out of the pan and put them in the serving dish. Pour the white wine into the pan and let it bubble fiercely, stirring so that it amalgamates with the juices and all the little bits left behind in the pan. When it has thickened to a syrupy consistency, add a very little finely chopped parsley and pour the sauce over the scallops.

The mixture of pork or bacon with the fish sounds odd, but it is an old-fashioned and delicious one, although the amount must not be overdone.

French Provincial Cooking

RAGOÛT OF SHELLFISH

12 cooked scampi or Dublin Bay prawns, 4 pints (2.25 l) mussels, 6 scallops, ¼ lb (120 g) mushrooms, ½ pint (280 ml) white wine, 1 tablespoon concentrated tomato purée, 1 tablespoon flour, 1 onion, 4 cloves of garlic, seasoning, herbs, 1 dessertspoon sugar, 1 oz (30 g) butter, parsley.

First of all split the scampi tails in half, retaining 6 halves in their shells for the garnish. From the remaining shells remove the flesh and cut it into fairly large pieces.

In a fairly deep pan sauté a sliced onion in butter, when golden add the tomato purée, the chopped garlic, salt, pepper, and the sugar and herbs. Simmer 5 minutes. Stir in the flour. When thick pour over the heated wine, and cook this sauce for 15 to 20 minutes. Add the flesh of the scampi, the sliced mushrooms, the scallops cut into two rounds each, and the mussels, which should have been very carefully cleaned. Turn up the heat and cook until the mussels have opened. At the last minute add the reserved scampi in their shells. Turn into a tureen or deep dish, squeeze over a little lemon, sprinkle with parsley, and serve very hot, in soup plates. The black shells of the mussels and the pink of the prawns make a very decorative dish.

The tails of large crawfish (*langouste*) can be used instead of the prawns, but of course fewer will be needed, and they can be cut into four or six pieces each.

Enough for 4–6 people as a first course.

Mediterranean Food
chosen by Cecile Harris

LOBSTER COURCHAMPS

For one freshly boiled, medium large (about 1½ lb/675 g) hen lobster or *langouste* (if you are boiling the creature at home, you can always add the large goblet of Madeira called for in the original recipe), the ingredients for the sauce are 2 small shallots, a heaped teaspoon of tarragon leaves, 2 tablespoons of chopped parsley, salt, pepper, a scant teaspoon of strong yellow French mustard, 24 to 30 drops of soy sauce, approximately 6 tablespoons of mildly fruity Provence olive oil, the juice of half a rather small lemon, 1 teaspoon of anisette de Bordeaux.

From the split lobster extract all the red and creamy parts. Pound them in a mortar. Mix with the finely chopped shallots, tarragon and parsley. Add the seasonings and the soy sauce, then gradually stir in the olive oil; add lemon juice. Finally, the anisette. Divide the sauce into two portions, and serve it in little bowls or squat glasses placed on each person's plate so that the lobster can be dipped into it. The lobster meat can be cut into scallops and piled neatly back into the shells.

Apart from its sheer deliciousness (most cold lobster sauces, including mayonnaise, are on the heavy side for what is already rich and solid food) this sauce has other points to recommend it. Anisette is not a liqueur which, speaking at least for myself, one has a great compulsion to swig down in quantity; in my cupboard a bottle lasts for years. A half-crown's worth of soy sauce also tends – unless you are keen on

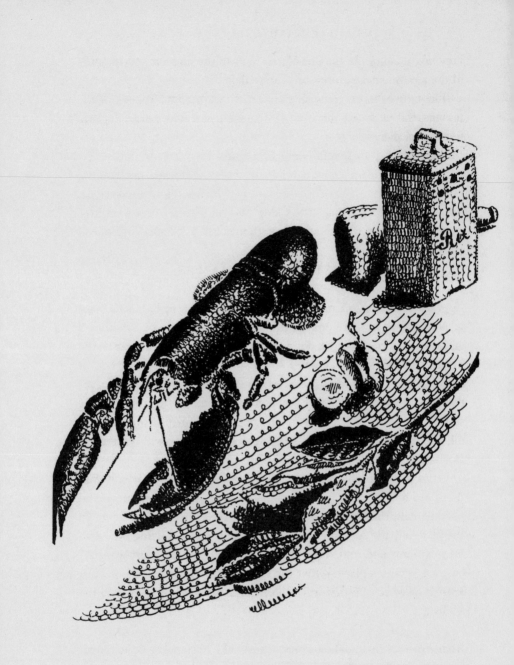

Chinese cooking – to remain an old faithful among the stores; and although nothing can quite compare with fresh tarragon, it is perfectly possible to use the excellent Chiltern Herb Farm dried version. The makings of your sauce, then, are always with you. All you need is the freshly boiled hen lobster ... And, as it is not a classic regional or other recognized traditional dish, you can call it what you please. It has no name of its own. I have named it after the Comte de Courchamps, author of the first of the three books[1] in which I found the recipe. The others were by Dumas the Elder[2] and the Baron Brisse.[3] Highly imaginative as they were, all three gentlemen called it Sauce for Boiled Lobster.

An Omelette and a Glass of Wine
chosen by Simon Hopkinson

LANGOUSTE COMME CHEZ NÉNETTE

You have decided upon your meal, and Madame, in her black dress, has moved majestically towards the kitchen to attend to your wishes. A bottle of cooled white wine is already in front of you, and from the big table in the centre of the restaurant a waiter brings hors-d'œuvre, to keep you amused and occupied while more serious dishes are being prepared. Now, in spite of all that grave gastronomes are in the habit of saying about the pernicious custom of starting off a meal with a lot of little oddments and titbits, it is nevertheless a fact that the quality of a restaurant may very largely be judged by the way in which the hors-d'œuvre are planned and presented. At Nénette's they bring you quantities of little prawns, freshly boiled, with just the right amount

1. *Néo-Physiologie du Goût par Ordre Alphabétique: Dictionnaire Général de la Cuisine Française Ancienne et Moderne ainsi que de l'Office et de la Pharmacie domestique*, Paris, Henri Plon. Published anonymously in 1839, reprinted 1853 and 1866. Vicaire asserts that the book was the work of Maurice Cousin, Comte de Courchamps. In the preface to the book it is claimed that a number of the recipes came from unpublished papers of Grimod de la Reynière. The recipe in question might well be from his hand.
2. *Grand Dictionnaire de Cuisine*, Alexandre Dumas, 1873.
3. *Les 366 Menus de Baron Brisse*, 2nd edition 1875, first published *c.* 1867.

of salt, and a most stimulating smell of the sea into the bargain, heaped up in a big yellow bowl; another bowl filled with green olives; good salty bread; and a positive monolith of butter, towering up from a wooden board. These things are put upon the table, and you help yourself, shelling your prawns, biting into your olives, enjoying the first draught of your wine. Gradually you take in your surroundings: the light and sunny dining-room, neither too big nor too small, the comfortably worn flowered wallpaper, the country flowers on the tables, and the shady garden which you can see through the open window at the far end of the dining-room.

You settle in, realizing that you are in a serious restaurant, and a serious provincial restaurant at that. You have no anxiety about the meal to come, and you are quite right. For any international Palace Hotel or expense-account restaurant can serve you oysters and *foie gras*, smoked salmon and caviar, in the very pink of condition (this is a question of good buying and has nothing to do with the chefs) and still follow them up with the deadliest of dull dinners. But the eye which picked out those bowls, the taste which decreed what was to go into them, and the hand which carved that butter into its meticulously studied carelessness of shape are scarcely likely to falter when it comes to the silver sea-bass roasted over a vinewood fire, the *langouste* in its tomato and brandy and garlic-scented sauce, the salad dressed with the fruity olive oil of Provence. Upon this last point, however, one must not enlarge too much. For we are at Montpellier, and as Madame Nénette observed, in tones of only very mild reproof, in answer to my question about her lobster dish, '*Ah, nous ne sommes pas en Provence, Madame, ici c'est le Languedoc.*' So Madame Nénette's lobster or, rather, crawfish dish is her own special version of *langouste à la sètoise* or *civet de langouste*, a dish quite remarkably similar to the famous *homard à l'américaine*.

'Cut a live crawfish into not too large pieces; put them at once into a wide and shallow pan containing a little smoking olive oil, add salt and pepper, and cook until the shell turns red. Add some finely chopped shallots and a clove or two of garlic, crushed and first cooked separately in a little oil.

'Pour in a small glass of good cognac and set light to it; when the flames have gone out, add a half bottle of still champagne or chablis, and a spoonful of tomato purée. Cover the pan and cook over a steady heat for about 20 minutes. Remove the pieces of crawfish, which are now cooked, and keep them hot.

'Press the sauce through a very fine sieve, let it boil up again, season with a scrap of cayenne and, at the last minute, add 3 good spoonfuls of *aïoli*.

'Pour the sauce over the crawfish and sprinkle a little finely chopped parsley over the dish.'

French Provincial Cooking

Elizabeth contributed regularly to *Vogue* for about three years in the mid-fifties; I admired her greatly. At first, however, her articles consisted of straightforward cookery details, and I was especially happy that I succeeded in coaxing her into giving a personal background to her recipes. That approach started in May 1957 with the first of her French Regional Cooking series – which became the basis of *French Provincial Cooking*. In those articles Elizabeth took the reader into the whole experience of coming upon a dish in a household or restaurant, and finding out all about it from its creator. The recipe which emerged from this encounter had infinitely more appeal than the usual list of ingredients and instructions.

Audrey Withers

BAR À LA MARSEILLAISE

Bar or *loup de mer* is one of the most delicate fish of the Mediterranean; grilled on a bed of fennel stalks it makes the famous Provençal *grillade au fenouil*. The bass which come from Cornwall are the English equivalent; they don't appear very often, but are well worth buying when they do.

The ingredients for this dish, for four people, are a bass weighing 2½–3 lb (1–1.5 kg), a coffee-cupful of olive oil, a small glass of dry white wine, a little bouquet of fennel leaves, 2 cloves of garlic, ½ lb (225 g) mushrooms, ½ lb (225 g) onions, 1 lb (450 g) yellow waxy potatoes.

Put the fish in a baking dish, pour over it the oil and wine, cover with the chopped fennel and garlic, round it arrange the sliced onions, mushrooms and thinly sliced potatoes. Season with salt and pepper, add 1 pint (550 ml) water and cook in a fairly hot oven (200°C/400°F/ Gas Mark 6) for about an hour.

Serve with an *aïoli* (page 93) or *sauce rouille* (page 260).

Summer Cooking

TRUITE SAUMONÉE AU FOUR

Few of us now possess fish kettles in which a large whole fish can be poached, but the system of wrapping the fish in greaseproof paper or foil and cooking it in the oven produces, if anything, better results.

Cut a piece of aluminium foil about 6 inches (15 cm) longer than your fish. Butter it copiously, or if the fish is to be served cold, paint it with oil. Lay the fish in the middle, gather up the edges and twist them together, so that no juices can escape. Also twist the two ends very securely, taking particular care that the paper touching the tail and the head is well buttered or oiled, as these are the parts which stick easily.

Have your oven already heated for 10 minutes at a very low temperature, 140°C/290°F/Gas Mark 1. Place your wrapped fish on a baking sheet and leave it severely alone for the whole cooking time – 1 hour for a 2-lb (900-g) fish. All you have to do when it is cooked is to lay it on the warmed serving dish, unwrap the paper, and slide the fish and all its juices off the paper on to the dish. A hot salmon trout does not really need any sauce other than its own juices and a little bowl of fresh melted butter. If it is to be served cold, have with it a *sauce verte* or Montpellier butter or, best of all, I think, Escoffier's horseradish and walnut-flavoured sauce. It also makes serving easier if the skin is removed while the fish is still warm; this is not difficult so long as the fish has not been overcooked but, of course, it must be done gently and patiently.

There is one more point. A cold salmon trout eaten a couple of hours after it is cooked is infinitely superior to one cooked and kept until the following day.

Sea-bass (*loup de mer*) is excellent cooked in the same way.

French Provincial Cooking

AÏOLI

'Provençal *aïoli* – dish of the farmhouse and the *cabanon**– triumph of the Provençal kitchen, is composed of a garlic mayonnaise and an assortment, as varied as possible, of fresh vegetables cooked in salted water, white fish cooked in *court-bouillon* and cold meats.'

EUGÈNE BLANCARD: *Mets de Provence* (1926)

Aïoli is indeed one of the most famous and most beloved of all Provençal dishes. The magnificent shining golden ointment which is the sauce is often affectionately referred to as the 'butter of Provence'. With this wonderful sauce are served boiled salt cod, potatoes, beetroot, sweet peppers, either raw or cooked, carrots, a fine boiled fish such as a bream or mullet, hard-boiled eggs, sometimes little inkfish or octopus, French beans, globe artichokes, even little snails, and perhaps a salad of chick peas.

The *aïoli garni* is, in fact, a Friday dish as well as one of the

---

* *Cabanons* are the huts of the *gardians* of the Camargue.

93

traditional Christmas Eve dishes; on non-fasting days the beef from the *pot-au-feu* or even a boiled chicken may form part of the dish: it then becomes *le grand aïoli*. It will be seen, then, that with all these different accompaniments, the *aïoli garni* is essentially a dish for a large family or a party of intimate friends, although personally I could quite well dispense with all the rest provided there were a large bowl of potatoes boiled in their skins and perhaps some raw peppers and celery to go with the *aïoli*.

In a small country restaurant in Provence where I once asked, at short notice, if it were possible to produce an *aïoli garni* for dinner, it was too late for the *patron* to go out and buy anything specially, but he produced a handsome dish of ham accompanied by potatoes and the vegetables in season, with the *aïoli* in a bowl in the centre of the dish. It was an excellent demonstration of the sort of impromptu *aïoli* which can be produced with ingredients to hand.

To make the *aïoli* sauce:

Allow roughly 2 large cloves of garlic per person and, for eight people, the yolks of 3 eggs and nearly 1 pint (550 ml) very good quality olive oil – failing Provençal olive oil, the best Italian or Spanish will do. Crush the peeled garlic in a mortar until it is reduced absolutely to pulp. Add the yolks and a pinch of salt. Stir with a wooden spoon. When the eggs and garlic are well amalgamated, start adding the oil, very slowly at first, drop by drop, until the *aïoli* begins to thicken. This takes longer than with a straightforward mayonnaise because the garlic has thinned the yolks to a certain extent. When about half the oil has been used, the *aïoli* should be a very thick mass, and the oil can now be added in a slow but steady stream. The sauce gets thicker and thicker, and this is as it should be; a good *aïoli* is practically solid. Add a very little lemon juice at the end, and serve the sauce either in the kitchen mortar in which you have made it or piled up in a small salad bowl. Should the *aïoli* separate through the oil having been added too fast, put a fresh yolk into another bowl and gradually add the curdled mixture to it. The *aïoli* then comes back to life.

Now as to the amount of garlic: you can, of course, use less but you are likely to find that the mass of eggs and oil is then too heavy and rich. A true *aïoli* is a remarkable mixture of the smooth mayonnaise combined with the powerful garlic flavour which tingles in your throat as you swallow it. One Provençal writer suggests that those who find the *aïoli* indigestible should take a *trou* or *coup du milieu* in the form of a little glass of *marc* in the middle of the meal.

French Provincial Cooking

LA BOURRIDE DE CHARLES BÉROT

Bourride is one of the great dishes of Provence. There are various different ways of presenting it but the essential characteristic is that *aïoli* or garlic-flavoured mayonnaise is added to the stock in which the fish has cooked to make a beautiful smooth pale yellow sauce – and of this there must be plenty for it is the main point of the dish.

M. Bérot, once *chef des cuisines* on the *Île de France* – a liner celebrated for its good cooking – served us his own version of this dish at the Escale, a hospitable and charming restaurant at Carry-le-Rouet, a little seaside place west of Marseille.

The ingredients you need for four people are 4 fine thick fillets of a rather fleshy white fish. M. Bérot uses *baudroie* or angler fish, but at home I have made the dish with fillets of John Dory, of turbot, of brill (*barbue*).

In any case, whatever fish you choose, be sure to get the head and the carcase with your fillets. Apart from these you need a couple of leeks, a lemon, a tablespoon of wine vinegar, at least 4 cloves of garlic, 2 or 3 egg yolks, about ⅓ pint (185 ml) olive oil, a couple of tablespoons of cream, and seasonings. To accompany the *bourride* you need plain boiled new potatoes and slices of French bread fried in oil.

First make your stock by putting the head and carcase of the fish into a saucepan with a sliced leek, a few parsley stalks, a teaspoon of salt, a slice of lemon, the wine vinegar, and about 1¼ pints (700 ml) of water. Let all this simmer gently for 25–30 minutes. Then strain it.

While it is cooking make your *aïoli* with the egg yolks, 3 cloves of garlic, and olive oil as explained in the previous recipe.

Now put a tablespoon of olive oil and the white of the second leek,

95

finely sliced, into the largest shallow metal or other fireproof pan you have; let it heat, add the spare clove of garlic, crushed; put in the lightly seasoned fillets; cover with the stock; let them gently poach for 15–25 minutes, according to how thick they are.

Have ready warming a big serving dish; take the fillets from the pan with a fish slice and lay them in the dish; cover them and put them in a low oven to keep warm.

Reduce the stock in your pan by letting it boil as fast as possible until there is only about a third of the original quantity left. Now stir in the cream and let it bubble a few seconds.

Have your *aïoli* ready in a big bowl or a jug over which you can fit a conical or other sauce sieve. Through this pour your hot sauce; quickly stir and amalgamate it with the *aïoli*. It should all turn out about the consistency of thick cream. Pour it over your fish fillets. On top strew a little chopped parsley and the dish is ready.

I know that all this sounds a tremendous performance, and indeed I wouldn't recommend *bourride* for days when you have the kind of guests who make you nervous; but as a matter of fact when you have cooked it once (try it in half quantities, just for two) it all seems quite easy, and it's a very satisfactory dish to be able to make.

Incidentally, I usually cook the potatoes and fry the bread while the fish is poaching; both can be kept warm in the oven, and then at the last minute you can give your undivided attention to the sauce.

French Provincial Cooking
chosen by Katharine Whitehorn

CALAMARI IN UMIDO
(*Stewed squid*)

1 lb (450 g) squid, 2 large onions, 3 cloves of garlic, 2 or 3 tomatoes, tomato paste, red wine, oil, herbs.

To clean the squid, remove the insides from the pocket-like part of the fish, and pull out the thin transparent spine bone. Remove also the purplish outside skin, which comes off very easily in warm water.

From each side of the head remove the little ink bag (the whole operation is carried out in a bowl of water and is very quickly done) and take out the eyes and the hard beak-like object in the centre of the tentacles, of which Dumas remarks that it is *'non pas un nez, mais l'anus (au milieu du visage!)'*. Rinse the squid in running water until it is quite free of grit. When clean they are milky white.

Cut the body of the squid into rings, about ¼ in (5–6 mm) wide, and the tentacles into strips. Season them with salt and lemon juice. Now put the onions, cut into rings, into a pan in which you have warmed enough olive oil to cover the bottom. Let them turn golden and add the inkfish. After 2 minutes put in the chopped tomatoes, some marjoram and thyme, and the garlic, and after 2 more minutes pour in a small glassful of red wine; let this reduce a little and add a dessertspoonful, not more, of tomato purée. Add enough hot water to reach the level of the ingredients in the pan, put on the lid, and cook very slowly for 1½ hours. Serve with rice or with toasted French bread.

Will serve 3–4 people.

Italian Food

TRIGLIE ALLA GRIGLIA
(*Grilled red mullet*)

Medium-sized red mullet are the best for grilling, and grilling is the most delicious way of cooking these fish. You will need 1–2 per person, depending on size. Make a couple of incisions crosswise on each side of the fish, which should have its liver left in. Brush it with oil. Cook it under a hot grill for about 7 minutes on each side – it will be golden and crackling. If the fish is absolutely fresh, it has such a marvellous flavour of the sea that it is absurd to serve any sauce with it. Town fish can do with a little melted butter and parsley, or a *salsa verde*.

Italian Food

TRIGLIE ALLA VENEZIANA
(Red mullet marinated in white wine)

Put two leaves of fresh mint and a small piece of garlic inside each red mullet, medium-sized ones being best for the dish. Roll them in flour and fry them gently in oil; drain them and arrange them on a long dish. Prepare the following sauce, enough for 2 people. In a little oil sauté a small onion finely chopped; let it melt but not turn brown, then pour in about 6 fl oz (170 ml) of white wine and a tablespoonful of wine vinegar. Simmer the sauce for 10–15 minutes, until it has reduced by one third. When it has cooled, pour it over the red mullets. Serve them cold, garnished with a little parsley and slices of lemon or orange. Instead of frying the mullets, they can be scored across twice on each side and grilled, and the sauce then poured over them. They can also be eaten hot cooked in this way, and are excellent.

Italian Food

FISH PLAKÍ

This is a typical Greek way of cooking fish and appears over and over again in different forms.

Wash a large fish, such as bream, chicken turbot or John Dory. Sprinkle with pepper and salt and lemon juice, and put in a baking dish. Fry some onions, garlic and plenty of parsley in olive oil; when the onions are soft add some peeled tomatoes. Fry gently for a few minutes, add a little water, simmer for a few minutes longer, cover the fish with this mixture, add a glass of white wine, some more sliced tomatoes and thinly sliced lemon. Put in a moderate oven (180°C/ 350°F/Gas Mark 4) and cook about 45 minutes or longer if the fish is large.

Mediterranean Food

BRANDADE DE MORUE

A triumph of Provençal cooking, designed to abate the rigours of the Friday fast.

Take some good salt cod, about 2 lb (900 g) for 6 people, which has been soaked in cold water for 12 hours. Clean it well and put it into a pan of cold water; cover, and as soon as it comes to the boil remove from the heat. Carefully remove all the bones and put the pieces into a pan in which you have already crushed up a clove of garlic and place over a very low heat. In two other small saucepans have some milk and some olive oil, both keeping warm, but not hot. You now add the oil and the milk alternately to the fish, spoon by spoon, stirring hard the whole time, with a wooden spoon, and crushing the cod against the sides of the pan. (Hence the name *brandade – branler*: to crush or break.) When the whole mixture has attained the appearance of a thick cream the operation is finished; it should be observed however that all three ingredients must be kept merely tepid, or the oil will disintegrate and ruin the whole preparation. Also the stirring and breaking of the cod must be done with considerable energy; some people prefer to pound the cod in a mortar previous to adding the oil and the milk.

Brandade can be served hot or cold, if hot in a vol au vent or little pâtés, garnished with a few slices of truffle or simply with triangles of fried bread.

Mediterranean Food
chosen by Karen Hess

A Book of Mediterranean Food was my introduction to Elizabeth David, so it remains my favourite. I cannot say that it was this recipe that influenced my work more than any other, except that it does carry the fragrances of the French countryside to an extent that few other writers capture, certainly none in English. And it was the recipe from which I made my first brandade.

There are many things I could say about her influence on my work – how impressed I was by the terrible honesty of her writing, and her wonderful attitude of assuming intelligence on the part of her readers. None of that endeared her to American readers – their loss – but it was precisely those qualities that drew me so to her work; those, and a remarkable way of being able to zero into the crucial point of a dish: in this recipe, the point (seldom made) about not letting the mixture get actually hot. Karen Hess

BACCALÀ MANTECATO
(*Cream of baccalà*)

This dish, a speciality of Venice, and one of which the Venetians are very proud, is almost identical with the *brandade de morue* of Provence. Possibly the Nîmois cook who claimed to have invented it borrowed the idea from Venice – perhaps the origin of both dishes is Spanish.

For *baccalà mantecato* for 4 you need about 1½ lb (675 g) the best quality Bergen salt cod, cut from the middle, and fattest, part of the fish, which before being put to soak has been beaten until it has lost some of its toughness. (In Venice the bashing of the *baccalà* against the stone mooring-posts alongside the canals and in the market place is a familiar sight.)

Leave the cod under running cold water for 24 hours. Steam it in a double pan for about an hour, then remove all skin and bone. Put the pieces of fish into a heavy mortar and pound and pound, with the addition of a few tablespoonfuls of olive oil, until a thick creamy mass results. (*Baccalà mantecato* is rather less liquid than the *brandade*.) If the fish is not sufficiently fat, and so does not turn to a soft purée, add a little warmed milk.

Slices of polenta are served with *baccalà mantecato*.

Smoked cod fillets make a good dish cooked this way. They should be soaked for about 6 hours, when the skin will come off easily. Cook as described for the *baccalà*. The pounding takes about 10–15 minutes, and the amount of olive oil added should be about 6 tablespoonfuls, and half that quantity of milk or, better, cream. The dish will not come out beautifully white as does *baccalà*, but the combination of the fish and the olive oil is unfamiliar and good.

Serve piled up in a mound, surrounded with squares of fried bread. Enough for 4.

The fish can be reheated in the double saucepan without coming to harm.

Italian Food

Chez Barattero

From 1956 to 1961 I contributed a monthly cookery article to London *Vogue*. In those days cookery writers were very minor fry. Expenses were perks paid to photographers, fashion editors and other such exalted personages. Foreign currency allowances were severely restricted, so cookery contributors didn't come in for subsidised jaunts to Paris or marathons round three-star eating cathedrals. They were supposed to supply their articles out of some inexhaustible well of knowledge and their ingredients out of their own funds. At a monthly fee of £20 an article (increased at some stage, I think, to £25) it was quite a struggle to keep up the flow of properly tested recipes, backed up with informative background material, local colour and general chatter. So it was with gratitude that one year I accepted an offer from my editor, the original and enlightened Audrey Withers, to go on the occasional trip to France, provided with £100 from Condé Nast to help cover restaurant meals, hotels, petrol and so on. To be sure, £100 wasn't exactly princely even in those days, but it was double the ordinary currency allowance, and even though those trips were very much France on a shoestring, the knowledge I derived from them was valuable. In French provincial restaurants at that time local and regional dishes weren't always double-priced on a 'menu touristique'. Some, incredible as it now seems, would be listed as a matter of course on the everyday menus of quite ordinary restaurants. Asked nicely, a *patron* might come up with a speciality based, say, on some local farmhouse pork product, or on a cheese peculiar to the immediate district, perhaps an omelette of the chef's own devising, or a simple fish dish with an uncommon sauce. It was for ideas and stimulus that I was looking, not restaurant set pieces.

*Madame Barattero and her chef Monsieur Perrier outside the Hôtel du Midi,
photographed by Anthony Denney, c. 1959.*

On one trip, however, I came to make the acquaintance of Madame Barattero and her Hôtel du Midi at Lamastre in the Ardèche. Now, a hotel with a Michelin two-star restaurant attached might not seem exactly the appropriate choice for people on a restricted budget. As things turned out, that particular two-star restaurant-hotel proved, in the long run, very much cheaper, infinitely better value, and far more rewarding than most of the technically cheap places we'd found. Staying at Lamastre on half-pension terms was restful and comfortable. Every day we drove out to the countryside, usually taking a picnic, or lunching at a small town or village restaurant. In the evening we were provided by Madame Barattero with a delicious dinner made up of quite simple dishes geared to the price charged to *pensionnaires*. Prime ingredients and skilled cooking were, however, very much included in our *en pension* terms. That lesson was a valuable one, and seemed well worth passing on to my readers.

My account of the Hôtel du Midi was published in *Vogue* in September 1958. I should add that while much of the material published in *Vogue* as a result of my trips to France in the fifties was incorporated in *French Provincial Cooking*, this was one of several articles which got away. There did not seem to be a place for it in the book, and in fact it was, in its day, unique for a *Vogue* food article in that it included no recipes. It was, again, Audrey Withers who took the decision to publish an article quite unorthodox by the rules prevailing at the time. I appreciated her imaginative gesture. With Madame Barattero I remained on friendly terms for many years, receiving a moving welcome every time I visited her hotel. Two years ago, after a brief retirement, Madame Barattero died. Her declining years had been clouded by increasing deafness, by the withdrawal of one of her Michelin stars, and I believe other untoward happenings. The restaurant of the Hôtel du Midi is now in the hands of the same chef who was in charge of the kitchens all those years ago, and who had long since become a partner in the business. I have not visited Lamastre for several years now, so cannot express any opinion on the cooking. I am glad though to be able to republish my article, as a tribute to Madame Barattero's memory.

* * *

Rose Barattero is the euphonious name of the proprietress of the Hôtel du Midi at Lamastre in the Ardèche. Slim, elegant, her pretty grey hair in tight curls all over her head, the minuscule red ribbon of the Legion of Honour on her grey dress, Madame Barattero is an impressive little figure as she stands on the terrace of her hotel welcoming her guests as they drive into the main square of the small provincial town whose name she has made famous throughout France.

Here, in this town, in the modest hotel which stands back to back with her own, she was born. Her parents were hotel keepers, her brother inherited, and still runs, the old Hôtel de la Poste. Her sister has a hotel at St-Vallier down on the Rhône. Her husband, a *niçois*, and a relation of the Escoffier family, started his career as an apprentice at the Carlton in London, and was already making a name for himself as a promising chef when she married him and they set up on their own at the Hôtel du Midi.

When M. Barattero died in 1941 the hotel was already celebrated for its cooking. His young widow took over the running of the hotel and the restaurant, putting the kitchen in the charge of a hard-working and modest chef who had started as Barattero's apprentice. His wife looks after the accounts and the reception work. During the past fifteen years or so the fame of Barattero's at Lamastre has spread throughout France; Madame Barattero's name is among the most respected in the entire French restaurant industry.

In the fiercely competitive world of the French catering business this is no ordinary achievement. Lamastre is a town of little over three thousand inhabitants. It is not on a main road; the country round about, although magnificent and infinitely varied, is not known to tourists in the way in which, let us say, Provence or the château country of the Loire are known, for there is not very much left in the way of architectural or historical interest for the ordinary sightseer. In other words, a place like Barattero's must rely, not on the local population and the passing tourist, but upon those customers who make the journey to Lamastre expressly for the cooking.

Michelin awards Madame Barattero two stars. Now, although Michelin one-star restaurants are very much on the chancy side, both as regards quality and price, and such of their three-star establishments (there are only eleven in the whole of France) into which I have penetrated, either a little too rarefied in atmosphere for my taste – or, as Raymond Mortimer observed recently of a famous Paris house, the food is too rich and so are the customers – it is rare to find the two-star places at fault. As far as the provinces are concerned these two-star establishments (there are fifty-nine of them in the whole country, about twenty of which are in Paris) offer very remarkable value. I do not mean to suggest that they are places for the impecunious, but rather that while the cooking which they have to offer is unique, the charges compare more than favourably with those prevailing in hundreds of other French establishments where the surroundings vary between the grandiose and the squalid and where the cooking, while probably sound enough, is uneven or without distinction.

I have often heard the criticism that these modest establishments of two-star quality, offering, as most of them do, no more than half a dozen specialities at most, are places whose resources are exhausted after a couple of meals, or alternatively that the accommodation which they have to offer is not up to the standard of the cooking. So tourists make their pilgrimage to eat a meal at a place like the Midi at Lamastre, the Chapon Fin at Thoissey, or the Armes de France at Ammerschwihr and move on without knowing that they could have stayed for several days, not only in comfort and quiet and enjoying a variety of beautifully cooked dishes, but quite often at considerably reduced prices for pension or half-pension terms.

Early last summer we drove from Lyon down the western bank of the Rhône towards St-Péray, and there turned off up the steep and beautiful road which leads to Lamastre and St-Agrève. We had been warned that the forty-odd kilometres from St-Péray to Lamastre would take us twice as long as we expected because of the sinuous road, so we had allowed plenty of time, and arrived in front of the Hôtel du Midi while the afternoon sun was still shining over the little *place*. Our welcome from Madame Baraterro was so warm and the rooms we were shown so airy, light and sympathetically furnished, the bathroom so immense and shining, the little garden below our terrace so pretty and orderly, that we decided there and then to stay several days. We discussed half-pension terms with Madame and then made ourselves scarce until dinner time.

Now it must be explained that chez Baraterro there are five special dishes for which the house is renowned. They are *galantine de caneton*, a *pain d'écrevisses sauce cardinal*, a *poularde en vessie*, a *saucisse en feuilletage* and a dish of artichoke hearts with a creamy sauce which they call *artichauts Escoffier*. If you were really trying you could, I suppose, taste them all at one meal (indeed four of them figure on the 1,800 franc menu, the most expensive one, the others being 1,600 and 1,200) but we could take our time and enjoy them gradually. We left the choice of our menus to Madame. Indeed, there was little alternative but to do so. For although she does not herself do the cooking Madame has been studying her guests and composing menus for them for thirty-four years and she neither likes being contradicted nor is capable of making a mistake in this respect. She knew without being told that we didn't want to overload ourselves with food, however delicious; with an unerring touch she provided us night after night with menus which I think it is worth describing if only to demonstrate one or two important points about French restaurant cooking. First, how varied the food can be even in a place where the advertised specialities are very limited; secondly, how well worth while it is eating even the simplest of the routine dishes of French cookery produced in an absolutely first-class manner. ('One does not come here to eat something as ordinary as *œufs en gelée*,' the archbishop-like head waiter in a famous Paris restaurant once said to me. He was wrong. Such simple things are the test of a really good establishment.) And thirdly, how very much a good dish gains by being served quite on its own, without fussy garnish or heaps of vegetables to overfill you and to get in the way of your sauce, to distract from the main flavours of the chicken or the fish and to sicken you of the sight of food long before the end of the meal.

We could have started every meal with soup had we so wished, but in fact we did so only once or twice because they were so good that we should have eaten too much. And the last part of the meal always consisted of a fine platter of cheeses and either strawberries, cherries or an ice, so I will leave those items out of the following account of our menus.

The wines we drank were mostly recent Rhône vintages, the current wines of the house, for many of which, especially the red Hermitages, the Cornas and the Côte Rôtie, I have a particular affection. Among the whites we tried were St-Péray, Chapoutier's Chante Alouette, Jaboulet's La Chapelle Hermitage 1950; for those who prefer, and can afford, old burgundies and bordeaux there is a well-stocked cellar of fine vintages.

Tuesday

Galantine de caneton: The name is misleading to English ears. It is a whole boned duck, its flesh mixed with finely minced pork, truffles, brandy and foie gras, sewn up in the skin of the duck and cooked in the oven; the result resembles a long fat sausage with the feet of the duck protruding at one end. This pâté has a flavour of very great delicacy, and is served sliced and quite unadorned. The lettuce leaves and the little heap of potato salad which, I have an uneasy feeling, would be the inevitable garnish provided by an English restaurateur, is simply unthinkable here.

Sole meunière: Perfectly cooked whole sole with quantities of hissing and foaming butter. Again, no garnish of any kind, and none needed.

Blettes à la crème au gratin: Blettes, or chard, that spinach-like vegetable with fleshy white stalks is, to me, only tolerable when cooked by a master hand, but as the Barattero chef has that hand, and makes a particularly excellent cream sauce, all was well.

Wednesday

After an exhausting day's driving in bad weather, and a good and not expensive lunch at the Cygne (but unsettling contemporary decor in an old hotel) in the rather depressing town of Le Puy, we returned to dinner at Lamastre.

Potage de légumes: The routine vegetable soup of the day, but the mixture of carrots, potatoes and other vegetables was so delicate, so buttery, so full of flavour, that this alone would serve to make the reputation of a lesser restaurant. Note: although so full of flavour this soup was quite thin. I think we make our vegetable soups too thick in this country.

Ris de veau à la crème: I have eaten too many ambitiously conceived but ill-executed dishes of sweetbreads ever again to order them of my own accord, so I was grateful to Madame Barattero for showing me how good they can be when properly done. There were mushrooms in the sauce. Perfect.

Petit pois à la française: A big bowl of very small fresh peas (even in good restaurants it is rare nowadays not to get *petits pois de conserve*) cooked with little shreds of lettuce but without the little onions usually associated with the *à la française* manner of cooking them. The result was very creamy and good. I doubt if I shall ever again put onions with my peas.

Thursday

Pain d'écrevisses sauce cardinal: A very remarkable dish. A variety of *quenelle*, but unlike the pasty *quenelles* one eats elsewhere, even in the much cracked-up Lyon restaurants; as light as a puff of air, with the subtle and inimitable flavour of river crayfish permeating both *quenelle* and the rich cream sauce. The garnish of the dish consisted of a few whole scarlet crayfish and crescents of puff pastry.

Poularde en vessie: A 3-lb Bresse chicken, stuffed with its own liver, a little foie gras and slices of truffle, is tied up inside a pig's bladder and cooked extremely gently in a marmite of barely simmering water for 1½ hours. As Madame Barattero said, a chicken poached in the ordinary way, however carefully, cannot help but be *'un peu délavé'*, a trifle washed out. By this system, which is an ancient one, the chicken, untouched by the cooking liquid, emerges with all its juices and flavours intact. When it is cold, as it was served to us, these juices formed inside the bladder have solidified to a small amount of clear and delicately flavoured jelly. Madame asserted that nothing was easier to cook than this dish – 'What do you mean, why can you not get a pig's bladder in England? You have pigs, do you not?' – and upheld her point by adding that the chef's eight-year-old son already knows how to prepare the *poulardes en vessie.* A green salad with cream in the dressing was the only accompaniment to the chicken.

Friday and Saturday

The most important part of Friday's meal was a sad disappointment. It was a dish of tiny grilled lamb cutlets, obviously beautiful meat, but much too undercooked for our taste.

On Saturday evening, when *épaule d'agneau* was announced, I explained the trouble. The little shoulder appeared cooked to what was, for us, perfection. A beautiful golden brown on the outside and just faintly pink in the middle. It has been preceded by a delicious *omelette aux champignons* and was accompanied by a *gratin* of courgettes and tomatoes, just slightly flavoured with garlic and cooked in butter instead of olive oil as it would have been in Provence. It went admirably with the lamb, and this was a good example of a very nice dinner of quite ordinary French dishes without any particular regional flavour or speciality of the house.

Sunday

Next day was Whitsunday and we stayed in to lunch as well as to dinner, for, as the weekend drew near, we had been observing with fascinated interest the preparations afoot for the large number of customers expected for the *fêtes.* The chef had prepared fifteen of his boned and stuffed ducks and by lunchtime on Sunday dozens of *poulardes* tied up in pig's bladders and scores of *pain d'écrevisses* were ready, all gently murmuring in their respective copper marmites.

Until now the service at meal times had been performed entirely by Marthe and Marie, the two pretty, expertly trained young girls in black frocks and starched white aprons who also brought our breakfasts and looked after our rooms. Now two waiters and Madame's sister from St-Vallier appeared upon the scene. There was no bustle and no panic or noise. Everything went like clockwork. And this I think partly explains what must seem a mystery to many visitors: how these unassuming places, in which the hotel part of the business is only incidental, can manage to maintain, day after day, cooking of a quality which simply could not be found in England and which is rare even in France. The answer is that they are organized and run in a way which a Guards sergeant-major would envy, and are as well equipped to deal with a banquet for three hundred people or a steady stream of holiday visitors as they are to provide comfort and an intimate atmosphere for a handful of regular guests out of season.

From a peaceful Sunday morning gossip in the charming blue and turquoise and cream tiled *charcuterie* run by M. and Madame Montagne (where there is a good restaurant in a French town or village you may be sure that a good *charcuterie* is not far away), I returned to Barattero's for the promised Sunday feast. Customers were arriving from Valence, from Marseille, from Lyon. A huge shining silver-grey Rolls-Bentley was parked in the square (it was the first English car we had seen). A party of young people flung themselves off their Lambrettas and clattered round a large table. They evidently took the cooking and its reputation for granted, for they hadn't dressed up or put on Sunday voices as we would have here for such an occasion. It was enjoyable to watch them, and all the other customers who were there simply because they were going to enjoy the food, for there was none of that holy hush which to some of us makes the grander eating places such a sore trial.

This was our luncheon menu:

Saucisse en feuilletage: This might be called the apotheosis of the sausage roll. A fresh, pure pork sausage (from the Montagne establishment, as I had already learned), coarsely cut and weighing about ¾ lb, is poached and then encased in flaky pastry, baked, and served hot, cut in slices. Both sausage and pastry were first class. A delicious hors-d'œuvre.

Pain d'écrevisses sauce cardinal: This seemed even better, if possible, than the first time we had eaten it, and this is quite a test, for one is inclined to be more critical when tasting a famous dish for the second time. The chef at Barattero's has been cooking the *pain d'écrevisses*, and the other specialities of the house, almost every day for some thirty years, but even so I suppose it is possible that they might vary.

Artichauts Escoffier: I am always in two minds about dishes of this kind. The cream sauce with mushrooms was very light and did not overwhelm the artichoke hearts, but all the same I wonder if they are not better quite plain; at La Mère Brazier's in Lyon we had a salad of whole artichoke hearts and lettuce dressed simply with a little oil and lemon, which, in its extreme simplicity, was quite delicious and the best artichoke dish I have ever eaten.

Poulet roti: A *poulet de grain* (the equivalent of a spring chicken) for two people, perfectly roasted in butter, already carved but reconstituted into its original shape, served on a long platter with a nest of miniature *pommes rissolées* beside it. No other garnish.

For dinner that evening we tasted again the wonderful duck pâté, to be followed by a little roast *gigot* and another dish of those tender little *petits pois*. When we told the waiter how much we had enjoyed the lamb, he replied yes, certainly, it must be a treat to us after the mutton boiled with mint of English cookery. Some very quaint notions of English food are current in France.

The last customers were only just leaving as we ourselves said goodbye to Madame Barattero after dinner, for we were leaving early next morning. The place had seemed full to us, but it was the time of the Algerian crisis, and had it not been for *les évènements*, Madame said, there would have been twice as many people. Customers would have come even from Paris. In her long, arduous and successful career as restaurateur and hotel keeper she has learned that you can never be quite sure what to expect, and even with her tremendous experience it is impossible to know how many people to cater for. As she says: 'Thirty-four years in the hotel business, what a stint, hein?'

An Omelette and a Glass of Wine
chosen by Peter Carson, Terence Conran,
Veronica Nicholson and Richard Olney

Elizabeth's books shot a ray of sunshine through the damp, grey cloud that hung over post-war Britain. Suddenly, here was a woman writing about food with equal measures of passion and intelligence, in a style that was a curious hybrid of the enthusiastic school mistress and the dowager duchess. Her books conjured up the atmosphere of the Mediterranean, and sent wafts of perfume into our fugged-up lives. They were eye-opening and educational, and they captured my imagination as strongly as they captured the spirit of France and Italy and Spain.

For me, Elizabeth's books formed an important part of the learning process that led to Habitat. In evoking the Mediterranean countries, she pinpointed the essential, simple bounty of their cooking equipment – the heavy pots and pans, enamelled casseroles and salt-glazed pottery that would form the core of our kitchen department. We even featured Elizabeth in one of the Habitat catalogues in the 1970s, so I'm sure we passed the test.

It's difficult to pick out recipes as particular favourites: I think the value of her books is primarily in the way they teach an understanding and appreciation of food and the art of cooking. Of course, they set the ball rolling in terms of the transformation in the eating habits of the British, but you can't cook from Elizabeth's recipes in the way you can from most cookbooks which spoon-feed the reader. I like to browse in them for inspiration, to get the creative and gastric juices flowing.

For me, probably the most evocative piece she ever wrote is 'Chez Barattero'. The descriptions are so vivid and the writing so precise that when, on Elizabeth's advice, I visited the hotel myself, it was exactly what the article had led me to expect. Re-reading the piece recently, I was struck by just how many of her observations have informed my own views on food and restaurant business. With fetishistic precision, she describes the meals that she and her companion enjoyed over their six-day stay. 'How very much a good dish gains by being served quite on its own, without fussy garnish or heaps of vegetables to overfill you,' she observes, and it strikes an immediate chord.

Terence Conran

Recommended by Elizabeth, we stayed at the 'Midi' and ate the lovely food they prepared. The first night we were there, a fire broke out in the hotel opposite. Fire engines, firemen and hose-pipes were mustered. There were sharp orders and sharper counter-orders, shouting, excitement. It was *son et lumière* at its best. The next morning when the fun was over we asked Mme

Barattero whether she had feared that her own hotel might catch fire. She stiffened – 'The Hôtel du Midi is made of marble,' she told us. Later we reported this to Elizabeth who was much amused. 'But *of course*,' she said.

Veronica Nicholson

Elizabeth David's correspondence archive contains several letters and post-cards (see below) from people who went because of her article, and found everything exactly as expected – especially Madame Barattero who 'gave us such a welcome when we mentioned your name', and who often added a few lines to the postcard. These comments stretch over a quarter of a century to the early 1980s, when Madame was no longer alive but Bernard Perrier, the son of her partner, continued her tradition of hospitality and excellence.

J.N.

La Charcuterie

A great deal is said and written about the innate cooking skill of every French housewife and every *patron-chef* of every other *auberge*, restaurant and transport café in the land. While not wishing in any way to belittle the culinary talents so lavishly bestowed by Providence upon the French, and so brilliantly cultivated by them, it should be observed that both housewife and restaurateur frequently lean heavily upon their local *charcutiers* and *pâtissiers*. If a housewife has but little time for cooking, she is able to rely upon the terrines and pâtés, the sausages, the hams, and all the miscellaneous pork products of the *charcutier* to make a quick midday meal for her family or a first course for her lunch party. If the talents of her cook do not lie in the direction of pastry-making, she can with perfect confidence order a vol-au-vent to fill with a rich creamy sea-food mixture, or a cake, a handsome fruit flan or a *savarin* to serve as dessert, while she and her cook concentrate upon the meat, the fish and the vegetables.

The reputation of many a small restaurateur has been built upon the products of the local *charcutier*. A careful look at the details of restaurant specialities given in the Michelin and other guides shows that not a few of them owe their star to some kind of sausage, or pâté, *andouillette* or *pieds de porc truffés*. Ten to one you will find that not far away from that restaurant is a first-class pork butcher. Or it may be that the pork butcher himself has gone into the restaurant business as an outlet for his products. In fact, this is partly the reason that the English tourist often finds that the one-star restaurant is a disappointment, for the rest of the cooking is not always up to the standard of the *charcuterie*.

I cannot say that Lamastre in the Ardèche is typical of any small French provincial town, for it has been made famous throughout France by Madame Barattero and the lovely food she has been serving there for thirty years at the Hôtel du Midi. Neither can it be suggested that Madame Barattero relies upon the local *charcutier*, for, first by her husband and, after he died, by her chef, the same few beautiful and high-class dishes have been produced almost every day of those thirty years. But the first-class *charcutier* is there all right and works in cooperation with the hotel, supplying it with at least one of its renowned specialities, a sausage which the Barattero chef cooks and presents wrapped in the lightest and most melting of puff pastries. . . .

Into Montagne's beautiful blue- and cream-tiled shop, hidden away in a narrow, unprepossessing street in Lamastre, I strolled, therefore, one Whitsunday morning to see what might be going on while all the housewives and restaurateurs in the town would be busy preparing their Sunday midday feast.

Besides the sausages and the hams, the pâtés and the local Ardéchois specialities called *jambonnettes*, *cayettes* and *rosettes* (unexpectedly, this is a *salame* type of sausage also popular in Lyon but better made here, I thought – it is identifiable by the coarse-meshed net in which it is presented for sale), there were all sorts of special things for the fêtes. There were trays of snails, their shells almost bursting with fresh-looking parsley butter, and Sunday hors-d'œuvre of cones of raw ham alternating with little chicken liver pâtés moulded in sparkling aspic jelly, all arranged by Madame Montagne herself on long narrow-plated dishes and ready to take away. There was a huge supply of *quenelles de brochet* (you can't get away from them in these parts) and on the magnificent butcher's block of smooth scrubbed wood was a tank-sized two-handled pan of pale orange-coloured sauce full of chopped olives, to serve with the *quenelles*. Beside it was one of those monolithic loaves of butter which never fail to have their effect upon English eyes accustomed to seeing only little half-pound slabs in paper wrappings.

There was a steady stream of customers making last-minute purchases for their Sunday lunches. One woman came in with her saucepan and took away her sauce in it, all ready to put upon the stove and to serve with her *quenelles*. For another, Madame Montagne swiftly cut half a pound of *jambon de pays* in the requisite postcard-thin slices. (The French don't always take sufficient care about this point. I have seen the otherwise excellent *jambon d'Auvergne* absolutely murdered by being slashed into doorsteps.) A small boy had been sent by his mother to buy an extra chicken to roast. There was none left. What about some sausages instead? The cooking sausages from chez Montagne are the very ones which go into the *feuilletage* at Barattero's, and, as we were to discover presently, made those of Lyon appear very coarse in comparison. And in between serving her customers, Madame Montagne told me how the *jambonnettes* are cut from the knuckle end of a ham, boned, stuffed with fresh pork meat, and sewn up into a fat little cushion shape; how the *rosette* is called after the particular kind of sausage skin in which it is encased, a thick and fat skin which, during the curing process, nourishes the meat inside, and gives it its characteristically fresh and moist quality; how a mixture of leg and shoulder meat is used for this kind of sausage and how it is the favourite *charcuterie* speciality of the Ardèche, so that out of every four pigs killed the legs of two only are made into hams, the others, and the shoulders, being used for *rosettes*; how the fresh dry air up here at Lamastre is more propitious for the manufacture of sausages than the notorious fog and damp of Lyon; how they do not care here for that ancient traditional *saucisse aux herbes* which is still made down on the Rhône, but how the same sort of mixture of pork with cabbage, spinach and *blettes* is made into *cayettes*. These resemble rather large rissoles, cooked in the oven, all browned and very appetizing-looking in serried rows on their baking trays. Madame Montagne said she didn't think I'd like them, but they have a not unattractive, coarse flavour which collectors of genuinely rustic dishes would appreciate.

Another speciality, Madame Montagne told me, her green almond eyes curious that I should want to know all these things, was the pâté made largely with *grattons*, the little browned scraps which are the residue after the pork fat has been melted down, and which were also the original ingredient of the renowned *rillettes de Tours*.

And the interesting decoration of the shop? Who had created it? It was designed twenty-five years ago by M. Montagne's grandfather; the lapis-coloured tiles were really to discourage flies, for it is well known that blue repels them but, using the blue as his starting point, old M. Reymond achieved a most original and oddly beautiful combination, a kind of mosaic of sea colours which turns the *charcuterie* into a cool and orderly grotto, if such a thing can be imagined, with the rows of hanging sausages and hams for stalactites. The young Montagnes are very go-ahead (the family have been in the *charcuterie* business for some eighty years) and would like to install a large refrigerated cabinet – but it would mean destroying some of *grandpère*'s work and that would break the old man's heart. And I hope that even after he is dead the young couple will leave his shop intact, for it is the work of a man who was an artist in design as well as in *charcuterie*.

Madame Montagne told me that many foreign customers who come to Lamastre to eat Madame Barattero's food also come and buy the *charcuterie* products (once again, the link between the restaurant and the local shopkeepers), Germans, Belgians, Swiss, even Italians. She did not, I think, realize what a compliment this is, for it is not common to find sausages anywhere in Europe as good as those of Italy. And all these visitors would surely be sorry to see the old decoration and the elegant little façade of the shop replaced with gleaming glass and chromium.

French Provincial Cooking
chosen by Richard Binns

In the early sixties I bought a copy of *French Provincial Cooking* for my wife. A new dimension was added to our love of France, both at home, in our kitchen, and across the Channel. Her masterpiece became our bible: no paperback (we still have the original edition and two reprints) has ever returned such handsome dividends.

A classic example of Elizabeth at her best – the clever way she used her evocative writing skills to encourage you to find out more for yourself –

was in the piece devoted to Lamastre, Mme Barattero and the Montagne *charcuterie*. In the mid-'sixties we headed up into the hills to see the little town for ourselves. Decades later I was able to add an intriguing footnote to her tale: Elizabeth had never known that, in the thirties, Mme Barattero's chef/husband Joseph had won three Michelin stars in the out-of-the-way Ardèche town. She, like me, would see the irony in that: today, such an unpretentious hotel would never win three stars – the rules have been changed! Richard Binns

MEAT

LA DAUBE DE BŒUF PROVENÇALE

There must be scores of different recipes for *daubes* in Provence alone, as well as all those which have been borrowed from Provence by other regions, for a *daube* of beef is essentially a country housewife's dish. In some *daubes* the meat is cut up, in others it is cooked in the piece; what goes in apart from the meat is largely a matter of what is available, and the way it is served is again a question of local taste.

This is an easy recipe, but it has all the rich savour of these slowly cooked wine-flavoured stews. The pot to cook it in may be earthenware, cast iron or a copper oven pot of about 2 pints' (1.1 l) capacity, wide rather than deep.

The ingredients are 2 lb (900 g) top rump of beef, about 6 oz (170 g) unsmoked streaky bacon or salt pork, about 3 oz (90 g) fresh pork rinds, 2 onions, 2 carrots, 2 tomatoes, 2 cloves of garlic, a bouquet of thyme, bay leaf, parsley and a little strip of orange peel, 2 tablespoons of olive oil, a glass (4 fl oz/120 ml) of red wine, seasoning.

Have the meat cut into squares about the size of half a postcard and about ⅓ inch (8 mm) thick. Buy the bacon or salt pork in the piece and cut it into small cubes.

Scrape and slice the carrots on the cross; peel and slice the onions. Cut the rinds, which should have scarcely any fat adhering to them and are there to give body as well as savour to the stew, into little squares. Skin and slice the tomatoes.

In the bottom of the pot put the olive oil, then the bacon, then the vegetables, and half the pork rinds. Arrange the meat carefully on top, the slices overlapping each other. Bury the garlic cloves, flattened with a knife, and the bouquet, in the centre. Cover with the rest of the pork rinds. With the pan uncovered, start the cooking on a moderate heat on top of the stove.

After about 10 minutes, put the wine into another saucepan; bring it to a fast boil; set light to it; rotate the pan so that the flames spread. When they have died down pour the wine bubbling over the meat. Cover the pot with greaseproof paper or foil, and a well fitting lid. Transfer to a very slow oven (140°C/290°F/Gas Mark 1) and leave for 2½ hours.

To serve, arrange the meat with the bacon and the little pieces of rind on a hot dish; pour off some of the fat from the sauce, extract the bouquet, and pour the sauce round the meat. If you can, keep the dish hot over a spirit lamp after it is brought to table. At the serving stage, a *persillade* of finely chopped garlic and parsley, with perhaps an anchovy and a few capers, can be sprinkled over the top. Or stoned black olives can be added to the stew half an hour before the end of the cooking time.

Although in Italy pasta is never served with a meat dish, in Provence it quite often is. The cooked and drained noodles, or whatever pasta you have chosen, are mixed with some of the gravy from the stew, and in this case the fat is not removed from the gravy, because it lubricates the pasta. Sometimes this *macaronade*, as it is called, is served first, to be followed by the meat.

Nowadays, since rice has been successfully cultivated in the reclaimed areas of the Camargue, it is also quite usual to find a dish of rice, often flavoured with saffron, served with a meat stew.

This *daube* is a useful dish for those who have to get a dinner ready when they get home from the office. It can be cooked for 1½ hours the previous evening and finished on the night itself. Provided they have not been overcooked to start with, these beef and wine stews are all the better for a second or even third heating up. The amounts I have given are the smallest quantities in which it is worth cooking such a stew, and will serve four or five people, but of course they can be doubled or even trebled for a large party; if the meat is piled up in layers in a deep pan it will naturally need longer cooking than if it is spread out in a shallow one.

French Provincial Cooking
chosen by John Ruden

BŒUF À LA BOURGUIGNONNE

This is a favourite among those carefully composed, slowly cooked dishes which are the domain of French housewives and owner-cooks of modest restaurants rather than of professional chefs. Generally supposed to be of Burgundian origin (although Alfred Contour's *Cuisinier Bourguignon* gives no recipe for it) *bœuf à la bourguignonne* has long been a nationally popular French dish, and is often referred to, or written down on menus, simply as '*bourguignon*'. Such dishes do not, of course, have a rigid formula, each cook interpreting it according to her taste, and the following recipe is just one version. Incidentally, when I helped in a soup kitchen in France many years ago, this was the dish for feast-days and holidays.

2 lb (900 g) topside of beef, 4 oz (120 g) salt pork or streaky bacon (unsmoked for preference), a large onion, thyme, parsley and bay leaves, ¼ pint (150 ml) red wine, 2 tablespoons of olive oil, ½ pint (280 ml) meat stock, preferably veal, a clove of garlic, 1 tablespoon flour, meat dripping. For the garnish, ½ lb (225 g) small mushrooms, a dozen or so small whole onions.

Cut the meat into slices about 2½ inches (6 cm) square and ¼ inch (6 mm) thick. Put them into a china or earthenware dish, seasoned with salt and pepper, covered with the large sliced onion, herbs, olive oil and red wine. Leave to marinate from 3–6 hours.

Put a good tablespoon of beef dripping into a heavy stewing-pan of about 4 pints (3 l) capacity. In this melt the salt pork or bacon, cut into ¼-inch (6-mm) thick match-length strips. Add the whole peeled small onions, and let them brown, turning them over frequently and keeping the heat low. Take out the bacon when its fat becomes transparent, and remove the onions when they are nicely coloured. Set them aside with the bacon. Now put into the fat the drained and dried pieces of meat and brown them quickly on each side. Sprinkle them with the flour, shaking the pan so that the flour amalgamates with the fat and absorbs it. Pour over the strained marinade. Let it bubble half a minute; add the stock. Put in a clove of garlic and a bouquet of thyme, parsley and bay leaf tied with a thread. Cover the pan with a close-fitting lid and let it barely simmer on top of the stove for about 2 hours.

Now add the bacon and onions, and the whole mushrooms washed but not peeled and already cooked in butter or dripping for a minute or so to rid them of some of their moisture. Cook the stew another half-hour. Remove the bouquet and garlic before serving.

There should be enough for 4–6 people.

If more convenient, the first 2 hours' cooking can be done in advance, the stew left to cool and the fat removed; it can then be reheated gently with the bacon, mushrooms and onions added. There are those who maintain that the dish is improved by being heated up a second time; the meat has time to mature, as it were, in the sauce.

To make a cheaper dish, chuck (shoulder) beef may be used instead of topside, and an extra 45 minutes' cooking time allowed. And when really small onions are not available it is best simply to cook a chopped onion or two with the stew, and to leave onions out of the garnish, because large ones are not suitable for the purpose.

For formal occasions a boned joint of beef may be cooked whole and served with a similar sauce and garnish, and then becomes *pièce de bœuf à la bourguignonne.*

French Provincial Cooking
chosen by Rupert Grey

BŒUF À LA GARDIANE

A dish from western Provence and the Camargue demonstrating the stewing of a tough piece of meat in red wine without the addition of any stock or thickening for the sauce.

Ingredients for 4 people are 2 lb (900 g) top rump of beef, 4 tablespoons of brandy, 1 large glass (6 fl oz/170 ml) of red wine, a bouquet of thyme, parsley and bay leaf, plus a little strip of orange peel and a crushed clove of garlic, butter and olive oil; and about 6 oz (170 g) stoned black olives.

The meat should be cut into small neat cubes, not more than an inch (2.5 cm) square. Brown them in a mixture of olive oil and butter. Warm the brandy in a soup ladle, pour it over the meat, set light to it, shake the pan until the flames go out. Add the red wine; let it bubble fast for about half a minute. Season with only very little salt and pepper, put in the bouquet tied with thread, turn the heat as low as possible, cover the pan with at least two layers of greaseproof paper or foil and the lid.

Cook as gently as possible, on top of the stove, with a mat underneath the pan, for about 3½ hours. Ten minutes before serving, remove the bouquet and put in the stoned black olives. Taste for seasoning before serving. A dish of plain boiled rice can be served separately.

The flaming with brandy, although not absolutely essential, burns up the excess fat and makes quite a difference to the flavour of the finished sauce, which will be a short one, most of the liquid having been absorbed by the meat. The old Nîmoise cook who showed me how to make this particular version of the dish used Châteauneuf du Pape to cook it in (we were in the district, so it wasn't so extravagant as it sounds, and it most definitely pays to use a decent and full-bodied wine for these beef stews) and she garnished the dish with heart-shaped croûtons of fried bread instead of rice.

French Provincial Cooking
chosen by Barbara Kafka, Jacqueline Korn and John Ruden

I wrote my first article about food in 1959. It was the same year that I first came across Elizabeth David's writing, in two thin paperbacks from Penguin: *A Book of Mediterranean Food* and *French Country Cooking*. They cost sixty-five and ninety cents respectively. I know, because they are sitting, yellowed, their cheap paper cracking off at the edges and their covers loosened from their spines, on my desk as I write. These two 1959 events had no causal relationship – but the coincidence is pleasing.

My own work took a comparative perspective as I wrote about the sweet and sour foods of Italy, Germany, Russia and China, and foods from around the world wrapped in dough. At the same time, the deceptively simple, and often sketchy, recipes of the two little paperbacks stayed in my mind. They were so appealing, so direct, the prose so authoritative. I read them again and again, and they helped to direct me back to other kinds of food that I enjoyed, simple hearty dishes often of the French and Italian Mediterranean coast.

For years, mindful of a pleasant debt due, I have paid homage in the introduction to various recipes of my own based on one of Elizabeth David's, a recipe for a *daube* that was clearly etched in my mind along with its introducing me to *daubières*. I had a recipe for short ribs and another for oxtail stew. Writing today, I went back to those two little books looking for my original impetus. Enjoying myself as I browsed, I was taken aback not to find the stew I sought or the words on *daubières* that I remembered. I found close matches: the Bœuf en Daube à la Niçoise in the *Mediterranean Food* book and the Estouffade de Bœuf à la Provençale in the *French Country* book which also had some evocative notes on earthenware pots. It was only when I turned to the later *French Provincial Cooking*, brought out in America in 1962, that I finally found Bœuf à la Gardiane and a brief note on *daubières*. The recipe is the most direct antecedent of my own (which are less of clones than I had thought) and shares ingredients with the recipes from the earlier books.

I was not disappointed. I realized that Mrs David had given me incomparable gifts. She had stimulated me to research on pots and she had given me the tools and inspiration for invention in recipes of my own. Even knowing the truth behind my memories, I wouldn't change a word of my introductions. When I finally met her, I received another gift, the surprise of her physical beauty. She remained Mrs David to me, not a friend but a respected and graceful mentor, as she was to much of my generation.   Barbara Kafka

LA QUEUE DE BŒUF DES VIGNERONS
(*Oxtail stewed with white grapes*)

Oxtail 'as cooked by the winegrowers' is a lovely dish made out of what should be inexpensive ingredients, but as in England grapes are not to be had just for the picking, one should perhaps only attempt it when imported grapes are plentiful and cheap. To make the lengthy cooking worth while buy at least 2 oxtails, cut into the usual 2-inch (5-cm) lengths by the butcher. The other ingredients are 3–4 oz (90–120 g) of salt pork or of a cheap cut of fat unsmoked bacon bought in one piece, 2 large onions, 4 large carrots, and 2 lb (900 g) white grapes. Seasonings include, besides salt and freshly milled pepper, a little mace or allspice, a bouquet of 2 bay leaves, parsley, thyme and 2 crushed cloves of garlic tied in a little bunch.

Steep the oxtail in cold water for a minimum of 2 hours, so that the blood soaks out.

Cut the bacon, without the rind, into little cubes. Chop the onions and dice the carrots. At the bottom of a heavy cooking pot put the bacon with the vegetables on top. Start off on a low flame and cook for 10 minutes until the fat from the bacon is running. Now put in the pieces of oxtail, and put the bouquet in the centre. Season the meat. Cover the pot and cook gently for 20 minutes. Now add the grapes, which you have picked off their stalks and crushed slightly in a bowl. Cover the pot with 2 sheets of greaseproof paper and the lid. Transfer to a very slow oven (140°C/290°F/Gas Mark 1), and cook for a minimum of 3½ hours. Oxtail varies very much in quality, and sometimes takes a good deal longer, and unless the meat is so soft and tender it is almost falling from the bones it will not be good. Once cooked, quickly transfer the pieces of oxtail and a few of the little bits of bacon to another terrine or to a serving dish, and keep them hot while you sieve all the rest of the ingredients through the finest mesh of the *mouli-légumes*. Pour the resulting sauce over the oxtail. A dish of potatoes boiled in their skins, or a potato purée, should accompany the dish.

An alternative method is to cook the dish for half an hour less, take out the oxtail, and leave the sieved sauce separately so that excess fat can be removed from the top when it is cold. Having done this, pour the sauce, warmed, over the meat and heat on top of the stove rather than in the oven, because all-round heat tends to make the sauce oily, whereas with direct heat it will retain its consistency. The dish can, as a matter of fact, be reheated two or three times without damage.

Two oxtails should make six to eight ample helpings.

French Provincial Cooking
chosen by Eleo Gordon

Oxtail stew 'in the fashion of Mpishi the cook' appeared regularly on the lunch table during my childhood in Uganda. One day a particularly splendid version was planned by Mpishi to celebrate the arrival of an uncle from England. He piled more and more bones into the pressure cooker, put it on the high flame, with the obvious result – oxtail all over the ceiling, pan in a million pieces and Mpishi lying on the floor, totally unharmed but moaning that he was dead.

Many years later the same uncle was treated – more successfully this time – to Elizabeth's divine Oxtail with Grapes. *Her* recipe recommends long, slow cooking. Eleo Gordon

SUSSEX STEWED STEAK

This is one of the excellent old English dishes in which mushroom ketchup and ale or stout make a rich-looking and interesting gravy.

Ingredients are 2½ lb (1 kg) a cheap cut such as chuck steak, top rump or thick flank cut in one piece, an onion, a tablespoon or two of flour, 2½ fl oz (75 ml) each of port and stout, 2 tablespoons of mushroom ketchup or wine vinegar, salt and pepper.

The whole dish takes scarcely five minutes to prepare for cooking.

Season the meat, rub flour on both sides. Put it flat in a shallow baking dish in which it just fits. Over it slice a large onion. Pour in the wine, stout, and ketchup or vinegar. Cover with a double sheet of greaseproof paper, and the lid of the dish. Put it in a very low oven (140°C/280°F/Gas Mark 1) and leave it for about 3 hours – a little less or longer won't matter. The toughest piece of meat emerges beautifully tender, and the gravy rich, bright brown, excellently flavoured.

Creamy mashed potatoes and perhaps a few fried or grilled mushrooms – if you can get large flat ones – go well with this casserole of steak.

Spices, Salt and Aromatics
chosen by John Ruden

COLD BAKED SILVERSIDE OF BEEF

Salt silverside is a true English speciality often overlooked when it comes to home entertaining. A pity, for it can be delicious and, especially when cooked to be eaten cold, is economical and presents the minimum of cooking and serving problems.

5–6 lb (2.25–2.75 kg) of salt silverside of beef, onions, carrots, garlic, bay leaves, peppercorns. Optional: a tumbler of red wine or cider.

Give your butcher due warning that you will be needing a handsome piece of salt beef, otherwise he may not have any which has been long enough in the pickle.

Before cooking it, soak it in cold water for a couple of hours.

Put the beef in a deep ovenproof pot in which there is not too much room to spare. Surround it with a couple of large carrots and onions sliced, a crushed clove of garlic, 2 bay leaves, a half dozen peppercorns and, if you are using it, the wine or cider (all these extra flavourings not only improve the taste of the meat but help to produce a stock which, next day, will make the basis of a beautiful beetroot or onion soup), and fill up the pot with water. Cover the pot closely.

Place low down in a very moderate oven (150°–170°C/300°–330°F/ Gas Mark 2–3) and leave untouched for 3 to 4 hours. Test to see if the meat is tender. Don't let it overcook, or it will crumble when carved. Take the joint from the liquid, wrap it in greaseproof paper, put it in a deep bowl, on top of it put a tea plate or small board, and a 2 lb (1 kg) weight. Leave until next day.

With the beef have tomato and cucumber salads, and a mild fruit chutney.

Spices, Salt and Aromatics

SPICED BEEF FOR CHRISTMAS

Dry-pickled or spiced beef is very different in flavour from the brine-pickled or salt beef sold by the butchers. It used to be a regular Christmas dish in a great many English country houses and farms. 'This is more a Christmas dish than any other time of the year,' says John Simpson, cook to the Marquis of Buckingham, in his *Complete System of Cookery* (1806), 'not but it may be done any time, and is equally good.' He calls it rather grandly *Bœuf de Chasse* but under the names of Hunting Beef, or Beef à l'Écarlate, or simply Spiced Beef, various forms of the recipe have certainly been known for at least three hundred years.

In former times huge rounds of beef weighing upwards of 20 lb (9 kg) were required to lie in pickle for 3 to 4 weeks. A 5–12 lb (2.25– 5.5 kg) piece will however be ready for cooking after 10 to 14 days.

Here are two prescriptions for the spices worked out for varying quantities of meat. The presence of juniper berries among the pickling spices makes the recipe somewhat unusual. They appear in old recipes from Yorkshire, Cumberland, Wales, Sussex – those areas, in fact, where the juniper shrub grows wild on the hills. The dried berries can be bought from grocers who specialize in spices, and from any of the small kitchen shops which now sell herbs and spices.

For a 10–12 lb (4.5–5.5 kg) joint   For a 5–6 lb (2.25–2.75 kg) joint

5–6 oz (150–170 g)	light brown Barbados or other brown cane sugar	3 oz (90 g)
1 oz (30 g)	saltpetre (to be bought from chemists)	½ oz (15 g)
6 oz (170 g)	sea or rock salt	4 oz (120 g)
2 oz (60 g)	black peppercorns	1 oz (30 g)
1 oz (30 g)	allspice berries (also known as pimento and Jamaica pepper. To be bought from the same shops as the juniper berries)	½ oz (15 g)
2 oz (60 g)	juniper berries	1 oz (30 g)

For cooking the beef you will need only water, greaseproof paper or foil, and a big heavy cast-iron oven pot.

Ask the butcher for the best quality round or silverside beef and explain to him what it is for. He will probably be incredulous but will know how to cut and skewer it.

First rub the beef all over with the brown sugar and leave it for two days in a glazed stoneware crock or bowl. Crush all the spices, with the salt and saltpetre in a mortar. They should be well broken up but need not be reduced to a powder. With this mixture you rub the beef thoroughly each day for 9 to 14 days according to the size. Gradually, with the salt and sugar, the beef produces a certain amount of its own liquid, and it smells most appetizing. But keep it covered, and in a cool airy place, not in a stuffy kitchen.

When the time comes to cook the beef, take it from the crock, rinse off any of the spices which are adhering to it, but without sousing the meat in cold water. Put it in a big deep cast-iron pot preferably oval, in which it fits with very little space to spare. Pour in about ½ pint (280 ml) water. In the old days the meat would now have been covered with shredded suet to keep in the moisture, then with a thick crust made from 1 lb (450 g) of flour and 2 oz (60 g) lard, but the suet and the sealing crust can both be dispensed with, two or three layers of greaseproof paper or foil being used instead, to make sure there is no evaporation of juices. Put the lid on the pot. Bake in a very low oven (140°C/290°F/Gas Mark 1) for 5 hours for a 5–6 lb (2.25–2.75 kg) joint. Take it from the oven carefully, for there will be a certain amount of liquid round the beef. Leave it to cool for 2–3 hours. But before the fat sets, pour off all the liquid and remove the beef to a board. Wrap it in foil or greaseproof paper and put another board or a plate on top, and a 2–4 lb (1–2 kg) weight. Leave it until next day.

The beef will carve thinly and evenly, and has a rich, mellow, spicy flavour which does seem to convey to us some sort of idea of the food eaten by our forebears. Once cooked the beef will keep fresh for several days, in an ordinary larder *provided* it is kept wrapped in clean greaseproof paper frequently renewed. It can also be stored in a refrigerator so long as it is taken out and kept at room temperature for a couple of hours or so before it is to be eaten.

Silverside of beef dry-spiced according to the above recipe is prepared and sold ready for cooking at Harrods' meat counter. Produced on a large scale, and from expertly cut and very high quality Aberdeen Angus meat, Harrods' spiced beef used to be a better product than most of us could achieve at home.

It was thanks to the initiative of Mr Ducat, master-butcher and creator of the famous French *boucherie* at Harrods, that this marvellous dish has been rescued from neglect. In 1958, when I told Mr Ducat that I was going to publish my own version of the ancient Sussex recipe for spiced beef in the Christmas number of *Vogue* magazine, he suggested that he might try preparing the beef and offering it for sale ready for cooking. Since those days Harrods have been selling something like 2½ to 3 tons a year of their dry-spiced beef. It is, however, important to order in advance and to stipulate that the meat spends the requisite time in the spicing mixture. If the spices and salt have not penetrated the meat it will be tough and uninteresting.

On no account should anyone allow themselves to be persuaded that dry-spiced beef should be boiled or simmered on top of the stove.

Spices, Salt and Aromatics
chosen by Julia Caffyn, Chris Grey

PAUPIETTES DE VEAU BOURBONNAISE

Paupiettes, or *alouettes sans tête*, are to be found everywhere in France and, indeed, in Belgium and Italy as well, but every cook has a different recipe for them.

They are primarily designed to use up small quantities of cooked meat which go into the stuffing, although this does not by any means imply a makeshift dish; with good veal and a nicely blended and seasoned stuffing they often make a 'speciality of the house' in France, and at restaurants there is a great demand for them when the *patron*'s recipe is known to be a good one.

For this particular version the ingredients are 6 slices of veal cut as for small escalopes, beaten out thin, and weighing between 2 and 3 oz (60–90 g) each. For the stuffing about 2 oz (60 g) of unsmoked bacon and the same quantity of cold boiled beef or chicken or a mixture of both, parsley, a small clove of garlic or a shallot, 2 tablespoons of fine breadcrumbs, 1 egg, seasoning, a few drops of cognac if possible. To cook the paupiettes, 1 oz (30 g) butter, a small glass of red or white wine, a small onion, a little stock or broth.

Chop all the ingredients for the stuffing quite small (mincing them makes too close-textured a mixture), season with salt and pepper, add the breadcrumbs, the beaten egg and the cognac. There should be enough stuffing to fill a teacup, closely packed. Spread the veal slices out flat; season them with salt, pepper and lemon juice. Divide the stuffing into six portions and put one on each slice of veal. Roll them up, tuck in the ends to prevent the stuffing escaping, tie each round with two circles of string. In a sauté pan melt the butter, put in the finely sliced onion; as soon as it turns very pale yellow put in the paupiettes; leave them over a moderate heat a minute or two; pour over the wine, let it bubble, then add the stock. Transfer the dish to the oven, and cook gently, uncovered, for just under an hour at 170°C/330°F/Gas Mark 3. The sauce should be fairly reduced and does not need any thickening. Simply transfer the *paupiettes*, minus their string, to a heated serving dish and pour the sauce over them; add a very little chopped parsley. Enough for three.

The same dish can be made with beef (very thin slices of topside or skirt steak) and, of course, the stuffing can be varied according to what is available, but don't resort to sausage meat, which makes too heavy a stuffing. If you like, a very light purée of potatoes can go with the paupiettes, or triangles of fried bread.

The preliminary preparation of onions in butter which forms the basis of the sauce is, I think, particular to this recipe from a Bourbonnais cook.

French Provincial Cooking

ESCALOPES DE VEAU EN AÏLLADE

4 escalopes of veal cut from the leg, 1 lb (450 g) tomatoes, olive oil, 4 or 5 cloves of garlic, a handful of dried breadcrumbs, salt, pepper, a bunch of parsley.

Cover the bottom of a thick sauté pan with olive oil. When it is hot (but not boiling) put in the seasoned escalopes. Cook them gently so that they are just golden on each side. Add the skinned and chopped tomatoes and, as soon as they have melted, the breadcrumbs, the chopped garlic and parsley, and cook another 8–10 minutes, by which time most of the oil should be absorbed, and the tomatoes turned to a thick sauce.

Summer Cooking
chosen by Julia Caffyn

My mother Priscilla (one of Elizabeth's sisters) used to cook this for almost every supper party. The veal is good-tempered and will keep warm on the stove with a mat underneath while a dinner party assembles. It never seems to spoil. The tomatoes, parsley and garlic give it a lovely fresh flavour.

Julia Caffyn

VITELLO TONNATO
(*Veal with tunny fish sauce*)

Roast a 2 lb (900 g) piece of boned leg of veal or fillet. Leave it to cool. Having poured the fat from the pan, make a little stock from the juices in the pan with the addition of a cupful of water. (No flour.)

Make a tunny fish mayonnaise as described below, thinning it to the consistency of thick cream with the prepared stock. Pour the mayonnaise over the sliced veal, and serve next day with a green salad. Serves four.

Italian Food

MAIONESE TONNATA
(*Tunny fish mayonnaise*)

Make a stiff mayonnaise with 2 yolks of eggs, a little salt, 4 fl oz (120 ml) olive oil, and a very little lemon juice.

Pound or put through a sieve about 2 oz (60 g) tinned tunny fish in oil. Incorporate the purée gradually into the mayonnaise.

Excellent for all kinds of cold dishes, particularly chicken or hard-boiled eggs, for sandwiches, or for filling raw tomatoes for an hors-d'œuvre.

Italian Food

NORMAN'S RECIPE

Thin escalopes of veal, raw ham or *prosciutto*, fresh sage leaves, fresh tomato sauce, flour, butter.

On each piece of seasoned veal place a slice of raw ham the same size, and then 1 leaf of sage. Roll and tie with thread. Roll in flour and fry them in butter. Finish cooking them in a well-seasoned tomato sauce (about 15 minutes) – see p. 265.

Mediterranean Food

COSTOLETTE ALLA BOLOGNESE

A good escalope of veal and ½ oz (15 g) grated Parmesan per person, butter, stock, Marsala.

Cut the escalopes from a fillet of veal or from the boned leg; they should be about ¼ in (6 mm) thick and weigh about 3 oz (90 g) each. Season them with salt and pepper, flour them lightly, and brown them in plenty of butter on a fairly high heat; add 2 tablespoonfuls of Marsala, stirring it into the butter. On top of each escalope spread a generous amount of grated Parmesan, and then moisten each with a few drops of stock; at the same time add a tablespoonful of stock to the sauce. Turn down the flame, cover the pan, and cook gently for another 5 minutes, until the meat is tender and the cheese melted. In Bologna, the region of rich and delicious cooking, they would add, in season, some sliced white Piedmont truffles to this ingenious dish.

A dish of French beans goes well with these escalopes; so do braised endives, with their slightly bitter aftertaste which counteracts the richness of the cheese and wine mixture.

Italian Food
chosen by Jacqueline Korn

OSSI BUCHI MILANESE

2 lb (900 g) shin of veal (if from a full-grown calf allow 4 lb/1.8 kg) sawn into pieces 2 in (5 cm) thick, ¼ pint (150 ml) each white wine and stock, ¾ lb (350 g) tomatoes, parsley, a lemon, a clove of garlic, 2 oz (60 g) butter.

Brown the slices of shin of veal in the butter. Once browned arrange them in the pan so that they remain upright, in order that the marrow in the bone may not fall out as the meat cooks. Pour the white wine over them, let it cook for 10 minutes, then add the skinned and chopped tomatoes; let them reduce; add the stock. Season. Cook for 1½ to 2 hours.

Prepare a handful of chopped parsley, a clove of garlic chopped, and the grated peel of half a lemon. The Milanese call this mixture *gremolata*, and it is an essential part of the traditional *ossi buchi Milanese*. It is to be sprinkled on the top of the *ossi buchi* before serving. Serves four.

To make the dish as it should be, very tender veal from an animal not more than three months old should be used. A dish of risotto Milanese (see p. 234) always accompanies *ossi buchi*.

Italian Food
chosen by Julia Drysdale and John Ruden

Elizabeth was very particular that it should always be Ossi, and not the singular Osso, which is inclined to confuse everybody even though it is correct. I consider it a summer dish for if it is made with large ripe tomatoes you will never taste better. Julia Drysdale

FEGATO ALLA VENEZIANA

A dish to be found all over Italy, but at its best in Venice.

2 lb (900 g) onions, 1 lb (450 g) calf's liver, olive oil. Slice the onions very finely. Cover the bottom of a thick shallow pan with oil. When it is warmed, not smoking, put in the onions. They are to stew very gently, turning soft and golden yellow, not brown. Salt them lightly. When they are ready (about 30–40 minutes, cooked with the cover on the pan) add the prepared liver. This should ideally be the very tenderest calf's liver, so soft that you could put a finger through it as if it were bread. It should be cut in the thinnest possible slices, like little scraps of tissue paper, and it needs only a minute's cooking on each side. Serve as quickly as possible. Serves 3–4.

When obliged to use tough liver for this dish, have it cut as thinly as possible, but cook it slowly with the onions, for 10–15 minutes. It will still make an excellent dish, although it will not have the finesse of genuine *fegato alla Veneziana*.

Italian Food
chosen by Jonna Dwinger

SAUCE AU VIN DU MÉDOC
(Beef, rabbit and pork or hare stewed in red wine)

Here is a dish which is something of a collector's piece. I did not have to search for the recipe because I did not know of its existence. It fell, in a most felicitous way, into my outstretched hands through the kindness of Miss Patricia Green, a highly enterprising young woman who has made a study of wine and wine production on the spot in the Médoc.

From Madame Bernard, the wife of a wine-grower of Cissac-Médoc, Miss Green obtained this recipe and passed it on to me exactly as it was given to her; and she told me that Madame Bernard knew as much as there was to know of the peasant cooking of the region. I should also perhaps add that the name of the dish is not a printer's error, nor does it mean you throw away the meat and only eat the sauce; for, although the meat is cooked so slowly for so long that it practically *is* sauce, it is not uncommon in country districts of France to hear a stew of this kind referred to as *la sauce*.

Here is the recipe, unaltered in any particular. You may think it needs an act of faith to try it but when you read the recipe carefully you see that it is not really so strange and wild as it seems at a first glance.

1 rabbit, 1½ lb (675 g) stewing beef, 1 hare or 1½ lb (675 g) lean pork, 6 shallots, 4 cloves of garlic, 1 bay leaf, small sprig of thyme, large bundle of parsley, 1 dessertspoon of flour, salt, sugar, 1 square of plain chocolate, 1 bottle red wine, equal quantity of water, 3 large carrots, pork dripping or oil.

This is essentially a peasant dish, '*la grosse cuisine de la campagne*', and it should therefore be as rich and vulgarly hearty a savoury stew as possible when finished. It will be spoilt if the meat is cut into too delicate pieces or the carrots carefully sliced.

Heat the oil or, better still, pork dripping in a large, thick saucepan which has a closely fitting lid. Cut the shallots very finely, and slowly and gently brown them in the hot fat, adding the carrots carefully peeled but cut only in 2 or 3 pieces. Sprinkle generously with salt, and when well browned add the meat. For pork and beef, trim off gristle and excess fat and cut into rather large chunks. For hare and rabbit, dry the joints well before adding to the frying vegetables. Brown the meat well all over, then add the garlic finely sliced, and the herbs, sprinkle with flour, and mix all well together. Now pour on a bottle of red wine and bring quickly to the boil and bubble vigorously for about 5 minutes, reduce the heat, add an equal quantity of water, stir well, add a teaspoon of sugar and 1 small square of plain chocolate. Put on the lid and simmer, just a murmur, for about 3 hours.

Allow to get quite cold. On the second day simmer again for about 2 hours before serving. Taste before doing so and adjust seasoning; it may be a little sharp, in which case a sprinkle more sugar will usually put matters right.

The choice of meats, as you see, is left pretty well to individual taste (shin of beef cut from the bone and spare rib or hand of pork *on* the bone with its skin is what I use, plus a hare or rabbit if either happens to be available). A whole bottle of wine and an equal quantity of water seems a lot of liquid, and this question is one which frequently arises in French recipes of this type, because the French peasants and workmen reckon on filling out their meal with a great deal of bread soaked in the sauce; in fact, two-thirds of the quantities can be used, but less I think would deprive the dish of its character. If there is a lot of sauce left over, serve it with poached eggs, or poured round a mousseline of potatoes.

As for the chocolate, of which rather less than an ounce is needed, it is not an uncommon ingredient in Italian and Spanish cookery, particularly in hare dishes, and is there as a sweetening and thickening for the sauce. Its use perhaps filtered down to the Bordelais through the channel of Basque and Béarnais cookery. And Bayonne, for generations one of the great chocolate-manufacturing centres of France, is not far off.

French Provincial Cooking
chosen by Judy Rogers

If no other books on the topics of French or Italian cookery had ever been compiled, those cuisines could *still* be honoured and revered thanks to these works. Any time I think about compiling my own recipes I look at Elizabeth David's work and I sigh – knowing hers are the seminal recipes and her voice cannot be improved upon.

I have selected a couple of recipes I use and love. The Pommes Sablées are tricky to pull off but delightful to eat. Sauce au Vin du Médoc is one of those seminal recipes I use, re-use, transform, modify. The comment about using leftover sauce with poached eggs is, for me, a perfect example of her *knowing* and her sense of what is true in food and nourishment. Also, I nearly always refer to and hand out her essay on omelettes in *French Provincial Cooking* which should be required reading in culinary schools.

Judy Rogers

ENCHAUD DE PORC À LA PÉRIGOURDINE
(*Loin of pork stuffed with truffles*)

For those who like pork, this is one of the loveliest dishes in the whole repertoire of south-western French cookery. It cannot very often be made in England in its full beauty because the pork should be studded with black truffles. Occasionally, though, when one feels like a little extra extravagance, even quite a small tin of truffles is sufficient to give the right flavour to the meat. It is one of the dishes which I like to make at Christmas as an alternative to the turkey, or to serve as a cold dish for a large lunch party.

Have a fine piece, about 4 lb (1.8 kg) or more of loin of pork, boned and with the rind removed. Lay the meat on a board, salt and pepper it, cut 2 or 3 truffles into thick little pieces, and lay them at intervals along the meat. Add a few little spikes of garlic and some salt and pepper as well. Roll the meat up and tie it round with string so that it is the shape of a long, narrow bolster. Put in a baking dish with the bones, the rind cut into strips and all the trimmings. Let it cook about 30 minutes in a low oven (170°C/330°F/Gas Mark 3). When the meat has turned golden, pour in about 1 pint (550 ml) clear hot meat stock or ¾ pint (400 ml) water and ¼ pint (150 ml) white wine, plus the liquid from the tin of truffles. Now cover the dish and leave the meat to cook for another 2 to 2½ hours.

Pour off the sauce and remove the fat when it has set. Chop the jelly which remains beneath the fat and arrange it round the cold pork in the serving dish. Enough for about ten people.

The beautifully flavoured fat from this pork dish can be spread on slices of toasted French bread and makes a treat for the children at tea-time, as used to be our own toast and beef dripping.

Without the truffles, this pork dish is sometimes cooked at the time of the grape harvest, and La Mazille, author of *La Bonne Cuisine en Périgord*, says that slices of bread spread with the dripping and a piece of the cold pork topped with a pickled gherkin are distributed to the harvesters for their collation.

Remember, also, that this beautifully flavoured pork dripping is a wonderful fat in which to fry bread or little whole potatoes.

French Provincial Cooking
chosen by Jack Andrews

In the early fifties I was fortunate in meeting the late Lesley O'Malley who, over the years, became a very good friend. Dinner at Lesley's was always a special affair for, as I soon realized, she was a close and much admired friend of Elizabeth David, and as such presented many of E.D.'s dishes to her friends. Very shortly after our meeting Lesley moved to the basement flat of Elizabeth's house, giving her a distinct advantage over other hostesses in sw3. For the flat was not self-contained but separated from the main house by a short staircase on which stood a 'shared' refrigerator. So one had the pleasure of enjoying not only Lesley's own cooking but, as often was the case, some delicious pâté or mushroom soup left over from Elizabeth's own lunch party. A great bonus!

As I got to know Elizabeth better, I had the good fortune to share meals with her in her own kitchen and, encouraged by Lesley, cooked dinner for her myself on more than one occasion. It should be recorded here that this latter exercise was neither daunting nor difficult provided you kept your head. Discussion of the menu was inevitable, of course, but I find it hard to recall a more appreciative and amusing guest than Elizabeth.

Nothing, however, sticks out more in my mind than those early dinners in Lesley's kitchen after a pre-dinner drink with Elizabeth upstairs. This is a dish that she often served, followed by a salad, baked apricots and cream cheese.

Jack Andrews

NOISETTES DE PORC AUX PRUNEAUX

This dish, a speciality of Tours, is a sumptuous one, rich and handsome in appearance as well as in its flavours. But it is not one to try out for the first time on guests, unless you can be sure of ten minutes or so uninterrupted in the kitchen while you make the sauce. Neither is the dish exactly a light one, and is perhaps best eaten, as pork dishes are always supposed to be, at midday rather than in the evening.

Ingredients are 6 to 8 *noisettes* cut from the boned and skinned chump end of the loin of pork, each one weighing about 3 oz (90 g); 1 lb (450 g) very fine large juicy prunes (there should be approximately 2 dozen, and the best Californian prunes are perfect for the dish); a half-bottle of wine, which should, by rights, be white Vouvray, a tablespoon of red-currant jelly, approximately ½ pint (280 ml) of thick cream (you may not use it all but it is as well to have this quantity, as I will explain presently), 2 oz (60 g) butter, a little flour, seasonings.

Both the utensil for cooking the pork and the dish to serve it in are important. The first should be a shallow and heavy pan to go on top of the stove, either a sauté pan or the kind of dish in which a whole flat fish is poached; failing this the meat will first have to be browned in a frying-pan and then transferred to an oven dish. The serving dish should be a big oval one, preferably one which can go for a few minutes into the oven without risk.

First, put the prunes to steep in a bowl covered with ½ pint (280 ml) of the wine; this is supposed to be done overnight, but with good prunes a half-day will be sufficient. After which, cover them and put them in a very low oven (110°C/230°F/Gas Mark ¼) to cook. They can stay there an hour or more. They should be quite tender but not mushy, and the wine must not evaporate.

Season the pork very well with freshly milled pepper and salt and sprinkle each *noisette* with flour. Melt the butter in the pan; put in the meat; let it gently take colour on one side and turn it. Keep the heat low because the butter must not brown. After 10 minutes pour in the remaining 2 tablespoons or so of the white wine. Cover the pan. Cook very gently, covered, on top of the stove, or in the oven if necessary, for approximately 45 minutes to an hour, but the timing must depend upon the quality of the meat. Test it with a skewer to see if it is tender.

When it is nearly ready (but it will not, being pork, come to harm if left a bit longer even after it is tender), pour the juice from the prunes over the meat – this, of course, must be done over direct heat on top of the stove – and keep the prunes themselves hot in the oven. When the juice has bubbled and reduced a little, transfer the meat to the serving dish and keep it hot.

To the sauce in the pan add the redcurrant jelly and stir until it has dissolved. Now pour in some of the cream; if the pan is wide enough it will almost instantly start bubbling and thickening; stir it, shake the pan and add a little more cream, and when the sauce is just beginning to get shiny and really thick, pour it over the meat, arrange the prunes all round and serve it quickly.

The amount of cream you use depends both on how much juice there was from the prunes and how quickly the sauce has thickened; sometimes it gets too thick too quickly, and a little more cream must be added. In any case there should be enough sauce to cover the meat, but not, of course, the prunes. These are served as they are, not 'boned', as the French cooks say.

On the whole, I think it is better to drink red wine than white with this dish. And, of course, you do not serve any vegetables with it.

Even with light first and last-course dishes, 8 *noisettes* should be enough for four people.

French Provincial Cooking

BAKED PORK WITH WINE AND ORANGES

A joint or loin of pork, weighing about 4 lb (1.8 kg) boned, skinned and tied in a sausage shape; ¼ pint (150 ml) clear meat or chicken stock; herbs (parsley, dried marjoram, dried rosemary), salt and pepper; 4 tablespoons of Madeira, white wine or dry vermouth; breadcrumbs; 3 oranges; a little olive oil; 1 or 2 cloves of garlic.

Chop a clove or two of garlic with a little parsley, marjoram, a scrap of rosemary, and salt and pepper. Rub this all over the meat, pressing it well in along the lean side of the joint. Pour a tablespoon of olive oil into a baking dish, put in the meat and all the bones and skin which have been removed. Let it cook for 10–15 minutes in a fairly hot oven at 200°C/400°F/Gas Mark 6, before adding the hot stock. Then cook uncovered in a very slow oven (150°C/300°F/Gas Mark 2) for 2½ to 3 hours.

From time to time baste it with a little of its own liquid. A quarter of an hour before the end of cooking, take out the bones and skin, squeeze the juice of half an orange over the meat and add the wine. Strew the breadcrumbs on the fat side of the joint and return it to the oven.

Slice the remaining 2½ oranges into thin rounds, and blanch them for about 3 minutes in boiling water. Drain carefully, and put them in the sauce round the meat for the last 5 minutes of cooking time.

Serve with sliced oranges all round the meat, and the sauce separately. This dish is even better cold than hot, and if this is how you intend to serve it, cook the sauce for an extra half-hour or so after the meat has been removed, strain it into a bowl, chill it and remove the fat before serving it.

Those who like a rather more fat joint could economize by using boned and rolled fore-end of pork, which is appreciably cheaper than leg and loin.

Spices, Salt and Aromatics
chosen by John Ruden

ARISTA FIORENTINA

Remove the rind and, should there be an excessive amount, some of the fat from a piece of loin of pork weighing about 3–4 lb (1.4–1.8 kg).

Press 2 or 3 cloves of garlic into the meat, with a few leaves of rosemary and 2 or 3 whole cloves. Rub the meat with salt and pepper and put it into a roasting pan with water, about 2 in (5 cm) deep. Cook it in a moderate oven (170°C/330°F/Gas Mark 3) in an open pan.

It will take somewhat longer than the normal method of roasting; allow about 45 minutes to the pound. The meat emerges tender and moist. Let it cool a little in its own juice, then pour off the liquid (don't throw this away – there will be good pork fat on the top when it has set) and serve the pork cold. Serves 6.

Italian Food

ARISTA PERUGINA

The method is the same as for the *arista fiorentina*, but instead of rosemary flavour the pork with fennel leaves and garlic, or if there are no fennel leaves available a few pieces of the fennel bulb or fennel seeds. Although it is not orthodox, I find the flavour of the meat is greatly enhanced by rubbing the cloves of garlic in a few crushed coriander seeds before putting them into the meat.

A nice accompaniment is a potato salad flavoured with a very little fennel.

Italian Food

MAIALE AL LATTE
(*Pork cooked in milk*)

About 1½ lb (675 g) loin of pork, or boned leg, without the rind, rolled into a sausage shape, 1½ pints (850 ml) milk, 1½ oz (45 g) butter, 1½ oz (45 g) ham, salt and pepper, an onion, garlic, coriander seeds; marjoram, basil or fennel.

Melt the butter, brown the finely chopped onion in it, then the ham, also finely chopped.

Stick a clove of garlic inside the rolled meat, together with 3 or 4 coriander seeds and a little marjoram, basil or fennel. Rub it with salt and pepper and brown it in the butter with the onion and ham. In the meantime heat the milk to boiling point in another pan. When the meat has browned pour the milk over it. Add no more salt or pepper. Keep the pan steadily simmering at a moderate pace, uncovered. Gradually a golden web of skin begins to form over the top of the meat while the milk is bubbling away underneath. Don't disturb it until it has been cooking for a good hour. At this moment break the skin and scrape the sides of the pan, stirring it all into the remaining milk, which will be beginning to get thick. In about another 30 minutes the milk should have reduced to about a small cupful, full of all the delicious little bits of bacon and onion, and the meat should be encased in a fine crust formed by the milk, while it is moist and tender inside. It is at this moment that any meat or bird cooked in milk should be carefully watched, for the remaining sauce evaporates with disconcerting rapidity, leaving the meat to stick and burn.

To serve, pour the sauce, with all its grainy little pieces, over the meat. Can be eaten hot or cold. But best cold, I think. Serves four.

Whatever the weight of the piece of meat to be cooked in this fashion, allow roughly a pint (550 ml) milk per pound (450 g).

One or two readers have told me they find this recipe very tricky. It can be made easier by transferring the dish, uncovered, to a moderate oven (170°C/330°F/Gas Mark 3) after the web has formed. When the meat is cooked, return the pan to the top of the stove and reduce the sauce.

Italian Food
chosen by John Ruden

THE COOKING OF GAMMON JOINTS

One of the very nicest of all cold meat dishes is a piece of Wiltshire-cured, home-cooked gammon on the bone. It has so much more flavour and character than the steamed, boned, defatted product of the cooked-meat shop.

For a special occasion, or to last a small household for several days, the best cut is a piece of middle leg or a corner. These are lean joints, and easy to carve.

Many provision merchants and grocers nowadays tell you not to soak gammon before cooking it, but in my own mind there is no doubt that it is necessary to do so. Not only is there a risk of its being too salt if this preliminary is omitted, but it should be remembered that all curing processes imply a certain amount of hardening and drying out of the meat, especially when it is also smoked, as most of our gammon is. The steeping in water allows it once more to swell and soften.

BAKED MIDDLE GAMMON

Suppose you have a 5 lb (2.25 kg) piece of middle leg, soak it for a minimum of twenty-four hours, and preferably for thirty-six, in cold water to cover (and also keep a cloth or dish over the basin). Change the water two or three times.

When the time comes to cook the gammon wrap it in two sheets of aluminium cooking foil, twisting the edges together so that the joint is completely enclosed.

Stand this parcel on a grid placed in a baking tin. Half fill the tin with water – the steam coming from it during cooking helps to keep the gammon moist.

Place low down in a very moderate oven (170°C/330°F/Gas Mark 3) and allow approximately 50 minutes to the pound (450 g). The only attention you have to give it is simply to turn the parcel over at half-time.

When the cooking time is up, remove the gammon, still in its tin, from the oven, and leave it for about 40 minutes before unwrapping the parcel and carefully removing the rind, which peels away very easily in one piece without damage to the fat so long as the gammon is still warm. Press home-made golden breadcrumbs into the exposed fat surface. Wrap up the joint again, put it in a bowl or dish and if practicable put a board or plate on the top, weight it, and leave until next day.

This compressing of the joint is not vital, but does make carving easier.

Accompaniments. American-style sweet and spiced fruit garnishes and sauces – pineapple, peach, cranberry and the like – are acceptable with a dry gamey-flavoured and highly cured meat such as a genuine Virginia ham, but mild, moist, English-cured gammons and bacon are best, I think, accompanied by simple lettuce, potato, or other vegetable salads with a straightforward French dressing of olive oil and wine vinegar.

Whether you keep your cooked gammon or bacon in a refrigerator or a larder do keep it wrapped in clean greaseproof paper, constantly renewed. In this way it will keep sweet and moist down to the last slice.

BARBADOS BAKED AND GLAZED GAMMON

Cook a 4–5 lb (2–2.25 kg) piece of corner or middle gammon as described above, allowing 45 minutes instead of 50 to the pound (450 g).

Remove from the oven, unwrap the foil, and peel off the rind – this is very easily done while the gammon is still hot – and score the fat in diamond shapes. Replace the gammon in the rinsed-out baking tin.

Have ready the following mixture: 2 heaped tablespoons of soft brown sugar, 1 teaspoon of made mustard and 4 tablespoons of milk, all stirred together. Pour this mixture over the gammon, pressing some of it well down into the fat. If you feel you must, stud the fat with whole cloves.

Place the tin near the top of the oven – still at the same temperature – and cook the gammon for another 20 to 35 minutes, basting frequently with the milk and sugar mixture, which will eventually turn into a beautiful dark golden shining glaze.

Serve hot with creamed spinach and jacket potatoes or a purée of red lentils, or cold with a salad of cubed honeydew melon seasoned with lemon juice and a pinch of powdered ginger.

N.B. The sugar, mustard and milk-glaze mixture is by far the most effective, as well as the cheapest and most simple, of any I have ever tried. There really is no need for fanciful additions of rum, orange juice, pineapple chunks and all the rest of the fruit cocktail so often nowadays advocated in the colour-cookery pages of magazines.

Spices, Salt and Aromatics
chosen by Julia Drysdale

The pig fascinated Elizabeth and she claimed that you could eat every part of it except the ear drums. I think she would have liked to be brave enough to write the ultimate book on the subject, but it would have been impossible in a small London house with all the brining and pickling to test.

Julia Drysdale

ÉPAULE D'AGNEAU BOULANGÈRE

'She was a capital cook; and her method of boning and rolling up a shoulder of mutton like a large Bologna sausage was a mystery which cost me a considerably long post-prandial lucubration to penetrate.'

GEORGE MUSGRAVE, writing of the Hôtel du Louvre at
Pont-Audemer in *A Ramble Through Normandy (1855)*

The boning and rolling of a shoulder of lamb or mutton is not really such a mystery as it seemed to George Musgrave; any decent butcher will do it for you, and the system certainly does make the joint very simple to carve. This particular way of cooking a boned shoulder owes its name to the fact that, like the *carbonnade nîmoise*, it was a dish which would be prepared at home and carried to the bakery to be cooked in the oven after the bread was baked. It makes an excellent and quite economical dish for a large household.

The boned shoulder will weigh about 4 lb (1.8 kg). Press salt, pepper, chopped fresh thyme or marjoram, and, for those who like it, garlic, into the inside of the rolled meat. People who like the flavour of garlic without wishing to find it in the meat might try putting a clove or two under the joint in the pan while it is cooking. In this way it will flavour the gravy and the potatoes, but will scarcely be perceptible in the meat itself. Personally, I find a little garlic with lamb as indispensable as others find mint sauce.

Melt 1 oz (30 g) butter and a tablespoon of oil in a large pan; brown the seasoned meat in it. Transfer it to an oven dish; put in the garlic and 2 lb (900 g) whole new potatoes. In the same fat fry a sliced onion until it turns golden; pour over 2 teacups of meat *bouillon* or stock, which can have been made from the bones of the joint, cook a minute or so, and pour over the meat and potatoes. Cover with a buttered greaseproof paper and the lid of the dish. Cook in a slow oven (170°C/330°F/Gas Mark 3) for 2 hours or a little under if you like the meat faintly pink. Before serving salt the potatoes and sprinkle with more fresh herbs. The stock, reduced a little by fast boiling, will serve as a sauce.

French Provincial Cooking
chosen by Alex Crawford

DAUBE À L'AVIGNONNAISE

4 lb (1.8 kg) leg of lamb or mutton, 4 large onions, 2 or 3 carrots, ½ bottle of red wine, salt, pepper, herbs, 4 cloves of garlic, a piece of orange peel, 4 oz (120 g) fat salt pork or bacon, a handful of parsley, 1 small glass of brandy, olive oil.

Cut the meat into fair-sized pieces, each weighing about 3 oz (90 g). Into each piece of meat insert a small piece of salt pork or bacon which has been rolled in the parsley chopped with a clove of garlic. You will need about 1 oz (30 g) of the 4 oz (120 g) pork or bacon.

Put the prepared meat into an earthenware dish with 2 onions, and carrots cut up, salt, pepper, and herbs (thyme, bay leaf, marjoram). Pour the red wine over, and the brandy, and leave to marinate 4 or 5 hours.

Into a heavy stewpan put the rest of the pork cut in squares and 4 or 5 tablespoons of olive oil, and let the bacon melt a little in the oil. Now add the other 2 onions, sliced, and let them brown, then put in the pieces of mutton, with some fresh herbs and seasoning, the orange peel and 3 cloves of garlic. Pour over the wine in which the meat has marinated and let it bubble until it has reduced by about one-third. Just cover the meat with boiling water. Put the lid on the pan and simmer very slowly for 4–5 hours.

The *daube* can be made the day before it is wanted, any surplus fat skimmed off the sauce when it is cold, and gently reheated. A few stoned black olives and ½ oz (15 g) dried cèpes added before the water is put in add to the very southern flavour of the *daube*.

The nicest accompaniment is a dish of dried white haricot beans, cooked with a piece of salt pork and a garlic sausage, and moistened before serving with some of the sauce from the *daube*.

French Country Cooking

LAMB ON THE BONE

In the country districts of Greece, and the islands, the household cooking arrangements are fairly primitive and dishes such as this one are prepared early and sent to the village oven; they emerge deliciously cooked, better than they could ever be in a gas oven, but this method by no means ensures that the food will be served hot. The Greeks in fact prefer their food tepid, and it is useless to argue with them.

Saw a leg of lamb into 4 or 5 pieces, leaving the meat on the bone. Insert a clove of garlic into each piece of meat, season well and sprinkle with rosemary.

Cook in a shallow pan in the oven or over a slow heat, with oil or dripping. About 30 minutes before the meat is done add sliced potatoes and tomatoes. Instead of potatoes, partly cooked rice can be added. In this case, drain off the fat and add plenty of thin tomato purée, which will be absorbed by the rice.

The meat must be very well cooked and almost falling off the bone. Sometimes aubergines cut in half lengthways with the skins left on are added with the potatoes and tomatoes.

Mediterranean Food
chosen by Katharine Whitehorn

When I got around to looking out favourite Elizabeth David pieces, I was reminded but not surprised to see how often she evokes the right atmosphere by a quotation from her prodigious range of knowledge. I am not sure how good any suggestions about recipes might be, but do include the recipe for Lamb on the Bone, which contains that superb crack about the Greeks liking their food tepid; and one of the Bourride recipes which seems to bring out the lyrical in her. Also, I suppose, something on stuffed cabbage – I used constantly to make it until I realized that I actually don't like the stuff much, I just found her descriptions of it irresistible. The Mushrooms and Cream recipe has a scrap of reminiscence in it which makes it extra enjoyable.

It is not just laziness, by the way, that makes me go for her early works: though I cook from the later works, I liked her best at the beginning when she was greedier and less scholarly.   Katharine Whitehorn

TURKISH STUFFING FOR A WHOLE ROAST SHEEP

2 cups partly cooked rice, 1 dozen cooked chestnuts, 1 cup currants, 1 cup shelled pistachio nuts, salt, cayenne pepper, 1 teaspoon ground cinnamon, 4 oz (120 g) butter.

Chop the chestnuts and the pistachio nuts finely, mix with the other ingredients. Melt the butter and cook the stuffing in it gently, stirring until all the ingredients are well amalgamated.

This stuffing can also be used for chicken and turkey.

Mediterranean Food

Elizabeth maintained that John Lehmann accepted *Mediterranean Food* for publication because of this recipe. Some time after the book appeared she learned that his reader, Julia Strachey, had been so entranced by the impracticality of a stuffing for a whole sheep when the meat ration was only a few ounces a week in post-war Britain, that she persuaded him to publish on the strength of it.   J.N.

LAMB AND AUBERGINE STEW

When there are aubergines on the market, this dish is worth trying. It can be cooked in a frying pan or sauté pan, or any wide and shallow utensil of rather large capacity.

1½–2 lb (675–900 g) shoulder or middle neck of lamb, 2 small aubergines, 1 large onion, ½ lb (225 g) tomatoes, fresh or dried mint or basil, salt, pepper, a clove of garlic, 4 tablespoons of oil, and 2 heaped teaspoons of cumin seeds or ground cumin if you prefer.

Have the lamb boned and cut into 1 inch (2.5 cm) cubes.

Slice the unpeeled aubergines into quarters and then into half-inch (1.25 cm) cubes, put them in a colander, sprinkle them with a table-spoon of salt, put a plate and a weight on the top and leave them for at least an hour so that the excess moisture drains out. Before cooking them press them as dry as you can.

Heat the oil in a heavy 10–12-inch (25–30 cm) frying or sauté pan and put in the thinly sliced onion. When it has just begun to take colour put in the meat, plentifully sprinkled with the herbs, salt and pepper. Turn the meat cubes over and over until they are nicely browned. (If this operation is neglected the dish will be pallid and sad-looking.) Remove the meat and onions to a dish with a draining spoon and into the same oil put the aubergine cubes. Cover the pan and let them cook gently for 10 minutes, giving a stir from time to time.

Now return the meat and onions to the pan, add the skinned and roughly chopped tomatoes, the crushed garlic and the heated and pounded cumin seeds. Cover the pan again, let it simmer very gently for 1 hour. Or if it is more convenient cook it only for 45 minutes and then heat it up very slowly for half an hour next day. Strew with more mint or basil before serving. Plain boiled rice or pilau rice goes with this dish.

Ample for four.

Spices, Salt and Aromatics
chosen by Myrtle Allen and Gerald Asher

POITRINE D'AGNEAU STE. MÉNÉHOULD
(*Braised and grilled breast of lamb*)

One of the breadcrumb-grilled dishes I like best is the one called breast of lamb Ste. Ménéhould. It is very cheap (breast of English lamb was 8d. a pound at Harrods last Saturday – one often finds a cheap cut cheaper and of better quality in a high-class butchery than in a so-called cheap one, and 2½ lb (1 kg) was plenty for four), but I am not pretending it is a dish for ten-minute cooks. It is one for those who have the time and the urge to get real value out of cheap ingredients.

First you have to braise or bake the meat in the oven with sliced carrots, an onion or two, a bunch of herbs and, if you like, a little something extra in the way of flavouring such as 2–3 oz (60–90 g) of a cheap little bit of bacon or salt pork, plus seasonings and about a pint (550 ml) of water. It takes about 2½–3 hours – depending on the quality of the meat – covered, in a slow oven (140°C/280°F/Gas Mark 1). Then, while the meat is still warm, you slip out the bones, leave the meat to cool, preferably with a weight on it, and then slice it into strips slightly on the bias and about 1½–2 inches (3.5–5 cm) wide. Next, spread each strip with a little mustard, paint it with beaten egg (one will be enough for 2½ lb [1 kg] meat), then coat it with the breadcrumbs, pressing them well down into the meat and round the sides.

(I always use breadcrumbs which I've made myself from a French loaf, sliced, and dried in the plate drawer underneath the oven. I know people who think this business of making breadcrumbs is a terrible worry, but once the bread is dried it's a matter of minutes to pound it up with a rolling pin or with a pestle – quicker than doing it in the electric blender.)

All this breadcrumbing finished, you can put the meat on a grid over a baking dish and leave it until you are ready to cook it. Then it goes into a moderate oven (180°C/350°F/Gas Mark 4) for about 20 minutes, because if you put it straight under the grill the outside gets browned before the meat itself is hot. As you transfer the whole lot to the grill pour a very little melted butter over each slice, put them close to the heat, then keep a sharp look-out and turn each piece as the first signs of sizzling and scorching appear. The plates and dishes should be sizzling too, and some sort of sharp, oil-based sauce – a vinaigrette, a tartare, a mustardy mayonnaise – usually goes with this kind of dish.

As a matter of fact it can be made with a good deal less fiddling about in a way described to me by M. Kaufeler, the head chef at the Dorchester. No need, he said, for the boning and slicing of the meat once it's cooked. Just grill it whole or in large chunks. He added that in his youth he and his fellow apprentice cooks used to eat this dish frequently. They called it Park Railings. (It's a system of cooking which evidently engenders picturesque names. Once in a Lyonnais restaurant I had a hefty slab of tripe grilled in this way. It was called Fireman's Apron and even to a non-tripe-eater was made delicious by the lovely crackling crust.) I tried M. Kaufeler's method, and although I did not think it as successful as the Ste. Ménéhould one, I found that it did work a treat for the American cut of spare-ribs of pork (not the fore-end joint we call spare-rib, but a belly piece) which Sainsbury's are now selling at about 2s. a pound. Not much meat on these cuts, but what there is, tender and sweet. It needs less initial cooking time than the lamb – about 1 hour. It's the kind of food you have to pick up in your fingers, and I rather like something of this sort for Sunday lunch. The first cooking is light work for Saturday and the breadcrumbing business is a soothing occupation when you've had enough of the Sunday papers.

An Omelette and a Glass of Wine
chosen by Simon Hopkinson

It is very exciting when you find even one recipe in a cookery book that truly appeals. To find two, is fortunate indeed. When a collection of recipes and attendant prose are all published together from one's favourite cookery writer, one really does feel pampered.

When Elizabeth David's collection of articles and recipes was published in 1984, all at once, it promptly became my favoured reference book, bedtime reading, cookery book and muse. It still is – and even more especially so, because when I met E.D. when she came to dine at Hilaire for the first time, in the book's year of publication, I just happened to have a copy of *Omelette* in the kitchen. So it is a signed edition.

Two recipes that are now fairly splattered and thumbed, not only remain favourites, but also seem such perfect examples of true cookery and cookery writing that each is timeless and, at one and the same time, also seems new and inspired. The Breast of Lamb Ste. Ménéhould may use a cut of lamb that many turn up their noses at, but there are few who realize the delicacy of such meat when treated thus. And for what it is worth, the finished dish is as sophisticated – if not much, much more so – than many little plates of neatly trimmed loins of lamb, cut into perfect pink slices and daubed with shiny brown reductions.

The sauce for boiled lobster, as described under the dish called Lobster Courchamps, is one of the finest sauces (almost a dressing really) I know. In true tradition with many of the recipes that one finds in Elizabeth David, it carries amusing lineage. It seems that it had appeared in three different volumes of French cuisine, each unconnected with the other and all published around the middle of the nineteenth century. So plagiarism was rife in cookery book circles even then. Simon Hopkinson

Have It Your Way

'Always do as you please, and send everybody to Hell, and take the consequences. Damned good Rule of Life. N.' I think we must both have been more than a little tipsy the evening Norman wrote those words on the back page of my copy of *Old Calabria*. They are in a pencilled untidy scrawl that is very different from the neat pen-and-ink inscription, dated 21 May 1940, on the flyleaf of the book, and from the methodical list of 'misprints etc.' written on the title page when he gave me the book. 'Old-fashioned stuff, my dear. Heavy going. I don't know whether you'll be able to get through it.'

I have forgotten the occasion that gave rise to Norman's ferociously worded advice, although I fancy the message was written after a dinner during which he had tried to jolt me out of an entanglement which, as he could see without being told, had already become a burden to me. And the gentleman concerned was not very much to his liking.

'You are leaving with him because you think it is your duty. Duty? Ha! Stay here with me. Let him make do without you.'

'I can't, Norman. I have to go.'

'Have it your way, my dear, have it your way.'

Had I listened to Norman's advice I should have been saved a deal of trouble. Also, I should not, perhaps, have seen Greece and the islands, not spent the war years working in Alexandria and Cairo, not have married and gone to India, not have returned to England, not become involved in the painful business of learning to write about food and cookery. And I should not now be writing this long-overdue tribute to Norman Douglas. Was he right? Was he wrong? Does it matter? I did what I pleased at the time. I took the consequences. That is all that Norman would have wanted to know.

When I met him first, Norman Douglas was seventy-two. I was twenty-four. It was that period in Norman's life when, exiled from his home in Florence and from his possessions, he was living in far-from-prosperous circumstances in a room in the Place Macé in Antibes.

Quite often we met for drinks or a meal together in one or another of the cafés or restaurants of the old lower town, a rather seedy place in those days. There was little evidence of that bacchanal existence that legend attributes to all Riviera resorts.

The establishment Norman chose when he fancied a pasta meal was in a narrow street near the old port. 'We'll meet at George's and have a drink. Then we'll go and tell them we're coming for lunch. No sense in letting them know sooner. If we do, they'll boil the macaroni in advance. Then all we shall get is heated-up muck. Worthless, my dear. We'll give them just twenty minutes. Mind you meet me on the dot.'

At the restaurant, he would produce from his pocket a hunk of Parmesan cheese. 'Ask Pascal to be so good as to grate this at our table. Poor stuff, my dear, that Gruyère they give you in France. Useless for macaroni.' And a bunch of fresh basil for the sauce. 'Tear the leaves, mind. Don't chop them. Spoils the flavour.'

Now and again Norman would waylay me as I was buying provisions in the market. 'Let's get out of this hole. Leave that basket at George's. We'll take the bus up toward Vence and go for a little stroll.'

The prospect of a day in Norman's company was exhilarating; that little stroll rather less so. A feeble and unwilling walker, then as now, I found it arduous work trying to keep up with Norman. The way he went stumping up and down those steep and stony paths, myself shambling behind, reversed our ages. And well he knew it.

'Had enough?'

'Nearly.'

'Can you tackle another half kilometre?'

'Why can't we stop here?'

'*Pazienza*. You'll see.'

'I hope so.'

At that time I had not yet come to understand that in every step Norman took there was a perfectly sound purpose, and so was innocently impressed when at the end of that half kilometre, out in the scrub, at the back of beyond, there was a café. One of those two-chair, one-table, one-woman-and-a-dog establishments. Blessed scruffy café. Blessed crumbling crone and mangy dog.

'Can we deal with a litre?'

'Yes, and I'm hungry too.'

'Ha! You won't get much out of *her*. Nothing but bread and that beastly ham. Miserable insipid stuff.' From out of his pocket came a hunk of salami and a clasp knife.

'Do you always carry your own provisions in your pocket?'

'Ha! I should say so. I should advise you to adopt the same rule. Otherwise you may have to put up with what you get. No telling what it may be, nowadays.'

Certain famous passages in Norman Douglas' work, among them Count Caloveglia's dissertation in *South Wind* on the qualities neces-sary to a good cook, in *Siren Land* the explosive denunciation of Neapolitan fish soup, in *Alone* the passage in which he describes the authentic pre-1914 macaroni, 'those macaroni of a lily-like candour' (enviable phrase – who else could have written it?), have led many people to believe that Norman Douglas was a great epicure in matters gastronomical, and so he was – in an uncommon way; in a way few mortals can ever hope to become. His way was most certainly not the way of the solemn wine sipper or of the grave debater of recipes. Connoisseurship of this particular kind he left to others. He himself preferred the study of the original sources of his food and wine. Authenticity in these matters was of the first importance to him. (Of this, plenty of evidence can be found by those who care to look into *Old Calabria*, *Together*, *Siren Land*, *Alone* and *Late Harvest*.) Cause and effect were eminently his concerns, and in their application he taught me some unforgettable lessons.

Once during that last summer of his life, on Capri (he was then eighty-three), I took him a basket of figs from the market in the piazza. He asked me from which stall I had bought them. 'That one down nearest to the steps.'

'Not bad, my dear, not bad. Next time, you could try Graziella. I fancy you'll find her figs are sweeter; just wait a few days, if you can.'

He knew, who better, from which garden those figs came; he was

familiar with the history of the trees, he knew their age and in what
type of soil they grew; he knew by which tempests, blights, invasions
and plagues that particular property had or had not been affected
during the past three hundred years; how many times it had changed
hands, in what lawsuits the owners had been involved; that the son
now grown up was a man less grasping than his neighbours and was
consequently in less of a hurry to pick and sell his fruit before it
ripened . . . I may add that it was not Norman's way to give lectures.
These pieces of information emerged gradually, in the course of walks,
sessions at the tavern, apropos a chance remark. It was up to you to
put two and two together if you were sufficiently interested.

Knowing, as he made it his business wherever he lived and travelled
to know, every innkeeper and restaurant owner on the island (including, naturally, Miss Gracie Fields; these two remarkable human beings
were much to each other's taste) and all their families and their staff
as well, still Norman would rarely go to eat in any establishment
without first, in the morning, having looked in; or if he felt too poorly
in those latter days, sent a message. What was to be had that day?
What fish had come in? Was the mozzarella cheese dripping, positively
dripping fresh? Otherwise we should have to have it fried. 'Giovanni's
wine will slip down all right, my dear. At least he doesn't pick his
grapes green.' When things did not go according to plan – and on
Capri this could happen even to Norman Douglas – he wasted no
time in recriminations. 'Come on. Nothing to be gained by staying
here. Can you deal with a little glass up at the Cercola? Off we go
then.'

Well-meaning people nowadays are always telling us to complain
when we get a bad meal, to send back a dish if it is not as it should
be. I remember, one bleak February day in 1962, reading that a British
Cabinet Minister had told the hotel-keepers and caterers assembled
at Olympia for the opening of their bi-annual exhibition of icing-sugar
buses and models of Windsor Forest in chocolate-work, 'If the food
you have in a restaurant is lousy, condemn it . . .'

At the time Norman Douglas was much in my mind, for it was
round about the tenth anniversary of his death. How would he have
reacted to this piece of advice? The inelegance of the phrase would
not have been to his taste, of that much one can be certain. And from

the Shades I think I hear a snort, that snort he gave when he caught you out in a piece of woolly thinking. 'Condemn it? Ha! That won't get you far. Better see you don't have cause for complaint, I'd say. No sense in growling when it's too late.'

An Omelette and a Glass of Wine
chosen by Sybille Bedford, Richard Olney
and Jeremiah Tower

Pomiane, Master of the Unsacrosanct

'Art demands an impeccable technique; science a little understanding.'
Today the mention of art in connection with cookery is taken for
pretention. Science and cookery make a combination even more suspect. Because he was a scientist by profession, making no claims to
being an artist, Docteur de Pomiane's observation was a statement of
belief, made in all humility. Vainglory is totally missing from de
Pomiane's work. He knew that the attainment of impeccable technique
meant a lifetime – in de Pomiane's case an exceptionally long one –
of experiment and discipline. Out of it all he appears to have extracted,
and given, an uncommon amount of pleasure.

Docteur Edouard de Pomiane's real name was Edouard Pozerski.
He was of purely Polish origin, the son of emigrés who had fled Poland
and settled in Paris after the Revolution of 1863. Born and brought
up in Montmartre, he was educated at the Ecole Polonaise – an
establishment described by Henri Babinski, another celebrated
Franco-Polish cookery writer, as one of ferocious austerity – and
subsequently at the Lycée Condorcet. Pomiane chose for his career
the study of biology, specializing in food chemistry and dietetics.
Before long he had invented a new science called Gastrotechnology,
which he defined simply as the scientific explanation of accepted
principles of cookery. For a half-century – interrupted only by his
war service from 1914 to 1918 – de Pomiane also made cookery and
cookery writing his hobby and second profession. After his retirement
from the Institut Pasteur, where he lectured for some fifty years, he
devoted himself entirely to his cookery studies. He was eighty-nine
when he died in January 1964.

De Pomiane's output was immense – some dozen cookery books,

countless scores of articles, broadcasts, lectures. In France his books were best-sellers; among French cookery writers his place is one very much apart.

Many before him had attempted to explain cookery in scientific terms and had succeeded only in turning both science and cookery into the deadliest of bores.

De Pomiane was the first writer to propound such happenings as the fusion of egg yolks and olive oil in a mayonnaise, the sizzling of a potato chip when plunged into fat for deep-frying, in language so straightforward, so graphic, that even the least scientifically minded could grasp the principles instead of simply learning the rules. In cooking, the possibility of muffing a dish is always with us. Nobody can eliminate that. What de Pomaine did by explaining the cause, was to banish the *fear* of failure.

Adored by his public and his pupils, feared by the phoney, derided by the reactionary, de Pomiane's irreverent attitude to established tradition, his independence of mind backed up by scientific training, earned him the reputation of being something of a Candide, a provocative rebel disturbing the grave conclaves of French gastronomes, questioning the holy rites of the 'white-vestured officiating priests' of classical French cookery. It was understandable that not all his colleagues appreciated de Pomiane's particular brand of irony:

'As to the fish, everyone agrees that it must be served between the soup and the meat. The sacred position of the fish before the meat course implies that one must eat fish *and* meat. Now such a meal, as any dietician will tell you, is far too rich in nitrogenous substances, since fish has just as much assimilable albumen as meat, and contains a great deal more phosphorus . . .' Good for Dr de Pomiane. Too bad for us that so few of his readers – or listeners – paid attention to his liberating words.

It does, on any count, seem extraordinary that thirty years after de Pomiane's heyday, the dispiriting progress from soup to fish, from fish to meat and on, remorselessly on, to salad, cheese, a piece of pastry, a crème caramel or an ice cream, still constitutes the standard menu throughout the entire French-influenced world of hotels and catering establishments.

Reading some of de Pomiane's neat menus (from *365 Menus, 365*

Recettes, Albin Michel 1938) it is so easy to see how little effort is required to transform the dull, overcharged, stereotyped meal into one with a fresh emphasis and a proper balance:

Tomates à la crème
Côtelettes de porc
Purée de farine de marrons
Salade de mâche à la betterave
Poires

An unambitious enough menu – and what a delicious surprise it would be to encounter such a meal at any one of those country town Hôtels des Voyageurs, du Commerce, du Lion d'Or, to which my own business affairs in France now take me. In these establishments, where one stays because there is no choice, the food is of a mediocrity, a predictability redeemed for me only by the good bread, the fresh eggs in the omelettes, the still relatively civilized presentation – which in Paris is becoming rare – the soup brought to table in a tureen, the hors-d'œuvre on the familiar, plain little white dishes, the salad in a simple glass bowl. If it all tasted as beguiling as it looks, every dish would be a feast. Two courses out of the whole menu would be more than enough.

Now that little meal of de Pomiane's is a feast, as a whole entity. It is also a real lesson in how to avoid the obvious without being freakish, how to start with the stimulus of a hot vegetable dish, how to vary the eternal purée of potatoes with your meat (lacking chestnut flour we could try instead a purée of lentils or split peas), how to follow it with a fresh, bright, unexpected salad (that excellent mixture of corn salad and beetroot – how often does one meet with it nowadays?) and since by that time most people would have had enough without embarking on cheese, de Pomiane is brave enough to leave it out. How much harm has that tyrannical maxim of Brillat Savarin's about a meal without cheese done to all our waistlines and our digestions?

For a hot first dish, de Pomiane's recipe for *tomates à la crème* is worth knowing. His method makes tomatoes taste so startlingly unlike any other dish of cooked tomatoes that any restaurateur who put it on his menu would, in all probability, soon find it listed in the guide books as a regional speciality. De Pomiane himself said the recipe came from his Polish mother. That would not prevent anyone from calling it what he pleases:

TOMATES À LA CRÈME

'Take six tomatoes. Cut them in halves. In your frying pan melt a lump of butter. Put in the tomatoes, cut side downwards, with a sharply-pointed knife puncturing here and there the rounded sides of the tomatoes. Let them heat for five minutes. Turn them over. Cook them for another ten minutes. Turn them again. The juices run out and spread into the pan. Once more turn the tomatoes cut side upwards. Around them put 80 grammes (3 oz. near enough) of thick cream. Mix it with the juices. As soon as it bubbles, slip the tomatoes and all their sauce on to a hot dish. Serve instantly, very hot.'

The faults of the orthodox menu were by no means the only facet of so-called classic French cooking upon which de Pomiane turned his analytical intelligence. Recipes accepted as great and sacrosanct are not always compatible with sense. Dr de Pomiane's radar eye saw through them: '*Homard à l'américaine* is a cacophony . . . it offends a basic principle of taste.' I rather wish he had gone to work on some of the astonishing things Escoffier and his contemporaries did to fruit. Choice pears masked with chocolate sauce and cream, beautiful fresh peaches smothered in raspberry purée and set around with vanilla ice seem to me offences to nature, let alone to art or basic principles. How very rum that people still write of these inventions with breathless awe.

De Pomiane, however, was a man too civilized, too subtle, to labour his points. He passes speedily from the absurdities of haute cuisine to the shortcomings of folk cookery, and deals a swift right and left to those writers whose reverent genuflections before the glory and wonder of every last piece of peasant cookery-lore make much journalistic cookery writing so tedious. By the simple device of warning his readers to expect the worst, de Pomiane gets his message across. From a village baker-woman of venerable age, he obtains an ancestral recipe for a cherry tart made on a basis of butter-enriched bread dough. He passes on the recipe, modified to suit himself, and carrying with it the characteristically deflating note:

'When you open the oven door you will have a shock. It is not a pretty sight. The edges of the tart are slightly burnt and the top layer of cherries blackened in places . . . It will be received without much enthusiasm for, frankly, it is not too prepossessing.

'Don't be discouraged. Cut the first slice and the juice will run out. Now try it. A surprise. The pastry is neither crisp nor soggy, and just tinged with cherry juice. The cherries have kept all their flavour and the juice is not sticky – just pure cherry juice. They had some good ideas in 1865.'

Of a dish from the Swiss mountains, Dr de Pomiane observes that it is 'a peasant dish, rustic and vigorous. It is not everybody's taste. But one can improve upon it. Let us get to work.' This same recipe provides an instructive example of the way in which Dr de Pomiane thinks we should go to work improving a primitive dish to our own taste while preserving its character intact. Enthusiastic beginners might add olives, parsley, red peppers. Dr Pomiane is scarcely that simple. The school-trained professional might be tempted to superimpose cream, wine, mushrooms, upon his rough and rustic dish. That is not de Pomiane's way. His way is the way of the artist; of the man who can add one sure touch, one only, and thereby create an effect of the pre-ordained, the inevitable, the entirely right and proper:

TRANCHES AU FROMAGE

'Black bread – a huge slice weighing 5 to 7 oz., French mustard, 8 oz. Gruyère.

'The slice of bread should be as big as a dessert plate and nearly 1 inch thick. Spread it with a layer of French mustard and cover the whole surface of the bread with strips of cheese about ½ in. thick. Put the slice of bread on a fireproof dish and under the grill. The cheese softens and turns golden brown. Just before it begins to run, remove the dish and carry it to the table. Sprinkle it with salt and pepper. Cut the slice in four and put it on to four hot plates. Pour out the white wine and taste your cheese slice. In the mountains this would seem delicious. Here it is all wrong. But you can put it right. Over each slice pour some melted butter. A mountaineer from the Valais would be shocked, but my friends are enthusiastic, and that is good enough for me.'

This is the best kind of cookery writing. It is courageous, courteous, adult. It is creative in the true sense of that ill-used word, creative because it invites the reader to use his own critical and inventive faculties, sends him out to make discoveries, form his own opinions, observe things for himself, instead of slavishly accepting what the books tell him. That little trick, for example, of spreading the mustard on the bread *underneath* the cheese in de Pomiane's Swiss mountain dish is, for those who notice such things, worth a volume of admonition. So is the little tomato recipe quoted above.

All de Pomiane's vegetable dishes are interesting, freshly observed. He is particularly fond of hot beetroot, recommending it as an accompaniment to roast saddle of hare – a delicious combination. It was especially in his original approach to vegetables and sauces that de Pomiane provoked the criticism of hidebound French professional chefs. Perhaps they were not aware that in this respect de Pomiane was often simply harking back to his Polish origins, thereby refreshing French cookery in the perfectly traditional way. De Pomiane gives, incidentally, the only way (the non-orthodox way) to braise Belgian endive with success – no water, no blanching, just butter and slow cooking.

The English public knows little of de Pomiane's work and it is missing something of great value. Although his *Cooking in Ten Minutes*, a lighthearted treatise on how to make the most of charcuterie or delicatessen food – first published in England in 1948 – has proved a great favourite, there exists a much more representative book, a collection of lectures, radio talks, recipes and articles, called *Cooking with Pomiane*. It is most adroitly put together and translated into English cookery usage by Mrs Peggie Benton. Published four years ago and still relatively unknown, the book is modest in appearance and in size, its jacket is the reverse of eyecatching, there are no colour photographs, no packaging. It is just a very good and immensely sane book.

The Sunday Times Colour Supplement, 22 January 1967

Many a time, in the years since the explosion of *nouvelle cuisine*, I have wanted to write more of Dr de Pomiane and his unorthodox approach to classic French cookery. I wonder how many of the younger of today's professional chefs realize that the origins of their great rebellion of the late 1960s and early 1970s stem, at least in part, from the days of Dr de Pomiane and his protests against illogical and harmful eating habits. At any rate, some of those rebel chefs must surely know, even if they don't acknowledge as much, that some of their most publicized inventions were not their inventions at all, but were derived, however indirectly, from the Polish and Jewish recipes published or described by Pomiane in his books and radio talks of the 1930s. That *confiture d'oignons*, for instance, for which the recipe appeared in Michel Guérard's *Cuisine Gourmande* and which has since made the *tour du monde* surely derived from Pomiane's dish of sweet-sour onions in which the sweetening elements were sultanas and *pain d'épices*, the spiced honey cake of central Europe, and which Pomiane had in turn borrowed from the Jewish cookery of his native Poland. True, Guérard uses sugar rather than *pain d'épices*, adds red wine, sherry vinegar, and grenadine syrup 'to warm up the purple colour', and suggests that as well as sultanas, prunes or little pieces of dried apricot may be added. Again, Guérard gives a recipe for saddle of hare with hot beetroot which differs only in minor respects from the one Pomiane published two or three times and which I myself used often in the fifties, and eventually quoted, with acknowledgements, in *French Provincial Cooking*. As I mentioned in the *Sunday Times* article, Pomiane was fond of hot beetroot, and used it often, mixing vinegar and cream with it, a very un-French combination, and by no means the only one of his unconventional suggestions in the domain of vegetable cookery to arouse the scorn of reactionaries.

In the days when Pomiane was writing, chefs did not dream of braising vegetables – lettuces, leeks, Belgian endives, for example – without a preliminary blanching. That rule was immutable, and woe betide anyone who disregarded it. Dr de Pomiane bypassed it, and I adopted his method, particularly his recipe for cooking Belgian endives in butter and entirely without a prior water baptism. That sort of unorthodoxy got one into trouble. I have referred, in my Introduction [to *An Omelette and a Glass of Wine*], to the venerable French chef who in the fifties pursued me and my *Sunday Times* cookery articles with a zeal worthy of a Spanish inquisitor. One of his more intemperate outbursts, I recall, concerned a recipe for dipping sliced young fennel bulbs, mushrooms and scallops in batter and deep frying them in oil to make a *fritto misto* in the Italian manner. That idea was already red rag enough to the old gentleman. Worse was my omission of any mention of the essential ordeal by blanching of the vegetables, and of course of the scallops. In those days a French chef simply did not serve vegetables crisp. They *had* to be soft and woolly. (I have remembered for many years the *patronne* of a restaurant in the little Norman port of Barfleur who refused to cook artichokes for dinner that night – it was then 6.30 p.m. – on the grounds that they required two hours boiling. I'm afraid she meant it.) As for the idea that scallops might be cooked in one minute and no more, that old chef was genuinely outraged by it. There was just *one* way he, as a man who had risen to eminence in his profession, had learned to do things. It was the classical French way. There *was* no other. It did not occur to him that there might be. Today's chefs have very properly outlawed that preliminary blanching which spelled ruin to so many vegetables – of course there are still those such as celeriac and turnips which may need it – and one of their most fiercely held tenets concerns the brief cooking of fish, in particular of the fragile scallop. Heaven knows it was not before time that reformation in that respect came about. I hope it has penetrated the middle and lower échelons of French restaurant chefs. How many times have I nearly wept at the destruction of delicate little scallops at the hands of ignorant or insensitive chefs?

The uninformed criticism of the narrow-minded, whether it came from members of the cooking profession or from old-fashioned gourmets among his own colleagues, did not worry Dr de Pomiane one jot. His own unorthodox approach extended to his study of historical cookery and even to his choice of words when describing an ancient recipe he wanted to revive. That particular trend, now a flood, was something of a novelty in Pomiane's day. A sauce he adapted from *Les Dix Livres de Cuisine d'Apicius*, of which a French translation by the cookery historian Bertrand Guégan appeared in 1933, providing the starting point of the new trend, was one containing dates, almonds and a very large amount of chopped parsley. The way Pomiane chose to convey the necessary quantity to his listeners – he must have been a compelling radio talker – and later to his readers was in terms of 'a bunch as large as a bunch of violets'. Everybody in Paris and indeed in all France knows what a flower seller's bunch of violets looks like, but whoever heard of such a cookery direction, let alone of a sauce containing a mixture of dates and parsley? To the conventional, whether professional cooks or serious gourmets, this sort of thing was at best perverse and eccentric, at worst a blasphemous crime committed on the sacred body politic of *la cuisine française*. To me, and to the hundreds of ordinary French housewives who listened to his talks and read his books, his ideas and his attitude to cookery were stimulating and liberating. Now that we have become accustomed to reading about, if not to eating, such unconventional combinations of foods as duck *foie gras* with turnips in a sweet-sour sauce composed of wine vinegar, sugar, sherry *and* port, plus the odd 30 grammes of truffles; paupiettes of crayfish garnished with leaves of Brussels sprouts; lobster mould with a sauce of carrots and port blended in turn with a *sauce américaine*, Pomiane's innovations don't sound very audacious. Nobody is surprised by the idea of spirals of black Spanish radish, forerunners of the Troisgros *serpentins* de légumes, as part of an hors-d'œuvre, or lettuce dressed with orange juice as well as oil and vinegar. Turnip salad with capers is no shock today and raw choucroûte salad, an idea Pomiane had picked up in Moscow – buy very fresh choucroûte from the charcutier and stop at the village pump to wash it thoroughly, he told those of his French readers who went in for picnics on canoeing and automobile excursions[1] – should be the joy of vegetarians. Even apples filled with honey, spiced with cumin or dried mint and baked in pastry, another adaptation from Apicius, seems timid in comparison with Michel Guérard's *Ali baba*, two fantasy *babas* made with 120 grammes of mixed candied fruits and sultanas to only 250 grammes of brioche batter. The cooked babas are hollowed out, filled with confectioners' custard, sugared, *gratinés* in the oven, chilled in the refrigerator, and ultimately served with a *coulis* of raspberries or caramelized peaches. Altogether more of a Second Empire kind of guzzle than a Roman treat, that invention.

A long time ago, in 1956, I published a little review of a new edition of Pomiane's delightful and much loved *Cooking in Ten Minutes* in my *Sunday Times* cookery column. He wrote me a touching letter of thanks. 'J'ai été très heureux d'avoir été compris par une si aimable

1. *La Cuisine en plein air*, 1934.

Anglaise', he said, and ended 'if you were French I should give you a kiss. But I believe in England that is not done'. If I have really understood Dr de Pomiane all right, I fancy that while an extravaganza such as Maître Guérard's *Ali Babà* would not have met with his unqualified acclaim, with many of the *nouvelle cuisine* innovations he would surely have been in sympathy. I think he would have been amused rather than otherwise at finding his own dishes reappearing as specialities of the starry restaurants of the 1970s, and pleased that reforms in the matter of lighter meals and more logical sauce and vegetable cookery which he had preached in the 1930s have at last been put into practice. If there are lapses, obsessions, aberrations – and few would deny that there are – in the practice of the new style chefs, well, Pomiane was a man with a sense of humour and without a sense of self-importance. He would have smiled and said those are the foibles of innovators, they must be excused, and you are not after all obliged to mop up all those pools of *beurre blanc* which appear on your plate in such quantity. Nobody forces you to consume the equivalent of half a dozen eggs at one meal, but it is very easy to do so, so if you have eaten a *mousseline* of scallops, red mullet, and *écrevisses* floating in a lake of *sabayon* sauce, then do not follow it with a honey ice cream or one of those *ali baba* affairs nor with a peach charlotte containing five egg yolks, but rather with a *tarte fine chaude aux pommes acidulées*, which is nothing more outlandish or richer than an old-fashioned apple tart made on a base of puff pastry. Come to think of it, myself I would just as soon have a try at Doctor de Pomiane's honey-filled and cumin-spiced Apician apples. The recipe may be found on p. 203 of *Cooking with Pomiane*. If obtaining a copy of either version should entail a search, I do not think anyone will regret the time spent on it.

An Omelette and a Glass of Wine
chosen by Lindsey Bareham, Sybille Bedford
and Michael Zyw

POULTRY AND GAME

KUBAB CHICKEN

For a 2–2½ lb (900 g–1 kg) roasting chicken, dressed and drawn weight, prepare the following spice mixture: 2 teaspoons of coriander seeds, 12 black peppercorns, the seeds from 6 cardamom pods, ½ teaspoon of ground cloves, 1 teaspoon of salt, ½ oz (15 g) sliced green ginger (gross weight – there is a good deal of waste when you have peeled the root). Pound all these ingredients together until they are a paste, then work them with about ½ oz (15 g) butter, preferably clarified.

Draw back the skin of the chicken and with a small knife make incisions in the legs and breast. Spread the spice mixture into the incisions and draw the skin back into place. Leave for a couple of hours before cooking.

Put 2 oz (60 g) clarified butter into a deep heavy oven pot and heat it. Put in the chicken, lying on its side. Cover the pot closely. Bake in a moderate oven (180°C/350°F/Gas Mark 4) for 50 minutes to an hour, turning it over at half-time. Then remove the lid and turn the chicken breast upwards for 10 minutes.

Serve the chicken with the cooking liquid poured over, and lemon quarters round the dish. Boiled rice or saffron rice makes a good accompaniment, although I prefer a salad.

On occasion I have varied the spice mixture, omitting the green ginger and cloves, using cinnamon, saffron, cardamom and a little ground ginger. The salt is important. Serves 4.

Spices, Salt and Aromatics
chosen by George Elliot

CHICKEN POT-ROASTED WITH FENNEL AND HAM

For a 2¾ lb (1.2 kg) dressed and drawn roasting chicken the other ingredients are a half dozen each of dried fennel stalks and whole bay leaves; 4–6 oz (120–170 g) mild cooked ham in one piece; 2 or 3 garlic

172

cloves; a strip of lemon peel; 2 oz (60 g) butter; a half dozen whole black peppercorns. Optionally, 4 tablespoons of brandy.

Tie the fennel stalks and bay leaves into a bunch. Put them into an earthenware or cast-iron cocotte or pot. On top put the chicken (lying on its side) stuffed with the peeled garlic cloves, the strip of lemon peel and the ham cut into finger-thick strips and liberally sprinkled with coarsely crushed black peppercorns (no salt). Add the butter in small pieces. Cover the pot, put it low down into a medium-hot oven (200°C/400°F/Gas Mark 6). Leave for 45 minutes. Now turn the chicken, basting it with the butter, and return it to the oven. Cook for another 45–50 minutes.

Now uncover the pot, turn the chicken breast upwards and leave it to brown in the oven for 10–15 minutes.

To give the dish a spectacular finish, and to bring out to their full extent the scents and flavours of the aromatic herbs, transfer the pot to mild heat on top of the stove. Pour the brandy into a ladle, warm it, ignite it, pour it flaming over the chicken, rotate the pan so that the flames spread. After they have died down transfer the chicken to an ovenproof serving dish but leave the juices in the casserole to cook and mature for another 3 or 4 minutes. Pour them off into a sauceboat.

For serving, arrange the fennel stalks and bay leaves on the dish with the chicken.

When the chicken is served, make sure that everybody has a share of the little strips of ham from the inside of the bird. Serves 4.

Basically, this is a dish of the old-fashioned country cooking of Tuscany. The final blaze of brandy is a modern flourish.

Spices, Salt and Aromatics
chosen by Jack Andrews

PARSLEY AND LEMON STUFFING FOR A CHRISTMAS TURKEY OR CAPON

For a 10–12 lb (4.5–5.5 kg) turkey stuffing: ½ lb (225 g) dried bread-crumbs, 2 large lemons, 6 tablespoonfuls of finely-chopped parsley, 1 teaspoonful of dried marjoram, the same of lemon thyme when available; ½ lb (225 g) unsalted butter, 3 whole eggs, salt, freshly milled pepper.

To prepare the breadcrumbs for the stuffing, cut the crusts from a sliced white loaf, dry the slices on a baking sheet in a low oven until they are quite brittle, but not coloured. Pound them to crumbs with a rolling pin, or in the electric blender.

To make the stuffing, mix the breadcrumbs with the parsley (be sure to wash it before chopping it), add the marjoram, the grated peel of the two lemons and the strained juice of one. Beat in the eggs, then the softened butter. Season very lightly. Stuff the bird (body and crop) and secure the flaps with small metal skewers, so that the stuffing will not burst out during cooking.

For a 6–7 lb (2.75–3 kg) capon, reduce the quantities by one-third.

Spices, Salt and Aromatics

POULET À L'ESTRAGON

Tarragon is a herb which has a quite remarkable affinity with chicken and a *poulet à l'estragon*, made with fresh tarragon, is one of the great treats of the summer. There are any amount of different ways of cooking a tarragon-flavoured chicken dish: here is a particularly successful one.

For a plump roasting chicken weighing about 2 lb (900 g) when plucked and drawn, knead a good 1 oz (30 g) butter with a tablespoon of tarragon leaves, half a clove of garlic, salt and pepper. Put this inside the bird, which should be well coated with olive oil. Roast the bird lying on its side on a grid in a baking dish. Turn it over at half-time (45 minutes altogether in a pretty hot oven (200°C/400°F/ Gas Mark 6) or an hour in a moderate oven (180°C/350°F/Gas Mark 4) should be sufficient; those who have a roomy grill might try grilling it, which takes about 20 minutes, and gives much more the impression of a spit-roasted bird, but it must be constantly watched and turned over very carefully, so that the legs are as well done as the breast).

When the bird is cooked, heat a small glass of brandy in a soup ladle, set light to it, pour it flaming over the chicken, and rotate the dish so that the flames spread and continue to burn as long as possible. Return the bird to a low oven for 5 minutes, during which time the brandy sauce will mature and lose its raw flavour. At this moment you can, if you like, enrich the sauce with a few spoonfuls of thick cream and, at la Mère Michel's Paris restaurant, from where the recipe originally came, they add Madeira to the sauce. Good though this is, it seems to me a needless complication. Serves 3–4.

French Provincial Cooking
chosen by Jonna Dwinger

POULET SAUTÉ AUX OLIVES DE PROVENCE

For two people, buy a 1¾- to 2-lb (800–900-g) chicken split in two as for grilling. The success of all dishes in which the chicken is cut before cooking lies in having presentable portions. Nothing is more dismal than those *poulets sautés* and *fricassées de poulet*, in which all you get on your plate is an unidentifiable and bony little joint from which the dry flesh is detached only with great determination. Some skill is needed to joint a chicken into several pieces and, on the whole, it is more satisfactory to buy smaller chickens and simply split them, or have them split, in half.

Season the halves of chicken, rub them with lemon juice, and insert a very small piece of garlic and a little sprig of thyme or basil under the skin of each piece. Dust with flour. In an ordinary heavy frying-pan heat a coffee-cup (after-dinner size) of olive oil. Make it fairly hot and put in the pieces of chicken skin-side down. When they are golden on one side turn them over and, when both sides are seized, turn them over again, turn the heat low and cover the pan, removing the lid only from time to time to turn the chicken. After 20 minutes, transfer the chicken and nearly all the oil to a baking dish and put in a very low oven (140°C/280°F/Gas Mark 1), covered, while the sauce is made.

For this have ready 4 large ripe tomatoes, skinned and chopped; 2 anchovy fillets roughly pounded with 2 cloves of garlic; a sprig each of thyme, marjoram and basil, dried if no fresh is available; a small glass of wine, white for preference but red if it is easier; and 4 oz (120 g) stoned black olives.

First pour in the wine, detaching any brown pieces and juices which may have adhered to the pan. Let it bubble and reduce. Add the anchovy and garlic mixture, stir well in, then add the tomatoes and the herbs. Simmer until the sauce is thick, add the olives, let them get hot, and taste the sauce for seasoning.

Test the chicken by running a skewer through the thick part of the leg and, if the juices come out white, it is cooked. If still red, leave a little longer in the oven. For serving, arrange the chicken in a long dish *on top* of the very hot sauce.

French Provincial Cooking
chosen by John Ruden

ALEPPO CHICKEN

1 boiling chicken weighing 3 lb (1.3 kg), 1 lemon, carrots, onions, celery, garlic, ½ lb (225 g) mushrooms, ¼ lb (120 g) blanched almonds, half a glass of sherry, 4 egg yolks, 1 glass cream.

Rub the chicken over with salt, pepper and lemon juice, insert a piece of lemon peel in the inside of the bird. Boil with the vegetables in the usual way and when cooked take the pan off the heat, and with a ladle pour out about 1 pint (550 ml) of the stock into another pan. Add to this the juice of half a lemon, the sherry, the almonds and the previously sautéd mushrooms, and when hot pour it spoon by spoon on to the eggs beaten up with the cream. Heat gently and when it has thickened put the chicken on a hot dish, and pour the sauce all over and around it. Serves 4–5.

Mediterranean Food

SPICED CHICKEN COOKED IN MILK

A small boiling chicken (2–2½ lb/900 g–1 kg), a pint (550 ml) of milk to every pound (450 g) which the chicken weighs when ready for cooking, 1 oz (30 g) green ginger, a teaspoonful of coriander seeds, a teaspoonful of cardamoms, ¼ teaspoonful of ground cloves, salt, pepper, lemon, 2 eggs, a few pistachio nuts or roasted almonds.

Roast the coriander seeds for 2 or 3 minutes in the oven; peel the green ginger; pound both in a mortar with the cardamoms and the ground cloves; remove the husks of the cardamoms. Add salt and ground black pepper. Prick the chicken all over with a fork, rub it with lemon then press some of the spices into the chicken, and put some more in the inside. Leave for an hour or two. Bring the milk to the boil with the remainder of the spices. Pour it over the chicken and cook very slowly for about 2½ hours, for the first hour on top of the stove, with the pan covered, for the remainder of the time in the oven (140°C/280°F/Gas Mark 1) without the lid. When the chicken is quite tender, take it out and leave to cool. When cold, cut all the flesh from the chicken in nice neat pieces; measure about 1 pint (550 ml) of the sauce, heat it up. Add to two whole beaten eggs, through a sieve, and heat it in a double boiler till thick and pour it over the chicken. Serve cold, garnished with a few halves of pistachio nuts or roasted almonds and quarters of lemon. Serves 4.

Summer Cooking

POULET AU RIZ BASQUAIS

1 fine chicken weighing 2–2½ lb (900 g–1 kg), 1 lb (450 g) tomatoes, 3 or 4 sweet red peppers, 1 lb (450 g) coarse pork sausage (the Basques have their own particular sausages, called *Loukenkas*, very highly spiced), ½ lb (225 g) rice, herbs, salt and pepper, garlic, spices, a piece of orange peel, onions, paprika.

Brown the chicken, whole, in goose or pork fat, with a sliced onion, a branch of thyme, a bay leaf, salt and pepper. When it is golden all over, pour over warm water just to cover it, add the sausage, in one piece, and the orange peel, and simmer with the cover on the pan until it is tender; this will take about 40 minutes if it is a tender roasting chicken, anything up to 3 hours if it is one of those purple boiling fowls, so if you are not sure of the quality of the bird, better start it early – heating up later can hardly hurt it.

In the meantime make a *ragoût* of the tomatoes and peppers by sautéing the peppers cut in strips, in goose dripping, and when they are half cooked add the tomatoes, chopped, and seasoned with salt, pepper, and marjoram or thyme. Let them simmer until they are cooked, but don't reduce them to a pulp; stir in a tablespoon of paprika (in the Basque country they have a condiment called *Piment Basquais*, a coarsely ground red pepper stronger than paprika, the colour of cayenne, but nothing like so fiery).

When the chicken is nearly ready, put the rice into a large pan of boiling salted water: cook it for 12–15 minutes, until it is nearly, but not quite, done; strain it and put it in a fireproof pan in which it can be served; now take the chicken and the sausage out of the liquid in which they have cooked; pour a ladle or two of the stock over the rice, and stir it over a very gentle fire; carve the chicken into suitable pieces, and when the rice has absorbed the stock and is quite tender but not mushy put the chicken on the top, pour all round the tomato and pepper mixture, and garnish it with the sausage cut into squares.

The result should be a melting dish of rice, softer than a *pilaff* or a *paëlla*, and not so compact as a risotto, more in fact resembling the *Poulet au Riz*, but with the characteristic Basque flavouring of sweet pepper, tomato and spiced sausage. Serves 6.

A stewing pheasant cooked in the same way is quite excellent.

French Country Cooking
chosen by Julia Drysdale

DUCK WITH FIGS

Put 16 fresh figs to marinate in a half bottle of Sauternes for 24 hours.

Season the duck (weighing about 2½ lb [3 kg]) with salt and pepper and put a piece of butter and a piece of orange peel inside the bird. In a deep earthenware terrine with a lid put 2 oz (60 g) butter, and put the duck in the terrine, breast downwards, and another 1 oz (30 g) butter on top of the duck. Let it brown in a fairly hot oven (200°C/ 400°F/Gas Mark 6), without the lid, for 15 minutes; now pour the butter off, turn the duck over, and pour in the wine from the figs; let this cook 5 minutes and add about ½ pint (280 ml) stock made from veal bones, the giblets of the duck, 2 sliced onions, 2 carrots, a clove of garlic crushed, and a branch of thyme or marjoram. Put the cover on the casserole and cook in a slow oven (170°C/330°F/Gas Mark 3) for 1 hour, until the duck is tender.

Now take out the duck and remove the vegetables and giblets; leave the lid off the casserole, turn the oven up and let the juice bubble for 15 minutes to reduce it; put in the figs, and let them cook 5 minutes if they are the very ripe purple ones, 10 minutes if they are green figs; take them out and arrange them round the duck. Leave the stock to cool. Remove the fat and pour the liquid over the duck and figs; it should set to a light jelly.

Serve the duck with a plain green salad. Serves 4.

French Country Cooking
chosen by Derek Hill

WELSH SALT DUCK

This method of salting and cooking a duck is adapted from a Welsh recipe dating back at least a century. (So far as I know, the first time it appeared in print was in Lady Llanover's *Good Cookery* published in 1867.) In the original, the duck was eaten hot, with an onion sauce, which would have been rather heavy, but both the preliminary salting and the slow-cooking methods are worth reviving; they produce a deliciously flavoured and tender duck; and the melon goes to perfection with cold duck. It goes without saying that, if you prefer, the salad of sliced oranges more usual with duck can be substituted.

1 large duck (about 6 lb [2.75 kg] gross weight), 4 oz (120 g) sea or rock salt or coarse kitchen salt, 1 honeydew melon, lemon juice.

Buy your duck three days in advance. Place it in a deep dish. Rub it all over with salt. Repeat this process twice a day for three days. Keep the duck covered, and in a cool place, (use the giblets at once for stock, and the liver for an omelette) ideally in a larder rather than the refrigerator.

In the morning for the evening, cook the duck as follows: first rinse off excess salt; then place the bird in a deep oven-dish. (I use a large oval enamelled casserole, which will stand inside a baking tin.) Cover the duck with cold water, put water also in the outer tin. Transfer the whole contraption to the centre of a very low oven (150°C/300°F/Gas Mark 2), and cook, uncovered, for just 2 hours. Remove the duck from its liquid (which will probably be rather too salt to use for stock) and leave it to cool.

Serve the duck quite plain and cold, its sole accompaniment the flesh of a honeydew melon cut into small cubes and seasoned only with lemon juice. Jacket potatoes could also be served with the duck, but are hardly necessary, and do nothing to help the appreciation of this very delicately flavoured bird.

Spices, Salt and Aromatics
chosen by John Ruden

I enjoy Elizabeth's books because they are essays on food – interesting, learned and clear. They are not cook books as Americans define them, where one finds simple formulas for dishes or long and elaborate instructions for creating the approximations of food served in expensive restaurants. Instead, her writing is a background or history of how people ate, and the simple recipes that follow are explanations of the concept of what is to be produced. Welsh Salt Duck, which I once enjoyed with her in her kitchen, is a perfect example. Chocolate Chinchilla is another example of how knowing the background of the dish is as much a pleasure as eating it. It is a wonderful dessert to have as a result of having made a mayonnaise to serve earlier with fresh crab, as Elizabeth and I did one summer. What could be easier to prepare than Sussex Stewed Steak, or more satisfying on a cold evening? Other cold evening pleasures are the Daube de Bœuf Provençale and Bœuf à la Gardiane, where a small strip of orange peel is essential in each. In spite of what some readers might have told her, there is little that is very tricky about her directions for Maiale al Latte, and it is wonderful either hot or cold.

Elizabeth's explanations for Vitello Tonnato could not be more simple, and the tunny fish sauce ignores the kitchen blender which so many writers imply came before the recipe. The recipe for Ossi Buchi Milanese is another example of simplicity itself. The fresh tomatoes, which are readily available in Sacramento from my mother's garden, are a necessity. The directions for Risotto alla Milanese, however, are far more detailed than most of her recipes, and they need to be since so many people haven't the slightest idea of what a risotto should be.

John Ruden

L'ALICOT *or* ABATIS D'OIE EN RAGOÛT
(*Goose giblet stew*)

A rich and savoury stew can be made from the goose giblets. This recipe is from south-western France.

Slice 2 or 3 large onions. Fry them very gently in a little goose fat. When they are pale golden, put in all the giblets except the liver, and a 6 oz (170 g) slice of salt pork or gammon. Let them take colour, add 3 or 4 sliced carrots, 3 large tomatoes, plenty of garlic, salt, pepper and a big bouquet of herbs.

Pour over ½ pint (280 ml) heated stock. Bring to simmering point; cover the pot; cook in a very low oven (140°C/280°F/Gas Mark 1) for 2½–3 hours. Serve with boiled white haricot beans, augmented if you like with a well-spiced, coarsely cut sausage of the type sold in delicatessen shops as Spanish sausages. Serves 2–3.

French Provincial Cooking

PERDRIX À L'AUVERGNATE
(*Partridges stewed in white wine*)

For four stewing partridges, the other ingredients are 2 oz (60 g) butter, 4 oz (120 g) salt pork or mild streaky bacon, 5 tablespoons of brandy, 8 of white wine, 4 of clear veal or other meat or game stock, a little bouquet of bay leaf, parsley, thyme and a crushed clove of garlic.

If salt pork is being used, steep it for 1 hour in water. Cut it in small cubes. Put it with 1 oz (30 g) of the butter in an earthenware or other heavy pan just large enough to hold the four birds. When the fat from the pork or bacon runs, put in the birds, breast downwards. (If they have been trussed for roasting by the poulterer, take out the wooden skewer before cooking them; it only makes the birds more difficult to fit into the pot and is a nuisance when it comes to serving them.) After 2 or 3 minutes pour in the warmed brandy; set light to it. Shake the pan so that the flames spread. When these die down, put in the white wine, warmed if you are cooking in an earthenware pan. Let it bubble a minute; add the stock and the bouquet. Cover the pan with paper or foil and a well-fitting lid. Transfer to a slow oven (170°C/330°F/Gas Mark 3), and cook for 1½–1¾ hours. Pour off all the liquid into a wide pan, and keep the birds hot in the serving dish. Reduce the liquid by fast boiling to about half its original volume. Off the heat, add the second ounce of butter and shake the pan until the butter has melted and given the sauce a slightly glazed appearance. Pour it over the partridges. Serve at the same time a purée of brown lentils or of celeriac and potatoes. Serves 4.

Young partridges are excellent cooked in the same way, but according to size take only 30–40 minutes or so in the oven. If you have no stock use water instead but do not use a bouillon cube. It would falsify the flavour of the birds.

French Provincial Cooking

FAISAN À LA CAUCHOISE
(Pheasant with cream, calvados and apple)

Cook a tender roasting pheasant in butter in a heavy iron or earthenware *cocotte* on top of the stove, turning it over once or twice so that each side is nicely browned. It will take about 40–45 minutes to cook. Carve it, transfer it to the serving dish, and keep it warm. Pour off the juices into a shallow pan; let them bubble; pour in a small glass of warmed Calvados (or brandy, *marc* or whisky), set light to it, shake the pan, and when the flames have burnt out add a good measure, 8–10 fl oz (225–280 ml), of thick cream. Shake the pan, lifting and stirring the cream until it thickens. Season with a very little salt and pepper. Pour the sauce over the pheasant. Serve separately a little dish of diced sweet apple, previously fried golden in butter and kept warm in the oven: 2 apples will be sufficient for one pheasant. Serves 4.

This is, I think, the best of the many versions of pheasant with apples and Calvados, usually called *faisan normand*.

French Provincial Cooking
chosen by Julia Drysdale

This is one of the easiest and most delicious ways to cook a good young bird, but it will not turn an old cock into a succulent dish. Elizabeth loved cooking with apples; they were nearly always sweet dessert apples instead of the more usual tart cooking apple.   Julia Drysdale

CONIGLIO AL MARSALA
(*Rabbit cooked in Marsala*)

Cut a rabbit into six or eight pieces. In a braising pan put 1 oz (30 g) butter and 1 oz (30 g) ham or bacon cut into small chunks, and a small stick of celery cut into ¼-in (6 mm) lengths, then the pieces of rabbit. Let them brown. Add 4 chopped tomatoes, crushing them with a wooden spoon as they start to cook. Stir in a chopped clove of garlic, some fresh marjoram, salt and black pepper. Now pour in a small glassful of Marsala and let it bubble until it is reduced by half. Add hot water or stock, enough to barely cover the pieces of rabbit; cover the pan and simmer slowly. Halfway through the cooking put in a small aubergine, unpeeled but cut into inch squares which should have been sprinkled with salt and left to drain for an hour; ten minutes before the rabbit is ready add a red or green pimento cut into strips. The sauce of this dish should be thickish, sufficient, but not too copious, and the pimento still a little bit firm. The whole dish will take about an hour to cook, providing the rabbit is a reasonably tender one. Serves 4.

A chicken can be cooked in the same way, but if it is a boiling fowl it will need 2 good hours of slow cooking.

Italian Food

LEPRE DI CEPHALONIA
(*Cephalonian hare*)

A dish from the Ionian Islands, but of Italian origin.

Cut up a hare and put it in a deep earthenware pot. Pour over it the juice of half a dozen lemons, add a little salt and pepper. Leave it to marinate for at least 12 hours.

When the time comes to cook it cover the bottom of a capacious and heavy pan with about ¼ in (6 mm) of fruity olive oil. When it is hot, put in a sliced onion. Let it brown slightly, then add the pieces of hare. Brown them on both sides. Add about a dozen cloves of garlic, salt, pepper, a generous amount of *origano*, and a wineglassful of red wine. (If the hare is being cooked in an earthenware pot heat the wine before pouring it in, or the pan may crack.) Cover the pan and simmer for 2½–3 hours.

This may sound an outlandish dish, but try it. The lemon flavour, the garlic and the olive oil have an excellent effect upon the cloying and dry qualities of hare. It is not, of course, a refined dish, and the wine to go with it should be chosen accordingly. Serves 4–5.

Italian Food

The Markets of France: Cavaillon

It is a Sunday evening in mid-June. The cafés of Cavaillon are crammed. There isn't an inch to park your car. The noise is tremendous. In the most possible of the hotels – it goes by the name of Toppin – all the rooms are taken by seven o'clock. But the little Auberge La Provençale in the rue Chabran is quite quiet and you can enjoy a good little dinner – nothing spectacular, but genuine and decently cooked food well served – and go to bed early. The chances are you won't sleep much though, because Monday is the big market day in Cavaillon and soon after midnight the carts and lorries and vans of the big fruit farmers' co-operatives, of the market gardeners, of the tomato and garlic and onion growers, will start rattling and roaring and rumbling into the great open market in the place du Clos.

At dawn they will be unloading their melons and asparagus, their strawberries and redcurrants and cherries, their apricots and peaches and pears and plums, their green almonds, beans, lettuces, shining new white onions, new potatoes, vast bunches of garlic. By six o'clock the ground will be covered with *cageots*, the chip vegetable and fruit baskets, making a sea of soft colours and shadowy shapes in the dawn light. The air of the Place is filled with the musky scent of those little early Cavaillon melons, and then you become aware of another powerfully conflicting smell – rich, clove-like, spicy. It is the scent of sweet basil, and it is coming from the far end of the market where a solitary wrinkled old man sits on an upturned basket, scores and scores of basil plants ringed all around him like a protective hedge. With a beady eye he watches the drama of the market place. The dealers, exporters and wholesalers walking round inspecting the produce, discussing prices, negotiating; the hangers-on standing about in groups

smoking, chatting; the market police and official inspectors strolling round seeing that all is in order.

On the whole the scene is quiet, quieter at least than you would expect considering that this is one of the most important wholesale fruit and vegetable markets in France, the great distributing centre for the *primeurs* of the astonishingly fertile and productive areas of the Vaucluse and the Comtat Venaissin – areas which less than a hundred years ago were desperately poor, inadequately irrigated, isolated for lack of roads and transport, earthquake-stricken, devastated by blights which destroyed the cereal crops and the vines.

It was with the building of the railways connecting Provence with Paris and the north, with Marseille and the ports of the Mediterranean to the south, that the possibilities of the Rhône and Durance valleys for intensive fruit and vegetable cultivation first began to be understood. New methods of irrigation, the planting of fruit trees in large areas where the vines had been stricken, the division of the land into small fields broken with tall cypress hedges as windbreaks against the scourging mistral, the ever-increasing demand in Paris and the big towns of the north for early vegetables, and the tremendous industry of these Provençal cultivators have done the rest. And to such effect that last year eighty thousand kilos of asparagus came into Cavaillon market alone between 15 April and 15 May; in the peak month of July three hundred tons of melons daily; five hundred tons of tomatoes every day in July and August. Altogether some hundred and sixty thousand tons of vegetables and fruit leave Cavaillon every year, about fifty per cent by rail, the rest by road. And Cavaillon, although the most important, is by no means the only big market centre in the neighbourhood. Avignon, Châteaurenard, Bollène, Pertuis, all dispatch their produce by special trains to the north; vast quantities of fruit are absorbed locally by the jam and fruit preserving industries of Apt and Carpentras; and every little town and village has its own retail vegetable and fruit market, every day in the bigger towns, once or twice a week in less populated places.

But now seven o'clock strikes in the market at Cavaillon. The lull is over. This is the moment when the goods change hands. Pandemonium breaks loose. The dealers snatch the baskets of produce they have bought and rush them to waiting lorries. A cartload of garlic vanishes from under your nose. A mountain of melons evaporates in a wink. If you try to speak to anybody you will be ignored, if you get in the way you'll be knocked down in the wild scramble to get goods away to Paris, London, Brussels, and all the great centres of northern and eastern France. Suddenly, the market place is deserted.

At eight o'clock you emerge from the café where you have had your breakfast coffee and croissant. The market place is, to put it mildly, astir once more. It is surrounded by vans and lorries disgorging cheap dresses and overalls, plastic kitchenware, shoes and scarves and bales of cotton, piles of plates and jugs, nails and screws and knives, farm implements and packets of seeds, cartons of dried-up-looking biscuits and trays of chemically-coloured sweets.

You dive down a side street where you have spied a festoon of pretty cotton squares, and there, under gaudy painted colonnades, lilac and orange, cinnamon and lemon and rose, in patterns more typical of Marseille or the Levant than of Cavaillon, the retail market stalls are already doing business. The displays seem rather tame after the wholesale market and there is not a melon to be seen. It is too early in the season, they are still too expensive for the housewives of Cavaillon. Five thousand francs a kilo they were fetching today, and a week later in London shops 12s. 6d. each for little tiny ones. But the street opposite the painted colonnades leads into the square where more and more food stalls are opening and the housewives are already busy marketing. Here you can buy everything for a picnic lunch. Beautiful sprawling ripe tomatoes, a Banon cheese wrapped in chestnut leaves, Arles sausages, pâté, black olives, butter cut from a towering monolith, apricots, cherries.

It is still early and you can drive out towards Apt and branch off across the Lubéron. The roads are sinuous but almost empty, and they will take you through some of the most beautiful country in Provence. Perched on the hillsides are typical old Provençal villages, some, like Oppède-le-Vieux, crumbling, haunted, half-deserted, others like Bonnieux with a flourishing modern village built below the old one, and up beyond Apt, through the dramatic stretch of ochre-mining country, the strange red-gold village of Roussillon appears to be toppling precariously on the edge of a craggy cliff. Round about here, the network of caves under the ochreous rocks has been turned into vast *champignonnières*, and at the modest little Restaurant David (no relation) you can eat the local cultivated mushrooms cooked *à la crème* or *à la provençale* with, naturally, olive oil, parsley and garlic. And the Rose d'Or, a little hotel opened only a few weeks ago, promises a welcome alternative to the establishments of Apt, Aix and Cavaillon.

An Omelette and a Glass of Wine
chosen by Paul Levy

My choice of the best of E.D. would be the articles she did on French markets. They reinforce my view that her greatest contribution was to restore morale to a war-weary Britain, by reminding the middle classes that, only a few miles away, was a land where the lemon trees still blossomed – despite the fact that, in post-rationing 1950's Britain, lemons were still rare, and aubergines, courgettes, red peppers, basil and olive oil almost unobtainable. Then her books were for the imagination more than they were for palate and stomach, and they gave heart to a lot of discouraged people.   Paul Levy

Trufflesville Regis

On Saturday morning the entire main shopping thoroughfare of the Piedmontese market town of Alba in the Italian province of Cuneo is closed to traffic. The stalls are set up in the middle of the street, and the awnings stretch right across it from pavement to pavement. Coming from the big Piazza Savona you pass first stall upon stall of clothes, bales of cloth, household wares, plastics and, on the ground, huge copper polenta pots. The vegetable, fruit and cheese stalls fill the vast piazza at the far end of the street and ramble right round and to the back of the great red *duomo*. (There are some very remarkable carved and inlaid choir stalls in Alba's cathedral. The artist, Bernardo Cidonio, has created magnificent fruitwood panels showing the local landscapes, castles and towers, architectural vistas, and still-lifes of the fruit and even of the cooking pots of the region. These treasures, dating from 1501, unheralded by guidebooks, shouldn't be missed.)

At this season in Alba there are beautiful pears and apples, and especially interesting red and yellow peppers, in shape rather like the outsize squashy tomatoes of Provence, very fleshy and sweet, a speciality of the neighbourhood. What we have really come to Alba to see and eat, though, are white truffles, and these are to be found in the poultry, egg and mushroom market held in yet another enormous piazza (Alba seems to be all piazzas, churches, red towers and white truffles), and will not start, they say, until nine-thirty. In the meantime there are baskets of prime mushrooms to look at and to smell, chestnut and ochre-coloured *funghi porcini*, the cèpes or *Boletus edulis* common in the wooded country of Piedmont, and some fine specimens of the beautiful red-headed *Amanita caesarea*, the young of which are enclosed in an egg-shaped white cocoon, or volva, which has earned them their name of *funghi uovali*, egg mushrooms – although in Piedmont, where everything possible is kingly, the *Amanita caesarea* are *funghi reali*, royal mushrooms. They are *oronges* considered by some French fungi-fanciers as well as by the Piedmontese to be the best of all mushrooms.

In Piedmont the royal mushroom is most commonly eaten as an hors-d'œuvre, sliced raw and very fine, prepared only when you order it. Since few Piedmontese restaurateurs supply printed menus, expecting their clients to be familiar with the specialities, it is well for tourists to know that they won't get fungi unless they ask for them. The basket will then be brought to your table, you pick out the ones you fancy, making as much fuss as possible about the freshness and size, instruct the waiter as to their preparation (*funghi porcini* are best grilled), and they are charged according to weight.

As far as the beautiful salad of tangerine-bordered, white-and-cream cross-sections of *funghi reali* is concerned, normally it is seasoned only with salt, olive oil and lemon juice, but at this season you have to be pretty quick off the mark to prevent the Piedmontese in general and the Albesi in particular from destroying this exquisite and delicate mushroom with a shower of *tartufi bianchi*.

It is not that the white truffles, which are not white but putty-coloured, are not entirely marvellous and extraordinary. It is simply that their scent is so overpowering and all-penetrating that nothing delicate can stand up to their assault. The one creation evolved by the Piedmontese that accords perfectly with the white truffle is the famous *fonduta*, a dish made from the fat, rich Val d'Aosta cheese called Fontina, cut into cubes and steeped in milk for an essential minimum of twelve hours, then cooked, by those very few who have the knack, to a velvety, egg-thickened cream with an appearance entirely guileless until the rain of truffles, sliced raw in flake-fine slivers with a special type of *mandoline*-cutter, descends upon it. There is something about Fontina cheese, a hint of corruption and decadence in its flavour, that gives it a true affinity with the rootless, mysterious tuber dug up out of the ground.

The black truffles (*Tuber melanosporum*) of Périgord are, tradition-ally, sniffed out by pigs. In Provence and the Languedoc, dogs are trained to locate and indicate the presence of truffles by scratching the patches of ground that conceal them. In Piedmont the white truffle

(*Tuber magnatum*) is located in the same way. In the village of Roddi, not far from Alba, there is a training establishment for truffle hounds. Most of the dogs are mongrels. Valuable property, these Bobbis and Fidos, to the farmers and peasants who go about their truffle-digging secretively by dawn light, bearing their little hatchets for extracting the treasure from the earth. No system of truffle cultivation in the technical sense has ever yet been evolved, but according to Professor Gagliardi and Doctor Persiani in their Italian book on mushrooms and truffles, truffles can be and are propagated successfully by the reburying of mature truffles and spores close to the lateral roots of oaks and beeches, and in chalky ground with a southerly aspect. In five to ten years the chosen area may or may not yield a truffle harvest. Truffle veins peter out in forty to fifty years; laying truffles down for the future seems to be a sensible precaution.

The season for the true *tartufi bianchi* is brief. It opens in September. During the second week of October, Alba is in full fête with banquets, speeches, visiting celebrities and its very own truffle queen. By November the truffles are at their most potent and plentiful. By the end of January the ball is over.

In the Morra family's Hôtel Savona in Alba, visitors staying in rooms on the side are likely to be wakened early during the truffle season. The Morra canning and truffle paste factory starts up at six in the morning. It is not so much the noise, a very moderate one as Italian noises go, that gets you out of bed, as the smell of the truffles being bashed to paste, emulsified with oil, and packed into tubes for a sandwich spread. 'Truffle paste? Is there such a thing?' asks a *cavaliere* whose little shop window in the main street of Alba is pasted over with newspaper clippings and announcements to the effect that he is the *principe dei tartufi*. Certainly, somebody is due to succeed the Morra dynasty, still regarded as kings of the Alba truffle domain, even though the Morra manner of running a hotel and restaurant (its Michelin star must be the most misplaced of any in the whole Guide) is not so much regal as reminiscent of a Hollywood gangster-farce. All the same, the Morra truffle paste not only exists but does retain something of the true scent and flavour, which tinned whole truffles rarely do.

Contradiction and confusion in all things concerning the white truffle are normal in Alba, where the most harmless questions are met with evasive answers and where, for all the information one would ever be able to extract from the truffle dealers, the things might be brought by storks or found under gooseberry bushes. In the market there is no display of the truffle merchants' wares. The knobbly brown nuggets are not weighed out and are not even to be seen unless you are a serious customer. Some three dozen silent men in sombre suits stand in a huddle outside the perimeter of the poultry market. Only if you ask to see the truffles will one of these truffle men extract from his pocket a little paper- or cloth-wrapped parcel. You buy by nose and a sound, dry appearance.

About the storage of truffles the Albesi are comparatively communicative, if not very enlightening. 'What is the best way to keep *tartufi*?'

'You wrap them in a piece of stuff . . .'

Another dealer interrupts, 'No, you keep them in a jar of rice.'

The *cavaliere* says this is nonsense. Rice, he says, makes the truffles wet, and they must have air. (Nobody here seems to have heard of the Bolognesi method of keeping truffles dry in sawdust or wood shavings.) The *cavaliere* says jauntily that the ones we buy from him will last ten days. They are packed in tissue paper in four-inch-square packing cases. They have so much air that on the drive back to Turin from Alba we are nearly strangled by the smell. It is glorious, but it is dissipating itself, and the truffles are weakening with every kilometre. By the time we get them back to London in three days they will be ghosts.

The *cavaliere*'s ten days was a hefty over-estimation, but his recommendation of the cooking at the Buoi Rossi (The Red Ox), the unmodernized Piedmontese country-town inn in the via Cavour, was worthwhile. In the quiet old courtyard, with its characteristic vista of Piedmontese arches and open loft stacked with the copper-red corn-cobs, we drank a bottle of red Dolcetto, a local wine and a dry and genuine one, and ate some bread and butter spread with truffles. (This is one of the best ways of eating them if you can ever persuade a Piedmontese to allow you such a simple treat.) We returned three days running for meals.

The Red Ox is not mentioned in Michelin and is a simple *albergo-ristorante* where honest, decent and cheap food, which includes a genuine *fonduta*, is to be had. There were also delicious pears baked in their skins and sprinkled with coarse sugar, and fresh, fat *fagioli alla regina*, oven-cooked. The local wines are all they should be. In typical Italian fashion the *padrona* was unable to tell us more about her first-class vintage Barolo than that it comes from her cousin, one Enrico Borgogno, a grower in Barolo itself, and that it was, she thought, ten years old. The finer points of vintages and vintage years do not preoccupy Italian inn-keepers. Unless it is standardized and commercialized out of all recognition, two bottles of precisely the same growth are likely to resemble each other in about the same degree as the black truffle of Périgord resembles the white one of Piedmont.

An Omelette and a Glass of Wine

VEGETABLES

BROAD BEANS WITH CREAM

2 lb (900 g) very young broad beans, 1½ oz (45 g) butter, 2 oz (60 g) cream, a teaspoon of flour, salt, sugar, pepper.

Melt the butter, put in the broad beans, and stir until they have absorbed most of the butter. Sprinkle with the flour, stir again, and just barely cover the beans with hot water. Add pepper and sugar, but salt only when the beans are practically cooked. Simmer steadily for 15 minutes, then stir in the cream previously boiled in another pan.

Enough for four.

Summer Cooking

BROAD BEANS AND YOGHOURT

1½ lb (675 g) broad beans, 2 tablespoons of rice, a clove of garlic, 1 egg, a small pot of yoghourt.

Boil the broad beans and the rice separately, strain them and mix them together while hot. Stir the pounded garlic into the yoghourt, season with salt and pepper and add the mixture to the beans and rice. Heat gently, then stir in the beaten egg. As soon as the sauce has thickened slightly, it is ready.

Can be eaten hot or cold and serves 3–4. A Middle Eastern dish, called *fistuaia*.

Summer Cooking

SPINACI CON UVETTA
(*Spinach with sultanas*)

2 lb (900 g) spinach, 1 oz (30 g) sultanas, 1 oz (30 g) pine nuts, a clove of garlic, 1 oz (30 g) butter, olive oil, salt and pepper.

Clean the spinach and put it into a large saucepan with a little salt but no water. Plenty of moisture comes out as it cooks. When it is cooked drain it, pressing it hard so that as much of the moisture as possible is removed. In a wide saucepan or frying pan warm the butter and 2 tablespoonfuls of olive oil. Add the spinach, the chopped garlic, and a little pepper. Turn the spinach over and over; it should not fry, and neither should the garlic. When it is thoroughly hot put in the sultanas, which should have soaked for 15 minutes in a cup of warm water, and the pine nuts. Cover the pan, and continue to cook very gently for another 15 minutes. Serves 4 people.

Italian Food

PISELLI AL PROSCIUTTO
(*Green peas and ham*)

The green peas which grow round about Rome are the most delicious I have ever tasted anywhere. Small, sweet, tender and very green, they are really best simply stewed in butter. Cooked in this way they make a most delicate sauce for finely-cut home-made *pasta*, or for *riso in bianco*. The Romans adore these green peas cooked with ham. Try this method with young English green peas before they become wrinkled and floury.

2 lb (900 g) peas, a small onion, lard or butter, 3 oz (90 g) very good cooked ham cut into strips.

Melt the chopped onion in the lard or butter, and let it cook very gently, so that it softens without browning. Put in the shelled peas and a very little water. After 5 minutes add the ham. In another 5–10 minutes the peas should be ready. Serves 4 people.

Italian Food

MUSHROOMS IN CREAM

My sisters and I had a Nanny who used to make these for us over the nursery fire, with mushrooms which we had gathered ourselves in the early morning. I don't suppose they will ever taste quite the same, for the sensations of childhood food elude us in later years – but as a recompense nothing will surely ever taste so hateful as nursery tapioca, or the appalling boiled cod of schooldays.

In the days when cream was plentiful (and nothing but fresh, thick cream will do), I experimented often with this mushroom dish, and the best way of doing it in this:

For four people you must have 1 lb (450 g) mushrooms, and they must be medium-sized, white, button mushrooms, perfectly fresh from the fields. Do not wash or peel them, but carefully rub each one with a clean cloth, and take off the stalks. Put about a teacup of water into a pan and bring it to the boil; add a teaspoon of salt. Put the mushrooms in and cook them for 3 or 4 minutes.

In the meantime, heat your cream, 8–10 fl oz (225–300 ml) in a small pan, and as it cooks it will reduce and get thicker. Now strain the water off the mushrooms, put the mushrooms back in their pan, and pour the hot cream over them. Cook for 2 or 3 more minutes and serve immediately, extremely hot, on hot plates, in solitary splendour. To have anything else with them would be absurd, but see that there is a pepper-mill on the table, as you cannot add pepper while they are cooking for fear of spoiling the look of the dish.

French Country Cooking
chosen by Katharine Whitehorn

CHAMPIGNONS CÉVENOLS

Clean 1 lb (450 g) medium-sized mushrooms by wiping them with a clean cloth; put aside the stalks. In a thick pan warm some olive oil, enough to allow the mushrooms to cook comfortably without actually frying. The mushrooms should be put in when the oil is warm, not smoking, and cooked gently for 10 minutes.

Remove them with a draining spoon on to a dish, then in the same oil sauté the stalks cut into small pieces; spread these over the mushrooms, adding a sprinkle of finely chopped garlic and parsley. Still into the same oil throw a handful of fresh white breadcrumbs, and when these are golden, pour oil and breadcrumbs over the mushrooms. Serves 4.

Serve the dish cold the following day; if carefully cooked, without the oil having been overheated, they will be excellent.

French Country Cooking

CÈPES À LA BORDELAISE

Wash the cèpes and take the stalks off. If the cèpes are large ones cut them in 2 or 3 pieces. Put a glass of good olive oil in a sauté pan and when it is hot put in the cèpes. Let them brown a little, then turn the heat down very low. In the meantime chop the stalks finely with a handful of parsley and as much garlic as you like. Sauté this mixture in a separate pan, also in oil, then add it to the cèpes. They need about 25–30 minutes' cooking.

This method of cooking can be applied to all kinds of mushrooms.

Mediterranean Food

MELANZANE RIPIENE
(*Stuffed aubergines*)

For the stuffing for 4 aubergines you need about 4 oz (120 g) white bread without the crust, 8 anchovy fillets, a dozen black olives, a handful of parsley, 2 or 3 cloves of garlic, a tablespoonful of capers.

Cut the aubergines in half and scoop out about half the flesh. Chop this with all the rest of the ingredients, having first softened the bread with a little milk or water. Season with pepper and marjoram or *origano*, but salt will probably not be necessary. Put the stuffing lightly back into the aubergines and arrange them in a baking dish. Pour a generous quantity of oil over them, cover the pan, and cook in a slow oven (150°C/300°F/Gas Mark 2) for about an hour.

Italian Food
chosen by Jacqueline Korn

PAPETON D'AUBERGINES

The story goes that one of the Avignon Popes complained that Provençal cooking was not as good as that of Rome, and his cook invented this recipe in order to prove that he was wrong. It is also recounted that the first *papeton* was presented to the Pope in the form of a mitre.

Peel 6 aubergines, cut them in thick slices, salt them and leave them to drain. Stew them in olive oil in a covered pan, so that they remain moist; drain them and chop or sieve them. Season and add a chopped clove of garlic, a teacupful of milk and three eggs. Turn in to a lightly oiled mould. Cook 25 minutes in a bain-marie. Turn out and serve covered with a thick fresh tomato sauce flavoured with garlic and fresh basil. Serves 4.

Instead of being turned out, the *papeton* can be served in the dish in which it has cooked, with the sauce poured on the top, or offered separately. A much easier system.

Summer Cooking
chosen by John Ruden

PEPERONATA
(Sweet pepper and tomato stew)

8 red pimentos, 10 good ripe tomatoes, a large onion, butter and oil.

Brown the sliced onion very lightly in a mixture of oil and butter. Add the pimentos, cleaned, the seeds removed, and cut into strips; season them with salt. Simmer them for about 15 minutes, with the cover on the pan. Now add the tomatoes, peeled and quartered, and cook another 30 minutes. There should not be too much oil, as the tomatoes provide enough liquid to cook the pimentos and the resulting mixture should be fairly dry. Garlic can be added if you like. These quantities make enough for six or seven people, but *peperonata* is so good when reheated that it is worth making a large amount at one time.

To store for a few days in the refrigerator, pack the *peperonata* in a jar, and float enough olive oil on the top to seal the contents.

Italian Food
chosen by Jean McAuliffe

Another delight which Mrs David introduced me to was peppers, charred under the grill or baked until the skins were slightly burnt – these skins were then removed and the flesh was sliced and soaked in the lovely green olive oil which she always had at hand, with a small quantity of fresh basil. Red peppers were preferred to green as they are supposed to be more digestible.

Jean McAuliffe

PIMENTOS STUFFED WITH RICE AND HERBS

4 medium-sized red pimentos, 1 teacupful of rice, olive oil, lemon juice, fresh parsley and herbs. Boil and drain the rice; season it, and mix with it 2 or 3 tablespoons of chopped fresh herbs (parsley, marjoram, thyme or lemon thyme, or fennel, or simply parsley and a little of the green part of spring onions, or chives). Squeeze in a little lemon juice.

Cut the pimentos in half lengthways, take out the seeds. Put about 2 tablespoons of the rice mixture into each half and pour over a little olive oil. Pour a thin film of oil into a baking dish, put in the pimentos, cover the dish and cook in a gentle oven (150°C/300°F/Gas Mark 2) for about an hour. From time to time baste the pimentos with the oil in the dish, to prevent a hard crust forming on top of the rice. Serves 4.

Summer Cooking
chosen by Jonna Dwinger

RATATOUILLE NIÇOISE

There are any amount of versions of this dish, the variations being mainly in the proportions of each vegetable employed, the vegetables themselves being nearly always the same ones: aubergines, sweet peppers, onions, tomatoes, with courgettes sometimes being added and occasionally potatoes as well. Some people add mushrooms, but this is a rather pointless addition because they get completely lost in the mass of other vegetables. Garlic is optional, but the cooking medium must be olive oil.

To make a dish of *ratatouille* sufficient for about eight people, the ingredients are 3 medium-sized onions, 3 large aubergines, 3 large sweet red peppers, 3 courgettes, 4 large tomatoes, 2 cloves of garlic, a few coriander seeds, fresh or dried basil if available, or parsley, 2 coffee-cups (after-dinner size) of olive oil.

Prepare the vegetables by slicing the onions thinly and cutting the unpeeled aubergines and courgettes into ¼-inch-thick (6-mm) rounds and then into cubes. The aubergines, and the courgettes if they are being used, should be sprinkled with salt and put into a colander with a plate and a weight on the top, so that excess moisture is pressed out. This will take an hour or so. Cut the peppers in half, remove the core and all the seeds, wash them, and slice them in thin strips. Skin the tomatoes.

Heat the olive oil in a wide, heavy and shallow pan. Put in the onions and, when they are soft – but not brown – add the aubergines, courgettes, peppers, and chopped garlic. Cover the pan and cook gently for 40 minutes. Now add the chopped and skinned tomatoes, a teaspoon or so of pounded coriander seeds, and taste for seasoning. Cook another 30 minutes until all the vegetables are quite soft, but not too mushy. Stir in the basil or parsley and serve hot as a separate dish, or cold as an hors-d'œuvre. *Ratatouille* is a dish which takes kindly to reheating but, of course, it can be made in smaller quantities. Also, it can perfectly well accompany a joint of lamb or veal, grilled chops, steaks, or sausages.

French Provincial Cooking
chosen by Anne Willan

Elizabeth David opens such vistas of untried delights – think of flavouring mushrooms with mint, or of pickling plums. Imagine potted venison, or fritters of elderflower, or teatime sandwiches of thinly sliced brown bread and chopped walnuts. In summer I eagerly follow her advice to add tansy, balm, marigold petals, nasturtium flowers and leaves, pennyroyal, burnet, rocket, sorrel or rue to plain lettuce salad. I would love to try Elizabeth's sweet tomato jam, too, but our tomatoes are always gobbled up at once. Her *ratatouille*, however, has been my standby ever since I tried it when *French Provincial Cooking* was first published in 1960. In those far-off, spice-less days the flavouring of coriander seed was a revelation.   Anne Willan

THE COOKING OF POTATOES

For *sauté potatoes* cook the potatoes in their skins; peel, slice and sauté them gently in dripping or butter, adding a little chopped onion and parsley at the end.

Potatoes for salad should also be cooked in their skins, peeled and mixed with the dressing or mayonnaise while still warm.

For *Pommes Pailles*, *Allumettes* and all variations of chips, the raw potatoes should be plunged into plenty of water to wash away the outer starch which otherwise makes them stick together in the cooking. Drain and dry them thoroughly before cooking.

Put *new potatoes* into boiling water.

Go to the extra trouble of *mashing* potatoes through a sieve and adding *warmed* milk.

To keep *boiled* potatoes hot cover them with a clean tea-cloth instead of the lid of the serving dish. This absorbs the moisture and results in dry and floury, instead of sodden, potatoes.

Mashed fried potatoes should be done in bacon fat, very little of it, and watched constantly.

Rub the outside of potatoes for *baking* with a coating of salt.

Baked potatoes are delicious eaten with *aïoli* instead of butter.

French Country Cooking

POMMES DE TERRE RISSOLÉES

1 lb (450 g) new potatoes, as much as possible all the same size, 2 oz (60 g) butter.

Choose a small thick pan in which the potatoes will just fit, all in one layer. Melt the butter in this pan, put in the potatoes, whole, cover the pan. Cook very slowly, so that the butter does not burn. Turn the potatoes round several times during the cooking, so that they turn golden all over.

Small potatoes should be cooked in 25–40 minutes (according to the size) by which time the butter will all be absorbed by the potatoes. Add salt only when the potatoes are cooked. Serves 4.

Summer Cooking

POMMES DE TERRE SABLÉES

Cook the potatoes as for *pommes de terre rissolées*. When they are tender, add a little more butter and throw in a handful of fresh white breadcrumbs and shake the pan so that the breadcrumbs absorb the butter and turn crisp within two or three minutes.

Particularly good with grilled meat. Serves 4.

Summer Cooking
chosen by Judy Rogers

GALETTE DE POMMES DE TERRE

Peel about 1½ lb (675 g) potatoes and slice them very thinly and evenly. Wash them in plenty of cold water. In a thick frying-pan heat a tablespoon of butter and one of oil (the mixture of butter and oil gives a good flavour, and the oil prevents the butter from burning).

Put the potatoes into the pan and spread them evenly; season with nutmeg, salt and ground black pepper; turn the heat down as soon as they start to cook, cover the pan and leave them cooking gently for 15 minutes; by this time the under surface will be browned and the potatoes coagulated in such a way as to form a pancake; turn the *galette* over and leave the other side to brown for 3 or 4 minutes; serve either turned out whole on to a flat dish or cut into quarters. Serves 4–5.

French Country Cooking
chosen by Pamela Vandyke Price

GRATIN DAUPHINOIS

Gratin dauphinois is a rich and filling regional dish from the Dauphiné. Some recipes, Escoffier's and Austin de Croze's among them, include cheese and eggs, making it very similar to a *gratin savoyard*: but other regional authorities declare that the authentic *gratin dauphinois* is made only with potatoes and thick fresh cream. I give the second version which is, I think, the better one; it is also the easier. And if it seems to the thrifty-minded outrageously extravagant to use ½ pint (280 ml) cream to 1 lb (450 g) potatoes, I can only say that to me it seems a more satisfactory way of enjoying cream than pouring it over tinned peaches or chocolate mousse.

Peel 1 lb (450 g) yellow potatoes, and slice them in even rounds no thicker than a penny; this operation is very easy with the aid of the *mandoline*. Rinse them thoroughly in cold water – this is most important – then shake them dry in a cloth. Put them in layers in a shallow *earthenware* dish which has been rubbed with garlic and well buttered. Season with pepper and salt. Pour ½ pint (280 ml) thick cream over them; strew with little pieces of butter; cook them for 1½ hours in a low oven (150°C/300°F/Gas Mark 2). During the last 10 minutes turn the oven up fairly high (200°C/400°F/Gas Mark 6) to get a fine golden crust on the potatoes. Serve in the dish in which they have cooked. It is not easy to say how many people this quantity will serve: two, or three, or four, according to their capacity, and what there is to follow.

Much depends also upon the quality of the potatoes used. Firm waxy varieties such as the *kipfler* and the fir-apple pink which appear occasionally on the London market make a gratin lighter and also more authentic than that made with routine commercial King Edwards or Majestics which are in every respect second best.

Two more points concerning the proportions of a *gratin dauphinois*: as the quantity of potatoes is increased the proportion of cream may be slightly diminished. Thus, for 3 lb (1.4 kg) potatoes, 1¼ pints (700 ml) cream will be amply sufficient; and the choice of cooking dish (for the appropriate shape, see the *tian*) is also important, for the potatoes and cream should, always, fill the dish to within approximately three-quarters of an inch of the top.

The best way, in my view, of appreciating the charm of a *gratin dauphinois* is to present the dish entirely on its own, as a first course to precede grilled or plain roast meat or poultry, or a cold joint to be eaten with a simple green salad.

French Provincial Cooking

chosen by Lindsey Bareham, and by Johnny Grey for the late Diana Grey

In this recipe for Gratin Dauphinois, every aspect of preparing the dish, from the various versions that are passed off as authentic, to the way the potatoes are prepared, the sort of cream used and the effect it has on the potatoes, to the choice of dish, the rubbing (rather than chopping) of the garlic (to impart subtle flavour), the slow and then fast cooking and, most importantly, the type of potato is exhaustively explored. There is no detail untouched.

This excellent dish, which is something to serve with almost any savoury accompaniment, is much valued. I also appreciate the suggestions 'to present the dish entirely on its own, as a first course to precede grilled or plain roast meat or poultry, or a cold joint to be eaten with a simple green salad'. Every eventuality is thought of.

For me, this is the best kind of recipe writing. Lindsey Bareham

COURGETTES FINES HERBES

Wash but do not peel the little courgettes. Slice them into thin bias-cut rounds. Sprinkle with salt; leave in a colander with a plate and a weight on top for an hour so that excess moisture drains off. Put them in a saucepan with a ladle of water and cook gently for 10 minutes. Drain. For 1 lb (450 g) courgettes heat 1 oz (30 g) butter in a frying-pan and let the courgettes finish cooking in this quite gently. Turn them over once or twice and shake the pan so that they do not stick. When they are tender, stir in a tablespoon of finely chopped parsley, chervil or chives and a squeeze of lemon juice. Enough for two or three.

Good with veal, chicken, steak and lamb, and as a separate vegetable dish.

French Provincial Cooking

COURGETTE MUSAKA

The more commonly known version of this excellent and useful dish is made with layers of aubergines, minced lamb and tomatoes, all rather highly flavoured with onions and spices and herbs, the whole arranged in layers and baked in a tin to make a rich, colourful and rather filling kind of pie. Sometimes courgettes or even potatoes are substituted for the aubergines, and the courgette version is particularly good.

Ingredients are 1 lb (450 g) small courgettes, 1 lb (450 g) finely chopped or minced meat which can be lamb or beef, cooked or uncooked, 1½ lb (675 g) tomatoes, a large onion, a clove of garlic, 2 eggs, 4 tablespoons of olive oil, seasonings of salt, pepper, a teaspoon each of freshly ground allspice and dried or fresh mint, 2 or 3 tablespoons each of stock and breadcrumbs.

Wash the courgettes but do not peel them. Cut each one lengthways into slices about ⅛ inch (3 mm) thick. Salt them slightly and leave them to drain for an hour or so. Shake them dry in a tea towel, fry them gently in olive oil until they are tender. When all are done put more oil into the pan and in this fry the finely sliced or chopped onion until it is pale yellow. Put in the meat. If it is already cooked just stir it round until it is amalgamated with the onion. If it is raw meat let it cook gently about 10 minutes until it is nicely browned. Add seasonings and herbs and, off the heat, stir in the beaten eggs.

In a separate pan put the skinned and chopped tomatoes and the crushed garlic clove and simmer until most of the moisture has evaporated. Season with salt and pepper.

Now coat a 2–2½ pt (1.1–1.4 l) square or round and not too deep cake tin lightly with oil. Put in a layer of courgettes, then one of meat, then one of tomatoes, and so on until all the ingredients are used up, finishing with a rather thick layer of the tomatoes. On top sprinkle breadcrumbs and then moisten with the stock. Cover the tin with a piece of foil. Cook, with the tin standing on a baking sheet, in a low oven (170°C/330°F/Gas Mark 3) for an hour, but at half-time remove the foil. If the musaka looks dry add a little more stock. Serve hot. Serves 4–6.

With the layers of pale green courgettes in between the red and brown of the meat and tomatoes, this is a very beautiful looking dish, which, provided it has not been overcooked to start with, can quite successfully be reheated.

For a musaka with aubergines instead of courgettes the proceeding is precisely the same, and you need 2 to 4 aubergines according to size, unpeeled, cut lengthways into thinnish slices and salted before being fried in oil.

Spices, Salt and Aromatics
chosen by George Elliot

FLORENTINE FENNEL WITH PARMESAN

This is a simple and refreshing vegetable dish; it is surprising that it is not better known; it consists of the bulbous root stems of the Florentine or sweet fennel – this form of fennel now arrives in England from Israel, Kenya, Morocco and sometimes from France and Italy, during the late summer and again in the very early spring. The sweet, aniseed-like flavour of the plant is not to everybody's taste, but to those who do like it, it is quite an addiction.

For this dish, allow a minimum of one large fennel bulb – for want of an alternative short name, that is what everyone calls these root stems – per person. Other ingredients are butter, grated Parmesan cheese and breadcrumbs. Trim the bulbs by slicing off the top stalks, the thick base, and removing all the stringy outer layers of leaves. There is a good deal of waste. Slice the bulbs in half, longitudinally. Plunge them into a saucepan of boiling salted water. According to size they should cook for 7–10 minutes. When tender enough to be pierced fairly easily with a skewer, drain them.

Have ready a buttered *gratin* dish or the appropriate number of individual dishes. In this arrange the fennel halves, cut side down. Strew breadcrumbs over them (approximately 1 tablespoon per bulb) then grated Parmesan (again, 1 tablespoon per bulb) and finally a few little knobs of butter. Put the *gratin* dish in a medium oven (180°C/ 350°F/Gas Mark 4) and leave for 10–15 minutes until the cheese and breadcrumbs are very pale gold, and bubbling.

An Omelette and a Glass of Wine
chosen by Jonna Dwinger and George Elliot

CARCIOFI RIPIENI ALLA MAFALDA
(*Mafalda's stuffed artichokes*)

Prepare the artichokes by removing the outside leaves, cutting off about 1 inch (2.5 cm) of the top of the leaves and scooping out the choke.

Make a stuffing (for 6 artichokes) with 2 tablespoonfuls of bread-crumbs, 4 chopped anchovy fillets, and 2 chopped cloves of garlic. Cover the bottom of a small deep pan with olive oil, and when it is warm put in the stuffed artichokes. Add a glassful of white wine. Simmer very gently for about an hour. Serve hot.

Italian Food

CARCIOFI ALLA VENEZIANA
(*Venetian artichokes*)

For this dish the small dark violet-leaved artichokes are used. Put 6
or 8 of them, with only the outer leaves cut away, into a braising pan,
covered with equal parts of olive oil, white wine and water. Stew them
gently, with the cover on the pan, for an hour, then take off the lid,
turn up the flame, and let the liquid reduce until only the oil is left.
Serves 3–4.

Italian Food
chosen by Leslie Zyw

ONIONS AGRODOLCE

Put about 25 peeled small onions in a heavy *sauteuse* with 3 tablespoons of olive oil. As soon as the onions start to brown, add a sherry glass of port, one of vinegar, 2 tablespoons of brown sugar, a handful of raisins, salt and cayenne pepper.

Simmer slowly until the onions are quite soft, and the sauce has turned to a thick syrup. Serves 4.

Mediterranean Food

STUFFED TOMATOES À LA GRECQUE

Displayed in enormous round shallow pans, these tomatoes, together with pimentos and small marrows cooked in the same way, are a feature of every Athenian *taverna*, where one goes into the kitchen and chooses one's meal from the pans arrayed on the stove. It is impossible to describe the effect of the marvellous smells which assail one's nose, and the sight of all those bright-coloured concoctions is overwhelming. Peering into every stewpan, trying a spoonful of this, a morsel of that, it is easy to lose one's head and order a dish of everything on the menu.

Cut off the tops of a dozen large tomatoes, scoop out the flesh and mix it with 2 cups of cooked rice. To this mixture add 2 tablespoons of chopped onion, 2 tablespoons of currants, some chopped garlic, pepper, salt, and, if you have it, some left-over lamb or beef. Stuff the tomatoes with this mixture and bake them in a covered dish in the oven (180°C/350°F/Gas Mark 4) with olive oil.

Mediterranean Food
chosen by Julia Drysdale

ENDIVES AU BEURRE

Allow 1½ to 2 endives per person. Peel off any brown outside leaves; wipe the endives with a cloth. With a stainless knife cut each into ½-inch (1.25-cm) lengths. Melt a good lump of butter in a frying-pan. Put in the vegetables; let them cook a few seconds, turning them about with a wooden spoon, before adding salt, turning down the heat and covering the pan. By this method they will be sufficiently cooked in about 10 minutes (as opposed to over an hour when they are cooked whole) but uncover them and shake the pan from time to time to make sure the endives are not sticking. Before serving add a squeeze of lemon juice.

A variation is to add a few little cubes of bacon or ham. Leeks are excellent prepared and cooked in the same way.

French Provincial Cooking
chosen by Jonna Dwinger

STUFFED CABBAGE DISHES

To show what can be done with a cabbage apart from the one and only, and far too notorious, way common to railway dining-cars, boarding-schools and hospitals (and, goodness knows, these are all places where we should be offered the maximum of consolation in the way of good food), I am giving several recipes, each with its regional characteristic, for turning cabbage into an acceptable main-course dish, inexpensive, but abounding in the rich aromas of slow cooking and careful preparation.

These dishes are admirable for Aga and other cookers of the same type. They can be left in the slow oven for hours, and forgotten until dinner-time.

French Country Cooking

CHOU FARÇI AUX CÂPRES

A fine large cabbage, about 6 oz (170 g) each of minced fresh pork or pure pork sausage meat, chicken livers, and breadcrumbs, 1 yolk of egg; seasonings, spices, herbs, capers, 1 small glass brandy, a *roux* made of 1 oz (30 g) butter, 1 oz (30 g) flour, ½ pint (280 ml) stock or tomato juice; 2 tablespoons of capers, 1 small glass of brandy.

Put the whole cabbage into boiling, salted water and let it blanch for 5 minutes; take it out, drain it and, placing it on a wooden board, unfold the cabbage leaf by leaf, gently, until it looks like an open flower.

Now carefully spread each leaf with the stuffing made from the pork, the chicken livers, the breadcrumbs, all finely minced and amalgamated, bound with the yolk of egg and seasoned with salt, pepper, a little powdered thyme or marjoram, a clove of garlic, nutmeg and a minced bay leaf. When all the stuffing is used up, press the leaves of the cabbage gently together and tie it into its original shape with tape.

Have ready in a deep earthenware marmite a *roux* made from the flour, butter and stock. Into this put your cabbage, stick 4 cloves into it, cover the pot and put it into a slow oven (150–170°C/300–330°F/ Gas Mark 2 or 3) for about 2 hours.

When the cabbage is cooked, take the tape away very carefully and transfer the cabbage with its sauce to a deep serving dish, strew it with the capers and finally pour the brandy over it.

French Country Cooking
chosen by Katharine Whitehorn

CHOU ROUGE LANDAIS

1 medium-sized red cabbage, 1 lb (450 g) cooking apples, 1 lb (450 g) onions, 2 smoked Frankfurter sausages per person, ¼ pint (150 ml) red wine, ¼ pint (150 ml) wine vinegar, 4 tablespoons brown sugar, herbs and seasoning, 2 sweet red peppers, garlic, a piece of dried orange peel.

Slice the cabbage crosswise into thin strips. Peel, core, and slice the apples, and slice the onions.

In the bottom of a deep casserole put a layer of cabbage, then one of onions, then apples. Season with salt, pepper, sugar, herbs, mace, ground cloves, garlic, and add the strips of raw sweet pepper and dried orange peel. Continue these layers until the casserole is full up. Moisten with the wine and the vinegar. Cover the casserole and cook in a very slow oven for 3–4 hours. 20 minutes before serving add the sausages, buried deep into the cabbage.

The aroma which emanates from the cooking of this dish is particularly appetizing.

To make the dish more substantial, a few thick slices of bacon can be added. A bacon or ham bone, or even bones from roast mutton cooked with the cabbage and removed before serving, enrich the flavour.

French Country Cooking
chosen by Jack Andrews and Julia Caffyn

This was a dish that my uncle Chris (husband of Liza's sister Diana) cooked with great relish. He cooked it for me once, with the frankfurters, and very good it was too. It is wonderful also with pheasant, venison, goose, pigeon – or beef (sometimes the spiced beef given here on page 129). The sweet/sour taste is a perfect balance for rich gamey meat. Julia Caffyn

Bruscandoli

One fine morning early in May, 1969, with my sister Diana Grey and her husband, I arrived at the island of Torcello to lunch at Cipriani's lovely little Locanda, famous both for its cooking and its charm. I knew the place of old, so did the fourth member of our party. To my sister and brother-in-law it was new. This was their first visit to Venice. For all of us the trip was a particularly magical one.

When we had settled at our table and ordered our food – the jugs of house wine were at our elbows as we sat down – I became aware of a couple at a neighbouring table exclaiming with rapture over their food. They were a handsome and elegant pair. I wondered what was so special about the rice dish which was giving them such pleasure. They in turn noticed my curiosity. With beautiful Italian manners they passed some across to me, explaining that it was a risotto unique to Venice and unique to this particular season. It was made with a green vegetable called *bruscandoli*, or *brucelando*. Wild asparagus, so they explained. It was so good that I called the waiter and changed my order. A most delicate and remarkable risotto it was. The manager of the restaurant told me that only during the first ten days of May can this particular wild asparagus be found in the Venetian countryside.

Next day, we all went to another of the lagoon islands, to lunch at Romano's on Burano. Surprise. There were our friends again, and again the green risotto was on the menu. They had of course ordered it. So did we. This time they told me I might find some *brucelando* in the Rialto market if I went early enough in the morning. Hurry though. The season ends any day now. When the charming and splendid pair had left, I asked the proprietor of the tavern who they were. Ah, you mean the Isotta-Fraschini? The inheritors of the name of that wonderful and glamorous automobile of the twenties and thirties, no less. No wonder they carried about them the aura of romance, and, he especially, of the authentic Italian magnifico. So, to me, the name of Isotta-Fraschini is now indissolubly linked with the memory of those extraordinary and subtle risotti of the Venetian lagoons.

We went again to Torcello to eat *bruscandoli*, I went to the Rialto market, found an old woman selling a few bunches of it – it's the last of the year, she said – took it back to my hotel, stuck it in a glass so that I could make a drawing of it. When I came back in the evening the zealous chambermaid had thrown it away. No, next morning there was no old lady selling *bruscandoli* in the market. For once it was true, that warning 'tomorrow it will be finished'.

I searched the cookery books and the dictionaries for more details of the wild asparagus. I could find no descriptions, no references. Months later in a little book about Venetian specialities I discovered the following sentence: *'le minestre piu usate sono quelle di riso: con bruscandoli (luppolo) kumo (finocchio selvatrico) . . .'* So *bruscandoli* is Venetian for *luppoli*. And *luppoli* or *cime di luppolo* are wild hop-shoots.

It is of course well known that hop-shoots have a flavour much akin to that of asparagus, and the confusion is a common one. All the same, it was curious that neither the local Venetians to whom I talked, nor the knowledgeable Isotta-Fraschini couple should have known that hop-shoots rather than asparagus were used in those famous risotti. Maybe they did but didn't know the alternative words (in the Milan region they have yet another name, *loertis*) and thought that wild asparagus was a near enough approximation. The truth is, that when I bought the *brucelando* in the market, it didn't look much like any kind of asparagus, so I was suspicious. But it didn't look like hops either. And wild hop-shoots I had never before seen.

Research has yielded various other regional Italian dishes made with *bruscandoli* or *luppoli*. In her little book *La Cucina Romana* dealing with the old specialities of Roman cooking, Ada Boni gives a recipe for a *zuppa di luppoli*, and I have heard of a *frittata* or flat omelette with hop-shoots in Tuscany and also in the more northerly region of Brianza. In Belgium hop-shoots are equally a speciality. They are called *jets de houblon*.

The *risotto al bruscandoli* of Torcello and Burano I have never had the opportunity to cook for myself, so I shall not attempt to give a recipe here. Indeed a Venetian risotto is a dish notoriously difficult to reproduce anywhere else. The finest quality of round-grained risotto rice from the Po valley, essential to the success of the dish, is hard to come by nowadays, and few English people appreciate its importance or are willing to accept the fact that long-grained pilau rice simply will not cook to the subtle, rich creaminess of texture characteristic of the refined and aristocratic *risotti* of the Veneto.

An Omelette and a Glass of Wine
chosen by Guy Cooper

For many years my partner, Gordon Taylor, and I have had an account with a bookshop near the King's Road originally owned by John Sandoe. One of his most amiable assistants was Felicité Gwynne who became a friend. One day in 1979 we mentioned that we had become co-directors of The Herb Society, an educational charity which aimed to disseminate information about herbs. Felicité said that her sister, Elizabeth David, would be fascinated to know more about it and the quarterly magazine, *The Herbal Review*.

Over the next few years we met Elizabeth quite often, usually to discuss her articles, either in proof stage or what she would like to contribute in an upcoming number. 'Bruscandoli' was one of the articles Elizabeth so generously wrote for the review. Expeditions to her Halsey Street house in Chelsea were often at midday. They were well-timed, by chance, to coincide with the first bottle of delicious white burgundy. Whatever the business reason for the meetings might have been, we will always remember the hospitality, laughter, erudition, and chats about food, literature, personalities and some good gossip.   Guy Cooper

Fresh Herbs

The use of herbs in cooking is so much a matter of tradition, almost of superstition, that the fact that it is also a question of personal taste is overlooked, and experiments are seldom tried; in fact the restriction of this herb to that dish is usually quite arbitrary, and because somebody long ago discovered that basil works some sort of spell with tomatoes, fennel with fish, and rosemary with pork, it occurs to few people to reverse the traditional usage; to take an example, fennel is an excellent complement to pork, adding the sharpness which is supplied in English cookery by apple sauce, while basil enhances almost anything with which it is cooked; for ideas one has only to look to the cooking of other countries to see how much the use of herbs as a flavouring can be varied. In England mint is considered to have an affinity for lamb, new potatoes, and green peas; the French regard the use of mint as a flavouring as yet another sign of English barbarism, and scarcely ever employ it, while all over the Middle East, where the cooking is far from uncivilized, mint is one of the most commonly used of herbs; it goes into soups, sauces, omelettes, salads, purées of dried vegetables and into the sweet cooling mint tea drunk by the Persians and Arabs. In Spain, where the cooking has been much influenced by the Arabs, it is also used in stews and soups; it is usually one of the ingredients of the sweet sour sauces which the Italians like, and which are a legacy from the Romans, and in modern Roman cooking wild mint gives a characteristic flavour to stewed mushrooms and to vegetable soups. The Indians make a fresh chutney from pounded mint, mangoes, onion and chillies, which is an excellent accompaniment to fish and cold meat as well as to curries. Mint is one of the cleanest tasting of herbs and will give a lively tang to many vegetables, carrots, tomatoes, mushrooms, lentils; a little finely chopped mint is good in fish soups and stews, and with braised duck; a cold roast duck served on a bed of freshly picked mint makes a lovely, fresh-smelling summer dish; a few leaves can be added to the orange salad to serve with it. Dried mint is one of the most useful of herbs for the winter, for it greatly enlivens purées and soups of dried peas, haricot beans and lentils. Finely powdered dried mint is a characteristic flavouring of Turkish, Egyptian and Lebanese cooking. It is particularly good in mixtures of tomatoes and aubergines, and with rice dishes cooked in olive oil.

In England basil is one of the traditional herbs for turtle soup, and it is well known that it brings out the flavour of tomato salads and sauces; although it was common at one time in English kitchen gardens it is now extremely hard to lay hands on fresh basil, a state of affairs which should be remedied as fast as possible, for, with its highly aromatic scent, it is one of the most delicious of all herbs. In Provence, in Italy, in Greece, basil grows and is used in great quantities. The Genoese could scarcely exist without their *pesto*, a thick compound of pounded basil, pine nuts, garlic, cheese and olive oil which is used as a sauce for every kind of pasta, for fish, particularly red mullet, and as a flavouring for soups and minestrones. The Niçois have their own version of this sauce called *pistou* which has given its name to the Soupe au Pistou made of french beans, potatoes and macaroni, flavoured with the *pistou* sauce. To the Greeks basil has a special significance, for the legend goes that basil was found growing on the site of the Crucifixion by the Empress Helena, who brought it back from Jerusalem to Greece, since when the plant has flourished all over the Greek world; scarcely a house in Greece is to be seen without its pot of basil in the window. Once you have become a basil addict it is hard to do without it; Mediterranean vegetables such as pimentos and aubergines, garlicky soups and wine-flavoured dishes of beef, salads dressed with the fruity olive oil of Provence or Liguria and all the dishes with tomato sauces need basil as a fish needs water, and there is no substitute.

Of that very English herb sage I have little to say except that, and this is where the question of personal taste comes in, it seems to me to be altogether too blatant, and used far too much; its all-pervading presence in stuffings and sausages is perhaps responsible for the distaste for herbs which many English people feel. The Italians are also very fond of sage, and use it a great deal with veal and with liver; it seems to give a musty rather than a fresh flavour, and I would always substitute mint or basil for sage in any recipe. The same applies to rosemary, which when fresh gives out a powerful oil which penetrates anything cooked with it; in southern France it is used to flavour roast lamb, pork and veal, but should be removed from the dish before it is served, as it is disagreeable to find those spiky little leaves in one's mouth; in Italy rosemary is stuffed in formidable quantities into roast sucking pig, and in the butchers' shops you see joints of pork tied up ready for roasting wreathed round and threaded with rosemary; it looks entrancing, but if you want to taste the meat, use only the smallest quantity, and never put it into stock destined for a consommé or for a sauce.

Thyme, marjoram and wild marjoram are all good and strong-flavoured herbs which can be used separately or together for robust stews of beef in red wine, for those aromatic country soups in which there are onions, garlic, bacon, wine, cabbage; the *garbures* of south-western France and the minestrones of northern Italy; one or other of these herbs should go into stuffings for chicken, goose and turkey, for pimentos and aubergines, into meat croquettes (accompanied by grated lemon peel), terrines of game, and stews of hare and rabbit; either thyme or marjoram is almost essential to strew in small quantities on mutton, pork and lamb chops and liver to be fried or grilled; wild marjoram is called *origano* in Italy and Spain and is used for any and every dish of veal and pork, for fish and fish soups, and is an essential ingredient of the Neapolitan pizza, that colourful, filling, peasant dish of bread dough baked with tomatoes, anchovies and cheese. The marjoram which grows wild in Greece and Cyprus called *rígani* is a variety which has a more powerful scent; the flowers as well as the leaves are dried and no kebab of mutton, lamb or kid is thinkable without it. Lemon thyme is at its best fresh rather than cooked and is particularly good in a buttery potato purée, and in salads; there are dozens of varieties of thyme each with its particular scent, the best for cooking being perhaps the common thyme which grows wild on the downs. A curious thyme which has a scent of caraway seeds is good with roast pork.

Fennel, both the leaves and stalks of the variety which grows rather too easily in English gardens, and the root-bulb of the Florentine fennel which is imported from France and Italy, has many uses besides the sauce for mackerel which is found in all old English cookery books. For the famous Provençal *grillade au fenouil* the sun-dried, brittle stalks of the fennel are used as a bed on which to grill sea-bass (*loup de mer*) or red mullet; there is a Tuscan chicken dish in which the bird is stuffed with thick strips of ham and pieces of fennel bulb and pot-roasted; in Perugia they stuff their sucking pig and pork with fennel leaves and garlic instead of the rosemary prevalent elsewhere in Italy; one of the best of Italian sausages is *finocchiona*, a Florentine pork *salame* flavoured with fennel seeds; if you like the aniseed taste of fennel use it chopped up raw in soups, particularly iced soups, and in vinaigrette sauces, in rice salads to give the crisp element so necessary to soft foods, in mixed vegetable salads, in fish mayonnaises, in the court-bouillon in which fish is to be poached, in stuffings for baked fish, in chicken salads, and mixed with parsley and juniper berries for a marinade for pork chops which are to be grilled. The leaves of dill are not unlike those of fennel, but the aniseed flavour is less pronounced; it is a herb much used in Scandinavian and Russian cooking, particularly to flavour pickled cucumber and for soups.

Tarragon is essentially a herb of French cookery; *poulet à l'estragon* and *œufs en gelée à l'estragon* are classics of the French kitchen; without tarragon there is no true Sauce Béarnaise; with chives and chervil (which also goes well with carrots, potatoes, and in salads) or parsley it is one of the *fines herbes* for omelettes, sauces, butters, and many dishes of grilled meat and fish. It is a herb to be used with care for its charm lies in its very distinct and odd flavour and too much of it spoils the effect, but a few leaves will give character to many dishes and particularly to smooth foods such as sole cooked in cream, eggs *en cocotte*, cream soups, bisques of shell fish, stewed scallops, potato purées and also to tomato salads. In Italy, tarragon is to be found only in and around Siena, where it is used in the stuffing for globe artichokes, and to flavour green salads. When buying tarragon plants be sure to insist on the true French tarragon. Common tarragon, sometimes called Russian tarragon, has a rank taste and no scent at all.

The routine *bouquet garni* of French cookery consists of a sprig of thyme, parsley and a bay leaf (which besides its well-known use in

soups and stews and marinades gives a good flavour to béchamel sauce
if put in the milk while it is heated, and then removed). Chives, with
their delicate onion flavour and brilliant green colouring, are one of
the best of summer garnishes for eggs, vegetables, salads and soups.
Borage is used by the Genoese to mix with the stuffing for ravioli,
and to make fritters; the finely chopped leaves give a delicate cucumber
taste to cream cheese, and its use in wine cups is traditional. The
Sardinians flavour roast pork with myrtle, the French consider savory
(*sarriette*) indispensable as a flavouring for broad beans; lovage, a
member of the *Umbelliferae* family, has a peppery leaf with a faint
hint of celery and gives an interesting taste to a salad of haricot beans
and to fish soups. Among its thousands of uses in the kitchen, parsley
is the perfect foil for garlic; the fresh leaves of angelica can be used
in salads, while the translucent green stalks have a very strong fresh
scent, which when candied give such a delicious flavour and elegant
appearance to sweet creams and cream cheese puddings; the leaf of
the sweet-scented geranium gives a lovely scent to a lemon water ice
and an incomparable flavour when cooked with blackberries for jelly.
The fresh leaves of coriander are much used in Oriental, Middle
Eastern and Mexican cookery, while the dried seeds are one of the
essential ingredients of nearly all curries and Oriental cooking; with
their slightly burnt orange peel taste they are also good to flavour
pork, mutton and venison, and in sauces for coarse fish; they can also
be used to flavour milk and cream puddings and junkets. All these
herbs and many others, tansy, violets, balm, marigold petals, nasturtium flowers and leaves, penny-royal, yarrow, costmary, burnet, rocket,
sorrel and rue, were familiar ingredients of country cookery all over
Europe until the twentieth century brought such a battery of chemical
flavourings and synthetic essences that the uses and virtues of fresh
plants have been almost forgotten. But when you are accustomed to
their presence in food they are as necessary as salt; during the summer
months while their flavours are fresh and their leaves green they add
enormously to the appearance as well as to the flavour of food.

The quantity in which any given herb is to be used is a matter of
taste rather than of rule. Cookery books are full of exhortations to
discretion in this matter, but much depends on the herb with which
you happen to be dealing, what food it is to flavour, whether the dish

in question is to be a long simmered one in which it is the sauce which will be ultimately flavoured with the herbs, or whether the herbs are to go into a stuffing for a bird or meat to be roasted, in which case the aromas will be more concentrated, or again whether the herbs will be cooked only a minute or two as in egg dishes, or not cooked at all, as when they are used to flavour a salad or a herb butter. Whether the herbs are fresh or dried is an important point. The oils in some herbs (rosemary, wild marjoram, sage) are very strong, and when these dry out the flavour is very much less powerful. But in the drying process nearly all herbs (mint is an exception) acquire a certain mustiness, so that although in theory one should be able to use dried herbs more freely than fresh ones, the opposite is in fact generally the case.

Some fresh herbs disperse their aromatic scent very quickly when in contact with heat; a few leaves of fresh tarragon steeped in a hot consommé for 20 minutes will give it a strong flavour, whereas if the tarragon is to flavour a salad considerably more will be necessary. Lemon thyme and marjoram are at their best raw, or only slightly cooked, as in an omelette; the flavour of fennel stalks is brought out by slow cooking; basil has a particular affinity with all dishes in which olive oil is an ingredient, whether cooked or in salads. Knowledge of the right quantities, and of interesting combinations of herbs, can be acquired by using egg dishes, salads and soups as a background. Even if the herbs have been dispensed with a less cautious hand than is usually advised the result will not be a disaster, as it can be when some musty dried herb has completely permeated a roast bird or an expensive piece of meat. You may, on the contrary, have discovered some delicious new combination of tastes, and certainly the use of fresh herbs will be a startling revelation to all those people who know herbs only as something bought in a packet called 'mixed dried herbs', and for which you might just as well substitute sawdust.

It is particularly to the dishes in which fresh herbs are an essential rather than an incidental flavouring that I would like to call attention, for it is this aspect of cookery which is passed over by those writers who enjoin so much caution in the use of herbs. Sometimes it is a good thing to forget that basil, parsley, mint, tarragon, fennel, are all bunched together under the collective word 'herbs' and to remember that the difference between leaf vegetables (sorrel, spinach, lettuce) and herbs is very small, and indeed at one time all these plants were known collectively as 'salad herbs'. Nobody tells you to 'use spinach with caution', and neither can you be 'discreet with the basil' when you are making a *pesto* sauce, because the basil is the essential flavouring (so for that matter is mint in mint sauce).

In a slightly different way, a plain consommé or potato soup can be used as a background for a flavouring of herbs, tarragon being a particularly good one for this purpose. An *omelette aux fines herbes* needs tarragon as well as parsley and chervil. So do many sauces; the delicious *sauce verte* and *sauce ravigote* are two of them; the wonderful Sauce Messine (the recipe is on page 260) is another.

For the dispensing of fresh herbs into salads and soups it is advisable to keep a pair of kitchen scissors handy, and for chopping larger quantities a two-handled, crescent-shaped chopper such as may now be obtained in the larger kitchen equipment stores. Small sturdy wooden bowls complete with a little axe-shaped chopper are also now obtainable in some stores and are invaluable in any kitchen where fresh herbs are frequently in use.

Summer Cooking
chosen by Martin Lam

PASTA, PULSES AND GRAINS

PASTA ASCIUTTA

On the 15th of November 1930, at a banquet at the restaurant Penna d'Oca in Milan, the famous Italian futurist poet Marinetti launched his much publicized campaign against all established forms of cooking and, in particular, against *pastasciutta*. 'Futurist cooking,' said Marinetti, 'will be liberated from the ancient obsession of weight and volume, and one of its principal aims will be the abolition of *pastasciutta*. *Pastasciutta*, however grateful to the palate, is an obsolete food; it is heavy, brutalizing, and gross; its nutritive qualities are deceptive; it induces scepticism, sloth, and pessimism.'

The day after this diatribe was delivered the Italian press broke into an uproar; all classes participated in the dispute which ensued. Every time *pastasciutta* was served either in a restaurant or a private house interminable arguments arose. One of Marinetti's supporters declared that 'our *pastasciutta*, like our rhetoric, suffices merely to fill the mouth'. Doctors, asked their opinions, were characteristically cautious: 'Habitual and exaggerated consumption of *pastasciutta* is definitely fattening.' 'Heavy consumers of *pastasciutta* have slow and placid characters; meat eaters are quick and aggressive.' 'A question of taste and of the cost of living. In any case, diet should be varied, and should never consist exclusively of one single element.' The Duke of Bovino, Mayor of Naples, plunged into the fight with happy abandon. 'The angels in Paradise,' he affirmed to a reporter, 'eat nothing but *vermicelli al pomidoro*.' To which Marinetti replied that this confirmed his suspicions with regard to the monotony of Paradise and of the life led by the angels.

Marinetti and his friends proceeded to divert themselves and outrage the public with the invention and publication of preposterous new dishes. Most of these were founded on the shock principle of combining unsuitable and exotic ingredients (*mortadella* with nougat, pineapple with sardines, cooked *salame* immersed in a bath of hot black coffee flavoured with eau-de-Cologne, an aphrodisiac drink composed of pineapple juice, eggs, cocoa, caviar, almond paste, red pepper, nutmeg, cloves, and Strega). Meals were to be eaten to the accompaniment of perfumes (warmed, so that the bald-headed should not suffer from the cold), to be sprayed over the diners, who, fork in the right hand, would stroke meanwhile with the left some suitable substance – velvet, silk, or emery paper.

Marinetti's bombshell contained a good deal of common sense; diet and methods of cookery must necessarily evolve at the same time as other habits and customs. But behind this amiable fooling lurked a sinister note: the fascist obsession with nationalism and patriotism, the war to come. '*Spaghetti* is no food for fighters.' In the 'conflict to come the victory will be to the swift,' '*Pastasciutta* is anti-virile . . . A weighty and encumbered stomach cannot be favourable to physical enthusiasm towards women.' The costly import of foreign flour for *pastasciutta* should be stopped, to boost the national cultivation of rice. The snobbery of the Italian aristocracy and haute bourgeoisie, who had lost their heads over American customs, cocktails parties, foreign films, German music, and French food, was damned by Marinetti as *esterofil* (pro-foreign) and anti-Italian. In future a bar should be known as a *quisibeve* (here-one-drinks), a sandwich as a *traidue* (between-two), a cocktail as a *polibibita* (multi-drink), the maître-d'hôtel would be addressed as *guidopalato* (palate-guide), an aphrodisiac drink was to be called a *guerra in letto* (war-in-the-bed), a sleeping draught a *pace in letto* (peace-in-the-bed). Marinetti's tongue was by no means wholly in his cheek. A message from Mussolini, to be published in *La Cucina Futurista* (F. Marinetti, 1932), was dedicated 'to my dear old friend of the first fascist battles, to the intrepid soldier whose indomitable passion for his country has been consecrated in blood'.

Marinetti's effort was not the first that had been made to reform the Italian diet. In the sixteenth century a Genoese doctor had denounced the abuse of *pasta*. Towards the end of the eighteenth century a campaign was instituted against the consumption of excessive quantities of macaroni. Innumerable volumes from the hands of eminent scientists and men of letters proved unavailing. Not only was the passion for *pastasciutta* too deeply rooted in the tastes of the people, but there was also a widely diffused superstition that macaroni was the antidote to all ills, the universal panacea.

Another effort was made in the first half of the nineteenth century by the scientist Michele Scropetta; he, again, achieved nothing concrete. Had it not been for the war Marinetti's campaign might have achieved a certain success; but however aware enlightened Italians may be of the unsuitability of *pasta* as a daily food, the fact remains that the majority of southern Italians (in the north it is replaced by rice or *polenta*) continue to eat *pastasciutta* at midday and probably some kind of *pasta in brodo* at night. Considering the cost of living, this is not surprising; freshly made *pasta* such as *tagliatelle* and *fettuccine* is cheap and versatile. According to circumstances it may be eaten economically with tomato sauce and cheese, with fresh tomatoes when they are cheap, with butter and cheese, with oil and garlic without cheese. The whole dish will cost rather less than two eggs, is immediately satisfying, and possesses the further advantage that every Italian could prepare a dish of spaghetti blindfold, standing on his head in his sleep.

Figure-conscious Italians claim that no fattening effect is produced by *pasta* provided no meat course is served afterwards; vegetables or a salad, cheese and fruit, are quite sufficient. People mindful of their digestions will also tell you that the wise drink water with their *spaghetti* and wait until it is finished before starting on the wine.

Italian Food
chosen by Bettina McNulty

In 1954 Elizabeth's *Italian Food* was published – well before the spate of Italian restaurants burst on the scene, firmly and permanently changing the eating-out habits of Londoners. The beginning of her chapter of Pasta Asciutta shows Elizabeth in full spate – funny, observant, informative, even irreverent.   Bettina McNulty

FETTUCCINE ALLA MARINARA
(*Fettuccine with fresh tomato sauce*)

Fettuccine are home-made ribbon noodles. The ready-made kind will, however, do just as well for this dish, which is Neapolitan. Cook them as usual; 5 minutes before they are ready make the sauce. Into a frying pan put a good covering of olive oil; into this when it is hot but not smoking throw at least 3 cloves of sliced garlic; let them cook half a minute. Add 6 or 7 ripe tomatoes, each cut in about 6 pieces; they are to cook for about 3 minutes only, the point of the sauce being that the tomatoes retain their natural flavour and are scarcely cooked, while the juice that comes out of them (they must, of course, be ripe tomatoes) amalgamates with the oil and will moisten the *pasta*. At the last moment stir in several leaves of fresh basil, simply torn into 2 or 3 pieces each, and season the sauce with salt and pepper. Pour the sauce on top of the *fettuccine* in the serving dish, and serve the grated cheese separately. Since basil is not common in England, mint makes a pleasant substitute, or parsley, but this will not, of course, be so aromatic.

This sauce is also thoroughly to be recommended for all kinds of *pasta*, rice, and dried vegetables such as haricot beans and chick peas.

Italian Food

RAVIOLI O GNOCCHI VERDI

Although this dish is now usually known as *gnocchi* (and the most delicious of all the tribe), they were originally, and in some parts of Tuscany still are, called *ravioli*, while what we know as *ravioli* have a host of other names.

The ingredients are 12 oz (340 g) cooked and chopped spinach (i.e. 1 lb/450 g to start with), 8 oz (225 g) *ricotta*, 1½ oz (45 g) grated Parmesan, 2 eggs, 3 tablespoonsful of flour, a little butter, salt, pepper, nutmeg, and for the sauce plenty of melted butter and grated Parmesan.

Cook the cleaned spinach with a little salt but no water. Drain it, press it absolutely dry, then chop it finely. Put it into a pan with salt, pepper, nutmeg, a nut of butter, and the *ricotta*. Stir all the ingredients together over a low flame for 5 minutes. Remove the pan from the heat and beat in the eggs, the grated Parmesan, and the flour. Leave the mixture in the refrigerator for several hours or, better, overnight.

Spread a pastry board with flour, form little croquettes about the size of a cork with the spinach mixture, roll them in the flour, and when they are all ready drop them carefully into a large pan of barely simmering, slightly salted water.

(Do not be alarmed if the mixture seems rather soft; the eggs and the flour hold the *gnocchi* together as soon as they are put into the boiling water.)

Either the *gnocchi* must be cooked in a very large saucepan or else the operation must be carried out in two or three relays, as there must be plenty of room for them in the pan. When they rise to the top, which will be in 5–8 minutes, they are ready. They will disintegrate if left too long. Take them out with a perforated draining spoon, drain them carefully in a colander or sieve, and when the first batch is ready slide them into a shallow fireproof dish already prepared with 1 oz (30 g) of melted butter and a thin layer of grated Parmesan cheese. Put the dish in the oven to keep hot while the rest of the *gnocchi* are cooked. When all are done, put another 1 oz (30 g) of butter and a generous amount of cheese over them and leave the dish in the oven (150°C/300°F/Gas Mark 2) for 5 minutes.

This quantity is sufficient for 4 people for a first course. If they are to be the mainstay of a meal make the quantities half as much again; but as the cooking of these *gnocchi* is an unfamiliar process to most people, it is advisable to try out the dish with not more than the quantities given.

I am indebted for this recipe to Mr Derek Hill's Florentine cook Giulia, who makes a most beautiful dish out of these green *ravioli*.

Italian Food
chosen by Derek Hill

LENTICCHIE IN UMIDO
(*Stewed lentils*)

12 oz (340 g) brown lentils, a small onion, mint, garlic, olive oil.

Wash the lentils and pick out any pieces of grit. There is no need to soak them. Cover the bottom of a thick pan with olive oil, and when it is warm melt the sliced onion in it. Add the lentils, and as soon as they have absorbed the oil pour 2 pints (1.1 l) hot water over them. Add a clove of garlic and a sprig of fresh mint. Cover the pan and stew steadily for 1¼–1½ hours. By that time the lentils should be soft and the liquid nearly all absorbed. Now season with salt and pepper. Also good cold, with the addition of fresh olive oil and hard-boiled eggs.

Enough for 4 or 5 people.

Brown lentils are whole (sometimes called German) lentils; they do not break up in the cooking, as do red lentils which are not suitable for this dish.

Italian Food

FOOL *or* EGYPTIAN BROWN BEANS

Fool (brown beans) are the staple food of the Egyptian peasant. 1 lb (450 g) of these beans and 6 tablespoons of red lentils are washed and put into an earthen or copper casserole with 3 cups of water. This is brought to the boil and then left for hours and hours – all night usually – on a low charcoal fire. If necessary more water can be added. Salt is not put in until the cooking is finished, and olive oil is poured over them in the plate, and sometimes hard-boiled eggs are served with them. The lid of the casserole should be removed as little as possible, or the beans will go black.

The way I cook Egyptian dried brown beans on a modern cooker is as follows: soak 8 oz (225 g) of them in cold water for about 12 hours. Put them into an earthenware pot well covered with fresh water (about ¾–1 pint [400–550 ml]). Put the covered pot in the lowest possible oven and leave undisturbed all day or all night, or for a minimum of 7 hours. When they are quite soft and most of the water is absorbed, decant them into a shallow serving bowl or dish, season with salt, moisten with plenty of fruity olive oil and lemon juice – or, better still, the juice of fresh limes. Serve separately a plate of hard-boiled eggs. This is a very filling, nourishing and cheap dish. Tins of ready-cooked Egyptian brown beans are also to be bought in Oriental shops; they are time-saving but still require a good hour of extra cooking, and of course the ritual seasoning of olive oil and lemon.

Mediterranean Food

FASŒIL AL FÙRN
(*Beans in the oven*)

A Piedmontese country dish which is made with dried red haricot (*borlotti*) beans, cooked all night in a slow oven and eaten the following day at lunch time. The Piedmontese custom is to put the dish to cook on Saturday night so that it is ready to take out of the oven when the family return from Mass on Sunday at midday.

Put 1 lb (450 g) haricot beans (white ones when red are unobtainable) to soak for 12 hours. Chop a good quantity of parsley with several cloves of garlic, and add pepper, cinnamon, ground cloves and mace. Spread this mixture on to wide strips of pork rind (or rashers of bacon), roll them up, put them at the bottom of a deep earthenware bean pot, cover them with the beans, and add enough water to cover the beans by about 2 in (5 cm). Put the cover on the pot, and cook in a very slow oven (140°C/280°F/Gas Mark 1) regulating the heat according to the time at which the beans are to be eaten. The slower they cook, the better the dish.

Serve in soup plates as a very substantial midday meal. A splendid dish when you are busy, hard up, and have hungry people to feed.

Italian Food

POLENTA

Polenta, yellow maize flour, is one of the staple foods of northern Italy, particularly of Lombardy and the Veneto, where boiled *polenta* very often takes the place of bread. There are different qualities of this *farina gialla*, coarsely or finely ground. Plainly boiled *polenta* is dull and rather stodgy, but left to get cold and then fried in oil, toasted on the grill, or baked in the oven, with meat or tomato sauce or with butter and cheese, it can be very good. In the Veneto it is the inevitable accompaniment to little roasted birds, and to *baccalà*. It can be made into *gnocchi*; into a kind of fried sandwich containing cheese and ham; and into a filling winter *pasticciata*, with a cheese sauce and white truffles.

To cook it, boil about 2½ pints (1.4 l) salted water in a fairly large saucepan. Pour in 1 lb (450 g) finely ground *polenta* (enough for at least 10 people). Stir it round with a wooden spoon until it is a thick smooth mass. Now let it cook very slowly, stirring frequently, for 20 minutes. See that there is enough salt. Turn the *polenta* out on to a large platter, or wooden board, or marble slab. It can be eaten at once, with butter and cheese, or with a meat or tomato sauce, with boiled broccoli or with roasted quails or other little birds on the top; or it can be left until cold, cut into squares or rounds and cooked in any of the ways already mentioned.

For coarsely-ground *polenta* use a little more water for the initial cooking.

In northern Italy every family has a special copper pot for cooking *polenta*, shaped rather like our own copper preserving pans, and it is stirred with a long stick. These implements figure over and over again in paintings of Venetian life, and the making of *polenta* will also be familiar to anyone who has read *I Promessi Sposi*, Manzoni's famous novel of seventeenth-century Lombardy.

Italian Food

RISOTTO ALLA MILANESE

There are various versions of *risotto alla Milanese*. The classic one is made simply with chicken broth and flavoured with saffron; butter and grated Parmesan cheese are stirred in at the end of the cooking, and more cheese and butter served with it. The second version is made with beef marrow and white wine; a third with Marsala. In each case saffron is used as a flavouring.

Risotto is such a simple and satisfactory dish, so universally appreciated that it is well worth mastering the principles of cooking the rice, after which any amount of different dishes can be improvised. It can be served absolutely plain with butter and cheese, or it can be elaborated by the addition of chicken, duck, game, lobster, mussels, oysters, prawns, mushrooms, truffles, goose or chicken livers, artichoke hearts, peas, aubergines, almost anything you like. But not more than one or two of such ingredients in one *risotto*.

For *risotto alla Milanese* with white wine, proceed as follows: into a heavy pan put a good ounce (30 g) butter (in northern Italy butter is always used for *risotto*, in the south it is very often made with oil). In the butter fry a small onion cut very fine; let it turn pale gold but not brown; then add 1 oz (30 g) beef marrow extracted from marrow bones; this gives a richer quality to the *risotto*, but can perfectly well be left out. Now add the rice, allowing about 3 oz (90 g) per person (in Italy they would allow a good deal more; the amount rather depends upon whether the *risotto* is to constitute a first course only or a main dish). Stir the rice until it is well impregnated with the butter. It must remain white. Now pour in two-thirds of a tumbler of dry white wine and let it cook on a moderate heat until the wine has almost evaporated. At this moment start adding the stock, which should be a light chicken consommé and which is kept barely simmering in another pan; add about a breakfastcupful (in American terms, a regular measuring cup) at a time, and keep your eye on the *risotto*, although at this stage it is not essential to stir continuously. As the stock becomes absorbed add more; in all you will need about 2 pints (1.1 l) for 10–12 oz (280–340 g) rice, and if this is not quite enough, dilute it with hot water. Towards the end of the cooking, which will take 20–30 minutes, stir continuously using a wooden fork rather than a spoon, which tends to crush the grains. When you see that the rice is tender, the mixture creamy but not sticky, add the saffron.

The proper way to do this is to pound the filaments to a powder (three or four will be enough for 12 oz [340 g] rice), steep the powder in a coffee-cupful of the broth for 5 minutes, and strain the liquid obtained into the rice. Having stirred in the saffron, add 1 oz (30 g) each of butter and grated Parmesan, and serve the *risotto* as soon as the cheese has melted. More butter and grated cheese must be served separately.

To make *risotto* with Marsala, proceed in exactly the same way, omitting the beef marrow, which would make too rich a combination, and using only half a glass of Marsala.

Italian Food
chosen by John Ruden

RISOTTO WITH MUSHROOMS

This is a very simple form of *risotto* and, needless to say, all sorts of things can be added – slices of chicken, sautéd chicken livers, beef marrow. It should also be noted that *risotto* is made with *Italian* rice which is a round, absorbent variety; no other will serve the purpose so well, the long Patna type of rice being wasted on this dish, for it is not sufficiently absorbent and makes your *risotto* tough and brittle, whereas a poor quality or small-grained rice will turn into a pudding.

Take 2 cups of Italian rice, 2 pints (1.1 l) chicken stock, 1 medium onion chopped fine, 2 cloves of garlic, 1 wineglass of oil, 4 oz (120 g) of white mushrooms cut into slices. Into a heavy sauté pan put the oil and as soon as it is warm put in the onion, the garlic and the mushrooms. As soon as the onion begins to brown, add the rice and stir until it takes on a transparent look. This is the moment to start adding the stock, which should be kept just on the boil by the side of the heat. Pour in about 2 cups at a time, and go on stirring, and adding stock each time it has been absorbed. The whole process is done over a low heat, and in about 45–50 minutes, the *risotto* should be ready. It should be creamy, homogeneous, but on no account reduced to porridge. One must be able to *taste* each grain of rice although it is not separated as in a pilaff. Grated Parmesan cheese is served with it, and sometimes stirred in before bringing the *risotto* to the table. In any case a *risotto* must be eaten immediately it is ready, and cannot be kept warm in the oven, steamed over a pan of boiling water, or otherwise kept waiting. Serves 4.

Mediterranean Food

RISOTTO AUX FRUITS DE MER

For 4 people you need:

4 or 5 pints (2 kg) mussels, 1 pint (500 g) prawns, ½ lb (225 g) rice, a glass of white wine, 2 shallots or small onions, a clove of garlic, grated cheese, olive oil, black pepper, 2 or 3 tomatoes, and a green or red pimento.

Clean the mussels and put them to cook with 2 pints (1.1 l) water and the white wine, a chopped clove of garlic and shallot, and ground black pepper. When they are open, strain the stock into a basin and leave it while you shell the mussels and the prawns. Now strain the stock through a muslin, and put it into a pan to heat up. In a heavy pan heat a little olive oil, enough to cover the bottom of the pan, and in it sauté a chopped shallot or onion; add the uncooked rice and stir it round in the oil until it is shiny all over, taking care not to let it stick to the pan; now add a large cupful of the mussel stock, which should be kept simmering on the stove; when the first cupful of stock has been absorbed, add some more; it is not necessary to stir continually, but the pan should be kept on a low heat, and stirred every time more stock is added; as the rice begins to swell and cook, larger quantities of stock can be added and care must be taken that the rice does not stick to the sides of the pan.

In the meantime sauté the tomatoes and the pimento in a little more olive oil, and when the rice is soft add the mussels and the prawns and let them get hot; add this mixture to the *risotto* only at the last minute, stirring it lightly round. Serve the grated cheese separately, and if you like garnish the dish with a few mussels which have been left in their shells; they make a good decoration.

Mediterranean Food

PILAU RICE

There are Egyptian, Turkish, Persian, Indian, Chinese and goodness knows how many other systems of cooking and flavouring pilau rice. This is one of my own recipes, evolved by combining an Indian method with flavourings which are predominantly Levantine.

Measurements for pilau rice cookery are nearly always based on volume rather than weight. The use of a cup or glass for measuring the rice simplifies the recipes because the cooking liquid is measured in the same vessel, the success of the process depending largely upon the correct proportions of liquid to rice. The cooking pot is also important, especially to those unfamiliar with the routine. Choose a saucepan or a two-handled casserole not too deep in proportion to its width. Whether of aluminium, iron, cast iron, copper or earthenware is not important provided the base is thick and even.

Those unfamiliar with rice cookery are advised to start by making a small quantity of pilau, enough for say two or three people. The recipe once mastered, it is easy to increase the quantities, in proportion, and to experiment with different flavourings. This quantity is for 2– 3 people.

Using the best quality thin-grain rice sold in the Indian shops under the name of Basmati, the initial ingredients and preparations are as follows: 1 tumbler of rice, 2 tumblers of water.

Put the rice in a bowl and cover it with water. Leave it to soak for an hour or so.

Cooking and flavouring ingredients are 1 oz (30 g) clarified butter (or ghee bought from an Indian provision store), 1 small onion, 4 cardamom pods, 2 teaspoons of cumin seeds, or ground cumin, a teaspoon of turmeric powder, 2 teaspoons of salt, a bay leaf or two, 2 tumblers of water.

Melt the butter in your rice-cooking pot or saucepan (for this quantity a 2½–3 pints [1.4–1.8 l] one is large enough) and in it cook the sliced onion for a few seconds, until it is translucent. It must not brown. This done, stir in the cardamom seeds extracted from their pods and the cumin seeds, both pounded in a mortar, and the turmeric. The latter is for colouring the rice a beautiful yellow, as well as for its flavour, and the object of cooking the spices in the fat is to develop their aromas before the rice is added. This is an important point.

Drain the rice, and put it into the butter and spice mixture. Stir it around until it glistens with the fat. Add the salt. Pour in the two tumblers of water and let it come to the boil fairly fast. Put in the bay leaf.

Let the rice cook steadily, uncovered, over medium heat until almost all the water is absorbed and holes begin to appear in the mass. This will take almost 10 minutes.

Now turn the heat as low as possible. Over the rice put a thickly folded absorbent tea cloth, and on top of the cloth (use an old one; the turmeric stains) the lid of the pan. Leave undisturbed, still over the lowest possible heat, for 20–25 minutes. At the end of this time the rice should be quite tender and each grain will be separated. Fork it round, turn into a warmed serving bowl.

The rice should be a fine yellow colour and mildly spiced.

The pilau can be eaten as an accompaniment to spiced lamb or beef kebabs, but to my mind is even nicer on its own, with the addition of a few sultanas or raisins, soaked for an hour in water, heated up in a little saucepan and mixed into the rice just before it is turned out of the saucepan for serving. Oven-toasted almonds or pine kernels make another attractive addition.

The tumbler I use for measuring holds 6 oz (170 g) Basmati rice and 6 fl oz or just over ¼ pint (150 ml) water.

In the following recipe the rice is simply washed under running cold water rather than soaked. I find that it does not produce quite such well-swollen and delicious rice, but many people hold that the quicker method is the better one.

QUICK PILAU RICE

If you are in a hurry, or have forgotten to soak the rice, simply put it in a sieve or colander, wash it very thoroughly under cold running water, and cook it as described for pilau rice – with or without spices – allowing a little longer, say five extra minutes, for the first part of the cooking.

Spices, Salt and Aromatics

GIULIA'S RISO RICCO

Giulia Piccini was Tuscan. She came from a hill village near Florence, and during the fifties she cooked for Derek Hill, the English painter, who at that time occupied the *villino* in the garden of I Tatti, Bernard Berenson's villa at Settignano. Giulia's cooking was like herself, elegant and delicate – in bearing she was more the fastidious aristocrat than the sturdy peasant – subtly seasoned, but with unexpected contrasts, as in a cold, uncooked tomato sauce which she served with hot dry rice. Conversely, *riso ricco*, or rich rice, consists of plain white rice left to cool until barely more than lukewarm, when a hot cheese sauce resembling a *fonduta* is poured over it. Not an easy dish to get right, but when it comes off, glorious. This is Giulia's own recipe written out by her husband, Emilio.

'For 500 gr. of rice: put 3 litres of water in a large boiling pot, and when it boils throw in the rice and a little salt, and cook it for about 15 to 17 minutes, stirring so that it doesn't stick. Turn it into a colander, and then into a buttered mould and leave it to cool. (The mould can be plain or with a central tube.)

'Meanwhile prepare the sauce: into ½ litre of barely tepid milk put 250 gr. of Gruyère cut in small thin slices; then leave them for about an hour in this tepid bath, until the cheese has softened and melted and is forming threads. At this point add 4 egg yolks, whisking them in to obtain a cream which you then cook over a very slow fire.

'The sauce made, turn the rice into a serving dish and pour the sauce over it, first putting little flakes of butter over the rice.'

Notes

The only point Giulia doesn't make quite clear is that the milk and Gruyère should be held 'barely tepid' during the hour it takes for the cheese to melt, so a bain-marie or a double saucepan is indicated. Provided the water underneath or surrounding the milk is hot when you add the cheese, there should not be any necessity for further cooking at this stage. But keep the milk and cheese covered.

When it comes to adding the egg yolks and the final cooking of the sauce to a smooth custard-like cream I find it necessary, for the sake of speed, to have recourse to the blender, giving the yolks and the milk-cheese mixture a quick whirl, then returning them to the saucepan to thicken over very gentle heat. The sauce is not supposed to be thicker than double cream.

Both for flavour and melting property I prefer the Italian Fontina cheese to Gruyère which in England is of such variable quality, and inclined to turn into rubbery knots when heated. The rice should be Italian round-grained risotto rice. Giulia reckoned 500 gr. for 6 people.

GIULIA'S TOMATO SAUCE AND DRY RICE

With a dish of dry rice cooked in the manner of a pilau, Giulia used to serve the simplest possible tomato sauce. She sliced ripe tomatoes into a bowl (I don't think she skinned them. I do, but that's a matter of choice), mixed them with olive oil, wine vinegar, salt, pepper and a scrap of onion. The important points are to prepare the mixture two hours in advance, and immediately before serving to stir in a pinch of sugar.

PASTA, PULSES AND GRAINS

For the *riso secco* use long-grain rice. Put half a small onion in a deep saucepan or casserole with olive oil and butter. When the onion turns pale gold, extract it, throw in 500 gr. of rice (for 6 people) and let it cook until it turns a pale blond colour; now pour in salted water or broth, and cook, covered, for 20 minutes. 'Take care that the rice is not too liquid; it is sufficient for the water to cover it by one finger's depth or less; when cooked turn it on to a serving dish and on top put, here and there, some flakes of butter and some grated cheese.'

The tomato sauce is served separately. '*Riso secco* may sound dull,' says Derek Hill, 'but the contrast of the hard hot rice and the cold tomato "salad" is absolutely delectable. It's most important I remember that the rice should not be shaken about or disturbed.'

An Omelette and a Glass of Wine
chosen by Derek Hill

SULEIMAN'S PILAFF
(*one of the most comforting dishes imaginable*)

Into a thick pan put 3 or 4 tablespoons of good dripping or oil, and when it is warm put in 2 cupfuls of rice and stir for a few minutes until the rice takes on a transparent look. Then pour over about 4 pints (2.25 l) of boiling water and cook very fast for about 12 minutes. The time of cooking varies according to the rice, but it should be rather under- than overdone.

In the meantime, have ready a savoury preparation of small pieces of cooked mutton, fried onions, raisins, currants, garlic, tomatoes and pine nuts, if you can get them, or roasted almonds, all sautéd in dripping with plenty of seasoning.

Put your strained rice into a thick pan and stir in the meat and onion mixture, add a little more dripping if necessary, and stir for a few minutes over a low flame before serving.

Hand with the pilaff a bowl of sour cream or yoghourt. Serves 4–5.

Mediterranean Food
chosen by George Lassalle

'The meeting with Elizabeth changed my rather jaundiced view of Cairo as a tawdry fly-infested slum. She was generous in sharing her food and her many devoted friends, and I found that, as the range of my culinary and social life expanded, I could face the world without my flywhisk.

'How can I try to describe the meals produced for guests by Elizabeth's Sudanese cook, Suleiman, master of the primus stove, when she herself has done it so inimitably in Fast and Fresh, one of the pieces in her collected journalism, *An Omelette and a Glass of Wine*.'

George Lassalle in his *Further Adventures of a Fish Cook*

Fast and Fresh

It isn't only the expense, the monotony and the false tastes of the food inside most tins and jars and packages which turn me every day more against them. The amount of space they take up, the clutter they make and the performance of opening the things also seem to me quite unnecessarily exasperating. However, even cookery journalists who spend most of their lives with a saucepan in one hand and a pen in the other can't dispense entirely with the kind of stores from which a meal can every now and again be improvised. What I personally require of such things is that there shall be no question whatever of their letting me down or giving me any unwelcome surprise. Out with any product which plays tricks or deteriorates easily. And out also with all the things of which one might say they'll do for an emergency. If something isn't good enough for every day, then it isn't good enough to offer friends, even if they have turned up demanding a meal without notice.

Twenty years ago, during the war years, which I spent in the Eastern Mediterranean, I became accustomed to planning meals from a fairly restricted range of provisions. Now I find myself returning more and more to the same sort of rather ancient and basic foods. They suit my taste and they are the kind of stores which will always produce a coherent and more or less complete meal, which is just what haphazardly bought tins and packages won't do. What happens when you have to open four tins, two jars and three packets in order to make one hasty cook-up is that you get a thoroughly unsatisfactory meal; and the contents of half-used tins and jars have got to be dealt with next day – or left to moulder in the fridge. Or else, like the suburban housewife in N. F. Simpson's *One Way Pendulum*, you've got to pay somebody to come in and eat the stuff up.

The only stores I had to bother about when I lived for a time in a small seashore village on an Ægean island were bread, olive oil, olives, salt fish, hard white cheese, dried figs, tomato paste, rice, dried beans, sugar, coffee and wine.

With fresh fish – mostly small fry or inkfish, but occasionally a treat such as red mullet or a langouste to be obtained from one of the fisher boys, with vegetables and fruit from the garden of the tavern-owner, eggs at about twopence a dozen, and meat – usually kid, lamb or pork – available only for feast days, the diet was certainly limited, but at least presented none of the meal-planning problems which, as I have learned from readers' letters, daily plague the better-off English housewife.

Subsequently, in war-time Egypt, I found, in spite of the comparative plenty and variety and the fact that in Greece I had often grumbled about the food, that the basic commodities of the Eastern Mediterranean shores were the ones which had begun to seem essential. Alexandrians, not surprisingly, knew how to prepare these commodities in a more civilized way than did the Greek islanders. The old-established merchant families of the city – Greek, Syrian, Jewish, English – appeared to have evolved a most delicious and unique blend of Levantine and European cookery and were at the same time most marvellously hospitable. I have seldom seen such wonderfully glamorous looking, and tasting, food as the Levantine cooks of Alexandria could produce for a party. And yet when you got down to analysing it, you would find that much the same ingredients had been used in dish after dish – only they were so differently treated, so skilfully blended and seasoned and spiced that each one had its own perfectly individual character and flavour.

In Cairo the dividing line between European and Eastern food was much sharper. It was uphill work trying to make English-trained Sudanese cooks produce interesting food. Most of them held a firm belief that the proper meal to set before English people consisted of roast or fried chicken, boiled vegetables and a pudding known to one and all as *grème garamel*.

My own cook, Suleiman, was a Sudanese who had previously worked only for Italian and Jewish families. He was erratic and forgetful, but singularly sweet-natured, devoted to his cooking pots and above all knew absolutely nothing of good, clean, English school-room food.

I used occasionally to try to teach him some French or English dish for which I had a nostalgic craving, but time for cooking was very limited, my kitchen facilities even more so, and on the whole I left him to his own devices.

So it came about that for three or four more years I lived mainly on rather rough but highly flavoured, colourful shining vegetable dishes, lentil or fresh tomato soups, delicious spiced pilaffs, lamb kebabs grilled over charcoal, salads with cool mint-flavoured yoghourt dressings, the Egyptian *fellahin* dish of black beans with olive oil and lemon and hard-boiled eggs – these things were not only attractive but also cheap and this was important because although Egypt was a land of fantastic plenty compared with war-time Europe, a lot of the better-class food was far beyond the means of young persons living on British Civil Service pay without foreign allowances, and tinned stores were out of the question because there was no room for them in the cave which my landlord was pleased to describe as a furnished flat.

What I found out when I returned to England to another five or six years of the awful dreary foods of rationing was that while my own standard of living in Egypt had perhaps not been very high, my food had always had some sort of life, colour, guts, stimulus; there had always been bite, flavour and inviting smells. Those elements were totally absent from English meals.

As imports came slowly back, I found once more, and still find, that it is the basic foods of the Mediterranean world which produce them in the highest degree. And it is curious how much more true variety can be extracted from a few of these basic commodities than from a whole supermarketful of products, none of which really taste of anything in particular.

So long as I have a supply of elementary fresh things like eggs, onions, parsley, lemons, oranges and bread and tomatoes – and I keep tinned tomatoes too – I find that my store cupboard will always provide the main part of an improvised meal. If this has to be made quickly it may be just a salad of anchovy fillets and black olives, hard-boiled eggs and olive oil, with bread and a bottle of wine. If it is a question of not being able to leave the house to go shopping, or of being too otherwise occupied to stand over the cooking pots, then there are white beans or brown lentils for slow cooking, and usually a piece of cured sausage or bacon to add to them, with onions and oil and possibly tomato. Apricots or other dried fruit can be baked in the oven at the same time, or I may have oranges for a fruit salad, and if it comes to the worst there'll at least be bread and butter and honey and jam. Or if I am given, say, forty-five minutes to get an unplanned meal ready – well, I have Italian and Patna rice and Parmesan, spices, herbs, currants, almonds, walnuts, to make a risotto or a pilaff. And perhaps tunny, with eggs to make mayonnaise, for an easy first dish. The countless number of permutations to be devised is part of the entertainment.

An Omelette and a Glass of Wine
chosen by Norma Grant

Elizabeth David had a great influence on me as a bride of twenty-one in 1950, still rationed. *Mediterranean Food* was only for inspiration – although I did cook Suleiman's Pilaff for a husband who had only eaten rice as a pudding, and raisins in a cake! I used *French Country Cooking* for making a tinned steak and kidney pudding 'presentable', as she put it. It also sent me to Parmigiani's emporium in Soho, where I was completely overawed and came out clutching a 2 oz brown paper bag of bay leaves – the smallest denomination I could think of when asked 'how many' – too frightened to ask for anything else in what was then a dark strange place with many unknown items hanging from hooks. I loved her for opening my mind to other worlds of which I was ignorant. I set off for Provence in 1952 with her in mind and tasted tomatoes and onions in oil and a French omelette for the first time.

Norma Grant

Mrs Leyel

House-bound after a temporarily incapacitating illness during the early nineteen-sixties I enjoyed my compulsory leisure re-reading old favourites in my cookery library. Some of the books had been my earliest kitchen companions and it was instructive to discover which had survived the passage of time and my own changes of taste, increased knowledge, experience of writing and publishing my own cookery books, and my travels in search of gastronomic information.

Among the authors who came out as sturdy survivors were, predictably, Marcel Boulestin and more surprisingly, Mrs Leyel of Culpeper House fame.

It was partly that Mrs Leyel's writing still appeared fresh and alluring even if her recipes struck me as sketchy in the extreme, more relevantly the growing realization, as I read through *The Gentle Art of Cookery*, that the book was yet another manifestation of the English love affair with Eastern food and Arabian Nights ingredients.

During the 1939 war years, circumstances had landed me in Alexandria and subsequently in Cairo. In my turn I fell under the spell of the beautiful food of the Levant – the warm flat bread, the freshly pressed tomato juice, the charcoal-grilled lamb, the oniony salads, the mint and yoghourt sauces, the sesame seed paste, the pistachios and the pomegranates and the apricots, the rosewater and the scented sweetmeats, and everywhere the warm spicy smell of cumin. Because I had so often pored over Mrs Leyel's cookery book without quite realizing what she was putting into my head, the food of the Levant appeared more attractive than perhaps I should have found it without the background of that book. Come to that, I wonder if I would ever have learned to cook at all had I been given a routine Mrs Beeton to learn from instead of the romantic Mrs Leyel, with her rather wild and imagination-catching recipes.

Below is the tribute to Hilda Leyel which came out of my re-reading of her books. It appeared in the *Spectator* in July 1963.

Although Hilda Leyel is better known as foundress of the Society of Herbalists and the Culpeper House herb shops, and as author of some half dozen books on herbs and herbal medicine than as a cookery writer, *The Gentle Art of Cookery* is a book which should have its place as a small classic of English culinary literature. My own feelings towards *The Gentle Art*, one of the first cookery books I ever owned, are of affection and gratitude as well as of respect.

One of the fallacies about the passing of judgement on cookery books is the application to the recipes of what is believed to be the acid test implied in the question do they work? A question which always reminds me of the Glendower–Hotspur exchange in *Henry IV*:

> I can call spirits from the vasty deep.
> Why so can I, or so can any man.
> But will they come when you do call for them?

The question I should have wanted to ask Glendower would have been not so much whether he expected the spirits to turn up as whether he really wanted them to and what he intended doing about it if they did.

What one requires to know about recipes is not so much do they work as what do they produce if they do work? A cookery book which gives foolproof recipes for seed cake and pears bottled in crème de menthe and straw potato nests is a good cookery book only to those in whose lives seed cake, pears bottled in crème de menthe and straw potato nests play an important part. A book which tells you as Mrs Leyel's did that you can make a purée from fresh green peas and eat it cold and that a cold roast duck will go very nicely with the purée is not necessarily a bad cookery book because it does not tell you for how long you must roast the duck nor how many pounds of peas you will need for the purée. I am not now speaking from the point of view of an experienced cook whose path has been crossed by a great many roasted ducks (and by no means all of them perfectly done, no matter how much one may know about timing, temperatures, basting, or not basting) and who with a modest effort of memory is able to recall that twelve ounces of shelled peas make just enough peas for two and that to get twelve ounces of shelled peas you must pick or buy one pound of peas in the pod, or perhaps two pounds if they are small or even three if they are very small. No. I am recalling rather the reactions to Mrs Leyel's book of a young woman quite ignorant of cooking techniques but easily, perhaps too easily, beguiled by the idea of food as unlike as could be to any produced by the conventional English cook of the time; and at this distance it is not difficult to perceive that Mrs Leyel's greatest asset was her ability to appeal to the imagination of the young.

Lack of technical instructions and vagueness as to quantities were faults – if faults they were – which didn't bother me because I did not know that they were faults, did not suspect what I was up against and would, I think, not have believed anybody who had tried to tell me.

Allowing for questions of temperament as well as of taste the young and totally inexperienced will usually prefer a book which provides stimulus to one which goes into technical details, makes strenuous efforts to keep the reader on the straight and keeps to the main roads of established cookery. At the age of nineteen one is better off having a stab at Mrs Leyel's 'marrons glacés in half an hour' than learning that the confection of professional marrons glacés involves no less than sixteen separate and distinct processes and that to make enough for two people is likely to mean a week's work.

Stimulus. That was the quality which Mrs Leyel's book provided, and in plenty, for she had the gift of making her recipes sound enticing. Re-reading The Gentle Art and some of those little books of Mrs Leyel's published by Routledge under the collective title of The Lure of Cookery, which includes Meals on a Tray, Picnics for Motorists, The Complete Jam Cupboard and Green Salads and Fruit Salads, it has to be admitted that Mrs Leyel suffered from incipient jellymania – the incidence of dishes set with gelatine and turned out of moulds is high even for an English cookery book – and here and there lost her head over a picturesque idea. A picnic dish of hollowed-out lemons stuffed with salmon mousse evokes an alluring freshness of sharp scent and cool flavour; how many dozen lemons I wonder would make enough containers for say four people and would the mousse still be in the lemons by the time you had driven the picnic basket from London to, say, the top of Firle Beacon? Small and carping criticisms, these, compared with the positive virtues of Mrs Leyel's attitude to cookery, the most attractive of which, I now see, was her love of fruit, vegetables and salad and her treatment of them almost as dishes to which meat and fish and poultry were little more than incidental accompaniments or scarcely necessary adjuncts of a meal. Indeed, *The Gentle Art* was notable for the way in which the recipes were classified. Appended to the vegetable chapter were two separate sections dealing with mushrooms and chestnuts respectively. How right of Mrs Leyel to emphasize the strangeness of these foods by separating them in the reader's mind from potatoes and sprouts and beans. The fruit chapter in *The Gentle Art* includes such rare recipes as a compote of pomegranates, an orange salad flavoured with sherry and lemon juice (a tablespoon of each to four oranges – she did give precise quantities when she knew that to overdo a flavouring would spoil the dish) and strewn with fresh mint leaves, a melon steeped in maraschino-flavoured syrup then filled with white grapes, white currants and pistachio nuts. In a five-page section devoted to recipes for almond creams, almond soups, almond puddings and almond pastes was a recipe for a rice cream to which ground almonds are added and 'when cool pour into a silver dish and sprinkle with powdered cinnamon and decorate with whole almonds'. When I first had Mrs Leyel's book nothing and nobody on earth could have sold me an English rice pudding, but a rice cream made with lemon and almonds and served in a silver dish, well, that gave one something to think about, silver dish and all.

Evidently much beguiled by the idea of Eastern cooking with its almonds and pistachio nuts, apricots and quinces, saffron and honey, rosewater, mint, dates and sweet spices, Mrs Leyel gave also in her book a little chapter of 'Dishes from the Arabian Nights' which, no doubt because of its vagueness and brevity, contained the true essence of magic and mystery.

'An Arabian way of cooking red mullet' – grilled in a sauce composed of tomatoes, onions, spices, shallots, salt, pepper, garlic, curry powder and saffron – sounded irresistible, so much so that even if you barely knew whether a red mullet was a bird, a flower or a fish you very quickly set about finding out. An hors-d'œuvre called *munkaczina*, alleged by Mrs Leyel to have been brought from the East by Anatole France (maddeningly, Mrs Leyel gives neither chapter nor verse), is a salad of sliced oranges strewn with finely chopped onion which in turn is covered with a layer of stoned black olives, the whole to be sprinkled with red pepper, salt and olive oil. Mrs Leyel certainly took one very far away indeed from the world of grapefruit and Scotch eggs to which a bed-sitter cook so easily succumbs. Her book turned out to be almost the equivalent in cookery of Walter de la Mare's unsurpassed poetry anthology *Come Hither* which had enlightened my childhood.

Spices, Salt and Aromatics
chosen by Alan Davidson

Elizabeth David was, to put it mildly, very widely read and was punctilious in acknowledging her debts, whether for information or inspiration, to other authors. But her most enthusiastic praise, of which this passage is a fine example, was bestowed sparingly, for she was a highly discriminating person.

Now, it so happened that Mrs Leyel's book was practically the first cookery book which I owned and used, and the quality of inspiration which it possesses still affects me almost fifty years later. Ah, the excitement when I first prepared Oeufs à la Constantinopolitaine! Judge then my delight when, long afterwards, I discovered that my next source of inspiration, Elizabeth, had herself derived so much information from the same author who gave me my first taste of it.

Alan Davidson

Officer of the Kitchen

Writing in the British India of the 1890s, under the pen name of Wyvern, Colonel Kenney-Herbert's cookery books were directed at the bewildered memsahibs who often found themselves transported from cosy suburban or small country houses into an uncomfortable situation as ruler of a whole hierarchy of Indian servants, incomprehensible in their ways and highly erratic in the performance of their duties.

Several good cookery books have been written by professional soldiers, and this is perhaps no coincidence. On the whole the most successful books of technical instruction, and this applies as much to cookery as to other subjects, are those in which the author expresses his views with soldierly precision and authority and is prepared to go to some lengths to defend them.

Colonel Kenney-Herbert's parade-ground voice is lowered in his books to lecture-room pitch, but commands no less attention for that. Copies of *Culinary Jottings*, *Fifty Breakfasts*, *Fifty Luncheons*, *Fifty Dinners*, *Vegetarian and simple Diet* are not uncommon in secondhand bookshops and I should recommend anyone with a taste for Victorian gastronomic literature to snap them up. His menu planning, modest though it was for his own times, is over-elaborate for ours, and many of his dishes now appear fussy and over-sauced; and, in the style of the period, his pages are peppered with italicized kitchen French. All the same his recipes for such things as consommés, omelettes, vegetables, curries, cold pies and pickled beef and tongues are so meticulous and clear, that the absolute beginner could follow them, yet at the same time he has much to teach even an experienced cook. His remarks about the conduct of the kitchen, the relationship between master and servant, his analysis of the shortcomings of Ramasamy, the Indian cook, compared and contrasted with those of Martha, his English counterpart, and his examination of the kitchen and its equipment provide illuminating and sometimes scarifying sidelights on domestic life in British India, where, wherever the memsahib's place may have been, it was certainly not in the kitchen.

The kitchen, in fact, was no part of the house proper, being 'part and parcel of a block of godowns (sheds) not unfrequently within easy access of the stables . . . the room is generally constructed with as little ventilation and light as possible, its position with regard to the sun is never thought of, and arrangements for its proper drainage are rare. There is no scullery or place for washing up . . . the consequence is that hard by many a cook-room in this Presidency, there is a noisome cesspool. . . . In the room itself there is no chimney you see, so the wall, up which the smoke is creeping towards an opening in the roof, is lined by an ancient coating of soot – the floor is of mother earth, greasy black and cruelly uneven in its surface.' 'How comes it to pass,' thunders the Colonel, 'that in India we continue year after year to be fully aware that the chamber set apart for the preparation of our food is, in ninety cases out of a hundred, the foulest in our premises – and are not ashamed? Why are so many of us satisfied with an equipment regarding the miserable inadequacy of which it would be as well to keep silence?' No question of the Colonel being one to keep silence. Not he. 'It is no exaggeration to say that not one Indian kitchen in twenty possesses a proper equipment . . . the batterie de cuisine of people with incomes of two thousand rupees a month, and more, is frequently inferior to that of a humble cottager in Britain.'

In Madras in the eighteen-seventies: 'there were many ladies who, when giving out stores for a dinner party, have no hesitation in using tins to the value of many rupees, but if asked for extra cream, butter, eggs, and gravy meat begin to consider themselves imposed upon.' It is the familiar trouble, that of the woman – there can be very few left today – who does not care to face the fact that the details of a meal may cost as much and need as much attention as its main features; in our idiom, the Colonel could simply have said that she had her priorities wrong. There must have been some pink faces in the Presidency in 1878 when *Culinary Jottings* appeared. The book was written, it must be remembered, at a period of change in the ways of living of British residents in India. Hitherto there had been little attempt to introduce a European atmosphere or European food into the houses of British officials. Curry and rice had been the accepted, routine food, and the cooks had been left to their own devices. When accelerated transport brought India nearer home the attempt to instil into wayward Indian servants the principles and virtues of English Victorian housekeepers focused attention upon the primitive conditions under which elaborate cookery was supposed to be carried out. 'Our dinners of today would indeed astonish our Anglo-Indian forefathers,' declares the Colonel. 'Quality has superseded quantity, and the molten curries and florid oriental compositions of the olden times – so fearfully and wonderfully made – have been gradually banished from our tables . . . men of moderate means have become hypercritical in the matter of their food, and demand a class of cooking which was not even attempted in the houses of the richest twenty years ago . . . dinners of sixteen or twenty, thoughtfully composed, are *de rigueur*; our menu cards discourse of dainty fare in its native French.'

No wonder that those squalid holes in the ground which passed for kitchens proved inadequate to the task. It is regrettable therefore, to have to record that seventy years later, as British rule in India was at its last gasp, the Colonel's reforming crusade had had sadly little effect. The kitchens which I myself had the opportunity of observing in New Delhi were still unbelievably primitive, and the food which came out of them an astonishing mixture of English nannies' puddings, cakes festooned in spectacular spun-sugar work, attempts at French dishes savagely flavoured with hot green chillies ('I make a French a-stew as good as you,' one of my Indian cooks remarked defiantly, and untruthfully), and, oddest of all, Edwardian fantasies of the school which liked to present food in any form but its own (mashed potatoes got up to resemble a roast chicken, mushrooms made out of meringue and the like).

This was just the sort of thing with which Colonel Kenney-Herbert had no patience whatever. When after thirty-two years' service in India, he returned to England, he wrote practical articles on the Arts of Dining, Cooking, and Management, which were published by the *Nineteenth Century*, and caused quite a stir. This unusual cavalry officer then proceeded to found a Commonsense Cookery Association, and eventually a school attached to this Association, with premises in Sloane Street. The Colonel's aims, as described to an interviewer from the *Epicure* magazine are worth quoting in full. They were so admirably put. Did anyone pay attention to them? Will they now, those cookery advisers whose faith is so firmly rooted in worked-over, worried, teased-up food?

'Briefly sketched the principles we advocate are economy in conjunction with thoroughly good cooking, no waste, and the production of good effects without the employment of ready-made sauces and flavourings. We are strongly opposed to over-ornamentation, the use of fancy colours in savoury cooking, and "poaching" on the confectioner's "preserves" by using forcing bags with pipe, etc., etc., in this branch. Finikin decoration – the making of "pretty-pretty" dishes at the cost of flavour and much valuable time – is a mistake in private houses where the kitchen staff consists of two or three persons. Besides, people of taste have declared against the practice. Simplicity in cooking, simplicity in materials, and simplicity in dishing up are consequently a feature in my teaching.'

The very thoroughness of Colonel Kenney-Herbert's instructions makes quotation of his recipes difficult. Just one of the shorter recipes from the chapter in *Culinary Jottings* entitled 'Our Curries' follows.

QUOORMA CURRY

'The "Quoorma", if well made, is undoubtedly an excellent curry. It used, I believe, to be one of the best at the Madras Club, in days when curries commanded closer attention than they do now.

'Cut up about a pound of very tender mutton without any bone, and stir the pieces about in a big bowl with a dessert-spoonful of pounded green ginger, and a sprinkling of salt. Melt a quarter of a pound of butter in a stew-pan, and throw into it a couple of white onions cut into rings, and a couple of cloves of garlic finely minced. Fry for about five minutes, and then add a teaspoonful of pounded coriander seed, one of pounded black pepper, half one of pounded cardamoms, and half one of pounded cloves. Cook this for five minutes, then put in the meat, and stir over a moderate fire until the pieces seem tender and have browned nicely. Now, take the pan from the fire, and work into it a strong infusion obtained from four ounces of well-pounded almonds, and a breakfast cupful of cream. Mix thoroughly, adding a dessert-spoonful of turmeric powder, and a tea-spoonful of sugar. Put the pan over a very low fire, and let the curry simmer as gently as possible for a quarter of an hour, finishing off with the juice of a couple of limes. This, it will be perceived, is another curry of a rich yet mild description. The total absence of chilli, indeed, constitutes, in the opinion of many, its chief attraction.'

Culinary Jottings for Madras, 'Wyvern' (Colonel Kenney-Herbert)
5th edition, 1885

Spices, Salt and Aromatics
selected by Myrtle Allen and Alan Davidson

Elizabeth David's first books did not have such a stunning impact on me as they seem to have had on everybody else. Perhaps this was because I was so immersed in farm and home in Co. Cork, with so many mouths to feed, that a better way to cook a turnip was more relevant.

It was the publication of *Spices, Salt and Aromatics* that finally won me over. I had spent three weeks in India and was so stunned by the spicy food that I suffered a sort of paralysis on my return home. Curry powder was thrown out and I found European food tasteless. I had no idea *how* to use fresh spices. To make matters worse, everyone expected me to produce new Indian miracles from the kitchen. Then I found the book and read:

> In the case of curries, the complexity and the preparation of the correct spices must have been a bit daunting for even the kitchen staffs of eighteenth- and nineteenth-century England, accustomed though they were to pounding and bashing, mashing and sieving. . . . Given the difficulties, it is not surprising that ready-prepared curry powders found and find such immediate acceptance in England, but for those who appreciate something a little less crude than dishes made with curry powders, a mixture of freshly pounded cardamom seeds, coriander, cumin, tumeric, and black or white pepper makes the basis of a very excellent spice compound, to my taste all the better for the absence of chillies, mustard seed, fenugreek and garlic. *But forget not the salt.* Forget not, also, that the development of the aromas of spices and spice mixtures is dependent upon the cooking

process. If you want to flavour a cooked dish, a sauce, a soup, or a kedgeree, say, with even just a sprinkling of a ready-made curry powder, the flavour will be enormously improved if the powder is put on a heat-proof plate in a low oven or in a dry frying-pan over a gentle heat for a few minutes before it is used.

Moreover, Elizabeth added Mrs Balbir Singh's tip for grinding spices in a coffee grinder.

This page unlocked a door. After that, I almost learned by heart her chapter on individual spices. Her recipes entered our repertoire and, I think, will stay on our tables for ever! Colonel Kenney-Herbert's Quoorma Curry and her own Lamb and Aubergine Stew in particular.   Myrtle Allen

One of the many features which I admired in Elizabeth was the generosity with which she acknowledged excellent writing by others when she found it – and especially if she found it in a book which was not well known but deserved to be. It is no coincidence that Colonel Kenney-Herbert is much better known now than he was when Elizabeth wrote about him. He is not alone in being, to some extent, rescued from relative obscurity by the deft and kindly use of her pen.   Alan Davidson

SAUCES

BOUILLON POUR LES SAUCES

When you have no meat stock available and when it is necessary to make a foundation for a sauce independently of the ingredients of the dish which it is to accompany, the following method will produce a well-flavoured clear stock without any great expense of either time or materials. It is a method simplified to the greatest possible degree for household cookery.

The ingredients are: ½ lb (225 g) each of lean stewing veal, preferably from the shin, and good quality minced beef; 2 scraped carrots, 2 halved tomatoes, 2 medium-sized onions, washed but not peeled, 2 sprigs of parsley with the stalks; no salt or pepper until a later stage.

Put all the ingredients in a small pot or saucepan which will go in the oven; cover with just over a pint (550 ml) water. Cover the pot and cook in a low oven (140°C/280°F/Gas Mark 1) for 1½ hours. Strain through an ordinary sieve. Leave in a bowl until the fat has set. Remove the fat. Heat up the stock, strain through a muslin to get rid of any sediment. There should now be about ¾ pint (425 ml) clear straw-coloured *bouillon* ready to make any sauce requiring stock.

As it has been cooked without salt, it can also be reduced to a thick syrup-like consistency, a sort of improvised meat glaze or *glace de viande*, in the following manner: put a large soup ladle of the *bouillon* into a 6-inch (15-cm) frying-pan or sauté pan. Let it bubble fairly gently for about 10 minutes, during which time you remove the little flecks of scum which come to the surface with a metal spoon dipped frequently in hot water. When the liquid starts to stick to the spoon and is reduced to about 2 tablespoons, it is done. The flavour is now three times as strong as it was to start with but, of course, had there been salt in it, it would have been uneatable. Pour it into a little jar, keep it covered, and when it is to be used heat it up in the jar standing in a pan of water. Although this has not the deep colour of professional meat glaze, it has the right amount of body to strengthen a sauce, plus a freshness and clarity of flavour unusual in the lengthily cooked, more elaborate confection of the chefs.

French Provincial Cooking

SAUCE BERCY
(*White wine and shallot sauce*)

A useful and excellent little hot sauce to be made when you have a small amount of natural concentrated gravy from a roast, a little jelly left over from a *bœuf mode* or some of the meat glaze described above; or for fish, some aromatic stock made from trimmings and bones, plus sliced onion and carrot.

Chop 4 shallots very finely. Put them in a small saucepan with half a claret glass of dry white wine. Let it boil until it is reduced by half. Add 2 tablespoons of the gravy (with, naturally, all fat removed) or melted meat glaze or fish stock; season; off the heat stir in 1 oz (30 g) good butter, a squeeze of lemon juice, and a small quantity of very finely chopped parsley.

Apart from grills of meat or fish, *sauce bercy* is delicious with eggs, fried or *sur le plat* or *en cocotte*, and with fried or grilled sausages.

French Provincial Cooking

SAUCE MESSINE

½ pint (280 ml) fresh cream, 2 oz (60 g) unsalted butter, a teaspoon of flour, 2 yolks of eggs, chervil, parsley, tarragon, 2 or 3 shallots, a lemon, a teaspoon of french mustard.

Chop the herbs and the shallots with a little lemon peel. Work the butter with the flour. Mix all the ingredients, except the lemon juice, together in a bowl, then put them in a double saucepan and heat, stirring all the time. Do not allow to boil. Season with salt and pepper. Squeeze in the juice of the lemon immediately before serving.

This sauce, which is perfectly exquisite, is intended to be served with a poached fish.

Auricoste de Lazarque, who gives the recipe in *La Cuisine Messine*, suggests that with this sauce the fish can be dispensed with; it can; it is perfect poured over hard-boiled eggs, or *œufs mollets*, either hot or cold.

Summer Cooking

SAUCE ROUILLE

1 clove garlic, 1 red pimento, breadcrumbs, olive oil.

Grill the pimento whole until the skin turns black. Take out the seeds, rub off the burnt skin, rinse the pimento in cold water, and pound it with the garlic. Soak a handful of breadcrumbs in water and squeeze them dry. Add them to the pimento and then stir in very slowly 4 tablespoons of olive oil. Thin the sauce with a few teaspoons of the stock from the fish with which it is to be served.

Mediterranean Food

CAPPON MAGRO SAUCE

A large bunch of parsley, a clove of garlic, a tablespoon of capers, 2 anchovy fillets, the yolks of 2 hard-boiled eggs, 6 green olives, fennel (either a bunch of the leaves or a slice of the fleshy root-stem), a handful of breadcrumbs, a large cupful of olive oil, a little vinegar.

Remove the thick stalks from the parsley, wash the leaves, put them into a mortar with a little salt and the clove of garlic. Pound until it is beginning to turn to a paste (this is not so arduous a task as might be supposed). Then add the capers, the anchovies, the stoned olives and the fennel. Continue pounding, and add the breadcrumbs, which should have been softened in a little milk or water and pressed dry. By this time there should be a thick sauce. Pound in the yolks of the hard-boiled eggs. Now start to add the olive oil, slowly, stirring vigorously with a wooden spoon as if making mayonnaise, and when the sauce is the consistency of a thick cream add about 2 tablespoonsful of vinegar.

This is the sauce which is poured over *cappon magro*, the celebrated Genoese fish salad made of about twenty different ingredients and built up into a splendid baroque edifice. The sauce is an excellent one for any coarse white fish, for cold meat, or for hard-boiled eggs.

Mediterranean Food

PURÉE D'OSEILLE
(*Sorrel sauce*)

Wash and chop very finely a small handful of sorrel leaves, not much more than 4 oz (120 g). Melt it gently in ½ oz (15 g) butter. Stir in, bit by bit, ¼ pint (150 ml) cream previously boiled (this is important, for sorrel is very acid and there is a risk of the cream curdling when the two come into contact) and then thin it with a tablespoon or two of the stock from the dish the sauce is to accompany – usually veal or fish. A very excellent little sauce, which also makes, in larger quantities, a good accompaniment to poached eggs.

It may be hard to believe, but a purée of green gooseberries, barely sweetened, with the same additions of cream and stock, is almost indistinguishable from a sorrel purée.

French Provincial Cooking
chosen by Caroline Conran

The fact that I know about sorrel is due to Elizabeth, and I think one of the best things to do in springtime is, as she suggests, to throw a handful of sorrel, finely cut into a chiffonade, into soup. It makes a huge difference to, for example, nettle or leek soup. One of the few *nouvelle cuisine* dishes which has lasted well is the combination of salmon with sorrel sauce, but in fact this delicious sauce is excellent with white fish too – as she pointed out in 1960.

Caroline Conran

MAIONESE

Italian mayonnaise is made only with eggs and olive oil, and sometimes a little lemon juice. Italians think it exceedingly comical that mustard should be added, as it often is in France. They may well be right, for the mayonnaise in Italy, when really good oil is used, is perfectly delicious, and the cooks are, as always, prodigal with the eggs.

To make a really good mayonnaise for four or five people use 3 yolks of eggs, about 8 fl oz (225 ml) olive oil, and salt.

Put the yolks of the eggs into a heavy bowl or mortar which will not slide about on the table (or stand the bowl on a newspaper or cloth). Stir the yolks with a wooden spoon for about a minute before adding 1 teaspoonful of salt, then start putting in the oil. It must be stirred in drop by drop until the mayonnaise starts to attain its characteristic consistency, so it is easier to have it in a small jug with a narrow lip rather than in the bottle. After a few minutes several drops can go in at a time, and gradually more and more until in the end the oil is being poured in in a thin but steady stream.

Stir all the time; the mayonnaise should be very thick, with a consistency almost like thick paint. If it starts to lose its shiny gloss it is a sign that the eggs have absorbed enough olive oil. The mayonnaise will not necessarily curdle, but it will become a creamy sauce rather than the jelly-like substance which sticks to the spoon and falls with such a delicious plop on to the plate. A very few drops of lemon juice can be added at the last moment. Should the oil have been added too recklessly or the mayonnaise curdle (that is, when the oil separates from the eggs), break another yolk into a clean bowl, stir it, add a little of the curdled mayonnaise, and then the rest, a spoonful at a time.

There is no necessity whatever to stand the bowl on ice when making mayonnaise, to keep the kitchen at some special temperature, or in any way to consider its confection as a mystery, a conjuring trick, or a technical achievement to be attempted only by highly skilled cooks.

MAIONESE VERDE

To a plain mayonnaise add a handful of pounded parsley or basil, pine nuts, and pistachio nuts.

Italian Food

SAUCE VERTE

This is, I think, one of the great achievements of the simpler French cooking, but when I say simple I mean simple in conception rather than in execution, for it is hard work to make in any quantity, and so far as I know there is no short cut.

First prepare a very thick mayonnaise with 2 or even 3 egg yolks, ⅓ to ½ pint (180–280 ml) of best olive oil, and a few drops of wine or tarragon vinegar. The other ingredients are 10 fine spinach leaves, 10 sprigs of watercress, 4 of tarragon, 4 of parsley. Pick the leaves of the watercress, tarragon and parsley from the stalks. Put all these leaves with the spinach into boiling water for 2 or 3 minutes. Strain, squeeze them quite dry, pound them, and put the resulting paste through a fine sieve. It should emerge a compact and dry purée. Stir it gradually into the mayonnaise but leave this final operation as late as possible before the sauce is to be served.

To the salmon of the summer months, lacking the exquisite curdy flesh of the early part of the year, *sauce verte* supplies the interest which might otherwise be lacking, but it need not be confined to fish. An hors-d'œuvre of hard-boiled eggs with this green sauce is just that much grander than an ordinary egg mayonnaise. It never fails to please.

French Provincial Cooking

SAUCE MOUTARDE AUX ŒUFS
or SAUCE BRETONNE

This is an egg and butter sauce reduced to its greatest possible simplicity. It has no relation to the *sauce bretonne* of the chefs.

Stir the yolks of 2 eggs in a bowl; add a pinch of salt and pepper and a teaspoon of yellow French mustard; then a few drops of tarragon vinegar; then a heaped teaspoon of fresh herbs finely chopped. These can be chosen according to what dish the sauce is to go with; fennel and parsley for fish; tarragon and chervil for steak; mint for grilled lamb cutlets, and so on. Have ready 2 oz (60 g) unsalted butter just barely melted over hot water, and not at all hot. Add this gradually to the eggs and stop stirring as soon as it has reached the consistency of a mayonnaise.

Sometimes, if the sauce is made in advance, it goes grainy as the butter coagulates. The remedy is to stand the bowl inside another containing a little hot water; stir until the sauce is smooth again.

This, although so little known, is an immensely useful sauce for those with little time to spare, for it can take the place of *hollandaise* or *béarnaise* to serve with steak, fish, grilled chicken, and so on, and for those who cannot eat olive oil it can even do duty instead of mayonnaise. It has not, however, the body which these sauces have, so it should always be served separately in a sauce-boat, not used as a *coating* sauce.

French Provincial Cooking

SALSA DI NOCI
(*Walnut sauce*)

2 oz (60 g) shelled walnuts, 1 coffee-cupful of oil, 2 tablespoonfuls of breadcrumbs, 1½ oz (45 g) butter, 1 large bunch of parsley, salt and pepper, 2 tablespoonfuls of cream or milk.

Take the skins off the shelled walnuts after pouring boiling water over them. Pound them in a mortar. Add the parsley, after having picked off all the large and coarse stalks. Put a little coarse salt with the parsley in the mortar – this will make it easier to pound. While reducing the parsley and the walnuts to a paste add from time to time some of the butter, softened or just melted by the side of the fire. Stir in the breadcrumbs and, gradually, the oil. The result should be a thick paste, very green; it need not be absolutely smooth, but it must be well amalgamated. Stir in the cream or milk. Season with a little more salt and ground black pepper. A bizarre sauce, but excellent with *tagliatelle*, or with fish, or as a filling for sandwiches.

Italian Food

SAUCE TOMATE *or* COULIS DE TOMATES

Although it is so well known, I find that many amateur cooks are uncertain about how to make a good tomato sauce from the fresh fruit. It is very useful and very easy but, all the same, demands a certain care in the seasoning, and judgement as to the length of the cooking time. Here it is, in its simplest form, without stock, wine, thickening or meat.

Ingredients are 1 small onion, 1¼–1½ lb (550–675 g) very ripe tomatoes, ½ oz (15 g) butter, 1 tablespoon of olive oil, 1 teaspoon salt, a lump of sugar, a teaspoon of chopped celery leaves or parsley, a clove of garlic, a couple of fresh or dried basil leaves if available.

Melt the butter and olive oil in a shallow wide pan and in this cook the finely sliced onion very gently until it turns yellow. Add the chopped tomatoes and all the other ingredients. Simmer over a moderate heat for 15–20 minutes. Put through the food mill. If it is at all watery, put it back into the rinsed-out pan and set it over a gentle heat until it has dried out a little. Taste for seasoning, as some tomatoes need more sugar than others.

As well as being the traditional accompaniment of spaghetti dishes, a tomato sauce goes well with fried chicken, with all manner of croquettes, with fried steak, and with fried eggs.

French Provincial Cooking

FRESH TOMATO SAUCE

This is an excellent sauce to make when tomatoes, either home-grown or imported, are plentiful and relatively cheap. The method of cooking makes it particularly useful for people who cook with solid fuel stoves.

Put from 2–3 lb (900 g–1.4 kg) or more, of very ripe tomatoes, whole and unskinned, into an earthenware or other oven pot. Add nothing whatsoever. Cover the pot. Put it into a moderate oven (170°C/330°F/Gas Mark 3), and leave it for almost an hour, or until the tomatoes are soft and squashy. Press them through a sieve or a mouli.

Heat the resulting purée in a thick saucepan, adding, for every pound (450 g) of tomatoes, a teaspoon each of salt and sugar, and optionally, a little ground ginger or cinnamon, dried or fresh basil or marjoram, and crushed garlic if you like. A tablespoon of port per pound (450 g) of tomatoes has a wonderfully mellowing effect on the sauce. For immediate use, cook the sauce as little as possible so that it retains its freshness of flavour and bright colour.

This is, basically, the tomato sauce given by Mrs Rundell in *A New System of Domestic Cookery* published in 1806. Mrs Rundell, whose formula appears to be one of the earliest published English recipes for tomato sauce, added chilli vinegar, pounded garlic and ground ginger to the tomato pulp, directed that the sauce should be stored in small, wide-mouthed bottles, well corked, and in a dry cool place. The sauce was intended for 'hot or cold meats'.

Mrs Rundell's method of baking the tomatoes is a most useful one to know. To my taste it is best minus the original vinegar and garlic. More or less reduced according to taste and stored in the refrigerator for current use (don't try to store it by Mrs Rundell's rather too rough and ready method) it is exceedingly good with pasta and with egg dishes. It can make also the basis of a luxurious and richly flavoured tomato soup.

Spices, Salt and Aromatics

RAGÙ

This is the true name of the Bolognese sauce which, in one form or another, has travelled round the world. In Bologna it is served mainly with *lasagne verdi*, but it can go with many other kinds of *pasta*. The ingredients to make enough sauce for six generous helpings of *pasta* are 8 oz (225 g) lean beef minced, 4 oz (120 g) chicken livers, 3 oz (90 g) bacon or uncooked ham (both fat and lean), 1 carrot, 1 onion, 1 small piece of celery, 3 tablespoonfuls of concentrated tomato purée, 1 wineglassful of white wine, 2 wineglassfuls of stock or water, butter, salt and pepper, nutmeg.

Cut the bacon or ham into very small pieces and brown them gently in a small saucepan in about ½ oz (15 g) butter. Add the onion, the carrot and the celery, all finely chopped. When they have browned, put in the raw minced beef, and then turn it over and over so that it all browns evenly. Now add the chopped chicken livers, and after 2 or 3 minutes the tomato purée, and then the white wine. Season with salt (having regard to the relative saltiness of the ham or bacon), pepper, and a scraping of nutmeg, and add the meat stock or water. Cover the pan and simmer the sauce very gently for 30–40 minutes. Some Bolognese cooks add at the last 1 cupful of cream or milk to the sauce, which makes it smoother. Another traditional variation is the addition of the *ovarine* or unlaid eggs which are found inside the hen, especially in the spring when the hens are laying. They are added at the same time as the chicken livers and form small golden globules when the sauce is finished. When the *ragù* is to be served with *spaghetti* or *tagliatelle*, mix it with the hot *pasta* in a heated dish so that the *pasta* is thoroughly impregnated with the sauce, and add a good piece of butter before serving. Hand the grated cheese separately.

This is the recipe given me by Zia Nerina, a splendid woman, titanic of proportion but angelic of face and manner who, in the 1950s owned and ran the Trattoria Nerina in Bologna. Zia Nerina's cooking was renowned far beyond the confines of her native city.

Italian Food
chosen by Elisabeth Lambert Ortiz

I first met Elizabeth when I was back in England, after years all over the world with my Mexican diplomat husband, César Ortiz Tinoco, for the Glenfiddich presentations. She told me then that the book she had most enjoyed writing was the Italian one, which was also my favourite.

I have a special affection for her piece on Mayonnaise. When I was about twelve, I sent off for the *Royal Baking Powder Cookbook* and in it found a proper recipe for mayonnaise – so no one has an excuse for the abomination called salad cream. I also love her piece on Pesto, written so long ago now. I am a fusspot, a purist, and so I rejoiced in the piece on Ragù, which points out that it isn't Spaghetti Bolognese.   Elisabeth Lambert Ortiz

ENGLISH SALAD SAUCE

Authentic mayonnaise is, as we all know, made with raw egg yolks and olive oil. In England it has never achieved true popularity, perhaps because as a nation we have always tended to regard olive oil as medicinal rather than as a marvellous and necessary table delicacy. It was English salad sauce, made with cooked egg yolks and cream, that was the basis of the commercial salad cream, wrongly called mayonnaise, which became, and remains, one of the major culinary disasters of this country. It is the acetic acid, the flour, the dried egg, the stabilizers, the emulsifiers and all the bag of trick ingredients which make English salad sauces, creams, and so-called mayonnaise the laughing stock of Europe. With the original recipe there was nothing wrong. Its name was perfectly explanatory, its ingredients honourable. As a sauce in its own right it is exceedingly good. With some salads – not with lettuce or straight green salads, but with compound cooked vegetable salads – and particularly with fish salads and with rich fish such as salmon it is perhaps preferable to mayonnaise because the combination of cooked egg yolk with cream produces a lighter sauce than that made of raw yolks with olive oil. As against that point the sauce is very easy to make. Here is the authentic pre-1914 recipe:

Ingredients: 1 large or 2 small hard-boiled egg yolks and 1 raw egg yolk; seasonings of salt, sugar, cayenne; ¼ pint (150 ml) double cream; 1 to 2 teaspoons of lemon juice or tarragon vinegar.

Pound the hard-boiled yolk to a paste, with a few drops of cold water. Stir in the raw yolk. Add seasonings with caution. Under-seasoning can be corrected later. Over-seasoning cannot. Then stir in, little by little, the cream. Finally add the lemon juice or vinegar.

This sauce is best made an hour or two ahead of time, the acid of the lemon or vinegar causing the cream to thicken to the correct consistency. To the basic mixture can be added, according to what may be available and the food which the sauce is to accompany, chopped herbs, anchovy fillets, finely grated horseradish, mustard.

Spices, Salts and Aromatics

CUMBERLAND SAUCE

This best of all sauces for cold meat – ham, pressed beef, tongue, venison, boar's head or pork brawn – can be made in small quantities and in a quick and economical way as follows:

With a potato parer cut the rind, very thinly, from two large oranges. Slice this into matchstick strips. Plunge them into boiling water and let them boil 5 minutes. Strain them.

Put them in a bowl with 4 tablespoons of redcurrant jelly, a heaped teaspoon of yellow Dijon mustard, a little freshly milled pepper, a pinch of salt and optionally a sprinkling of ground ginger.

Place this bowl over a saucepan of water, and heat, stirring all the time, until the jelly is melted and the mustard smooth. It may be necessary at this stage to sieve the jelly in order to smooth out the globules which will not dissolve. Return the sieved jelly to the bowl standing over its pan of hot water.

Now add 7 to 8 tablespoons (2½ fl oz/75 ml) of medium tawny port. Stir and cook for another 5 minutes. Serve cold. There will be enough for four people.

Made in double or triple quantities this sauce can be stored in covered jars and will keep for several weeks.

N.B. On no account should cornflour, gelatine or any other stiffening be added to Cumberland sauce. The mixture thickens as it cools, and the sauce is invariably served cold, even with a hot ham or tongue.

Spices, Salt and Aromatics
chosen by Kit Chapman

The name of Elizabeth David is instantly associated with the foods and cooking of France, Italy and the Mediterranean, and as a consequence it is widely assumed that she had little interest in or regard for England's culinary traditions. This, of course, is untrue.

For the past twenty years, and with the support of a succession of talented young chefs, I have tried to rehabilitate the gastronomic credentials of the British kitchen on the menus of the Castle Hotel. It has been a modest campaign waged against a tide of antipathy which, I think, is slowly beginning to dissolve as a new and more inquisitive generation of cooks discovers the joys of the British table. My beliefs and determination to pursue this line have been given backbone by the eloquence and authority of Mrs David's less populist writings.

From her *Spices, Salt and Aromatics* I have chosen Cumberland Sauce, Potted Tongue and Salted Almonds. 'Cumberland sauce', writes Elizabeth David, 'is certainly one of our most delicious sauces.' I agree. But although she believes potted tongue is 'the best and most subtle of all English potted meat inventions', we prefer game, duck, rabbit and pigeon, served with a few spiced pears. Very English. Very eighteenth century (when England was on a gastronomic high). And very delicious.   Kit Chapman

The Christmas Pudding is
Mediterranean Food

A white cube of a house, two box-like rooms and a nice large kitchen. No bath. No plumbing. A well and a fig tree outside the front door and five yards away from the Aegean. On the horizon a half circle of the islands of Andros, Tinos, Seriphos. In the village, about three dozen houses, two churches (one Orthodox, one Roman Catholic), one provision shop. Down on the shore one shack of a tavern, and in the village street a more important one, stacked with barrels and furnished with stout wooden tables. Christo, the owner of this second tavern, was one of the grandees of the village. He operated, in addition to the tavern, a small market garden, and sold his produce in the island's capital seven miles away. He also had a brother-in-law, called Yannaki. Yannaki was that stock Greek village character, the traveller come home after experiencing glamorous doings and glorious events in far-off places. True to type, he spoke a little Anglo-American and, more uncommonly, a little French; he was always on hand to help out if foreigners came to the village. He seemed a kind and cheerful man, rich too; at any rate, he owned a spare donkey and was prepared to lend me this animal, along with a boy to talk to it, so that I could ride into the town when I needed to stock up with fresh supplies of beans and oil, bottled wine, cheese, dried fruit, and boxes of the delicious Turkish Delight which was – still is – a speciality of the island.

Before long it transpired that the greatest favour I could bestow upon Yannaki in return for the loan of his transport would be some tomato soup in tins and perhaps also a jar or two of English 'picklies'.

Handing over to one of the brothers who owned the hotel and the Turkish Delight factory in the capital a bundle of drachmae which would have kept me in wine and cheese for a month, I got in return four tins, vintage, of the required soup. Of English piccalilli, which I took it was what Yannaki meant by picklies, there was no sign nor sniff, and very relieved I was. Many more such exotic luxuries, and it would be cheaper for me to leave my seashore village for Athens and a suite at the Grande-Bretagne.

The tomato soup gave Yannaki and Christo and their families a great deal of pleasure. It was the real thing, no mistaking it. In return I was offered baskets of eggs, lemons, oranges, freshly dug vegetables and salads, glass after glass of wine in the tavern. And, then, next time the picklies? I *was* English, wasn't I? Then I should certainly be able to produce these delicacies.

For days I scanned the horizon for sight of an English yacht. I could, in my turn, have bartered fresh vegetables and fruit for the jars of mustard pickles which I knew must grace the table of any English *lordos* grand enough to be roaming the Aegean seas. It was late in the season. That way no yacht came.

Anybody who has experience of the stubborn determination, courteous but quite unrelenting, of an Aegean islander when he has made up his mind about something will understand why, in the end, I was obliged to set to and make those confounded pickles myself.

Into the town then for mustard, vinegar, spices. Long mornings I spent cutting up cauliflower and onions, carrots and cucumbers. Afternoons, I squatted in my kitchen fanning the charcoal fires into a blaze brisk enough to boil the brew. The jars, the only ones I could find, which I had bought to pack the stuff in were of one oke capacity, three pounds, near enough. Also they were of rough earthenware, unglazed, and exceptionally porous. Before I could even give the filled jars away they were half empty again, the liquid all soaked up by that sponge-like clay. Every one had to be replenished with a fresh batch of pickle. To me the mixture seemed fairly odd, but with my village friends it was successful enough. In fact, on the barter system, I could have lived for nothing so long as I was prepared to dedicate my life to pickle-making. Before long, though, it was getting on for December, and references to 'Xmas pudding' began to crop up in the tavern talk. By now I had learned a little more about these kindly village tyrants. If Christmas pudding they wanted, Christmas pudding I should have to give them. But not, so help me, made on the improvized happy-go-lucky system I'd used for the mustard pickles. Once more then into the town (I never could stay five seconds on a horse or a mule or even a bicycle, but by that time I had at least found out how to sit on a donkey and get the animal moving over stony paths and up and down steep hills) to telegraph home for a recipe. When it arrived, it turned out to be one of those which calls for a pound of almost everything you can think of, which was lucky. Simply by multiplying each by three it was all turned into okes. A large-scale Christmas party was now simmering, so there wouldn't, I thought, be an oke too much.

Now, all those with their fine talk of the glories of Old English fare, have they ever actually made Christmas pudding, in large quantities, by Old English methods? Have they, for instance, ever tried cleaning and skinning, flouring, shredding, chopping beef kidney suet straight off the hoof? Have they ever stoned bunch after bunch of raisins hardly yet dry on the stalk and each one as sticky as a piece of warm toffee? And how long do they think it takes to bash up three pounds of breadcrumbs without an oven in which they could first dry the loaves? Come to that, what would they make of an attempt to boil, and to keep on the boil for nine to ten hours on two charcoal fires let into holes in the wall, some dozen large puddings? Well, I had nothing much else to do in those days and quite enjoyed all the work, but I'd certainly never let myself in for such an undertaking again. Nor, indeed, would I again attempt to explain the principles of a hay-box and the reasons for making one to peasants of whose language I had such a scanty knowledge and who are in any case notoriously unreceptive to the idea of having hot food, or for that matter hot water or hot coffee, hotter than tepid.

All things considered, my puddings turned out quite nicely. The ones which emerged from the hay-box were at just about the right temperature – luke-warm. They were sweet and dark and rich. My village friends were not as enthusiastic as they had been about the mustard pickles. What with so many of the company having partici-pated in the construction of the hay-box, my assurances that the raisins and the currants grown and dried there on the spot in the Greek sun were richer and more juicy than the artificially dried, hygienically treated and much-travelled variety we got at home, my observations on the incomparable island-made candied citron and orange peel (that was fun to cut up too) given me by the neighbours, and the memorable scent of violets and brilliantine given to the puddings by Athenian brandy, a certain amount of the English mystery had disappeared from our great national festive dish.

Spices, Salt and Aromatics
chosen by Celia Denney, Jackie Mallorca
and Anne Wilson

I find that it is a great mistake to pick up any of Elizabeth David's books unless you have an hour or two at your disposal, a comfortable chair and a pot of tea at your elbow. Her prose is as seductive as the dulcet tones of Greek sirens.

It is almost impossible to choose a favourite, but I do know that my education would be the poorer had she not fallen, in her own words, 'under the spell of the beautiful food of the Levant – the warm flat bread, the freshly pressed tomato juice, the charcoal-grilled lamb, the oniony salads, the mint and yoghourt sauces, the sesame seed paste, the pistachios and the pomegranates and the apricots, the rosewater and the scented sweetmeats, and everywhere the warm spicy smell of cumin.'

Living in northern California as I do, with its Mediterranean climate and wealth of fresh ingredients, it is quite easy to duplicate these dishes. They suit the land. Perhaps it is for this reason that I take such pleasures in her *Spices, Salt and Aromatics in the English Kitchen*, and so appreciate her commentary on the English preoccupation with the condiments of the near and far east.

At one point, many years ago, Elizabeth lived for a while on the Greek island of Syros. Delighted with this exotic foreigner in their midst, her Greek friends and neighbours were determined that she should provide them with English spiced 'picklies' and aromatic Christmas puddings. And so, under the most primitive of conditions, she made them both. Her description of these Herculean labours is a pure delight to read.   Jackie Mallorca

SWEET DISHES AND CAKES

MONTE BIANCO

1 lb (450 g) chestnuts, ½ lb (225 g) sugar, 4 fl oz (120 ml) cream, salt.

Score the chestnuts across the rounded sides and either boil them for 10 minutes or roast them in a slow oven for 15 minutes. While they are still hot (but not *red* hot – there is no necessity for burnt and bleeding fingers) remove the shells and the inner skins. Cover the chestnuts with plenty of water and simmer them for about an hour until they are perfectly tender. Strain off the water and mash the chestnuts with the sugar and a good pinch of salt. Put them through a potato ricer or a food mill with fairly large holes, held over the dish in which they are to be served. As the sieved chestnuts come out of the ricer they are to fall lightly into a cone-shaped mound.

Over the prepared chestnuts pour the whipped cream (flavoured, if you like, with a little brandy or Marsala or rum), but do not press it down or attempt to put the pudding into shape, or it will lose its lightness. If possible, prepare the *Monte Bianco* only a short while before it is to be served. Enough for 4.

Italian Food
chosen by Jacqueline Korn

CRÉMETS D'ANGERS

Whip ½ pint (280 ml) thick cream until it is absolutely stiff. Fold in the beaten whites of 3 eggs; turn into a clean muslin and place in little heart-shaped baskets or pierced moulds and leave to drain in a cool place for about 12 hours. Turn out on to a dish and cover with fresh cream. Serve with sugar. The best of all accompaniments for strawberries, raspberries and apricots. Serves 4.

Summer Cooking
chosen by Richard Hosking

'The best of all accompaniments for strawberries, raspberries and apricots' – what more could we want than the best? I have made this recipe more often than any other of Elizabeth David's. I love it. The charming, heart-shaped white china moulds used to be available at the Elizabeth David shop in Bourne Street (which is where I bought my set) but in practice I prefer to use metal ones: they give a clearer shape and are less cumbersome to use. I suppose you could simply line a colander with muslin and make the recipe in that – but the individual heart-shaped *crémet* is an important part of this recipe's great appeal.   R. Hosking

LEMON SOUFFLÉ

4 eggs, 3 tablespoons caster sugar, the juice and rind of one lemon: this is enough for 2 people.

Beat the yolks of the eggs with the sugar, the grated rind of the lemon and the juice, for several minutes. Whip the whites and fold them in. Pour into a buttered soufflé dish and cook for 10–12 minutes in a medium-hot oven (200°C/400°F/Gas Mark 6).

Soufflés made without the addition of flour are very light and creamy, but the whole operation should be performed with speed and the exact heat of the oven and the timing can only be learnt by experience.

French Country Cooking
chosen by Hilary Spurling

As a student in the 1960s I cooked my first omelette, my first spaghetti bolognese and my first beef stew (a Greek *stiphado* simmered over a whispering flame until 'the sauce is reduced almost to the consistency of jam') from a paperback copy of *Mediterranean Food*. For a beginner, Elizabeth David was the most consoling and encouraging of cooks. Others offered lists of utensils I hadn't got, comparative analyses of basic principles which bored me stiff, pages of step-by-step instructions I couldn't follow. With her, all you had to do was read the relevant paragraph, close the book and cook the recipe which, in my experience, *never failed*.

Books, plays, paintings, clothes, even friends have come and gone in my life since then but Elizabeth David's recipes have remained a staple for nearly forty years. My favourite could be any one of a dozen of her delicate French vegetable soups. Or something as rich and strange as Brillat Savarin's buttered spinach, and the Italian peasant's sweet-and-sour jugged hare, finished off with a glass three-quarters full of vinegar, sugar and grated chocolate. Dishes I could cook in my sleep include her fasoulia, her *pommes dauphinoises*, French apple tart, cinnamon ice cream, and her suave, coriander-flavoured cold pork cooked in milk. But if I have to choose one it is the Lemon Soufflé which has the lightness, simplicity and elegance of the very best minimalist art.

Hilary Spurling

CRÈME AUX FRAISES

Hull ¾ lb (340 g) strawberries and sieve them to a pulp, reserving half a dozen. Whisk ½ pint (280 ml) double cream, fold in one stiffly whisked egg white, then the strawberry pulp. Add a little caster sugar, about 2 or 3 tablespoons. Arrange the cream piled up in a shallow bowl; stir in the reserved whole strawberries before serving. Enough for 4 people.

This is a most exquisite cream which can also be made with raspberries or, most beautiful of all, *fraises des bois*. The recipe comes from a dictionary of French cooking of the period of the Second Empire.

French Provincial Cooking
chosen by Stafford Whiteaker

After a lengthy description of her ideal kitchen in which almost everything was hanging on a wall, my seven-year-old son anxiously asked Elizabeth David: 'What happens if your wall falls down?' Without hesitation, she replied, 'Open another bottle of wine.' This answer, containing as it does the essential ingredient of getting on with life, was typical of her response to my announcement that I was going to write a book devoted to the strawberry. 'You're mad, but that isn't important,' she said. 'Do it!'

Her support came in the form of postcards, letters, telephone calls and messages through mutual friends when some random thought had occurred or fact was discovered about the strawberry – ices, creams, sauces and waters; memories of strawberries when she lived in France, the recalling of a meal when strawberries had appeared at table. Stafford Whiteaker

SYLLABUB

It was Herbert Beerbohm Tree's wedding day. His half-brother had been called in to act as best man in place of his real brother who had vanished to Spain. At the celebration breakfast there were syllabubs. Herbert was beguiled by the biblical rhythm of the name. 'And Sillabub, the son of Sillabub reigned in his stead,' he intoned. His stepbrother, half-scandalized and wholly impressed by Herbert's levity, never forgot the episode. He had been ten years old at the time of Herbert's wedding; his name was Max Beerbohm; the story is recounted in Lord David Cecil's *Max, A Biography*; the date was 1882, and sillabub, added Max, was then his favourite dish.

Max Beerbohm's generation must have been the last to which the delicious syllabub was a familiar childhood treat. Already for nearly a century the syllabub had been keeping company with the trifle, and in due course the trifle came to reign in the syllabub's stead; and before long the party pudding of the English was not any more the fragile whip of cream contained in a little glass, concealing within its innocent white froth a powerful alcoholic punch, but a built-up confection of sponge fingers and ratafias soaked in wine and brandy, spread with jam, clothed in an egg-and-cream custard, topped with a syllabub and strewn with little coloured comfits. Came 1846, the year that Mr Alfred Bird brought forth custard powder; and Mr Bird's brain-child grew and grew until all the land was covered with custard made with custard powder and the trifle had become custard's favourite resting-place. The wine and lemon-flavoured cream whip or syllabub which had crowned the trifle had begun to disappear. Sponge cake left over from millions of nursery teas usurped the place of sponge fingers and the little bitter almond macaroons called ratafias. Kitchen sherry replaced Rhenish and Madeira and Lisbon wines. Brandy was banished. The little coloured comfits – sugar-coated coriander seeds and caraways – bright as tiny tiddlywinks, went into a decline and in their stead reigned candied angelica and nicely varnished glacé cherries.

Now seeking means to combat the Chemicals Age, we look to our forebears for help. We find that the syllabub can replace the synthetic ice cream which replaced the trifle which replaced the syllabub in the first place. The ingredients of a syllabub, we find, are simple and sumptuous. The skill demanded for its confection is minimal, the presentation is basic and elegant. Swiftly, now, before the deep-freezers, the dehydrators and the emulsifiers take the syllabub away from us and return it transformed and forever despoiled, let us discover how it was made in its heyday and what we can do to recapture something of its pristine charm.

In the beginning then, in the seventeenth and eighteenth centuries, there were three kinds of syllabub. There was the syllabub mixed in a punch bowl on a basis of cider or ale and sometimes both, sweetened with sugar and spiced with cinnamon or nutmeg. Into the bowl the milkmaid milked the cow so that the new warm milk fell in a foam and froth on to the cider. The contents of the bowl were left undisturbed for an hour or two, by which time a kind of honeycombed curd had formed on the top, leaving alcoholic whey underneath. Sometimes, on top of the milk curd, a layer of thick fresh cream was poured. This syllabub was more a drink than a whip, a diversion for country parties and rustic festivals.

Co-existing with the syllabub of pastoral England was one made with wine and spirits instead of cider and ale, and with cream instead of milk. This mixture was a more solid one. It was about four-fifths sweetened whipped cream, to be spooned rather than drunk out of the glasses in which it was served, and one-fifth of wine and whey which had separated from the whip, and which you drank when you reached the end of the cream. Then, at some stage, it was discovered that by reducing the proportions of wine and sugar to cream, the whip would remain thick and light without separating. This version was called a solid or everlasting syllabub. One eighteenth-century author, E. Smith, whose *Complete Housewife*, published in 1727, was also the first cookery book to be printed in America, claimed that her Everlasting Syllabubs would remain in perfect condition for nine or ten days, although at their best after three or four.

My own version of Everlasting Syllabub:

One small glass, or 4 fl oz (120 ml) of white wine or sherry, 2 tablespoons of brandy, one lemon, 2 oz (60 g) sugar, ½ pint (280 ml) double cream, nutmeg.

The day before the syllabub is to be made, put the thinly pared rind of the lemon and the juice in a bowl with the wine and brandy and leave overnight. Next day, strain the wine and lemon mixture into a large and deep bowl. Add the sugar and stir until it has dissolved. Pour in the cream slowly, stirring all the time. Grate in a little nutmeg. Now whisk the mixture until it thickens and will hold a soft peak on the whisk. The process may take 5 minutes, it may take as long as 15. It depends on the cream, the temperature and the method of whisking. Unless dealing with a large quantity of cream, an electric mixer can be perilous. A couple of seconds too long and the cream is a ruined and grainy mass. For a small amount of cream a wire whisk is perfectly satisfactory and just as quick as an electric beater. An old-fashioned wooden chocolate mill or whisk held upright and twirled between the palms of both hands is also a good implement for whisking cream. The important point is to learn to recognize the moment at which the whisking process is complete.

When the cream is ready, spoon it into glasses, which should be of very small capacity (2–2½ fl oz/60–70 ml) but filled to overflowing. Once in the glasses the cream will not spoil nor sink nor separate. As suggested by Sir Kenelm Digby, a tiny sprig of rosemary or a small twist of lemon peel can be stuck into each little filled glass. Keep the syllabubs in a cool place – not in the refrigerator – until you are ready to serve them. They can be made at least two days before they are needed. The quantities given will fill ten small syllabub or custard cups or sherry glasses and will be enough for four to six people. Though circumstances are so changed it is relevant to remember that in their heyday syllabubs were regarded as refreshments to be offered at card parties, ball suppers and at public entertainments, rather than just as a pudding for lunches and dinners, although they did quite often figure as part of the dessert in the days when a choice of sweetmeats, fruits, jellies, confectionery and creams was set out in a formal symmetrical array in the centre of the table.

An Omelette and a Glass of Wine
chosen by George Elliot

GOOSEBERRY FOOL

2 lb (900 g) green gooseberries; ½ lb (225 g) sugar; a minimum of ½ pint (280 ml) of double cream.

Wash the gooseberries. There is no need to top and tail them. Put them in the top half of a double saucepan with the sugar, and steam them (or if it is easier bake them in a covered jar in a low oven) until they are quite soft. Sieve them through the *mouli* having first strained off surplus liquid which would make the fool watery. When the purée is quite cold add the cream. More sugar may be necessary.

Later in the season when gooseberries are over, delicious fools can be made with uncooked strawberries; a mixture of raspberries and redcurrants, also uncooked; and blackberries, cooked as for gooseberries; but in this case I think that cream spoils the rich colour of the fruit and should be offered separately.

To me it is essential to serve fruit fools in glasses or in simple white cups, and with shortbread or other such biscuits to go with them.

An Omelette and a Glass of Wine
chosen by Jonna Dwinger

GLACE MOKA
(*Coffee ice cream*)

A luxury ice cream, with a mild but true coffee flavour and a very fine texture.

First put 4 oz (120 g) freshly roasted coffee beans in a marble mortar. Do not crush them but simply bruise them with the pestle, so that the beans are cracked rather than broken up. Put them in a saucepan with a pint (550 ml) of single cream, the yolks of 3 eggs well beaten, a strip of lemon peel, and 3 oz (90 g) pale brown sugar (*cassonade*). Cook this mixture over very gentle heat, stirring constantly until it thickens. Take from the heat and go on stirring until it is cool. Strain through a fine sieve. When this cream is quite cold and thick, into it

282

fold ¼ pint (150 ml) double cream lightly whipped with a tablespoon of white sugar. Freeze in an ice cream maker or turn into a pint-sized (550 ml) freezing tray, cover with foil, and place in the ice-making compartment of the refrigerator, which should already be turned to maximum freezing point. Freeze for 3 hours; after the first hour stir the ice-cream, turning sides to middle. Turn out whole on to a flat dish and cut into four portions.

The coffee beans can be used again for a second batch of ice cream; and a less expensive mixture using a pint (550 ml) milk and 5 egg yolks still makes a very excellent ice. Always use a light roast of coffee.

French Provincial Cooking

CINNAMON ICE CREAM

The idea for this rather unexpected recipe came from that vast compendium, *Cassell's Dictionary of Cookery*, *circa* 1880. To judge by the measurements given in the Cassell's volume, the original recipe was of much earlier date.

The cinnamon makes an interesting and attractive flavour for an ice cream.

Put 1 pint (550 ml) double cream, 4 oz (120 g) white sugar, and ¼ oz (10 g) powdered cinnamon in the top half of a double boiler, or in a bowl fitting into a deep saucepan. Heat over gently simmering water. Beat together, preferably in a blender, 4 egg yolks and ½ pint (280 ml) milk. Amalgamate the two mixtures, and continue the steady cooking until you have obtained a fairly thick custard. Strain into a deep jug or bowl. Chill in the refrigerator before freezing.

Spices, Salt and Aromatics

CHOCOLATE CHINCHILLA

This is a splendid – and cheap – recipe for using up egg whites left from the making of mayonnaise, *béarnaise* or other egg-yolk based sauces. It is also a dish which demonstrates how excellent is the combination of chocolate with cinnamon. This flavouring stems from the sixteenth century, when the Spaniards first shipped the product of the cocoa bean from South America to Spain. Chocolate, both drinking and eating versions, spiced with cinnamon is still sometimes to be found in Spain, and also I believe in Mexico, although almost everywhere else cinnamon has long been superseded by vanilla as the favourite aromatic for flavouring chocolate.

Ingredients are 5 to 7 egg whites, 2 oz (60 g) unsweetened cocoa powder, 3 oz (90 g) caster sugar, 1 heaped teaspoon of ground cinnamon.

Mix together the cocoa, sugar and cinnamon. Whip the egg whites to a stiff snow. Tip the cocoa and sugar mixture on to the egg whites. Fold the two together, gently but thoroughly. A large metal spoon or a wide flexible spatula are the best implements to use for this operation.

Have ready a buttered ring mould, *kugelhopf*, or best of all a steamed-pudding mould with a central funnel and clip-on lid. Austrian and German cooks use these moulds for all puddings and cakes in which there is a high content of whisked egg white. The central funnel helps enormously in the even distribution of heat throughout the mixture, which in a soufflé dish or plain mould tends to remain moist in the centre for some minutes after the rest of the pudding is cooked. Whatever mould is used for this recipe, the capacity should be approximately 1½–2 pints (850 ml–1.1 l).

Having filled your mould with the prepared mixture, stand it, uncovered (for this particular recipe the lid of the mould is not necessary) in a baking tin with water to reach halfway up the dish or mould.

Cook the chinchilla – which is really a kind of soufflé without egg yolks – in the centre of a moderate oven (170°C/330°F/Gas Mark 3), for about 45–50 minutes. It will rise in a spectacular manner. But since it is to be eaten cold, it will sink in an even more spectacular fashion unless, when taken from the oven, it is left to cool in a warm place, protected from draughts and sudden changes of temperature. When cold, the pudding, although shrunk, will have become compact enough to turn out easily. It will have a good texture and a very rich dark colour.

With the chinchilla, serve fresh thin pouring cream to which has been added a little sherry, rum or brandy.

Spices, Salt and Aromatics
chosen by John Ruden

SOUFFLÉ AU CHOCOLAT

A chocolate soufflé is made on a somewhat different system from other soufflés, the melted chocolate itself being so thick that no other basic mixture is required. Also it cooks very quickly and equally quickly becomes dry, so careful timing is necessary, for to be good a chocolate soufflé must be creamy in the middle.

Melt 4 oz (120 g) bitter chocolate in the oven with 2 or 3 tablespoons of water, rum or brandy. Stir it smooth, add 2 tablespoons of sugar and the very well beaten yolks of 4 eggs, then fold in the beaten whites of 6. Turn into a 2-pint (1.1-l) buttered soufflé dish and cook with the dish standing on a baking sheet in a pre-heated hot oven (200°C/ 400°F/Gas Mark 6), for approximately 12 minutes. Enough for 4 people.

This is a soufflé which is improved by fresh cream served separately.

French Provincial Cooking
chosen by Jenny Dereham

CHOCOLATE MOUSSE

1 egg per person, 1 oz (30 g) plain or vanilla chocolate per person.

Melt the chocolate in a thick pan over a low flame with a tablespoon of water. A tablespoon of rum added will do no harm. Stir the chocolate until it is smooth. Separate the eggs and beat the yolks. Stir the melted chocolate into the yolks.

Whip the whites very stiffly and fold them over and over into the chocolate, so that they are perfectly blended, or the chocolate may sink to the bottom. Put the mousse into a soufflé dish so that the mixture just about comes to the top (nothing is sadder than a small amount of mousse hiding at the bottom of a huge glass bowl) and leave it in a cool place to set. Unless in a hurry, don't put it on ice, as this tends to make it too hard.

Instead of water, the chocolate can be melted in a tablespoon of black coffee.

French Country Cooking
chosen by Gerald Asher and Pamela Vandyke Price

MOUSSE AU CHOCOLAT À L'ORANGE

Nearly everyone knows and appreciates the old and reliable formula for a chocolate mousse – 4 yolks beaten into 4 oz (120 g) melted bitter chocolate, and the 4 whipped whites folded in. Here is a slightly different version, its faint orange flavour giving it originality.

Break 4 oz (120 g) good quality bitter chocolate into squares and put in a fireproof dish in a low oven. When the chocolate is soft, after a few minutes, take it from the oven, stir in 4 well-beaten yolks, then 1 oz (30 g) softened butter, then the juice of 1 orange. Use a Seville orange when in season; its aromatic flavour comes through better than that of the sweet orange.

Beat the 4 egg whites as for a soufflé and fold them into the chocolate mixture. Pour into little pots, glasses or coffee-cups. This quantity will fill 6. Put in the refrigerator or a cool larder until ready to serve.

Should you have some orange liqueur such as Grand Marnier or Curaçao, add a spoonful in place of the same amount of the orange juice.

French Provincial Cooking
chosen by Jacqueline Korn

SAINT ÉMILION AU CHOCOLAT

4 oz (120 g) butter, 4 oz (120 g) sugar, 1 egg, 8 oz (225 g) chocolate, 1 teacup milk, 12 to 16 macaroons.

Cream the butter and the sugar until they are well amalgamated. Scald the milk and let it cool, then mix it with the yolk of the egg. Melt the chocolate over the heat, with a very little water, then stir in the milk and egg mixture, then the butter and sugar. Stir this cream carefully until it is absolutely smooth.

In a soufflé dish arrange a layer of macaroons, soaked in a little rum or brandy; over these pour a layer of the chocolate cream, then put another layer of macaroons and so on until the dish is full, finishing with macaroons. Leave the dish in a cold place for at least 12 hours.

French Country Cooking
chosen by Julia Caffyn

TORRONE MOLLE

Torrone is the Italian name for all kinds of nougat. This sweet, literally 'soft nougat', is an ingenious invention, for it needs no cooking and can be successfully turned out by the least experienced of cooks. For six to eight people, the ingredients are 6 oz (170 g) each of cocoa, butter, sugar, ground almonds, and plain biscuits such as Petit Beurre or Osborne, plus 1 whole egg and 1 yolk.

Work the butter and the cocoa together until you have a soft paste, then stir in the ground almonds. Melt the sugar in a saucepan with a little water over a gentle heat and add it to the cocoa mixture. Stir in the eggs, and finally the biscuits cut into almond-sized pieces. This last operation must be performed gently so that the biscuits do not crumble. Turn the whole mixture into an oiled turban mould, or a cake tin with a removable base, and put it in the refrigerator or the coldest part of the larder. Turn it out on to a dish to serve. The *torrone* is infinitely better when prepared the day before it is to be eaten.

The combination of the plain biscuits with the chocolate mixture is reminiscent of that most admirable picnic food, a slab of bitter chocolate accompanied by a Petit Beurre biscuit.

Italian Food

GÂTEAU AU CHOCOLAT

This is a cake which can also be eaten as a pudding, and is neither expensive nor difficult to make.

4 oz (120 g) bitter chocolate, 4 oz (120 g) caster sugar, 2 tablespoons of flour, 3 eggs, 3 oz (90 g) butter.

Melt the chocolate in the oven; mix it with the softened butter, flour, sugar and beaten egg yolks. Fold in the stiffly beaten whites. Turn into a buttered 6-inch (15-cm) cake tin or 1¼-pint (700-ml) loaf tin and cook in a pre-heated moderate oven (180°C/350°F/Gas Mark 4) for 35 minutes. There will be a thin crust on top of the cake but if you test it with a skewer the inside will appear insufficiently cooked, which in fact is correct, as it gets firmer as it cools.

As soon as it is cool enough to handle, turn upside down on to a cake rack. When cool, the cake can either be covered with lightly whipped cream, or the following mixture.

Break up 3 oz (90 g) plain chocolate and melt it on a fireproof plate in the oven, with 4 or 5 lumps of sugar and 2 or 3 tablespoons of water. Stir it smooth; add 1 oz (30 g) butter. Let it cool a little, then with a palette knife cover the whole cake with the chocolate, smoothing it with a knife dipped in water. Leave it to set before serving.

The quantities given make a small cake, but it is somewhat solid and goes quite a long way.

French Provincial Cooking

The Elizabeth David chocolate cake which started off my endless chocolate cake making was Gâteau au Chocolat. I don't think Elizabeth's description of it as 'somewhat solid' is apt at all – it is simply rich with chocolate and softly dense, but at the same time quite delicate. A million miles away from a conventional, often dry, chocolate sponge. I couldn't count the number of variations on the same sort of theme that I've made since that first revelation. For better or worse, Elizabeth David helped chocolate to dominate my cake and pudding cooking.   Josceline Dimbleby

GÂTEAU AU CHOCOLAT ET AUX AMANDES

4 oz (120 g) bitter chocolate, 3 oz (90 g) each of butter, caster sugar, and ground almonds, 3 eggs, 1 tablespoon each of rum or brandy and black coffee.

Break the chocolate into small pieces; put them with the rum and coffee to melt in a cool oven. Stir the mixture well, put it with the butter, sugar and ground almonds in a saucepan and stir over a low heat for a few minutes until all the ingredients are blended smoothly together. Off the heat, stir in the well-beaten egg yolks, and then fold in the stiffly whipped whites. Turn into a lightly buttered shallow sponge-cake tin, of 7–8 inches (18–20 cm) diameter, or a tart tin with a removable base. Stand the tin on a baking sheet and cook in a very low oven (140°C/290°F/Gas Mark 1) for about 45 minutes. This cake, owing to the total absence of flour, is rather fragile, so turn it out, when it is cool, with the utmost caution. It can either be served as it is, or covered with lightly whipped and sweetened cream. It is a cake which is equally good for dessert or for tea-time.

French Provincial Cooking
chosen by Julia Caffyn

HONEY AND HAZEL NUT CAKE

This is not really a cake, but a kind of soufflé eaten cold, a Périgordine speciality.

Put ½ lb (225 g) honey in a jar in a saucepan of hot water so that it is easy to manipulate. Pour it over 5 or 6 yolks of eggs beaten in a large bowl; add gradually a teacup of sifted flour and a teacup of hazel nuts pounded in a mortar with a little caster sugar; bind the mixture either with a little milk or cream (about ½ cup) or the equivalent amount of butter.

Lastly, add the beaten whites of the eggs, and pour the whole mixture into a buttered cake tin or soufflé dish, and cook it for 40 minutes in a moderate oven (170°C/330°F/Gas Mark 3). When cold, turn the cake out.

It is also excellent made with walnuts instead of hazel nuts.

French Country Cooking

ORANGE AND ALMOND CAKE

The juice of 2 large or 3 small oranges, grated rind of 1 orange, 4 oz (120 g) ground almonds, 2 oz (60 g) fine dry breadcrumbs, 4 oz (120 g) sugar, 4 eggs, ½ teaspoon salt, cream and, if available, 1 tablespoon orange-flower water.

Mix together the breadcrumbs, orange juice and grated orange rind, add the ground almonds, and the orange-flower water.

Beat the egg yolks with the sugar and salt until almost white. Add to the first mixture. Fold in the stiffly beaten egg whites. Pour into a cake tin (2½ inches/5.5 cm deep, 1¾-pt/1–1 l capacity) buttered and sprinkled with breadcrumbs. Bake in a moderate oven (180°C/350°F/Gas Mark 4) for about 40 minutes.

When cold turn the cake out and cover the top with whipped cream (about ¼ pint [150 ml]). Very good and light, and excellent for a sweet at luncheon or dinner.

Mediterranean Food

RASPBERRY SHORTBREAD

6 oz (170 g) flour, 3½ oz (100 g) moist brown sugar, 2 oz (60 g) butter, ½ teaspoon ground ginger, 1 teaspoon baking powder, 1 lb (450 g) raspberries, a little white sugar.

Put the raspberries in a fairly large shallow pie dish, strew them with white sugar. Cut the butter into very small pieces and crumble it with the flour until it is thoroughly blended. Add the sugar, ginger and baking powder. Spread this mixture lightly over the raspberries, and smooth it out evenly, but do not press down. Bake in the centre of a medium oven (180–190°C/350–375°F/Gas Mark 4–5) for 25 minutes. Can be served hot or cold and is excellent.

Summer Cooking

SUMMER PUDDING

Although nearly everybody knows of this wonderful pudding, authentic recipes for it are rare.

For four people stew 1 lb (450 g) raspberries and ¼ lb (120 g) redcurrants with about ¼ lb (120 g) sugar. No water. Cook them only 2 or 3 minutes, and leave to cool. Line a round fairly deep dish (a soufflé dish does very well) with slices of one-day-old white bread with the crust removed. The bread should be of the thickness usual for sandwiches. The dish must be completely lined, bottom and sides, with no space through which the juice can escape. Fill up with the fruit, but reserve some of the juice. Cover the fruit with a complete layer of bread. On top put a plate which fits exactly inside the dish, and on the plate put a 2–3 lb (1–1.5 kg) weight. Leave overnight in a very cold larder or refrigerator. When ready to serve turn the pudding out on to a dish (not a completely flat one, or the juice will overflow) and pour over it the reserved juice.

Thick fresh cream is usually served with summer pudding, but it is almost more delicious without.

Summer Cooking

ARANCI CARAMELLIZZATI
(*Caramel oranges*)

This way of serving oranges is a speciality of the Taverna Fenice in Venice, a restaurant where the colours of Venetian painting are translated to the kitchen. Saffron-coloured *polenta* is cooking in copper pans next to an immense dish of artichokes, purple and dark green, stewing in a bath of white wine and olive oil. On the other side of the stove is a deep pot of red-brown Venetian bean soup, and simmering in a *bain-marie* is an orange and umber sauce of tomatoes, clams and onions. Translucent little squids sizzle on the grill; on a marble table are rose-coloured *scampi* and vermilion Adriatic crabs, and coils of pale-gold *fettuccine* are drying in plaited baskets. In the coolest part of the larder the oranges shine, luminous with their sugary coating. A particular variety of Sicilian oranges, without pips, is used for the confection of these caramel oranges, but even with the ordinary kinds, where the pips must be extracted as the fruit is eaten, the dish is well worth a trial.

Now, in 1987, caramel oranges have long ago became a cliché of London Italian restaurants, but they are better when made at home.

Peel 4 oranges extremely carefully with a very sharp knife, so that not one scrap of pith is left on them. Now prepare a syrup with 6 oz (170 g) sugar to a teacupful of water. When it is thick, dip the oranges into the syrup, turning them over so that the whole orange may be well coated with the sugar. They should be in the syrup for only 2 or 3 minutes. Take them out and arrange them on a large dish. Now cut the peel, as thin as possible (this can be done very successfully with a potato peeler), from two other oranges. Cut this peel into fine strips about the length of matches. Plunge into boiling water and cook for about 7 minutes, to rid the peel of its bitter taste. Drain, then cook in the syrup until the strips have begun to take on a transparent look and are becoming caramelized. Becoming is the operative word. Don't let them turn into toffee.

Put a spoonful of this caramelized peel on top of each orange. Serve the oranges very cold. The addition of a little kirsch to the syrup is, I consider, an improvement.

Italian Food

Lorraine

It was a late spring afternoon as, driving from the ancient city of Bar-le-Duc, we approached Nancy. It was already getting dark, and we preferred to see the capital of Lorraine for the first time in daylight. Turning back into the country, we spent the night in a seedy roadhouse on the banks of the Moselle, where the cooking was of about the same standard of artistry as the blue pottery gnomes with which the dining-room was unsparingly ornamented. It was just the sort of place in which the tourist is liable to land when too late and too tired to drive any farther, so we had only ourselves to thank for this bad beginning. In this case it was of little consequence (and it might have been worse, for we did manage to needle out some very acceptable local wine, the *vin gris* of Toul, the existence of which the landlord had done his best to conceal at the very end of a pretentious and expensive wine list) for we were all the more anxious to be up and away before breakfast, and to see the great Place Stanislas for the first time in the early morning sunlight.

The extreme elegance and aristocratic grace of the Place Stanislas, the beauty of Héré's columns and arcades, the delicacy and fantasy of Lamour's black and gilt wrought-iron balconies, and of the grilles and the gates which mark the four entrances to this square make a powerful impact when seen for the first time. As a monument to pure eighteenth-century taste the Place Stanislas must be unique in Europe. It was indeed of Nancy that Maurice Barrès, himself a native of Lorraine, wrote that 'here remains fixed the brief moment in which our society achieved its point of perfection'.

On our way from the Place Stanislas to the central food market we pass what seems, at least at breakfast time, to be an almost unbroken line of bakeries and pastry shops, wafting infinitely beguiling smells from their warm interiors. In the end, of course, we have not the strength of mind to pass another. As we go in to order our *croissants*, there in front of us upon the counter and all round the shop are piled hundreds of flat round orange and gilt tins, glinting and shining like little lamps in the pallid sunshine. The tops of the tins are decorated with pictures of the wrought-iron grilles of the Place Stanislas and in gilt lettering bear the words LES BERGAMOTTES DE NANCY. Upon inquiry the assistant tells me that these are little boiled sweets, scented with essence of Bergamot, and are one of the oldest specialities of Nancy. I had heard vaguely of these Bergamottes without having any precise idea as to whether they were a cake, a sweet, or perhaps some sort of candied flower petal, and as I walked away carrying my pretty little tin of childish sweets I thought how often some such trivial little discovery colours and alters in one's mind the whole aspect of a city or a countryside. On a former occasion it had been the crystallized violets of Toulouse which had caused that remarkable city of ferocious history and dignified rose and ochre buildings to show yet another side of its character; for frivolous little boxes of *violettes de Toulouse* tied up in pale mauve satin ribbons are displayed amid swirls of violet tulle in every confectioner's window.

The province of Lorraine is rich in such small associations. The first city you enter driving east from Champagne is Bar-le-Duc, ancient capital of the Dukes of Bar and Lorraine, but more familiar to me as the home of those magically translucent preserves, half-jam, half-jelly, of red currants, white currants or little strawberries, sold in miniature glass jars in luxury Paris grocery stores, and sometimes served at dessert with cream or cream cheese. At the little town of Commercy originated the small, fragile, shell-shaped cakes called *madeleines* so beloved of French children, and which have become celebrated in French literature because it was the taste of a *madeleine* dipped in a cup of tea which Proust used as the starting point of his long journey into the past. (How the English madeleine, a sort of castle pudding covered with jam and coconut, with a cherry on the top, came by the same name is something of a mystery.) The name Épinal on a signpost brings back another childish memory, of primitive coloured pictures and sheets of brightly uniformed soldiers, the *images d'Épinal* which have the same primitive charm as our penny-plain twopence-coloured prints. To Lunéville, where the château was built as a replica, on a small scale, of Versailles, belongs that thick white china sprayed with stylized pink and red roses which is, to me, inseparable from the memory of *café au lait* in bowls, and *croissants*, and crisp curls of very white butter on little oval dishes. On the map of Lorraine are also to be found Contrexéville and Vittel of the mineral waters, reminders of countless restaurant cars and wagon-lits; Baccarat of the crystal decanters and wine goblets; and on all the postcard stands are crude coloured pictures of a young woman serving a great flat cartwheel of a *quiche Lorraine* to some rough peasantry seated round a scrubbed farmhouse table. The pink wine of Toul may remind collectors of insignificant information that it was in that city that Claude Gelée, rather better known as le Lorrain, was apprenticed as a pastry-cook before he found his real vocation as a painter. Le Lorrain is, in fact, sometimes credited with the invention of puff pastry, but this is perhaps over-enthusiastic on the part of French cookery historians, for surely it was already known to Italian cooks before Lorrain's time. (He may of course have learnt how to make it in Italy, for he worked as pastry-cook to an Italian landscape painter in Rome.)

In the great covered market place of Nancy there are new sights to be seen. Here are big bowls of pale amber-green and gold *choucroute*, and stalls bulging with sausages, the special smoked ones to go with the *choucroute*, and large, coarsely cut but, as it turns out, most subtly flavoured sausages for boiling (our own sausage manufacturers could learn a thing or two from these Lorraine and Alsatian *charcutiers* if they cared to do so); smoked fillets and loins of pork, terrines and pâtés of pork, duck, tongue; and deep dishes in which pieces of pork lie embedded in a crystal clear jelly; this turns out to be the famous *porcelet en gelée*, an elegant brawn sucking pig which makes a fine hors-d'œuvre; then there are trays of highly flavoured salad made from pig's head, and flat square cuts of streaky bacon smothered in chopped parsley – 'to keep it fresh' – the delicious mild-cured pale pink hams of Luxeuil, strong creamy cheeses called *Géromé des Vosges*, and others studded with caraway seeds, the *Anisé* of the Lorraine farmhouses; and – but it is nearly lunchtime, and in a busy provincial town like Nancy it is as well to secure your table soon after midday, and we have already learned from the menu pinned up outside the Restaurant of the Capucin Gourmand that that famous *quiche* is cooked fresh for every customer, and we shall have to wait at least twenty minutes for it. . . .

French Provincial Cooking
chosen by Johnny Grey and Joe Hyam

PRESERVES

Adrian Daintrey.

APRICOT CHEESE

Halve the apricots, stone them, and steam them until soft. Sieve them. Add 1 lb (450 g) sugar to every pint (550 ml) of pulp. Cook, stirring frequently, until the purée starts to candy at the edges. Store in jars.

An excellent and very useful preserve, better than jam for omelettes and puddings, delicious with unsalted cream cheese, or mixed with whipped cream to make a fool for the winter. The flavour is even better if a few of the stones are cracked and the kernels added to the apricots when sieved. Or a few blanched split almonds can be used instead of the apricot kernels.

Summer Cooking

ENGLISH LEMON CURD

To make 1 lb (450 g) approximately, ingredients are: 2 large lemons, preferably thick-skinned; ½ lb (225 g) lump sugar; 4 whole large eggs; ¼ lb (120 g) of unsalted or slightly salted butter.

Rub sugar lumps on to the peel of the lemons, holding them over a bowl, until each lump starts crumbling, then start on another. About four lumps will rub sufficient outside peel and oil out of each lemon. Put all the sugar together into the bowl.

Squeeze the lemons, and strain the juice. Whisk the eggs very thoroughly with the strained juice.

Cut the butter into small cubes.

Set the bowl in, or over, a pan of water. When the sugar has dissolved add the eggs, then the butter. Stir until all ingredients are amalgamated and the whole mixture looks rather like thick honey, with about the same consistency. Remove the bowl (older cooks still find an old-fashioned stoneware jam jar the best vessel for making lemon curd. I prefer an open bowl. I like to see what's happening) and stir until the curd has cooled. Turn into small jars and cover with good quality kitchen parchment such as Bakewell, to be bought at W. H. Smith and other stationers.

To the straightforward lemon curd, a couple of sponge fingers, broken up, are sometimes added. They thicken the curd, giving it extra body and making it more stable when spread into flan cases or flat, open plate pies. A richer alternative is a small proportion of ground almonds. Allow up to 2 oz (60 g) for the quantities given.

Writers of old recipes often claimed that lemon curd keeps for years. Perhaps it does. I would say that three months is about the maximum, and that long before this period is up the confection, like a fresh fruit sorbet stored in the deep freeze, has lost its exquisite flavour and the edge has gone from the sharp scent.

Use lemon curd to make a delicious filling for little brown bread sandwiches to eat with ices, to spread on brioche or currant bread, or as a sauce for little yeast pancakes as well as for the traditional lemon curd pie made with rich, sweet short crust.

An Omelette and a Glass of Wine
chosen by Jonna Dwinger

COTIGNAC ORLÉANAIS

Peel, core and slice 4 lb (1.8 kg) quinces. Put them into a preserving pan with water not quite covering them. Bring them to the boil and cook for 30 minutes. Strain them through a muslin, pressing them so as to extract as much juice as possible.

In the juice cook another 3 lb (1.4 kg) quinces, peeled, sliced and cored, and 1 lb (450 g) oranges, skinned and quartered, with the pips removed. Simmer for 1 hour, and put the mixture through a sieve, so as to obtain a thick purée; weigh the purée, add an equal quantity of sugar, return to the pan and cook until the mixture begins to come away from the sides.

The *cotignac* can be stored in jars or tins.

Excellent eaten with soft cream cheese.

French Country Cooking
chosen by Pamela Vandyke Price

PÂTE DE COINGS
(*Quince paste*)

Here is the easiest country method of making thick quince paste. Rub the quinces with a cloth to remove the down. Put them, whole and unpeeled, into a big, tall earthenware crock or jar, without any water. Leave them, covered, in a low oven until they are soft but not breaking up. When they are cool enough to handle, slice them, without peeling them, into a bowl, discarding the cores and any bruised or hard pieces. Put the sliced fruit through the food mill. Weigh it. Add an equal quantity of white sugar. Boil in a preserving pan, stirring nearly all the time until the paste begins to candy and come away from the bottom as well as the sides of the pan. Take care to use a long-handled wooden spoon for stirring, and to wrap your hand in a cloth for the boiling paste erupts and spits. Continue stirring after the heat has been turned off until boiling has ceased. With a big soup ladle, fill shallow rectangular earthenware or tin dishes with the paste. Leave to get quite cold. Next day put these moulds into the lowest possible oven of a solid fuel cooker, or into the plate drawer of a gas or electric stove, while the oven is on for several hours, until the paste has dried out and is quite firm. Turn out the slabs of paste, wrap them in greaseproof paper or foil, and store them in tins in a dry larder.

This paste is cut into squares or lozenges to serve as a dessert or as a sweetmeat for the children.

If you have no suitable utensil for the initial cooking of the fruit in the oven, it can be softened in a steamer over a big saucepan of boiling water.

French Provincial Cooking
chosen by Priscilla Gwynne-Longland

During the mid to late 1950s when my sister Elizabeth was collecting and experimenting with recipes for *French Provincial Cooking*, my family and I lived in an old, rambling East Sussex farmhouse. We had a large and fine quince tree in the garden, at the front of the house. Whenever I took fresh quinces to Liza in Halsey Street she would receive them with cries of joy, and on my next visit there was sure to be an exciting array of quince conserves;

they would stand on shelves and dressers in her kitchen or in the narrow
hall.

The Quince Paste or Pâte de Coings turned out to be very popular with
my then teenage daughters and I have made it ever since, always following
Liza's recipe.   Priscilla Gwynne-Longland

(Postscript from Sabrina Harcourt-Smith:
My mother is too modest to mention that Liza considered Priscilla's Quince
Paste to be better than any other she knew.)

MINCEMEAT

Christmas mincemeat and Christmas plum pudding and cake are all
such typical examples of the English fondness for spiced fruit mixtures
that it seems almost unnecessary to include recipes for them in this
little book. It so happens though that I have been asked many times
for a good mincemeat recipe, so perhaps an interesting one is not all
that common. This is the one I use. The friend who passed it on to
me was very insistent that bought shredded suet should not be used.
It would prevent the mincemeat from keeping, so she told me. I am
afraid that I disobeyed her instructions and used bought packet suet.
(Shredding suet is a terrible task. I cannot make myself spend so much
time and effort on it.) The first batch of mincemeat I made using
ready-prepared suet kept for five years. The last jar *was* a bit dried
out. I added more brandy and it came back to life.

The ingredients are: 1½ lb (675 g) sharp apples, ¾ lb (340 g) stone-
less raisins, ¾ lb (340 g) currants, ¼ lb (120 g) mixed peel; ¾ lb (340 g)
suet, ¾ lb (340 g) sultanas, 2 oz (60 g) skinned and coarsely chopped
almonds, ½ teaspoon each of grated nutmeg, cinnamon, mace, ¾ lb
(340 g) sugar, rind and juice of 1 lemon and 1 orange, 2½ fl oz (70 ml)
of brandy or rum.

Wash and dry all fruit. Chop the peeled and carefully cored apples.
Mix all ingredients well together, adding brandy last.

Fill stoneware jars and tie them down with thick greaseproof paper, or alternatively pack the mincemeat into glass preserving-jars with screw or clip-on tops.

This amount makes approximately 6 lb (2.75 kg) of mincemeat.

Spices, Salt and Aromatics

APRICOT CHUTNEY

2 lb (900 g) ripe apricots, 10 oz (280 g) brown sugar, 1 onion, ¼ lb (120 g) sultanas, 1 teaspoon of grated green ginger root or ½ teaspoon of ground ginger, a tablespoon of salt, ½ pint (280 ml) Orléans vinegar, 1 teaspoon of coriander seeds, 2 or 3 cloves of garlic.

Halve the apricots and stone them. Slice the onion and the garlic. Put all the ingredients into a large pan and boil until the apricots are quite soft. Take them out and put into jars. Boil the rest of the liquid rapidly until it turns to a thickish syrup, and pour into the jars. Seal down.

A mild chutney which goes well with cold boiled gammon or tongue.

Summer Cooking

PUMPKIN AND TOMATO CHUTNEY

It is not generally known that pumpkin can make an excellent chutney, rich and dark. The recipe below produces a mixture with a taste which is spicy but not too sharp; the pumpkin slices retain something of their shape, and shine translucently through the glass jars.

Greengrocers very often sell pumpkins by the piece at about a shilling a pound. A whole one is of course cheaper, but remember that once it is cut it will not keep longer than about ten days.

Ingredients are a 2½ lb (1.1 kg) piece of pumpkin (gross weight), 1 lb (450 g) of ripe tomatoes, ½ lb (225 g) onions, 2 oz (60 g) of sultanas, ¾ lb (340 g) each of soft dark brown sugar and white caster sugar, 2 tablespoons of salt, 2 scant teaspoons each of ground ginger, *black* peppercorns and allspice berries, 2 cloves of garlic, 1¼ pints (700 ml) white, red or rosé wine vinegar or cider vinegar.

Peel the pumpkin, discard seeds and cottony centre. Slice, then cut into pieces roughly 2 inches (5 cm) wide and long and ½ inch (12 mm) thick. Pour boiling water over the tomatoes, skin and slice them. Peel and slice the onions and the garlic.

Put all solid ingredients, including spices (crush the peppercorns and allspice berries in a mortar) and sugar, in your preserving pan. (For chutneys, always use heavy aluminium, never untinned copper jam pans.) Add vinegar. Bring gently to the boil, and then cook steadily, but not at a gallop, until the mixture is jammy. Skim from time to time, and towards the end of the cooking, which will take altogether about 50 minutes, stir very frequently. Chutney can be a disastrous sticker if you don't give it your full attention during the final stages.

This is a long-keeping chutney but, like most chutneys, it is best if cooked to a moderate set only; in other words it should still be a little bit runny; if too solid it will quickly dry up.

Ladle into pots, which should be filled right to the brim. When cold, cover with rounds of waxed paper, and then with a double layer of thick greaseproof paper. Transparent covers which let in the light are not suitable for chutney.

The yield from these quantities will be approximately 3½ lb (1.5 kg); and although it may be a little more extravagant as regards fuel and materials, I find chutney cooked in small batches more satisfactory than when produced on a large scale.

It is worth noting that should it be more convenient, all ingredients for the chutney can be prepared, mixed with the sugar and vinegar, and left for several hours or overnight (but not longer than 12 hours) in a covered bowl before cooking.

Spices, Salt and Aromatics

ESCOFFIER'S PIMENTO CHUTNEY

Unexpected recipes from authors regarded as classic are always interesting, provided one knows and trusts the taste of that author. I have
to confess that in this respect I do not invariably feel confidence in
Escoffier – I find for example that his fruit and ice cream dishes are
unnecessarily recherché and fussy, although it must be allowed that
the over-working of food and a professional reluctance to present a
peach, a nectarine, a pear or a bunch of muscat grapes as nature made
them was the tendency of Escoffier's time. A point about his work
which it is more rewarding to remember is that he was a Provençal
who was born and spent his early boyhood in Villeneuve-Loubet in
the Alpes Maritimes. One has the impression from his post-*Guide
Culinaire* books and from articles written for professional publications
that he did not ever entirely lose the taste for the village cooking of
his very humble childhood and that sometimes he was bored – as who
is not by his own public image – with exquisite subtlety and the
standards of perfection he had himself created, and had wistful hanker-
ings for the primitive food of his childhood. Today's interest in all
regional cooking and in particular in the dishes of his own native
Provence would surely have been welcome to him.

I do not know whether Escoffier's sweet pepper and onion mixture,
a cross between a chutney and a sauce to be eaten with cold meat, was
derived from a Provençal recipe – it is a little reminiscent of the Italian
peperonata – whether he evolved it from some other source, or invented
it entirely. It is an uncommonly interesting and unusual sauce; Escoffier
calls it simply *piments pour viandes froides* and the recipe is to be found
in his *Ma Cuisine*, published by Flammarion in 1934, the year before
the author's death at the age of eighty-nine. This Escoffier sauce, one
which evidently never found its way into the bottles of the Peckham
factory he founded in 1898 is one which became a favourite of mine
during the years I lived in Egypt. The ingredients were all to hand,
cheap and common, and the sauce was a great enlivener for the local
meat. My own slightly simplified and reduced version of the recipe
is no longer quite that of Escoffier.

You need 2 large, fat, fleshy, sweet and very ripe red peppers (about

1 lb [450 g] gross weight), ½ lb (225 g) mild Spanish onions, 1 lb (450 g) ripe tomatoes, 1 clove of garlic, 4 oz (120 g) of raisins, half a teaspoon each of salt, powdered ginger (or grated dried root-ginger) and mixed spices such as allspice, mace and nutmeg, 8 oz (225 g) white sugar, 4 tablespoons of olive oil and ¼ pint (150 ml) fine wine vinegar.

Melt the finely chopped onions in the olive oil, add the chopped peppers (well washed, all core and seeds removed), salt and spices, and after 10 minutes the peeled and chopped tomatoes and the raisins, garlic and sugar; lastly the vinegar. Cook extremely slowly, covered, for at least one hour and a quarter.

A tall marmite-type pot rather than a wide preserving pan should be used for the cooking of this confection. The sauce does not, and I think is not supposed to, turn into a jam-like substance. It is an iridescent bronze dish, *mordoré* to use the marvellous French word.

Bottled in screw-top jars the mixture keeps well for two or three weeks, although I have never made enough at one time to report as to whether it has a more enduring shelf life. It is good with cold lamb and salt beef.

Spices, Salt and Aromatics

SALTED ALMONDS

With drinks, the cashews and peanuts of commerce make wretched substitutes for salted almonds; and salted almonds, whatever the promises held out by the words vacuum-sealed or oven-fresh on tins and jars are not to be bought. They must be prepared at home, and on the day they are to be eaten. Five or six hours after the almonds come out of the oven they are at their best. Within twenty-four hours they have already lost their pristine freshness. It is, goodness knows, easy to prepare almonds for salting. They cost half the price of salted almonds in jars or tins and taste twice as good.

If blanched whole almonds are not to be found, the skinning process is a matter of minutes. Plunge the almonds into boiling water. When the water has again boiled, turn the almonds out into a colander. While they are still warm, slip off the skins. This part of the operation can be done in advance.

All that is needed apart from the blanched almonds is an oven, a baking tin, kitchen salt and kitchen paper and, if possible, a tiny phial of sweet almond oil bought from the chemist, and cayenne pepper in a sprinkler. Butter, very highly refined olive oil or deodorized ground-nut oil will pass instead of almond oil. Corn oil, with its detestable taste and greasy cling, will not pass for this, nor so far as I am concerned, for any other purpose whatsoever.

It was a Sudanese cook called Suleiman who cooked for me in Egypt who discovered how the best salted almonds are made. Suleiman used not more than a teaspoonful of almond oil or butter per 8 oz (225 g) of blanched almonds, and it does not matter whether Valencia or Jordan almonds are used. What you do is to put the prepared almonds in a baking tin rubbed with the oil or butter. The tin then goes into the centre of a very slow oven (the oven in my Cairo kitchen was a tin box perched over a primus stove. The magic of this primitive device can be very well reproduced with any gas, solid fuel, or oven at a temperature of approximately 110°C/230°F/Gas Mark ¼) and there leave it for about 45 minutes until the almonds are pale toast colour. Have ready on the table a sheet of greaseproof paper and some *gros sel* (about three tablespoons to the 8 oz [225 g]. Free-running table salt is to be avoided for this purpose. Empty the toasted almonds on to the paper. Swish them round in the salt. Gather up the corners of the paper and twist them so that you have a tightly fastened little parcel which you put away in a drawer, or in the kitchen cupboard. This part of the ritual is not so much a matter of witchcraft as of plain common sense. In my experience, it is necessary to conceal salted almonds from all eyes until the appropriate time comes for them to be produced. Nothing yet invented so sets the gastric juices to work as the sight of a plateful of freshly toasted and salted almonds. Even to say the words or see them written does the trick. (Whoever thought of calling the cocktail bar at the old Trocadero the *Salted Almond* knew a thing or two.) Left where anybody can see them, a pound (450 g) of salted almonds will be devoured within fifteen minutes.

When therefore the moment to set out the almonds arrives, unwrap the parcel, shake the almonds free of excess salt and over them shake an infinitesimal sprinkling of cayenne pepper.

There is very little question of salted almonds left over from one evening being produced again the next. There never are any left over. Should there be, re-toast them in a slow oven – but they will not be the same. Suleiman used to put any left over into a rice dish. And he could not be persuaded to make salted almonds in a hurry. He held it essential to give them their few hours in the salt. He was right. The important points about salted almonds are that they must be so dry from the slow toasting in the oven that they squeak as you bite into them; at the same time they must be salty in taste but not to the extent that their own flavour is killed.

Spices, Salt and Aromatics
chosen by Gerald Asher, Peter Carson,
Kit Chapman and Alan Davidson

Having spent two years in Cairo at the end of the 1950s, and having come to know Elizabeth David shortly afterwards through the kindness of a colleague who had been with her in Cairo during the war, I was always deeply curious about the time she spent there. Where did she live? What sort of kitchen, and how arranged? And so on. Scores of questions. I never ventured to pose any of these to Elizabeth – but I have cherished, ever since I first read the passage, this glimpse of her Sudanese cook and his oven in her Cairo kitchen.   Alan Davidson

Have We A Choice?

Now, I do not think, as do wholehearted wholefood campaigners, that all the ills of this country stem from the eating of white bread and the lack of bran in roller-milled white flour. I do think that there should be far more choice, and above all, that every responsible person should know what he is choosing. We are faced with an ironic situation. For centuries the working man envied the white bread of the privileged. Now he may very soon grow to envy them their brown wholewheat bread. This is certainly every bit as inaccessible to the majority as was the fine white manchet bread of the sixteenth century, perhaps more so. For while it is true that, legally, wholewheat bread bought from a baker must contain 95 to 100 per cent of the grain, and (1976) carry a maximum price of only 6p more than that of the white wrapped loaf of equivalent weight, there are very few bakers who make or sell the genuine article.

It should be, and is not, generally understood that what is sold by bakers as 'wheatmeal' or 'brown' bread is quite distinct from wholemeal, should not be designated as such and should be 2p cheaper for a 28 oz loaf. Many people who buy those brown loaves are under the impression that they are buying wholemeal while what in fact they are buying is or may be, *quite legally*, a loaf of white flour with 0.6 per cent fibre plus caramel colouring, or it may be white with added wheat germ or a malted meal, or just possibly a quite genuine 85 per cent wheatmeal.

In view of the widely differing content of brown flours and brown bread as sanctioned under the Regulations,[1] it is curious that these

1. *The Bread and Flour Regulations*, Statutory Instrument, 1963, no. 1345; see the *Food Standards Committee Second Report on Bread and Flour*, H.M.S.O., 1974.

are thought by our legislators to be so clearly defined that bakers are not required by law to label their products or to state what flour they have used for any given loaf. So the customer, not surprisingly, has little idea of what she is buying. In the 1974 survey of the bread industry conducted by a Manchester University research team,[1] it was found that out of ninety-three shops visited, only thirty-two had 'brown' or 'brownish' loaves for sale. Of these thirty-two, five only were accepted by a public analyst as being made from genuine wholewheat flour. Among the loaves rejected was one made from white flour coloured with caramel.

Caramel, of course, is a permitted colouring for bread. It is the only permitted one – so for the time being we are protected from blue or pink or green bread – but it is widely used and is even legally permitted in 100 per cent wholemeal bread. So are quite a few other unexpected additives. To quote the *Food Standards Committee Second Report on Bread and Flour* (1974) 'While consumers may purchase wholemeal bread in the belief that it contains no additives, it is in fact permitted to contain all the yeast stimulating preparations . . . preservatives, emulsifiers and stabilizers which are permitted in white bread and in addition caramel is permitted for standardizing the colour . . . all these types of additives are used by some if not all bakers. Thus while consumers may rely on wholemeal flour to contain no additives, the same cannot be said for wholemeal bread.'

For those, then, who are determined to eat bread made from authentic 100 per cent wholemeal or even 85 per cent wheatmeal, there is precious little alternative but to buy the flour and bake it themselves.

WHAT IS CHOICE AND WHO MAKES IT?

It was during the 1950s that the millers bought out the British bakery industry. What happened, briefly, was that Mr Garfield Weston, Canadian head of a powerful biscuit and flour confectionery group known as Allied Bakeries, started buying up the more vulnerable bakery

1. T.A.C.C. Report (*Bread. An Assessment of the Bread Industry in Britain*), 1974.

businesses throughout the country. These provided his company with valuable outlets for his products, increasing also its production facilities by using existing bakery plant. In time Mr Weston decided to by-pass the British milling trade and import his own flour direct from Canada. The loss of so large-scale a flour customer as Allied Bakeries – by this time they had acquired control of the Aerated Bread Company with its manufacturing plant, its teashops and retail outlets – was a serious blow to the millers. Before long two of the most powerful milling firms in the country, J. Rank Ltd and Spillers Ltd, retaliated by establishing their own bakery plants, thus maintaining assured outlets for the flour products of their mills. These companies also went shopping for the minor plant bakeries and family businesses. At the same time many of the smaller milling firms found themselves succumbing to the unequal competition and went out of business or allowed themselves to be taken over.

By the end of the decade all three of the new major baking concerns had set about ensuring that their products would be available in grocery shops and dairies throughout the country, thus creating thousands of hitherto untapped retail outlets for their mass-produced bread. It was no longer necessary for the housewife to go to the bakery on her daily shopping round. She could buy a wrapped loaf at any corner shop. With the early 1960s came the spectacular growth of supermarkets and self-service stores. Commercial television also came. Proprietary brands of bread manufactured by the great milling concerns – Mother's Pride, Wonderloaf, Sunblest – became household names. J. Rank Ltd swallowed the old-established Hovis business and the familiar McDougall milling concern. Rank Hovis McDougall and their Mother's Pride white loaf came to be synonymous with all that was – and is – the total antithesis of homely basic bread. As *Which?* observed mildly in its issue of June 1975, 'if you like wrapped sliced bakery bread you'll find it difficult to make something similar at home'.

By the mid 1960s the notorious Chorleywood Bread Process had been evolved. Unknown to the general public the instant factory loaf had superseded the plant loaf of the 1950s. Does Chorleywood bread represent a further deterioration in quality? It certainly does not lack detractors. One example, perhaps an extreme one – those who feel strongly about the white factory loaf tend to feel very strongly indeed – was a Mr Maurice Frohn, a London consultant surgeon, who wrote to the *Daily Telegraph* (6 June 1973) that 'not only does the white loaf do no good, it is actually harmful to the body. Every encouragement should be given to the abolition of this foul food . . . the white loaf is not even fit to be given away.'

Now, criticisms such as Mr Frohn's, and many less forcibly expressed, are dismissed by the spokesmen and the apologists of the milling-baking industry as emotive, unrealistic, alarmist, mischievous. The bread produced in its factories, the milling industry claims, is incontrovertibly what the overwhelming majority wants. They support their claim by telling us that two out of every three loaves bought today by the British housewife are loaves processed by one of the three major combines.[1] When these companies send out their market researchers with questionnaires, what are the reasons given by house-wives for their choice? They are 'availability', 'convenience' (which means, I think, that the slices are the appropriate size and shape for toast and sandwiches) and 'hygiene'. These are reasons which include no mention of anybody buying the bread because they actually like it, and reasons which appear also to imply a bored indifference to the bread itself. It happens to be there in the shop, so it is bought. The customers like it being wrapped in paper and they like the shape. Is that choice? What yardstick of comparison is offered? And what choice is left to the minority, which is after all quite a substantial minority? That this minority is also an articulate one, and that it can scarcely be shrugged off as biased, irresponsible and ignorant (it does after all include a growing body of medical opinion) was candidly admitted by the Flour Advisory Bureau when it stated in an advertisement issued to the national Press in April 1975 that 'the white loaf, which represents over 80 per cent of the bread bought in Britain, hardly ever gets a good word said for it'. It might be inferred from this statement that the Flour Advisory Bureau is itself a biased body. So in a sense it is. It is the milling industry's own paid public relations agency. Its advertising copy went on to tell us how good is the white loaf, how packed with proteins, minerals, iron, vitamins and – again – all those

1. Now only two. In 1978 Spillers French withdrew from the baking industry.

'nutrients' handed to us in exchange for 16p,[1] the then cost of a 28 oz sliced, wrapped white loaf. Somewhat reluctantly – or so it appeared – and in parentheses, the copy added that 'brown and wholemeal of course are extremely good nutritionally, and may be chosen by people requiring extra roughage'.

What we really need to discover is what would happen were there freedom of choice uninhibited by considerations either of price or of availability, and choice unprejudiced by massive one-sided advertising campaigns. The wholefood organizations and the independent bakers are not rich enough to launch million-pound advertising campaigns. Any movement towards more interesting, more authentic bread and a genuine choice must come from the public itself.

Bread and Yeast Cookery
chosen by Rosi Hanson

When I first worked at the Bourne Street shop, *Spices, Salt and Aromatics in the English Kitchen* had just come out, and Elizabeth was working on what became the bread book.

We usually brought lunch and ate it in the stockroom. (Incidentally, at that time one of the perks that went with this not very well-paid shop assistant's job, was a glass of *vin ordinaire* at lunchtime.) Elizabeth brought whatever she was trying out, offering tastes and inviting comments. Most of us caught the bread-making habit from her and she was solicitous and encouraging of our efforts. We sold everything you needed to make bread, including decent flour and proper household salt, and I remember assembling all the equipment at the end of a tiring Saturday to take home and make bread for the first time. Elizabeth gave me her home telephone number in case of a disaster. It turned out fine and I didn't need to use the emergency number. I have been using her recipe several times a week ever since.

The piece is a wonderful example of extensive research made readable. She was very angry about the millers and their power but she never let the anger get in the way of clarity. Rosi Hanson

1. 25p by November 1978.

BREAD AND YEAST COOKERY

WHOLEMEAL TIN BREAD

'Observe, brown bread is often recommended by medical men. When used as a matter of health, almost the only chance of succeeding, is by procuring the undressed meal, and making the bread at home. If bakers are applied to for brown bread they generally produce it by merely taking a portion of the regular dough, and sprinkling among it as much bran as will bring it to the colour required.'

Esther Copley, *The Complete Cottage Cookery*, 1849

Stone-ground 100 per cent wholemeal is in some ways – but only in some ways – simpler to deal with than white flour or finely ground brown flour from which the bran has been extracted. One hundred per cent wholemeal loaves to be baked in tins can be made with only one rising and very little kneading; the dough is improved by the addition of a small proportion of fat in the form of lard, butter, milk, fresh buttermilk or cream. Wholemeal loaves don't rise very much and require careful baking if they are not to be dry and brick-like, as those sold in health-food shops and wholefood restaurants so often are, or soggy and puddingy, as they will be if the dough is made too liquid, and since these wholemeals vary so enormously in the amount of liquid they will absorb it is virtually impossible to indicate the correct quantity of water to meal.

Given the erratic performance of wholemeals the following recipe is for guidance only, and given in quantities for one trial loaf to be baked in a 3- to 3½-pint (1.8–2.4-l) tin, or for two smaller loaves.

1 lb 4 oz–1 lb 6 oz of stone-ground 100 per cent wholemeal, ½ oz of yeast, ½ oz of salt, approximately ½ pint–12 fl oz of water, 2 tablespoons of buttermilk or thick cream or 4 of milk, fat for the tins, and extra meal for handling the dough.

Equivalent metric quantities: flour 550–600 g, yeast 15 g, salt 15 g, water approximately 280–340 ml, 2 tablespoons of buttermilk or thick cream or 4 of milk, fat for the tins, extra meal for handling dough. Tin sizes: one tin of 1 litre capacity or two of 0.5 litre capacity.

First weigh out the flour. I find it best to start with the smaller quantity, keeping the extra 2 oz (60 g) aside in case the dough turns out to be impossibly wet. Taking this precaution means that for next time one knows how much liquid to meal is needed. Warm the flour in its bowl for a few minutes in a very low oven, such as the simmering oven of a solid fuel cooker, or in the plate drawer of a gas or electric oven.

While the meal is warming – 5–7 minutes is ample – mix the cream or buttermilk, which in all probability will be ice cold from the refrigerator, with very warm water to make up a total of about 14 fl oz (400 ml). Use a little of this to cream the yeast, then add the salt to the liquid. Grease or butter your warmed tin or tins. When the meal is warm to the touch, make a well in the centre, pour in the yeast, then about 10 fl oz (280 ml) of the warm liquid, and mix the dough with your hands. Add as much more liquid as will make the dough manageable. It must not be dry. If, on the contrary, it handles like a mud pie, as well as looking like one, dry it out a little with some of the extra meal, until you have a mixture which can be more easily handled. All that is necessary is to mix a fairly coherent dough which can be shaped and transferred to the tin or tins without difficulty.

Fill the warmed and greased tin or tins by about three-quarters, smooth the top surface of the dough as much as possible, cover with a damp cloth or a sheet of polythene and leave them in a really warm place until the dough has reached the tops of the tins. This should not take longer than 45 minutes – the dough, having been mixed with all ingredients well warmed, generates its own internal heat, which makes the yeast act well and quickly, even with an exceptionally coarse meal.

Have the oven ready heated, and bake the bread at 220°–230°C/ 425°–450°F/Gas Mark 7–8, for 15–20 minutes, then reduce the heat to 190°C/375°F/Gas Mark 5, for another 15–20 minutes. By this time the loaf or loaves will have contracted and can be slipped out of the tins, but will not yet be quite cooked. Return them to the oven, upside down or on their sides, until they are ready, which is when the undersides are sufficiently baked to give out a hollow sound when tapped with the knuckles.

Leave them on their sides on a wire tray to cool, or balance them across the still warm empty tins, so that they are not subjected to a sudden draught of cold air.

English Bread and Yeast Cookery
chosen by Steve Grey

IRISH WHOLEWHEAT SODA BREAD

This is quickly made and delicious while fresh.

1 lb–1 lb 4 oz of 100 per cent whole wheatmeal; 1 level teaspoon of bicarbonate of soda; 2 level teaspoons of salt; approximately ½ pint of slightly sour buttermilk or milk sour enough to be just solid but without the slightest hint of a mouldy or acrid smell; 2 to 4 tablespoons of warm water.

Equivalent metric quantities: 100 per cent whole wheatmeal 450–550 g, bicarbonate of soda 1 level teaspoon, salt 2 level teaspoons, slightly sour buttermilk or milk approximately 280 ml, warm water 2 to 4 tablespoons.

Sift the salt and the bicarbonate very carefully throughout the mass of meal. Add the cold buttermilk or sour milk and mix to a dough, adding the warm water if the mixture is too dry.

Quickly divide the dough into two pieces, form them into nice round buns as tall as you can make them, place them on a non-stick baking sheet or a floured iron sheet. The alternative method of shaping the loaves is to make them rather flatter, like a scone, then make a deep cross cut, so that each loaf when baked will divide easily into four parts. Cover each loaf with a deep 6-inch (15-cm) or 7-inch (18-cm) cake tin. Put them immediately on the shelf above the centre of a hot oven, preheated for 5 minutes at 220°–230°C/425°–450°F/ Gas Marks 7–8, and bake for 30 minutes. Remove the tins and leave the loaves for another 10–15 minutes, until they have formed brown but not overbaked, crusts.

This bread is at its best when just cooled, but reheats successfully by the usual method, i.e. low down in a very moderate oven, and covered with a tin or bowl, for 7–10 minutes.

Notes: 1. If you cannot lay hands on buttermilk and have no sour milk, add 2 level teaspoons of cream of tartar to the bicarbonate of soda, and mix the dough with half fresh milk and half water. The cream of tartar provides acid in place of the sour milk or buttermilk. Should you have a little sour cream, say 2 to 4 fl oz (60–120 ml) to hand, use this made up to the right quantity of liquid with water. A little butter, up to 1 oz (30 g), can also be added.

2. The cake tin inverted over the bread while it is cooking helps it to rise a little – wholewheat soda bread never rises very much – and also to remain moist and not form too hard and dry a crust. It is an old dodge, helpful in today's gas and electric ovens.

English Bread and Yeast Cookery

TO MAKE A COBURG OR ROUND LOAF WITHOUT A TIN

I make these round loaves with 14 oz of strong plain unbleached flour, ¼ oz of fresh yeast, rather under ½ oz of salt, and slightly under 8 fl oz (1 cup U.S.) of warm water. Also needed is a floured baking sheet or heatproof earthenware platter.

Equivalent metric quantities: flour 400 g, fresh yeast 10 g, salt rather under 15 g, water slightly under 225 ml.

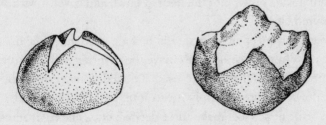

Mix the yeast to a cream with a little tepid water. Stir the salt into the flour, put the bowl, covered, into a very low oven for 5 minutes, just long enough to warm the flour. Mix the creamed yeast

into it, add the tepid water. The right temperature is about 37°
–38°C, 98°–100°F. Mix well and shape the dough into a ball. If
it is too wet, sprinkle with a little more flour. Cover, and leave in
a warm place to rise. The ideal temperature is from 21°–23°C,
70°–75°F.

In an hour to an hour and a half the dough should have doubled
in volume and feel spongy and light. Scoop it up, and slap it down
hard in the bowl or on a board. Repeat this three or four times. The
more the dough is knocked down at this stage the better the loaf will
be.

Now knead and roll the dough into a ball, place this in the centre
of the floured baking sheet. At this stage – and it is an important one
– fold the ball of dough all round, tucking the edges underneath, so
that the uncooked loaf looks like a little, round, plump cushion. If
this detail is omitted, the loaf will spread out flat. Getting the shape
right is a knack which may take a few tries to acquire. The correct
consistency of the dough also plays an important part. If it is too wet
nothing will prevent it spreading, so if you have used too much water
sprinkle in more flour as you shape the loaf. Try not to overdo the
addition of flour, or the finished loaf will turn out patchy.

It is advisable to cover the dough while it is rising for the second
time and the easiest way to do this is to invert a clean bowl over it.
For example, quickly rinse and dry the bowl used for mixing the
dough. Don't use it without cleaning it. An hour later it will be twice
as difficult to wash. An alternative method is to put the shaped ball
of dough upside down into the floured bowl, and cover it with a plate
or a floured cloth.

Three-quarters of an hour should be long enough for the dough to
double its volume once again. Remove the covering bowl. If necessary
re-shape the loaf. (If you have used the method of proving the loaf
upside down in a bowl, simply invert it on to the baking sheet.) With
a sharp knife or scissors make three deepish cuts, one right across the
loaf, the other two from the outer edges inward to the centre, so that
they meet the first cut and form a cross. As the cuts open the loaf is
ready to go into the oven.

Have the oven heated to 230°C/450°F/Gas Mark 8. Bake the loaf
on the centre shelf for 15 minutes at this temperature, another 15 at

200°C/400°F/Gas Mark 6, then turn it upside down and leave for 10–15 minutes with the oven turned off.

Cool on a rack.

English Bread and Yeast Cookery

A GRANARY LOAF

This is made from the proprietary granary meal packed in 3 lb (1.5 kg) bags by Granary Foods Ltd of Burton-on-Trent. It is a mixture of wheat and rye meals with a proportion of wheatkernels. Directions for making up the bread are given on the bag, but I find the malt flavour rather too strong, and so usually mix a proportion of plain flour, either 81 per cent wheatmeal or strong white, with the granary meal, and prefer to add fat in the form of olive oil rather than the lard recommended by the packers.

Home-made granary bread stays fresh and moist for an unusually long time, is particularly well-liked by the young, and the dough is very good tempered, exceptionally easy to mix and bake; taken all in all it has much to recommend it, especially to beginners in bread-making. My recipe is for a pan Coburg loaf, made as follows.

1 lb of granary meal, 4 oz of 81 or 85 per cent wheatmeal or strong plain unbleached flour, ½ oz of salt, ½ oz of yeast, 2 tablespoons of light olive oil, approximately ½ pint of water.

Equivalent metric quantities: granary meal 450 g, wheatmeal or strong plain unbleached flour 120 g, salt 15 g, yeast 15 g, light olive oil 2 tablespoons, water approximately 280 ml.

Mix the two flours or meals very thoroughly. Either add the salt directly to the flour or dissolve it in the warm water, whichever method you prefer to use. If the weather is cold, warm the flour in the oven as explained in the basic loaf recipe on page 314.

Cream the yeast with tepid water, mix it with the flour, make up the dough with the warm water; add the oil last. The dough will be very lithe and pliable, and will need little working or kneading at this stage. Form it into a ball, cover it, leave it to rise in the normal way, at room temperature in warm weather, in winter or whenever it is more convenient, over a pilot light or in some other warm place.

When the dough has at least doubled in bulk and is puffy, break it down, knead it for 2 or 3 minutes.

Have your round, sloping-sided tin or dish slightly warmed and well coated with olive oil or fat, put the ball of dough in the centre. Cover it, leave it for approximately 30 minutes, until it has filled the tin, and is beginning to rise above the rim. With a sharp knife make two deep cuts in the shape of a cross. These should start opening out immediately. Dough made with malted meal always takes the cuts most satisfactorily. Leave a few more minutes, until the dough has recovered its spring, before putting it into the oven.

Usually I bake this bread by the under-cover system (see p. 322), putting it on a low shelf, covered, with the oven turned on to 230°C/450°F/Gas Mark 8, but not preheated. The timing is approximately 45 minutes at this temperature, plus 20–25 minutes at 200°C/400°F/Gas Mark 6, with the loaf uncovered. If you use an earthenware dish or mould it will probably be necessary to give the loaf a further few minutes on the underside, after it has been turned out of the mould. This is because earthenware makes for a much softer undercrust than does metal.

N.B. The Fahrenheit and Celsius temperatures given in this recipe are those registered low down in the oven, not, as is usual with equivalent electricity and gas temperatures, in the centre.

English Bread and Yeast Cookery
chosen by Mick Caffyn

RICE BREAD

This is excellent bread for keeping, since the rice remains moist, and the texture is beautifully light and honeycombed. It is also a loaf which is very easy to mix and to bake.

Ingredients are 3 oz of rice (about ½ a U.S. cup) uncooked weight, three times its volume of water for cooking it, and for the dough 1 lb 2 oz of strong plain flour, ½ oz of yeast, ½–¾ oz of salt, rather under ½ pint of water, and fat for the tin. (If you use a larger saucepan you need extra water.)

Equivalent metric quantities: rice (uncooked) 85 g, three times its volume of water, strong plain flour 500 g, yeast 15 g, salt 15–20 g, water about ¼ litre, fat for the tin.

Put the rice in a thick saucepan of 1¾ to 2-pint (about 1 l) capacity, cover it with 1½ cups (340 ml) of water. Bring it to the boil, cover the saucepan, leave the rice to cook steadily until the water is absorbed and little holes have formed all over the surface of the rice.

While the rice is cooking, weigh out and prepare all the other ingredients. Cream the yeast with a little warm water. Put the salt in a measuring jug and dissolve it in ¼ pint (150 ml) of very hot water, then add cold water to make up the correct quantity.

When the rice is cooked, and while it is still very warm, amalgamate it, very thoroughly, with the flour. Now add the yeast, then the salted water, and mix the dough in the usual way. It will be rather soft. Cover it and leave it to rise for 1–1½ hours, until it is at least double in volume, and bubbly.

Probably the dough will be too soft to handle very much, so it may be necessary to dry it out a little by adding more flour before breaking it down and transferring it – very little kneading is necessary – to a warmed and well greased tin or tins. For the quantity given I use a sandwich loaf tin of 3–3½-pint (1.8–2 l) capacity. The dough should fill the tin by two-thirds. Cover it with a cloth or a sheet of polythene, leave it until it has risen above the top of the tin.

Bake the bread in the usual way, at 230°C/450°F/Gas Mark 8, for 15 minutes, then at 200°C/400°F/Gas Mark 6, for another 15 minutes, before turning the loaf out of its tin and returning it to the oven, on its side, for a final 15–20 minutes at the same temperature. If the crust shows signs of baking too hard and taking too much colour, cover the loaf with a large bowl or an inverted oval casserole.

English Bread and Yeast Cookery
chosen by Johnny Grey

UNDER-COVER BREADBAKING

Since it is so difficult in an ordinary household oven to create the steamy atmosphere required for the successful formation of a truly 'crusty' loaf, that is a loaf baked without benefit of a tin, and therefore crusty all round rather than just on the top, the 'undertin' method seemed to me to offer a clue worth following up. If a good loaf could be baked under an inverted tin, would it not be possible to apply the method to a crusty loaf, but using an earthenware or stoneware bowl or casserole instead of a tin? Experiment with this simple system proved enormously successful. The increase in the volume of a loaf baked for the first 15–30 or even 45 minutes under cover of a deep bowl is quite dramatic, the quality of the crust is much improved, and the crumb moist and evenly baked. What has happened is that the inverted bowl or casserole has become something like a small, domed, brick oven, a wonderful generator of moist heat. Within its confines the yeast in the dough grows with great rapidity and, as the loaf expands, it is drawn upwards, rather than spreading only sideways, as so often happens if your dough is a moist one. Under the dome, the crust forms gradually, allowing the crumb to grow to its full extent before the yeast cells are killed, and this eliminates the fault which spoils so many home-made crusty loaves – a crust which has formed so rapidly that it has become overcooked and hard long before the

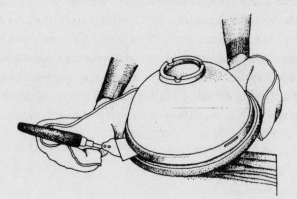

crumb has had a chance to expand, the resulting loaf being poorly formed and small with a rock-like crust and heavy crumb.

Now, to experiment with the under-cover method the only piece of required equipment not necessarily used in bread-baking is a large deep earthenware or stoneware bowl, which must, it goes without saying, be heat resistant. Whatever bowl or pot is used must be large enough to make, of itself, a kind of oven within the oven; there must be space for the dough to expand, and the finished loaf is not supposed to *fill* the pot, although to a minor extent it will take on something of the shape of the pot used. For a loaf made with 1¼ lb (675 g) flour, the bowls I use are approximately 9 inches (23 cm) in diameter and 4½ inches (12 cm) deep. Granary loaves and Coburgs are very successful baked by this method.

Mix the dough and leave it for its first rising in the ordinary way. Then, having broken down the dough, kneaded and shaped it on your baking sheet, or better, a flat earthenware platter, heat resistant, cover it with the inverted bowl and leave it to rise for the second time.

About 5 minutes before you intend baking the loaf reshape it and cut or slash it in the way you prefer; as soon as the cuts open, replace the bowl or pot, and put all into the oven, heated to 230°–240°C/450°–475°F/Gas Marks 8–9.

Leave the loaf for 30–35 minutes before removing the bowl to look at it. Make sure that you have a good thick cloth or oven gloves, and take the whole contraption, baking sheet, loaf and cover, from the oven before attempting to remove the cover or bowl. Slide a metal spatula or fish slice under the rim, tilting the bowl so that it is easy to lift it off. At this stage, depending upon the type of bread you are making and also upon your particular oven, the loaf should be very well grown while the crust will be only slightly coloured, or possibly not at all. Return the uncovered loaf to the oven, still at the same temperature.

After another 15 minutes, the crust should be golden, but may still be soft. In this case leave the loaf in the oven for another 10–15 minutes. At the end of the time the crust should be very beautiful, a mixture of gold and brown, with almost silvery patches where the cuts were made. The loaf will have shrunk a little while the crust has been baking to a proper crispness. If you prefer a soft crust, then leave the loaf covered throughout the whole of the cooking time, allowing an extra 10–15 minutes' baking time but at a reduced temperature.

Cool the loaf as usual on a rack. I find it a good idea to place the wire rack across the top of the bowl which is still warm from the oven. In this way the loaf cools gradually, instead of being subjected to a sudden draught of cold air.

English Bread and Yeast Cookery

CROISSANTS

I have only limited tolerance towards all the rolling and folding and turning involved in puff pastry. It is a process which gives me no pleasure. As in effect a *croissant* dough is just a yeast-leavened puff pastry I don't often embark on making *croissants*. When I do, I use the recipe from Julia Child's *Mastering the Art of French Cooking*, Volume 2. It is a long recipe, and that I have used it a couple of times with success proves that it is also a pretty foolproof one. I have to admit, though, that at the end of it all I do tend to suffer from combat fatigue, and question whether *croissants* are really worth all the production involved. However, now that at last Volume 2 of Mrs Child's extraordinary work is published in England (and before long will surely appear in paperback), those who are keen enough to have a try, and who have an aptitude for pastry-making, will be able to consult her *croissant* recipe direct. For a telescoped method, I suggest the following professional baker's recipe, which does of course assume that the reader knows all about the rolling out and folding of puff pastry. The author uses very slightly less butter to flour than is specified by Julia Child, gives the dough three turns to her four, and suggests only 30 minutes' resting period between turns where Mrs Child orders 1½ hours (it's a rest for the dough, not for the cook who probably needs it just as much), and a final proof period of 1 hour at 23°C/75°F.

I suggest that for a first try Mr Fance's recipe below could be used in half quantities, which should make twenty to twenty-four *croissants*.

Flour (strong) 2 lb 4 oz, salt ¾ oz, sugar 3 oz, yeast 1 oz, milk approx 1 lb 8 oz [i.e. 24 fl oz], butter for rolling in, 1 lb.'

Equivalent metric quantities: strong flour 1 kg, salt 20 g, sugar 85 g, yeast 30 g, milk approximately 670 ml, butter 450 g.

'Make a flying ferment [i.e. a preliminary sponge or batter] with the milk, yeast, sugar and 6 oz [170 g] of flour. Weigh up the other ingredients and make up a dough with the salt and the balance of the flour. The dough should be soft and well developed.

'Allow to rest for 30 minutes then roll the dough into a rectangle. Cover half the surface with the butter and fold the other half over on to the top. Give three half-turns, resting between turns if the dough toughens.

'When the dough is ready for finishing, it should be rolled out in a rectangle about ⅛ in (3 mm) thick and cut into strips 8 in (20 cm) wide, then cut into triangles to obtain a many-storied structure, allowing the dough pieces to roll up on themselves many times.

'The pieces are placed on to warmed and lightly greased baking sheets in the form of a crescent and egg washed. They are again egg washed after proof, before baking at 240°C/475°F/Gas Mark 9. The prover must not be too hot or the butter will melt and spoil the flaky structure.'

W. J. Fance and B. H. Wragg, *Up-to-Date Breadmaking*, 1968

Notes: A few details should, I think, be added to the above recipe.

1. The triangles of dough are rolled from the broad base towards the extended point; when rolled this point should come out on the top of the straight roll; with the next movement the ends are bent inwards to shape the crescent, and the point then comes to the front of the *croissant*.

2. As Mr Fance indicates, professional bakers have a proving box or cupboard heated to a controlled temperature, so to them the final rising or proving of the *croissants* is no problem. In a centrally heated domestic kitchen it is best to find a cool place for them, cover them with a sheet of polythene, and allow a good hour or longer for them to regain full volume before they go into the oven. It is preferable to delay the proving process rather than to allow them to get warm enough for the butter to run.

3. I find that in a small domestic oven 240°C/475°F/Gas Mark 9 is too hot for the baking of croissants, and that 12–15 minutes at

220°–230°C/425°–450°F/Gas Marks 7–8 with the tray on the shelf above centre, is about right. When there is more than one trayful it is advisable to bake them in two batches.

4. If you don't want all the croissants at once it is perfectly feasible to freeze some of the batch. They can be frozen either uncooked, at the full proof stage, or after baking and as soon as they have cooled.

5. *Please* don't use any fat but butter for croissants.

English Bread and Yeast Cookery
chosen by Prue Leith

CORNISH SAFFRON CAKE

Cornish saffron cake is really a spiced bread, delicate and light, and usually made without eggs. My recipe was evolved from several variations given in *Cornish Recipes Ancient and Modern*, compiled by Edith Martin and first published in 1929 by the Cornwall Federation of Women's Institutes, and from two other variations in a more recent and equally enterprising collection called *Devonshire Flavour*, published in 1970 by the Exeter branch of the YWCA.

It was from a recipe given in the latter book and attributed by Professor Arthur Hutchings to his Aunt Polly that I learned a valuable detail which no other recipe had made clear: that the little bits of saffron in the infusion which colours the cake are not strained out. This piece of information tells us that the good West Country cooks of the past used, and understood the advantages of, whole saffron filaments as opposed to ready-powdered saffron. Perhaps also it was a case of proper pride in the use of the best ingredients, just as at one time the specks of vanilla were left in ice cream to show that it had been flavoured with the bean rather than with essence. Further, Professor Hutchings adds that 'the true saffron yeast cake of the West Country should not be confused with travesties sold under the same name. They are not yeast cakes and they often have no saffron, but are coloured yellow and have a disgusting sickly taste of vanilla and far too much sweetening.' Having myself encountered those false, shameful saffron cakes when attempting to track down authentic West Country dishes, I can sympathize with the Professor's anger at the debauching of this fine old speciality, familiar to him since childhood.

The proportions I give here make a 2 lb (900 g) cake to be baked in one rectangular loaf tin of approximately 3-pint (1.8-l) capacity or in two smaller farmhouse-type tins each of 1¼ to 1½-pint (700–845 ml) capacity.

To 1 lb of plain flour, other ingredients are ½ oz of yeast, ¼ lb of butter or the equivalent in thick heavy cream, 2 oz of caster sugar, 2 oz each of sultanas and currants, rather over ¼ pint of milk, 1 teaspoon of salt, a scant saltspoon each of freshly grated nutmeg, powdered cinnamon and mixed sweet spice, approximately ½ teaspoon of saffron filaments. For glazing the cake an extra 2 tablespoons of milk and 1 tablespoon of sugar.

Equivalent metric quantities: plain flour 450 g, yeast 15 g, butter or thick cream 120 g, caster sugar 60 g, sultanas 60 g, currants 60 g, milk rather over 150 ml, salt 1 teaspoon, grated nutmeg, powdered cinnamon and mixed sweet spice a scant saltspoon each, saffron filaments approximately ½ teaspoon, extra milk 2 tablespoons and sugar 1 tablespoon (for glazing).

First prepare the saffron, and the yeast. Take about half the ¼ pint (150 ml) of milk and heat it to boiling point. Put the saffron filaments on an ovenproof saucer or small plate, place in a hot oven for about 5 minutes. Crumble the filaments into a coffee cup, pour a little of the hot milk over them and leave to infuse. Within 10 minutes the saffron will have dyed the milk a beautiful pale marigold colour.

Pour the remainder of the heated milk – which by this time will be only lukewarm – over the yeast and mix it to a cream.

Weigh out the flour, sugar, sultanas, currants and butter or cream.

Put the flour, sugar and salt into a warmed mixing bowl. Sprinkle in the dry spices. Stir in the creamed yeast. Now beat in the softened butter or the cream. This is best done with your hands. When it is well amalgamated, add the saffron infusion and the remainder of the milk. A little extra may be needed. Much depends upon the flour. The dough should be soft but not runny. Finally mix in the warmed currants and sultanas and make sure that they are well distributed throughout the dough. Cover the bowl, leave the dough to rise for a couple of hours, or longer if it is more convenient.

When the dough has at least doubled in volume, break it down very lightly, sprinkle it with flour, transfer it to the warmed and buttered tin, pat it into shape and leave it to rise for the second time. This is a slow-rising dough and will take a minimum of 45 minutes to an hour to return to life and reach almost to the top of the tin. When sufficiently risen, bake the cake in the centre of a fairly hot oven (190°–200°C/375°–400°F/Gas Mark 5–6) for 15 minutes, then move the tin to the lower shelf and leave it for a further 10–15 minutes at the same temperature.

As soon as you take the cake from the oven, brush it with the heated sugar and milk glaze. Leave it for about 15 minutes before turning out of the tin.

Saffron cake is at its best eaten when freshly baked and just cooled, although it *can* be reheated in a very low oven. It is for this reason that it is important not to overbake it in the first instance. This particular cake makes an original and subtle accompaniment to a glass of sweet Sauternes or any dessert wine of your fancy. A Madeira or the charming Italian soft white Orvieto called *amabile* would be other possibilities.

English Bread and Yeast Cookery

CRUMPETS AND MUFFINS

'If I sells three dozen muffins at ½d each, and twice that in crumpets, it's a werry fair day, werry fair; all beyond that is a *good* day.'
Henry Mayhew, *London Labour and the London Poor*, 1851

'Children are, in general, fondest of crumpets; but muffins are alone introduced at coffee-houses, etc. in London.'
The Family Receipt Book, London, 1853

To commence at the beginning, as the 1906 edition of *Mrs Beeton's Book of Household Management* said of bread storage, today's colloquialism or slang meaning of the word crumpet as a piece of skirt, any likely young woman, a girl with whom someone is having a passing affair, and other less polite interpretations, seems to have taken over from muffin, which once had the same or similar connotations. *The Oxford English Dictionary* quotes examples dating from 1856 and Miss Isabella Bird's observations during her travels in Canada: 'Every unmarried gentleman, who chooses to do so, selects a young lady to be his companion in the numerous amusements of the season . . . when she acquiesces [she] is called a "muffin".' Another evocative one is attributed to a Major A. Griffiths, 1904: 'A pleasant *tête-a-tête* drive for many miles . . . with your "muffin" by your side.' The *O.E.D.* concludes that the use of the word muffin in this sense is of Canadian origin.

Muffins are on the left, crumpets on the right. And which are pikelets?

Now for some slightly more literal interpretations of the two words:

'Muffin . . . connected with old French *moufflet*, soft, said of bread.'[1]

'Muffin-worry *colloq.*, a tea-party . . . an old ladies' tea party.'[2]

'The probable origin of the word crumpet is the Welsh *crempog*, a pancake or fritter. For some reason or other, probably because they are in some degree similar, and yet differing greatly, it is customary to associate muffins with crumpets, it being a rare occurrence for either to appear at the table separately.

1. *The Oxford English Dictionary.*   2. ibid.

Both are made of batter, both require re-cooking, and both are served hot and well buttered; yet there is so marked a difference between the two in flavour and constitution that most persons have a decided preference for one or the other."[1]

Crumpets, or at least terrible travesties of them, can still be bought in England, although they are more commonly sold packeted by grocers or supermarkets than by bakers. Perhaps indeed they are delivered direct from a plastics recycling plant, and have never been near a bakery.

Muffins one rarely sees – although Sainsbury's sell packets of a thing they *call* a muffin – and hears about only when the spasmodic wave of nostalgia for bygone popular specialities breaks over the British Press and its cookery contributors, when there is much talk of the muffin-man and his bell from feature writers far too young ever to have heard that bell or eaten the wares which the muffin-man cried through the streets; at such times there is nearly always reference to the past glories of the British breakfast (I remember the muffin-man ringing his bell on Primrose Hill when I lived there in the 1930s; it was always at weekends and in the afternoon, in time for tea, so if you wanted them for breakfast you had to keep them until the next day) and also to a solitary surviving muffin-man who still supplies the occupants of Buckingham Palace.

Well, what are or were the crumpets and muffins which Mayhew's muffin-man used to sell for a ½d each? What is the difference between them? Which have holes, which are baked in rings? Which are made from a pouring batter, which from a soft dough similar to the one used for baps and rolls? Is a pikelet the equivalent of a muffin or of a crumpet? What is the relation of an oatcake to either? Should muffins and/or crumpets be split and/or toasted or should they not? Are muffins and crumpets made from identical ingredients? If so, what are they? Flour, yeast, water, salt? Or flour and yeast plus milk, fat and eggs? Or flour, fat and eggs with a chemical raising agent? Anybody who knows the answers to more than two or three of these queries is wiser than I, although not necessarily more certain of their own beliefs

1. *The Encyclopaedia of Practical Cookery*, ed. Theodore Francis Garrett, 1899.

than professional bakers, cooking-school teachers, contributors to Women's Institute recipe anthologies and such redoubtable authorities on English household cooking as Florence Jack, Florence White and Dorothy Hartley.

English Bread and Yeast Cookery
chosen by Kit Chapman

Spices, of course, feature prominently in *English Bread and Yeast Cookery*, but if I am to choose one section, it must be Elizabeth David's brilliant, and sometimes tartly amusing, essay on the subject of Crumpets and Muffins. The reason for my choice is deeply Proustian. Crumpets and muffins are the *madeleines* of my childhood. I remember devouring them greedily at my grandmother's house in Sussex – dribbling warm butter and strawberry jam, staining her immaculate lace tablecloth and making her quite cross. Forty years on, middle age, girth and guilt are still no defences against the sensual comforts of hot buttered crumpets on a cold winter's afternoon.

Kit Chapman

THE ITALIAN PIZZA AND
THE FRENCH PISSALADIÈRE

In colloquial Italian the word *pizza* denotes a pie of almost any kind, savoury or sweet, open or covered, and with a basis of any variety of pastry or of leavened dough, and to the English-speaking world a *pizza* means a flat, round, open pie with a filling of tomato and onion topped with melting cheese.

In short, the *pizza* which has travelled the world, reached almost every deep-freeze cabinet in Europe and America, become a mainstay of the take-away food counters, and is manufactured by the ton in the food-processing factories, was originally the Neapolitan interpretation of an ancient method of dealing with a piece of bread dough in a rough and ready fashion, strewing it with a few onions, a handful of salt sardines or anchovies, or a sprinkling of pork scrapple left from the rendering down of lard. To us the *pizza* may be indissolubly associated with the tomato, but it did of course exist long before tomatoes were cultivated in Europe. Something like it was familiar to the Greeks

and to the Romans, probably the early Arabs had a version of it –
they certainly have one now – and the Armenians claim that they
invented it (perhaps they did); there are variations to be found in
Spain where it is called *coca*, meaning a kind of cake, and in Provence
where it was once known as *pissaladeira*, and has now all but merged
with the universal *pizza*. In eastern France the quiche of Lorraine,
almost as much a victim of current fashion and factory production as
the *pizza*, was originally made on a basis of bread dough, and a quiche
was not committed exclusively to a filling of bacon and cream and
eggs. It could be, and often was, the basis for a spread of fresh plums
or cherries, which baked to a delicious sticky, sugary mass. This brings
it all nearer home, to our own lardy cakes and fruit-enriched doughs.
For surely, anywhere there was leavened bread there was likely to be
left-over dough, to be quickly made up and baked to provide something
cheap and filling for children, for the poor, the hungry.

What seems extraordinary is that so many people in so many places
can be induced into paying so high a price for something so simple
and cheap to make at home and so difficult to reproduce in mass-market
terms as the Neapolitan *pizza*. Even taking into consideration your
own time and work plus the cost of the oven fuel, a home-made *pizza*
is something of a bargain, making the mass-produced 'pizza pie' –
many are made with a baking powder dough, not a yeast-leavened
one, hence their incredible toughness – seem rather more of a confidence trick than most products of its kind. This is probably because
being an alien import with an unfamiliar name it contains a built-in
mystique. Equivalent prices for a hot cheese sandwich or a take-away
portion of cottage pie would soon meet with resistance.

Now, it must be said that the authentic Neapolitan *pizza* was – and
is – heavy going, and lies uneasy on any but the most robust of
stomachs. It became popular because it was cheap, and the original
pizzeria, or pizza house, furnished with its own brick oven in which
every *pizza* was baked to order, was a refuge – if rather a noisy one
– where the hungry and hard-up could eat their hefty round of
cheese-topped *pizza* and drink a glass or two of cheap wine for the
equivalent of a few pence. As late as 1950 the *pizzeria* was an almost
exclusively southern Italian institution. The beehive-shaped brick
oven installed in the *pizzeria* was a conscious survival, or revival, of

the ancient, traditional bread oven, and it was then rare to find a *pizzeria* north of Rome, whereas now there must be one or more in almost every town throughout the Italian peninsula.

Along the Mediterranean coast, west beyond Genoa and across the borders of Provence a different version of *pizza* was to be bought from the bakeries. It was baked and displayed for sale in huge rectangular iron oven trays from which the customers could buy slices at the same time as they bought their morning bread. On the Ligurian coast this *pizza* was known as a *sardenara*, because originally salted sardines were part of the top dressing, the basis of which was onion and tomato. In Provence between Nice and Marseille the *pissaladeira*, very similar to the *sardenara*, owed its name to *pissala*, a brined and potted mixture of small-fry peculiar to the coasts of the County of Nice and of Provence. By the time I first encountered the *pissaladeira*, in the 1930s, anchovies had taken the place of the *pissala*, and there were basically two kinds of dressings for the bread dough, one mainly of onions stewed in olive oil, with black olives added, the other with tomatoes, anchovies and, again, black olives. A third, called *anchoïade*, was an anchovy and garlic mixture. This one is now nearly always made on a basis of ready cooked, fresh and thick bread slices, but is much nicer spread on the raw dough and then baked. None of these versions featured the cheese of the Neapolitan *pizza*.

These variations, then, are the ones upon which I base my own *pizza* mixtures: onion, tomato, anchovy, black olives, in varying proportions and not necessarily all at once, but always cooked in olive oil and flavoured with oregano, the wild marjoram of Italy. Sometimes, but not invariably, garlic goes into the mixture. I don't include any top dressing of chewy cheese. The *pizza* manufacturers, evidently believing it to be an essential selling point, use either processed Cheddar or a specially developed '*pizza* Mozzarella'. Both seem to me quite pointless. The mass-market product would be better as well as cheaper without them.

The dough I use is what the Italians would call *casalinga*, a household dough rather than a baker's basic bread dough, which means it is made rather lighter, with an egg or two and olive oil – or butter if you prefer it – so that what it amounts to is a very modified form of brioche dough.

Once you have acquired the knack of making this dough – it was through the *pizza* that I first discovered how easy it is to work with yeast – it is no trouble whatever to make a *pizza* in any size or form you please.

One word of advice, though, as to the filling or dressing for the dough. A great many English people make the mistake of thinking that the more oddments added in the way of bits of sausage, bacon, mushrooms, prawns and anything else that comes to hand, the better the *pizza* will be. In fact the reverse is true. The black olives for example, can be eliminated – it is now very difficult to find the right kind, and it is better not to attempt any substitute for them. There *is* no substitute. But you *can* use a few extra anchovies, which are more easily obtainable. And tomato is not obligatory any more than is cheese. Just onions, if you like them, slowly, slowly stewed in olive oil, and with a final addition of anchovy fillets before the dough goes into the oven, make an excellent *pizza*. For those allergic to onions, a tomato filling without them is perfectly feasible. There is really no problem and not many rules. The idea is, basically, that what you spread on the dough sinks *into* it, amalgamates itself with, and becomes an integral part of, the bread as it bakes. A mass of bitty things won't do this. They will just stay on top of the dough, toughen and probably burn as the *pizza* cooks. It is insufficient understanding of the nature and behaviour of leavened dough which causes English cooks to attempt so many non-viable additions and substitutions. Or is it the English propensity for treating every basic dish, so long as it is a foreign one, as a dustbin for the reception of left-overs?

LIGURIAN PIZZA OR SARDENARA

For those unfamiliar with yeast leavened dough and its workings, this is the easiest way to start, and the best way to ensure that a presentable *pizza* will be produced at the first attempt.

For a *pizza* to be baked in a 7- to 8-inch (18–20 cm) shallow tart tin with a removable base, ingredients and quantities are as follows:

For the filling: 1 lb of ripe tomatoes, or half and half fresh and

Italian tinned tomatoes, 2 small onions, 2 cloves of garlic, salt, sugar, freshly milled pepper, dried oregano (the Italian name for wild marjoram), olive oil, one 2 oz tin of flat anchovy fillets in olive oil, a dozen very small black olives.

For the dough: ¼ oz of yeast, 2 tablespoons of milk, ¼ lb of plain white flour – strong bread flour for preference, 1 whole egg, 2 tablespoons of olive oil, 1 teaspoon of salt.

Equivalent metric quantities, for the filling: tomatoes 450 g, small onions 2, garlic 2 cloves, salt, sugar, freshly milled pepper, dried oregano, olive oil, anchovy fillets one 50 g tin, very small black olives 12; for the dough: yeast approximately 10 g, milk 2 tablespoons, plain white flour 125 g, 1 whole egg, olive oil 2 tablespoons, salt 1 teaspoon.

To make the dough: Put the yeast into a cup with the milk. Mix it to a cream. Put the flour into a bowl with the salt, warm it for 4 or 5 minutes – no longer – in a very low oven; add the yeast mixture, then the whole egg and the olive oil. Mix all well together, then with your hands work the dough rapidly until it is smooth. Form it into a ball. Shake a little extra flour over it. Cover the bowl. Put it in a warm place and leave for 1½–2 hours until the dough is well risen and very light.

To make the filling: Pour boiling water over the tomatoes, leave them a couple of minutes, then slip off the skins. Chop the tomatoes roughly. Peel the onions, slice them into the thinnest possible rounds. Peel the garlic cloves. Crush them with the flat of a knife.

Into a heavy 10-inch (25-cm) frying pan or sauté pan put enough olive oil to cover the surface. Let the oil warm over low heat then put in the onions. They should stew gently, without frying, for about 7 minutes. Add the crushed garlic cloves, then the fresh tomatoes. With the pan uncovered, increase the heat, so that the water content of the tomatoes evaporates rapidly. Add seasonings of salt and a very little sugar. When the fresh tomatoes have reduced almost to a pulp add the tinned ones if you are using them. There is no need to chop them. Simply spoon them into the pan with some of their juice and crush them with a wooden spoon. Cook for a further few minutes, until the sauce has again reduced. Taste for seasoning – not forgetting that the olives and anchovies will provide extra salt – and scatter in a scant teaspoon of oregano. The basis of the *pizza* filling is now ready.

The olives and anchovies are added when the dough is spread with the tomato mixture and is all but ready to cook.

Prepare the olives by removing the stones with an olive- or cherry-stoner and halving them, or, if they are very small, simply rub them between thumb and first finger and push the stones out. (In Provence the bakers do not bother to stone the olives; the kind they use are so small it would not be feasible to do so.)

To make the final preparations for cooking the *pizza*: brush the tart tin, or a round iron sheet with slightly raised rim, or an earthenware plate of similar shape and size, with olive oil.

Break down the dough, which should have doubled in volume and feel puffy and soft, sprinkle it with flour so that it does not stick to your hands, reshape it into a ball which you put into the centre of the oiled tin. With your knuckles gently press out the dough until it fills the tin.

Turn the oven on to fairly hot, 220°–230°C/425°–450°F/Gas Mark 7–8, and have a baking sheet ready on the centre shelf.

Now spread the dough with the warm tomato mixture, break the anchovy fillets into inch-long pieces and arrange them at random on the top. Season them with a little black pepper from the mill. Scatter the black olives among the pieces of anchovy, add a final extra sprinkling of oregano and olive oil.

Leave the prepared *pizza* on the top of the stove for about 10 minutes, until the oven is really hot and the dough has started to rise again. Now slip the tin into the oven, leave it for 15 minutes, then decrease the heat to 190°C/375°F/Gas Mark 5, and cook for another 10–15 minutes. Alternatively, leave the oven at the same temperature and simply move the pizza to a lower shelf. If the filling begins to look dry, cover it with a piece of oiled foil or greaseproof paper.

Serve your *pizza* hot, with the base of the tart tin still underneath it, the whole on a flat serving platter.

These quantities should be enough for four people for a first dish, while for the hungry young, who will probably prefer to make a whole meal off a *pizza* and perhaps a salad, an 8-inch (20-cm) *pizza* will just about do for two.

For the filling for two 7–8-inch (18–20-cm) tins, you need only one and a half times the quantity of tomato and onion, but twice the number of olives and anchovy fillets.

After one or two tries, the confection of a *pizza* becomes so easy that any intelligent cook will be able to make it almost without reference to a recipe.

English Bread and Yeast Cookery
chosen by Jessica Douglas-Home and Johnny Grey

As very young children my brother and I were brought up by my father to believe that it was essential to eat brown wholemeal bread baked fresh each day – long before it was considered normal to have wholemeal bread in one's house. Along with home-made yoghourt such bread became the hall-mark of his table. Elizabeth David, who was my father's first cousin and who often visited us, loved his bread, which was surely a sub-conscious influence on her magnum opus *English Bread and Yeast Cookery*.

Going back a generation, it was their extraordinary aunt, the musician Violet Gordon Woodhouse, who was responsible for instilling a love of good food and pure ingredients both in Elizabeth and in my father. Elizabeth's father was Violet's favourite brother. After his premature death, Violet felt sorry for Elizabeth, who was only eleven, and brought her to stay at Nether Lypiatt Manor in Gloucestershire. Violet delegated every detail of the daily menu to her husband Gordon. His flamboyant recipes, with their fresh ingredients from Nether Lypiatt's large kitchen garden and orchards, and the produce from the farm close to the house (from which corn was used for the bread), built his reputation before the war as presiding over one of the best kitchens in England. His bread in particular was delicious.

Jessica Douglas-Home

A LARGE ROUND PIZZA

If you possess or can lay hands on a 12-inch (30-cm) flat oven platter, of rough or glazed earthenware, it is easy and cheap to make a pizza large enough for 7 to 10 ample helpings.

Make the dough with ½ lb of strong flour, ¼ oz yeast, 1 whole large egg, approximately 10 tablespoons of milk, 2 tablespoons of olive oil, 2 teaspoons of salt. Extra olive oil will be needed for the dish.

Equivalent metric quantities, for the dough: strong flour 225 g, yeast approximately 10 g, 1 whole large egg, milk approximately 10 tablespoons, olive oil 2 tablespoons, salt 2 teaspoons, extra olive oil for the dish.

The filling can be the tomato and onion mixture described in the previous pizza recipe using one and a half times the quantity (see the notes concerning the increase of quantities, on p. 336), or a variation in the Middle Eastern manner. This one is made with meat, spices, garlic and a good deal of tomato, as follows:

6–8 oz (170–225 g) cooked or raw minced lamb, a small onion, 2 or 3 cloves of garlic, one 8-oz (225-g) tin of peeled tomatoes, salt, olive oil, and seasonings of ground cinnamon, cumin, cloves and pepper. In Armenian and Lebanese cooking the seeds of a plant called sumach are much used as a spice and should go into this mixture. They are hard to come by in this country.[1] It is because, for most of us, the filling must be made without this spice that I call it 'in the Middle Eastern manner'. The dough is also different from the Levantine one.

To cook the filling, melt the chopped onion in olive oil. Add the meat and let it brown gently; put in the peeled and crushed garlic cloves, salt, a level teaspoon each of cinnamon and ground cumin, a half teaspoon of ground cloves, or of mixed sweet spice, and the same of freshly ground black pepper. Add the tomatoes from the tin, cover the pan and simmer gently until the juice from the tomatoes has evaporated and the whole mixture is fairly thick. Taste it for seasoning. It should be really well spiced, so may need more pepper and perhaps extra cumin. A teaspoon or two of sugar may be needed, and a little dried mint can also be added.

Having mixed the dough and left it to rise until very light and puffy, oil your large platter and spread the dough on it, taking it right up to the edges. Leave it, covered, for 15 minutes, until it has returned to life. Spread the warm filling over it. There should not be too thick a layer. Again leave the prepared pizza for 10–15 minutes before putting it into the oven, at the usual temperature for pizza, 220°C/425°F/Gas Mark 7. Cooking times are also as usual, 15 minutes at

1. Try Greek and Levantine provision shops.

high temperature, and another 15 at 190°–200°C/375°–400°F/Gas Mark 5–6, or alternatively at the original temperature but on a lower shelf. In either case it is a good idea to cover the pizza with a piece of oiled greaseproof paper at half time, as the filling should not dry out.

This is an excellent pizza, in some ways the best of all, and if you have lamb left from a joint it provides a splendid way of using it, and at very little cost.

English Bread and Yeast Cookery
chosen by George Elliot

TARTE AVEYRONNAISE *or* ROQUEFORT QUICHE

For the yeast pastry: 5 oz of plain, preferably unbleached, bread flour, ¼ oz of bakers' yeast, 1 whole egg, 1 teaspoon of salt, 3 tablespoons of thick ripe cream or unsalted butter.

For the Roquefort filling: 3½–4 oz Roquefort, 2 whole eggs, 4 tablespoons of milk, 3 tablespoons of thick cream, seasonings of nutmeg, freshly milled pepper, and salt if necessary. Roquefort is a salty cheese, and needs very little seasoning.

A 10-inch removable-base tart tin or two 6–7 inch tins.

Equivalent metric quantities, for the yeast pastry: plain unbleached bread flour 125 g, bakers' yeast approximately 10 g, 1 whole egg, salt 1 teaspoon, thick ripe cream or unsalted butter 3 tablespoons; for the Roquefort filling: Roquefort 100–120 g, eggs 2, milk 4 tablespoons, thick cream 3 tablespoons, nutmeg, pepper, salt if necessary. Tin size: a 25-cm removable-base tart tin or two 15–18-tins.

To make the pastry: Cream the yeast with a couple of tablespoons of tepid water. Warm the flour in a bowl, add the salt, then the whole egg and the creamed yeast. Mix all the ingredients into a light dough. Add the cream (or butter, softened but not melted) and with your hand beat the dough into a soft batter. Dry this by sprinkling it with a little flour, form it into a bun, cover the bowl with a plate or cloth. Leave in a warm place for approximately 2 hours, until the dough has doubled in volume and is light and spongy. Break it down, sprinkle again with flour, reshape into a bun. Unless you are going to use the dough at once, cover the bowl again, and this time leave it in a *cold* place – not the refrigerator – until next day.

To mix the filling: Mash the cheese to a paste. Add the cream. Stir rather gently until the two are amalgamated. Beat the eggs and the milk – the blender can be used for this operation but *not* for mixing the cheese and cream – and amalgamate the two mixtures. Gentle stirring with a fork or spoon is necessary now, and there is no cause for worry if there are a few recalcitrant lumps of cheese in the filling. They will smooth themselves out during the cooking. On the other hand, over-vigorous whisking can curdle the cream and the cheese, a minor disaster which does not affect the flavour but results in a rather flat filling when the quiche is cooked.

When the time comes to cook the quiche, butter and flour the tin, work the dough into a ball, put this into the centre of the tin. Sprinkling the dough with flour from time to time, press it out gently with your knuckles until it covers the base of the tin. Leave it, covered with a sheet of polythene or paper, and in a warm place, for about 25 minutes, until it has again become very pliable and is sufficiently risen to be gently pressed out again to line the sides of the tin.

To bake the quiche: Have the oven turned to 220°C/425°F/Gas Mark 7. Spoon the filling into the dough-lined tin, and put this quickly on to a baking sheet on the centre shelf of the oven.

Bake for 15 minutes before reducing the oven heat to 190°C/375°F/Gas Mark 5, covering the filling with buttered paper and cooking the quiche for another 10 minutes.

Serve quickly, before the filling sinks.

There should be enough for 4–6 people, depending upon whether the dish is to be eaten as a first, a main or a savoury course, and upon what else is to be offered.

Correctly cooked, and eaten hot and fresh, this Roquefort quiche is one of the most delicious things I know. Given the present price of Roquefort cheese it is also something of a luxury.

English Bread and Yeast Cookery

SAUSAGE IN BRIOCHE CRUST

For this excellent dish a large coarsely cut sausage weighing about 1 lb is first poached, or cooked in the oven, then wrapped in a brioche dough and baked.

In France the sausage used is a Lyonnais speciality, the *cervelas*, for which the sausage meat is brined, so that when cooked the inside is an appetizing pink – from the saltpetre – rather than the dead-looking grey of the traditional English sausage. And of course there is no bread filling in the French product. It is pure pork meat, sometimes lightly spiced, sometimes truffled.

Although it is difficult to get the right type of sausage in England, the time may well come when it will be obtainable from enterprising pork butchery specialists; alternatively it could be made at home[1] without too much difficulty, and there are other possibilities such as the Italian *cotechino* to be bought in Soho shops, or the English luncheon sausage made by Harrods butchery department from pure fresh pork meat without additional bread or rusk. Both these sausages will weigh 12 oz–1 lb (340–450 g), although the Italian variety may be a little heavier.

For the brioche dough, which is made in the morning for the evening, or in the evening for the next day's lunch, ingredients are:

8 oz of strong plain flour, ½ oz of yeast, a teaspoon each of salt and sugar, 3 tablespoons of milk, 4 oz of butter, 3 large eggs. For glazing the crust, a little cream.

Equivalent metric quantities: a large coarsely cut sausage (see above for suitable types) about 340–450 g; for the brioche dough: strong plain flour 225 g, yeast 15 g, salt 1 teaspoon, sugar 1 teaspoon, milk 3 tablespoons, butter 125 g, 3 large eggs, a little cream for glazing the crust.

Sprinkle the salt into the flour. Warm the flour very slightly, by putting it in its bowl in a cool oven for a few minutes. Cream the yeast with the sugar and the milk, made just tepid. Soften the butter

---

1. *See* Jane Grigson's admirable *Charcuterie and French Pork Cookery*, London, Michael Joseph, 1967; Penguin Books, 1970.

by putting it on a plate or in a bowl standing over a saucepan of hot water. None of these warming operations must be overdone.

Make a well in the flour. Pour in the yeast. Break in the eggs. Stir all together and mix to a paste. It will be rather sticky. Beat in the softened butter, using your hands. The dough will now be smooth and shiny. If it is too liquid, incorporate a little more flour. Form the dough into a ball, sprinkle it with flour, cover it and leave it in a warm – not too warm – place to rise until it has just about trebled in bulk and looks very light and spongy. Now break it down and knead it for a minute or two. Return it to a clean floured bowl. This time put the bowl in a *cold* place so that the dough remains quiescent overnight or for several hours.

Two hours or so before you intend making the dish, bring the dough back into the warm kitchen, so that it will come back to life slowly, while you deal with the sausage, which must be wholly cooked *before* it is wrapped in the brioche dough.

The easiest and least messy way to cook the sausage is to put it in a moderate oven and let it bake slowly, uncovered, at 170°–180°C/ 330°–350°F/Gas Mark 3–4. An English sausage will take 45 minutes to an hour to cook by this method. When it is cooked through – but not overcooked so that it shrinks – let it drain on paper towels, and leave it to cool a little before attempting to peel off the skin.

An Italian *cotechino* takes much longer to cook, and is best gently simmered in water to cover it, for about 2 hours. For this I use a narrow, rectangular, enamelled cast-iron pâté terrine in which the sausage fits neatly, or, if cooking more than one at a time, a small fish kettle (the kind known as a trout kettle) or an oval cocotte. Any of these can be used in the oven or on the hotplate.

When the sausage is ready, turn the dough on to a non-stick baking sheet or floured iron sheet, work it into a ball, pat it or roll it out into a rectangle, sprinkling it with flour as you do so. Put the skinned sausage in the centre, draw up the sides and ends of the dough, and dipping your fingers in cold water, pinch the seams together along the top and at the ends so that the dough entirely encloses the sausage, forming a nice plump bolster.

Using the back of a knife mark the top of the dough in a diamond pattern, then leave it for 10–15 minutes, just long enough for the dough to recover from the handling. Before putting it in the oven brush the dough with a little cream, to give a nice finish to the crust when it is baked.

Cook the sausage in the centre of a fairly hot oven, 220°C/425°F/ Gas Mark 7, for 20–25 minutes, until the crust is a good golden colour.

Slide the sausage on to a hot serving dish and leave it for 2 or 3 minutes before taking it to the table and carving it. The best way to do this is to start at the centre and work outwards towards the ends, cutting thick slices.

Sausage in brioche is always served as a hot first course, usually at the midday meal. No vegetable, salad or other accompaniment is ever served with it.

Notes: 1. The dough for this crust is a rather firmer one than that used for a brioche baked in a mould, which is too liquid to be handled with ease.

2. When mixing brioche dough take great care not to overheat any of the ingredients. The flour and milk should be just warmed, the butter softened so that it can be easily incorporated into the batter. If it is melted or 'oiled' it will separate from the flour, and a heavy dough will result.

3. The sausage should be warm when wrapped in the dough. If it is cold the dough will not adhere to it while baking, and when cut the slices of sausage will separate from the crust.

4. The joining of the seams of the dough with cold water when wrapping the sausage is important. If this step is omitted the dough will open during baking. This won't affect the taste but rather spoils the look of the finished dish.

5. The sausage should be completely cooked before it is wrapped in the crust. During the brief baking required for the brioche dough, the heat penetrates the crust sufficiently to make the sausage hot but does not allow for extra cooking.

6. Should your sausage weigh more than 1¼ lb (550 g), make rather more dough, say 10 oz (280 g) flour, 5 oz (150 g) butter, 5 tablespoons of milk. It will not be necessary to add extra yeast or eggs.

7. A good dish to follow a sausage in brioche crust is something

which has been slowly cooking low down in the oven while the sausage was baking, say a gratin of vegetables such as courgettes and tomatoes which can be transferred for its final browning to the centre or top shelf of the oven after the sausage has been taken out. A chicken baked slowly in a covered pot or in foil is another possibility. Or perhaps, for a simple but still ample meal, follow the hot sausage with a good fresh green salad, and finish with cheese or a compote of fruit.

English Bread and Yeast Cookery

Storage of Bread

'To put hot bread at once into a cool atmosphere is almost bound
to make it heavy.'

Florence Jack, *Cookery for Every Household*, 1914

Among the vital points to remember about the storage of bread are,
first, that the larger the loaf the longer it stays fresh; next, that a loaf
should never be wrapped up or put away until it is perfectly cool; and
that unless it is to be consigned to the deep freeze it keeps best if it
is allowed to breathe. A loaf enclosed in, for example, a sealed polythene
box or bag may appear to retain its moisture for a day or two but is
in fact giving it out; this moisture is condensing in the airtight container
and dampening the crust; the rapid formation of mould is inevitable.
The same happens, although not quite so quickly, when bread is
stored in a non-porous, highly glazed stoneware crock *unless* there is
an air-hole in the cover, or unless the cover can be raised slightly,
allowing air into the crock. This can be achieved by sticking tiny
wedges of cork at intervals round the rim of the crock, so that the
cover rests on them.

On street-market stalls and in antique shops one sometimes comes
across the old Doulton stoneware storage crocks for bread. It is a rare
occurrence to find one complete with its cover. This is because the
people who made these crocks, familiar with the problems of bread
storage, evolved specially designed lightweight steel covers, slightly
domed and perforated with small air holes in the centre. These covers
provided a very practical solution to the problems both of ventilation
and of weight. Unfortunately they were not rust proof, and few have
survived.

As practical as the old metal-covered stoneware crocks, lighter, and much cheaper were the common porous earthenware variety, the crock glazed on the inside only and the cover only on the outside. These crocks, called bread pans, were made in potteries specializing in rough clayware such as flower pots, dairy bowls, earthenware pans for bread-baking, and all manner of animal-feeding dishes and crocks. Although they cracked and chipped easily, bread pans were cheap to replace. Prices quoted in a catalogue dated 1900 range from 3s to 9s 6d including the covers. There were six sizes, from 12 inches to 20 inches in diameter. Such crocks have now become rarities, almost museum pieces – as indeed have ordinary clay flower pots – the only pottery whose interior-glazed terracotta or clayware crocks are nationally distributed being Brannams of Barnstaple in Devon. Brannams' products are usually to be found in the kitchen, hardware or china departments of such stores as those of the John Lewis group. Brannams' terracotta crocks are far from cheap and deliveries are irregular. It must be remembered that they are bulky, take up much space in the kiln, and are therefore uneconomical to produce. They are, however, solidly made and very much tougher than the old lightweight covered flower-pot type of crock, which incidentally is still occasionally to be found, although only by making an expedition to the premises of one of the few surviving producers of terracotta garden pots, such as the Harris family's establishment at Wrecclesham near Farnham in Surrey, or the Fareham pottery in Hampshire.

For bread storage, it is a help to stand earthenware crocks on a triangular wooden pot stand or a brick so that air circulates round

them. It is essential that bread crocks be frequently and meticulously cleared of crumbs, which generate mould. If you feel that the regular cleaning of the crock is too much bother there isn't much point in using one at all.

Metal containers, such as enamelled steel bins and roll top boxes are quite efficient for bread storage, although I find the latter difficult to keep clean and free of crumbs.

As an alternative to crocks and bins, a clean dry cloth wrapped round a loaf makes an effective protection. So does a porous earthenware bowl inverted over the loaf on a board or earthenware platter. For a cut loaf I find this the most effective of all short-term keeping methods, its disadvantage being the obvious one of the space it occupies.

In France bread is rarely stored from one day to the next. If it is, the long loaves are kept upright, like walking sticks, uncovered, in a tall basket. Round *pains de campagne* are stored in a cupboard, as indeed were their counterparts in England and most other European countries, until the old farmhouse food cupboards with carved and ventilated doors all disappeared into museums or were bought by private collectors probably unaware of the original purpose of these beautiful pieces of furniture. Taking into account, however, the quantity of bread baked at each firing of the oven, a storage cupboard, although a very necessary piece of equipment, would have been large enough only for the short-term storage of a few loaves, probably those already cut. For bulk storage some other solution had to be found. In Wales I have seen a splendid device, a huge wide cradle or crate of slatted wood suspended like a hammock from the ceiling. Two such bread crates are to be seen at the Welsh Folk Museum at St Fagans, near Cardiff, one in the great kitchen of the castle. In Normandy, a similar device on a smaller scale consisted of shelves, also slatted and suspended from the ceiling. Both systems seem to be very practical. So was the bread creel, the hammock-like device slung between cross bars hanging from the ceiling and used in Yorkshire for the storage of oatcakes.

THE FREEZING OF BREAD

The deep freeze is surely the best bread bin to date. If wrapped and consigned to the freezer just as soon as it has cooled, a loaf will retain its moisture intact, and when thawed will be difficult to distinguish from bread freshly made. The crust does of course suffer a bit, but less, I think, than it does when the loaf is stored in a crock or a metal container.

In effect, it is perhaps the deep freeze which has contributed most to the present revival of domestic breadmaking. We all know that it isn't going to be feasible to bake a new loaf whenever we may happen to want it, but it *is* possible always to have a fresh loaf or two in reserve. Many people who have a large enough freezer now do a weekly bake, rather as housewives did in the days of the brick oven. They find that good bread fully justifies the space it occupies in the freezer.

The sooner, after it has cooled, that a loaf is put into the freezer the fresher it will remain. Whatever wrappings you choose, see that they are well closed. Label and date them.

A large loaf takes three to four hours to thaw out at room temperature – a loaf still half-frozen in the centre is not an enticing proposition – but the process can be speeded by giving it a final half hour or so in a low oven, or you can transfer it straight from the freezer (having first unwrapped it) to a medium oven and let it re-bake for 30–40 minutes depending on the size of the loaf. Re-baking will if anything improve the bread, although only on a temporary basis. If it has to last for any length of time then it is best to let it thaw slowly. It is a good idea to take the loaf out of its freezer bag and wrap it in a towel while it thaws, otherwise moisture from the bag condenses on the loaf, making the crust leathery.

For cutting sandwiches, especially very thin ones, it is an advantage if the loaf is still slightly under-thawed.

Tin or pan loaves are the most practical for freezing, but small soft-crusted baps freeze well. So do fruit and spice loaves.

The refrigerator, by the way, is not a good place to store bread. The usual temperature of a refrigerator does indeed delay mould for a time, but is also just the one to draw out moisture.

English Bread and Yeast Cookery

Wine in the Kitchen

Nobody has ever been able to find out why the English regard a glass of wine added to a soup or stew as a reckless foreign extravagance and at the same time spend pounds on bottled sauces, gravy powders, soup cubes, ketchups and artificial flavourings. If every kitchen contained a bottle each of red wine, white wine and inexpensive port for cooking, hundreds of store cupboards could be swept clean for ever of the cluttering debris of commercial sauce bottles and all synthetic aids to flavouring.

To the basic sum of red, white and port I would add, if possible, brandy, and half a dozen miniature bottles of assorted liqueurs for flavouring sweet dishes and fruit salads, say Kirsch, Apricot Brandy, Grand Marnier, Orange Curaçao, Cointreau and Framboise. Sherry is a good addition, but should be used in cooking with the utmost discretion; it is vain to think that the addition of a large glass of poor sherry to the contents of a tin of soup is going to disguise it.

THE COOKING OF WINE

The fundamental fact to remember about the use of wine in cooking is that the wine is *cooked*. In the process the alcohol is volatilized and what remains is the wonderful flavour which perfumes the dish and fills the kitchen with an aroma of delicious things to come. In any dish which does not require long cooking the wine should be reduced to about half the quantity originally poured in the pan, by the process of very fast boiling. In certain soups, for instance, when the vegetables have been browned and the herbs and spices added, a glass of wine is poured in, the flame turned up, and the wine allowed to bubble fiercely for two or three minutes; when it starts to look a little syrupy on the bottom of the pan, add the water or stock; this process makes all the difference to the flavour and immediately gives the soup body and colour.

When making gravy for a roast, abolish the cabbage water, gravy browning and cornflour; instead, when you have strained off the fat pour a ½ glass of any wine round the roasting-pan, at the same time scraping up all the juice which has come out of the meat, let it sizzle for a minute or two, add a little water, cook gently another 2 minutes and your gravy is ready.

For a duck, add the juice of an orange and a tablespoon of redcurrant jelly; for fish which has been grilled add white wine to the butter in the pan, lemon juice, and chopped parsley or capers; to the butter in which you have fried escalopes of veal add a little red wine or Madeira, let it bubble and then pour in a ½ cup of cream.

TO FLAMBER

To *flamber* is to set light to a small quantity of brandy, liqueur or rum poured over the contents of the pan, which are left to flame until the alcohol has burnt away, leaving a delicately composed sauce in which any excess of fat or butter has been consumed in the flames. The brandy or liqueur will be easier to light if it is first placed in a warmed ladle, to release the spirit, which will then easily catch fire.

TO MARINATE IN WINE

To marinate meat, fish or game is to give it a bath lasting anything between 2 hours and several days in a marinade usually composed of a mixture of wine, herbs, garlic, onions and spices, sometimes with the addition of a little vinegar, olive oil, or water. A tough piece of stewing beef is improved by being left several hours in a marinade of red wine; it can then be braised or stewed in the marinade, strained of the vegetables and herbs which, by this time, have become sodden, and fresh ones added.

A leg of mutton can be given a taste approximating to venison by being marinaded for several days. It is then carefully dried and roasted, the strained marinade being reduced and used for the sauce.

For certain *terrines* I always marinate the prepared meat or game for two or three hours in white wine, but red can be used. Hare, I think, needs no marinade, unless it is ancient and tough, as the meat of a good hare has a perfect flavour which is entirely altered by being soaked in wine before cooking, although a glass or two of good red wine to French *civet de lièvre*, and of port to English jugged hare, is indispensable.

THE CHOICE OF THE WINE

There is no hard–and–fast rule as to the use of white or red wine, port or brandy for any particular dish. Generally speaking, of course, red wine is better for meat and game dishes, white for fish, but one can usually be substituted for the other, an exception being *Moules Marinière*, for which white wine is a necessity, as red turns the whole dish a rather disagreeable blue colour, and any essentially white dish, such as a delicate concoction of sole, must have white wine.

Incidentally, white wine for cooking should, except for certain dishes such as a cheese fondue, not be too dry, as it may give rather too acid a flavour; and beware of pouring white wine into any sauce containing milk or cream; to avoid curdling, the wine should be put in before the cream and well simmered to reduce the acidity, and the cream stirred in off the fire, and reheated very cautiously.

Don't be discouraged when you read lovely French regional recipes containing a particular and possibly little-known wine; remember that in their country of origin the *vin du pays* is always within arm's reach of the cook, so that while in Bordeaux a *matelote* of eel is cooked in wine of the Médoc, in Lyon the nuance is altered because Beaujolais is used, and cider in the apple country of Normandy. Here, too, a sweet omelette is *flambéd* with Calvados, in Gascony with Armagnac. In the same way the French frequently employ their own sweet wine, Frontignan, Muscat, or the Vin Cuit of Provence in place of port or marsala.

Cider is excellent for white fish, mussels, for cooking ham, and for rabbit, but it should be either draught or vintage cider.

Cheap wine is better than no wine at all, at any rate for cooking, but the better the wine the better the dish. By this I do not mean that fine old vintages should be poured into the saucepan, but that, for instance, a coq au vin, cooked in a pint of sound Mâcon or Beaujolais, will be a much finer dish than that cooked in fiery Algerian wine.

French Country Cooking
chosen by Julia Drysdale

Ladies' Halves

What on earth comes over wine waiters when they take the orders of a woman entertaining another woman in a restaurant? Twice in one week recently I have dined in different restaurants (not, admittedly, in the expense-account belt of the West End, where women executives have tables and bottles of 1945 Margaux permanently at the ready, or it's nice to think so, anyway) and with different women friends, on one occasion as the hostess and on the other as the guest. On both occasions, after the regulation lapse of twenty minutes, the wine waiter brought a half-bottle of the wine ordered instead of a whole one. Please don't think I have anything against half-bottles; on the contrary, I find they have a special charm of their own. There are occasions when a half is what one wants, a half and nothing else, in which case I really don't believe one has to be a master-woman to be capable of specifying one's wishes in the matter. I suppose the assumption on the part of wine waiters that women are too frail to consume or too stingy to pay for a whole bottle must be based on some sort of experience, but instead of having to go back to change the order (ten minutes the second time, one is getting edgy by then, and well into the second course; if they held up the food to synchronize with the wine one mightn't mind so much) he could inquire in the first place, in a discreet way. Or even in an indiscreet way, like the steward on the Edinburgh–London express a few years ago who yelled at me across the rattling crockery and two other bemused passengers, 'A bottle, madam? A *whole* bottle? Do you know how large a whole bottle is?'

An Omelette and a Glass of Wine
chosen by Lindsey Bareham, Arabella Boxer, Celia Denney

Between 1950 and 1977, that is to say between the publication of her first book, *A Book of Mediterranean Food*, and her penultimate, *English Bread and Yeast Cookery*, Elizabeth David's writing changed greatly. In the beginning, she wrote with a nostalgic hunger for the lands of the Mediterranean where she had lived throughout most of the war, before returning to a grey, post-war England. Gradually, as her store of memories dwindled, or her scholarly inclination started to assert itself, she began to rely on research for her material, and as her love for such pursuits grew, she lost me. I missed the romance and pleasure of her early books, and having by this time become a food writer myself, I was heartily sick of reading or writing recipes. The intricate niceties of comparing twenty-five similar receipts for muffins and crumpets failed to interest me, and I felt sad.

When, in 1984, *An Omelette and a Glass of Wine* appeared, with its enchanting cover of a Cedric Morris painting of eggs in a slipware dish, my delight knew no bounds. For this was Elizabeth at her best, in my opinion, as a companion as much as a writer: stimulating, opinionated, informative, moving, lyrical and, best of all, funny.

Finding a speck of humour in food writing is as rare as finding a pearl in an oyster, and I value it accordingly. I rarely find myself laughing out loud each time I re-read a favourite passage by any author, but I still fall about each time I glance at *Ladies' Halves*. It conjures up Elizabeth, sharing a table with strangers in a Pullman car, while being harangued by a bullying waiter. He, poor man, had misjudged his victim, for who knew better than Elizabeth just how large a *whole* bottle of wine is.   Arabella Boxer

Table Jewellery

Italy in the early decades of the seventeenth century was entering a new Ice Age. With their well-stocked snow wells and ice cellars the nobility of Rome, Florence and Naples could enjoy ice-cooled fruit and wines throughout the summer months. From June to September cherries, figs, grapes, peaches, plums, apricots, mulberries, strawberries, pears, were served either smothered in crushed snow (for storage snow was compacted into massive blocks and lasted even longer than ice) or set over a separate dish containing the snow or ice. Melons were invariably sliced and the snow was always underneath. Peeled peaches in wine were served in the same way. Jellies, junkets, creams, blancmanges of hashed chicken and ground almonds, were all kept in their pristine state by the indirect cooling system, and indications of innovations in the use of ice and snow appear in published records of the feasts of the 1620s. At a dinner in Rome on 2 July 1625, for example, for the first cold service – this was always provided by the butler's pantry and often differed little from the final dessert service, for which again the butler and his aides were responsible – there were not only the usual sliced melons and fresh figs with sugar over and snow under in separate dishes, and the expected junket set over snow and decorated with sugar and ribbons of rosewater-scented butter, but a showy centrepiece consisting of jelly (jellymania was rife in seventeenth-century Italy) in which was enclosed a hollow glass column filled with small pieces of ice, the whole resting on a wooden pedestal and surrounded with obelisks of variously coloured jellies, and pyramids of gilded wood. This remarkable piece of table décor reappears a number of times in the same compendium of records. On one occasion the glass column was filled with flowers, on another with

356

live fish swimming in water. The attendant obelisks and pyramids, both popular shapes for jellies at the time, were soon to be adapted for decorative ice centrepieces, later still for ice-creams. Indeed they survive to this day, little changed in outline.

The man who recorded these details of Roman feasting in the 1620s was Antonio Frugoli, a native of the then independent republic of Lucca, whose book *Pratica e Scalcaria*, a comprehensive volume on the art and practice of stewardship, was published in Rome in 1631. About half the book is taken up with detailed lists of the dishes served at eighty different dinners, suppers and banquets, six or seven for each month in the year, and covering the years 1618 to 1631.

No name-dropper, Frugoli does not reveal the identity of the host or the guests at any of his meals, and at no point tells us who his employer was – possibly it was that Cardinal Capponi, appointed Archbishop of Ravenna in 1621 and formerly papal legate in Bologna, to whom he dedicated his book – so although he asserts that he personally drew up all the lists of dishes and himself officiated on all but one of the occasions described, we have to be content with the information that this dinner was given in Rome, that one in Madrid, others in Bologna, Perugia, Ferrara. We also get glimpses of the kind of meal served to an important man on his travels through Italy. The dinner we are here chiefly concerned with, however, was a ceremonial one, given in Rome in 1623.

It is 15 August, the feast of the Assumption, then, as now, one of the most important festivals of the Italian year. Regardless of the sweltering heat of a Roman August, the dinner is in every way an exceptional one. There are altogether twenty-four cold dishes supplied by the *Credenza*, the pantry, in two services of twelve dishes each, one at the opening of the meal, one at the end. The pantry will also supply the dessert and the confectionery which conclude the banquet. From the kitchen proper there are twenty-four hot dishes in four services, each separated into two courses. Most unusually, both fish and meat are served, and in great variety, many of the meat and poultry dishes being garnished with small morsels of fish such as fried *calamaretti*, soft-shell crabs boiled in milk, then fried in butter, slices of pickled tunny alternating with the decoratively carved oranges and lemons for which, again, the butler and the pantry staff are responsible.

For a high summer afternoon in Rome the food is oppressively rich, heavy with sweet-sour sauces and syrups, everything strewn with sugar or sugar-coated comfits. Even to the reader it is a relief when the second course of the second hot service is cleared away, the napkins changed, and the dessert brought in. Compared to all that has gone before, this course is very low key. There are sliced truffles with carved oranges, a tart filled with conserve of rennet apples, three lobsters in the shell with a dressing of oil, pepper and clear verjuice (there was nearly always some kind of fish in the dessert course, usually oysters), pears and peaches in syrup strewn with aniseeds, more peaches in wine, Spanish olives, muscatel and early autumn grapes, a box of plum conserve, fresh pears, young sweet fennel, fresh peeled almonds, and six jars of the quince sweetmeat called *cotognata*. Perhaps to make up for the relative modesty of the dessert spread, the pantry has supplied a showy centrepiece: *un monte di diaccio con diversi frutti dentro*, a mountain of ice with divers fruits within, and in the centre a fountain spurting jets of cold orange flower water which lasted, says Frugoli proudly, 'more than half an hour'.

A pleasing sight indeed, that glittering icy Vesuvius, the fruit gleaming within its depths, the jets of perfumed water spouting from its crater, cooling the atmosphere, refreshing the eyes and reviving the flagging spirits of the company at dinner – there are only eight of them – and what a change, too, from the endless sugar paste and marzipan centrepieces or *trionfi* which at the time adorned every important feast. As Frugoli himself observes in his dedicatory epistle to his readers, 'every day we see new inventions', and this particular novelty was really quite a simple affair to create. An advance on Barclay's ice-encrusted fruit, all that was needed was a conical mould with a central tube, and a cover for the base. The mould was set on its narrow end and filled with different kinds of small fruit such as cherries, strawberries, plums and apricots. Water was then poured in, care being taken to leave a space for its expansion during freezing, and the covered mould buried in ice and salt. When released from its mould – a delicate operation – the ice mountain was set on a great dish, the clockwork fountain, devised by some skilled water engineer and not nearly such an innovation as the ice mountain (Leonardo, who died in 1519, had designed one), was placed in the centre, and

358

the sensational novelty was borne to the table to the sound, one surmises, of flutes, viols, and triumphal fanfares.

On only one other occasion in all the eighty dinner, supper and banquet lists he gives does Frugoli mention such an item as the *monte di diaccio*, and that was two years later, for a dinner on 18 May 1625 at the royal palace in Madrid, where he appears to have accompanied his master on a number of occasions. This time it was the feast of Pentecost and there were two fountains and two *monti di frutti diversi diacciate*, two mountains of divers iced fruit, by which it is difficult to tell if Frugoli meant fruit set in ice, or preserved and sugar-frosted fruit in pyramids, or simply fresh fruit with snow or crushed ice. Here indeed is a fair example of the kind of linguistic trap which has been responsible for many improbable legends concerning the early history of ices. It has been all too easy, to later generations, to interpret sixteenth- and seventeenth-century Italian and French allusions to plain ice, iced drinks, glazed creams, and sugar icing and frosting as meaning ices and ice-creams. In this instance, I think it likely from Frugoli's phrasing that he did mean the same kind of ice and fruit pyramids as had appeared at the Rome feast of 1623. The Spanish royal palaces were always plentifully supplied with ice, and as for the necessary moulds and table fountains, Frugoli, as was usual at the time, would have travelled with them in his luggage, along with a quantity of plate, serving dishes, and other such impedimenta.

If the ice pyramids were so new in the 1620s that Frugoli mentions them only twice, by the 1660s they seem to have become obligatory decoration at summer banquets. For the marriage celebrations in Florence in 1661 of Prince Cosimo de Medici and Princess Marguérite-Louise of Orléans, fluted silver moulds over a foot high were used for the freezing of the fruit and ice, and by the 1690s in Spanish Naples no summer wedding celebration, reception, banquet or outdoor party appears to have been complete without its quota of ice and fruit pyramids, about which one question remains unanswered. Was the fruit frozen into the ice regarded purely as decoration? Or did the company wait until the ice started to melt and then set about demolishing the pyramid and crunching the ice and fruit between their teeth?

Harvest of the Cold Months

Cathay to Caledonia

Anyone who believes that Marco Polo saw frozen milk on sale in the streets of Peking and that he returned to Italy with a recipe for Chinese ice-cream should try finding the tale in the account of his travels. At no point did he mention anything in China, or anywhere else, which even the most credulous could possibly construe as being frozen milk, nor anything in any way resembling ice-cream even at its most primitive. Indeed the only point in the whole of his narrative at which he makes more than a passing reference to milk of any kind is when he describes the dried milk and the *kumiss*, or fermented mare's milk, of Mongolia. That at some time somebody imagined that *kumiss* somehow equated with ice-cream is, I suppose, just conceivable. How otherwise to account for the persistent legend seems to me well nigh impossible, unless perhaps the tale was invented in fun and was later believed even by quite serious people. If only Marco had just once mentioned the Chinese use of ice, in his time already ancient, referred to the Imperial ice stores, or recorded the eating of ice-cooled melons or the restaurants specializing exclusively in iced foods, the assumption that he had also experienced some sort of icy milk delicacy would have been an easy step. But nowhere does he give so much as a passing hint of such usages. And that in itself is quite odd.

When the Polos arrived in China in the second half of the thirteenth century, Chinese methods of refrigeration already went back about 2,500 years, perhaps longer. The harvesting and storage of ice are recorded in a poem of circa 1100 BC in the *Shih Ching*, the famous collection of Food Canons, and there is mention of a festival held when the ice houses were opened for summer use: 'In the days of the second month, they hew out the ice . . . in the third month they convey it to the ice houses which they open in those of the fourth, early in the morning, having offered in sacrifice a lamb with scallions.'

Coming – in Chinese terms – to comparatively modern times, the T'ang rulers of AD 618–907 and their court used ice to cool their houses in summer as well as for preserving perishable foodstuffs. Cooling delicacies such as smooth mixtures of crystalline rice, cow's milk, camphor, and mysterious ingredients called dragon brain fragments and dragon eye ball powder were enclosed in metal tubes which were then lowered into an 'ice-pool' and thoroughly chilled. Professor Edward Schafer, of Berkeley University, California, describing this T'ang Imperial treat in his entrancing book *The Golden Peaches of Samarkand*, explains that camphor was probably chosen on account of its resemblance, when flaked, to ice and snow, and its consequent cooling effect. The idea of things looking cool making you feel cool must be even older than the most ancient of Chinese cultures, as old no doubt as mankind itself. As for camphor, it was prized in China for medicinal purposes as well as for its pretty, icy appearance. To me, it equates with the smell of mothballs. Note, by the way, that Professor Schafer is careful to emphasize that this 'clear wind rice' was 'thoroughly chilled'. It was not frozen. Nor was any attempt made to freeze it. The distinction is one to be borne in mind before anyone jumps to the conclusion that in 'clear wind rice' we have evidence of some ancient form of ice-cream.

As things turned out, the ice technology of China did in time come to exercise an important influence on our own, but that was not until late in the eighteenth century and had at first nothing much to do with the development of the ice-cream trade, then barely in its infancy. Primarily, it was the expansion of our fishing industry which we owed to Chinese expertise in the matter of transport and preservation of fresh fish by means of natural ice. The result was a dramatic increase in the demand for that commodity and the consequences were to be far-reaching.

The story is an interesting one, more prosaic perhaps than the fairytales of ice-cream mythology – Billingsgate-bound cargoes of fish packed in ice are not as romantic as argosies of sherbets and sugar, snow and fruit, carried on camel-back through the Holy Land to crusading warriors, or seaborne with attendant confectioners in papal galleons across the Mediterranean to attend a royal wedding in Marseille – but in its way the China to Scotland story, although fully substantiated, is every bit as unlikely.

In 1785 a Scottish gentleman named Alexander Dalrymple, an official of the British East India Company, who for the previous six years had been hydrographer to the Company (later he was to fill the same office for the Admiralty), was on a visit to London. One day, calling at East India House, Dalrymple chanced to meet Mr George Dempster, an eminent fellow Scot, Member of Parliament for the Perthshire burghs of Perth, St Andrews, Dundee, Forfar and Cupar (Fife) and a former director of the East India Company. The two men fell into conversation. In the course of their talk Dalrymple, who had spent several years on voyages of observation in the islands of the South Pacific and had also made himself familiar with the Chinese coastal trade and the Company's trading post in Canton, told Mr Dempster how the Chinese fishermen were in the habit of carrying ice on their boats in order to preserve their catches at sea.

What Alexander Dalrymple explained to George Dempster during their chance meeting at East India House was that the fishermen of the China coast drew their supplies of snow and ice from storehouses situated along the coastal areas and estuaries. Evidently the China coast in those days had ice houses and snow stores rather like the plains of La Mancha had windmills. All the employees and officers of the East India Company stationed at Canton during the eighteenth century could not but have been familiar with the sight of those little stores and with the use of ice by the Chinese fishermen. The Company's officers were themselves only too glad to have access to ice for cooling the wines of which they consumed such prodigious quantities. 'Claret, madeira and hock, all excellent and all made as cold as ice,' recorded William Hickey, describing a sumptuous dinner for thirty people held at the Company's establishment at Whampoa, the Canton anchorage for foreign trading vessels, during a prolonged visit there in the summer of 1769. How, in the stifling heat of a Canton summer, the wines had all been iced, Hickey did not reveal, although he could certainly have explained that the Chinese coastal ice stores were rather small above ground buildings, in outline not unlike English haystacks, very different from the cavernous underground ice houses already common in his day in English public and private parks and gardens, and essential to the caterers and confectioners of the capital. These unfamiliar little Chinese coastal stores were filled with ice harvested from low-lying surrounding fields deliberately flooded in winter and in summer given over to rice cultivation, an ingenious and economical way of obtaining ice for storage. Although it might have been supposed that summer storage of ice in above-ground buildings was not very practical, the opposite proved the case. Their insulation was so effective that the ice could be kept for as long as two years. If in a mild winter the ice crop was insufficient to fill the stores, there would still be plenty of the previous year's supply to fall back on.

The fish merchants likewise, Dalrymple revealed, used ice and snow to maintain their fish in a state of perfect preservation during transit over long distances inland. The information, although new to George Dempster, would not have been so to anyone who had read a similar first-hand story which had appeared in 1763 in *Travels from St Petersburg in Russia to Diverse Parts of Asia* by John Bell of Anter-mony, a compatriot of Dalrymple's. The book, which had attracted a good deal of favourable attention at the time of its publication, included a detailed account of a journey made by Bell, a doctor in the service of Czar Peter the Great of Russia, in his capacity as physician to an embassy from Russia to the Emperor of China. Arriving in Peking in November 1720 after an overland journey across Siberia lasting sixteen months, Dr Bell recorded that at Christmas a Jesuit priest, Father Paranim, 'sent us a present of a large sturgeon and some other fresh fish, brought from the river Amoor [nearly 1,000 miles north of Peking, on the border of what is now Manchuria]. These can only be carried to such a distance in the coldest season, when they are preserved by being kept frozen among the snow.' John Bell had perfectly understood the principle of preserving fish by rapid freezing: 'provided the fish is immediately exposed to the frost after being caught,' he wrote, 'it may be carried, in snow, for many miles, almost as fresh as when taken out of the water.' Bell would also, of course, have been familiar with the sight of frozen fish and entire frozen animal carcasses piled up in St Petersburg's winter market, hence his additional observation that 'the method of preservation by freezing is practised with success in northern countries'. His story had been written purely for the record, and apparently nobody who read it thought of attempting to apply the Chinese system of exposing fish to natural freezing for safe carriage from Scotland to the markets of London and Southern England. That was understandable. Climatic conditions in Scotland are not really such as to permit the development of natural freezing on a regular basis. The potential benefits of using ice as a temporary preservation for fish in transport were also unappreciated. The inauguration of a completely new method of carriage of perishable foodstuffs such as fish was still to come, awaiting a man, or men, with vision, initiative and the means of putting ideas to the practical test.

As things turned out, it was not until twenty years after the publication of John Bell's account of his stay in Peking that chance circumstances brought together a Scottish Member of Parliament and a Scottish official of the East India Company, and that this meeting, followed by prompt action on the part of a Scottish fish merchant, combined to bring about the innovation which was to revolutionize the Scottish and British fishing industries. In the course of that transformation, the British ice trade was also to grow from a spasmodic cottage industry, first into a major import business and ultimately into a great manufacturing and cold storage operation.

Just how much detail concerning the Chinese system of refrigerating perishable foodstuffs while in transit along the 1,100 miles of the Grand Canal – the oldest artificial waterway in the world – was known to Alexander Dalrymple and how much he in turn communicated to George Dempster is not on record. What we do know is that Dalrymple's story sufficiently impressed Dempster to cause him to write off – on the spot, according to his own testimony – to his salmon supplier in Scotland, a Mr Richardson, telling him of this Chinese custom of preserving fish in ice. Accordingly Richardson, although sceptical (again it is his own story), proceeded to make the experiment of packing freshly caught salmon in boxes filled with pounded ice (the Scottish lochs no doubt yielded ice in plenty) and sending them to London by sea. Surprise. It was found that the fish, after a six-day journey, were preserved in an excellent state. Thus, belatedly, and 160 years after Francis Bacon allegedly caught his fatal chill collecting snow in order to further his observations on its possible preservative effects on the flesh of a chicken, did the news of the use of ice as a preservative for fresh fish reach the British public.

The success of Richardson's initial consignment of salmon packed in ice had swift repercussions. In a letter published in the *Scots Magazine* of 3 October 1786, Richardson made a public declaration to the effect that the experiment had answered beyond expectation and that 'any benefit which might result from it either to the public or to individuals owes its beginning in this country to that patriotic gentleman Mr Dempster and to none else'. That Christmas Mr Richardson made a gift of £200 to Mr Dempster to buy 'a piece of plate' for Mrs Dempster. The sum was at that time a handsome one, evidence of the importance and financial value to the salmon trade of the newly evolved system of transport. In the previous July the Convention of Royal Burghs of Scotland had already recognized Dempster's services to Scottish trades, manufacturers and fisheries with a presentation of plate worth a hundred guineas. Dempster was indeed a man always open to new ideas. He is credited with innovations such as the building of the first lighthouses on the coast of Scotland, and the installation of a central heating system in his home in Perthshire, so it is in no way surprising that he was farsighted enough to perceive the significance of Alexander Dalrymple's account of the Chinese use of snow and ice in the preservation of fresh fish. To Dempster, therefore, goes the credit of instigating the introduction of a cold storage system, however tentative, to the British Isles. To Dalrymple's part in the innovation nobody gives more than a passing nod, but the value of his report on the Chinese methods of carrying ice both in the fishing boats and in the cross-country river and canal craft should not be underestimated. Without it, our own system of fish carriage in ice might have been delayed many more years.

It should here be explained that prior to the Dempster–Richardson innovation, the carriage of salmon to London from Scotland and other distant places had customarily ended with the approach of warmer weather in April. Carriage had been effected in baskets loaded on to packhorses, or by package in straw in light carts. Only occasionally, given the risks inherent in the vagaries of wind, weather and tides, had sea transport been successful. The use of ice as a preservative changed everything. Sailing delays no longer spelt disaster. Following

Richardson's lead, many Scottish fish merchants started conveying salmon from Aberdeen, Montrose, and Inverness, places 500, 600 and 700 miles distant from London. Before long, the salmon trade was transformed and seasonal sales of Scotch salmon at Billingsgate extended far into the summer months.

Although during the first years the use of ice in the fisheries was confined to the luxury trade in salmon, it was not long before the system was extended to the herring fisheries of the Forth. By 1794 Fife fish merchants were dispatching herrings, at that time plentiful in the Forth, in ice-filled boxes loaded in fast sailing smacks from Berwick to London. By 1815 the anonymous author of *The Epicure's Almanack*, a guide to London hotels, clubs, coffee houses, taverns, food markets, provision shops, confectioners and caterers, could write that all first-rate fish dealers had ice stores for the purpose of preserving their fish during hot weather, referring also to the Berwick smacks laden with salmon packed in ice arriving at Billingsgate during the season. Scottish turbot, the *Epicure* recorded, was also occasionally brought to London packed in ice. George Dempster, who lived on until 1818, had cause to be proud of the perceptive action which thirty years previously had wrought such a spectacular change in the fortunes of the Scottish fishing industry.

In 1838, a year after the accession of Queen Victoria, came another great innovation, the inauguration of a regular steamboat service carrying salmon in ice from Scotland to London. In four years the new service had proved so successful that in 1842 2,500 tons of salmon passed through Billingsgate, much of it in the peak summer months of June, July and August. 'Steam navigation has rendered the improvement perfect,' reported J. C. Platt, the enthusiastic contributor of an article on London's famous fish market published in the fourth volume of a collection of essays entitled *London*, published in 1843. Soon the railways would speed up those deliveries beyond recognition.

In the course of the fifty-odd years which had passed since George Dempster and Alexander Dalrymple had met and talked of ice and fish and the China Seas, the whole of the British fishing industry had been transformed, initially by the use of ice, and subsequently by the coming of steam.

Harvest of the Cold Months

A grey day in Cardiff. A London journalist, unable to get local work and homesick for the world of the international glossy magazines, postponed buying the rations for her RAF doctor husband and herself and turned into the cramped premises of a bookshop. She was vaguely looking for help and advice: her mama, the traditional 'good plain cook', had kept her out of the kitchen ('You should be studying') and shrugged off mentions of 'mucked about foreign food'. Husband and in-laws were of some assistance and had taken her abroad, but the furnished rooms in Wales were the first home with a kitchen.

Cookery books of the period were bewildering. Most devoted much space to cakes and puddings which the newly-weds didn't require. There were intimidating ingredients – 'a pint of white sauce made in the usual way', 'enough shortcrust pastry to cover a flan dish'. The jackets of such books as were on the 'cookery' shelf were garish with piped and decorated dishes except one which the bride picked out, a jacket brilliant with blue skies and sea and sunshine, with never a cooked creation in sight. Flipping the pages she began to read. Here was an erudite but inspiring writer, citing memories, encouraging the reader to attempt what seemed to be recipes that were simple yet, obviously, respected by people who travelled, who knew about *food*, not merely cakes and puddings and garnishes. *A Book of Mediterranean Food* was bought – and the next day I went back to buy *French Country Cooking*. The copies, later signed by the writer, are at my desk side to this day – the paperbacks, tattered and stained, reign in the kitchen.

Cautiously I experimented – and none of the recipes had to be rejected. I suppose I must have made Elizabeth's Galette de Pommes de Terre hundreds of times, with my own variations and additions. It was as if the writer was at one's elbow, luring on, warning and, always, making it simple to understand what one was doing. My mama shrieked in horror over the telephone when I told her I was using onions and olive oil, the local greengrocer asked if we kept dogs – 'all that garlic, said to be good for their blood'.

When we returned to London and my husband, on the staff of St Mary's Hospital, would invite home some of his students, I was grateful for economical recipes such as Riz au Chou à la Grecque – but when his chiefs came to supper they were treated to the sort of casserole that, I knew later, surprised them. Elizabeth's recipe for Chocolate Mousse was the routine pud.

By then I was back in the world of the glossies, having bluffed my way onto the staff of *House & Garden* by claiming, at the interview, that I was 'the best cook I know'. Gradually I came to know Elizabeth, though she was always reserved – I think she was genuinely shy. She was then writing for a rival publication, but I persuaded her to come and write for the organization to which I belonged. So I handled her copy. It might have been, but wasn't, the end of a friendship, for she was completely authoritative ('you know that what I do will be *right*') but difficult: 'Elizabeth, the art department must have only thirty lines on that first page, so may we cut the "and" in the penultimate line, put a comma and save the one word they need?' – 'No.'

She was ruthless in appraising her own books; especially she liked *Summer Cooking* although not its format. And she giggled once when I'd invited her to lunch and she brought one of her books to sign for me – she showed me that the proof readers had put '34' eggs in one recipe instead of '3 to 4'. And she was always delighted to learn more about food: the beautiful colour shot on the jacket of *French Provincial Cooking* was taken at a restaurant where my husband had suggested she might find good fare.

Never did she confuse chef cooking with the cuisine bourgeoise or cuisine paysanne that she taught so many of us to achieve and, if invited out (in those days I had a generous expense account because her name was, rightly, a big attraction) she would reject many chic, smart eating places – if she went to any of these she would always be impeccably couture-clad – for, possibly, a small Greek or Cypriot restaurant where she would order the food she liked and reminisce about her friend Norman Douglas. She had a wicked comment on many of the current cookery ladies ('they'll invent Lowestoft

Food next') and the decorated, piped, coloured trimmings were denounced and dismissed as 'Fair Isle food'. But she was a loving and sympathetic friend, as I knew when my husband died; once, when I spoke sharply about what was really a deplorable cookery book, she sighed and said, 'poor dear – perhaps she had to do it for the money'.

In her own domain, in her kitchen, quietly preparing something for friends to eat, offering glasses of wine, her hair usually covered with a kerchief, the hands – as creative as those of any sculptor – delicately at the work surfaces or the stove – there she was delightful company. I believe many manufacturers of kitchen cabinets offered to 'do' her kitchen, but the scrubbed wooden table and the occasional notebooks remained, and the herbs in the miniature garden outside while the books of her wonderful library were wedged in all the rooms and down the stairs. When John Ward made his exquisite sketch of her in that kitchen I was sitting at the end of the table, in the window seat, beside Squeaker, the cat. No hurry, no pronouncements, never more than the slightest references to the past – and the gentle tones of her voice would only deepen to a projected mezzo-soprano when she wished to point a jest.

She loved the classic French wines, especially the white Loires and the fine white Burgundies, yet I think that, like some other great authorities on food I have known, she wasn't ultimately fascinated by wine, as I have always been.

Her scholarship, as exemplified in several of her later books, was quietly impressive, remarkable and, like her personality, obsessive. She was a great lady – and as I write this, I can hear her soft laugh and wish she was still there to show her one of my chutneys, give her one of my pickles and, always, ask her about so many of the good things of life about which she taught me.

I have just turned up a card of hers, which ends: 'As always, I send you very much love.' How I miss her, how I think of her each time I take up the fruit squeezer she gave me ('it will take a grapefruit' – typically generous). I know that I am only one of many who must inscribe the adjectives 'inimitable, incomparable' when speaking of her – and, in our minds, hearing her say 'now let's cook something' – for she was one of those personalities who are always *giving*. Thank you, my very dear friend.

Pamela Vandyke Price

Index

Names of recipes and the *main* reference to these recipes are given in *italics* – all further references to the same recipes appear in roman type

TITLES of articles etc. are given in SMALL CAPITALS

Illustrations in this anthology

The illustrations on the listed pages are by:
Adrian Daintrey (*Summer Cooking*): frontispiece, 173 and 297
John Minton (*Mediterranean Food*): 1, 5, 8, 38, 51, 171, 185, 187 and 367
Juliet Renny (*French Provincial Cooking*): 11, 22, 28, 63, 84, 92, 114, 121, 124, 139, 144, 206, 211, 213, 219 and 293
Renato Guttuso (*Italian Food*): 59, 76, 196 and 226
John Minton (*French Country Cooking*): 44, 72, 119 and 275
Marie Alix (*An Omelette and a Glass of Wine*): 88, 258 and 350
Wendy Jones (*English Bread and Yeast Cookery*): 313, 317, 322, 329, 346, 347 and 348